MERITOCRACY AND ECONOMIC INEQUALITY

MERITOCRACY AND ECONOMIC INEQUALITY

Kenneth Arrow, Samuel Bowles, and
Steven Durlauf, Editors

PRINCETON UNIVERSITY PRESS   PRINCETON, NEW JERSEY

Library of Congress Cataloging-in-Publication Data

Meritocracy and economic inequality / Kenneth Arrow, Samuel Bowles,
and Steven Durlauf, editors.
p.   cm.
A collection of 12 original papers contributed by scholars, with
an introduction by the editors.
Includes bibliographical references and index.
ISBN 0-691-00467-6 (cl : alk. paper). — ISBN 0-691-00468-4 (pb :
alk. paper)
1. Income distribution.   2. Equality.   3. Elite (Social sciences).
4. Social mobility.   I. Arrow, Kenneth Joseph, 1921–   .
II. Bowles, Samuel.   III. Durlauf, Steven N.
HB523.M468   2000
305.5'13—dc21   99-39632

This book has been composed in Times Roman

The paper used in this publication meets the minimum requirements of
ANSI/NISO Z39.48-1992 (R1997) (*Permanence of Paper*)

http://pup.princeton.edu

Printed in the United States of America

10 9 8 7 6 5 4 3 2 1

10 9 8 7 6 5 4 3 2 1
(Pbk.)

Contents

Contributors

Kenneth Arrow, Joan Kenney Professor of Economics (Emeritus), Department of Economics, Stanford University

Orley Ashenfelter, Department of Economics, Princeton University, and National Bureau of Economic Research

Roland Bénabou, Department of Economics, New York University, CERAS-IDEI, GREMAQ-CNRS, and National Bureau of Economic Research, and Center for Economic Policy Research

Samuel Bowles, Department of Economics, University of Massachusetts at Amherst

Wendy Y. Carter, Department of Sociology, University of Wisconsin–Madison, and Center for Demography and Ecology

John Cawley, Department of Economics, University of Chicago

Freddy B. Christiansen, Department of Ecology and Genetics, University of Aarhus, Denmark

Steven Durlauf, Department of Economics, University of Wisconsin–Madison

Marcus W. Feldman, Department of Biological Sciences, Stanford University

James R. Flynn, Department of Political Studies, University of Otago, Dunedin, New Zealand

Herbert Gintis, Department of Economics, University of Massachusetts at Amherst

Robert M. Hauser, Department of Sociology, University of Wisconsin–Madison, and Center for Demography and Ecology

James Heckman, Department of Economics, University of Chicago

Min-Hsiung Huang, Department of Sociology, University of Wisconsin–Madison, and Center for Demography and Ecology

Sanders Korenman, School of Public Affairs, Baruch College, City University of New York, and National Bureau of Economic Research

Lance Lochner, Department of Economics, University of Rochester

Glenn Loury, Department of Economics, Boston University

Shelly J. Lundberg, Department of Economics, University of Washington

Sarah P. Otto, Department of Zoology, University of British Columbia, Vancouver, Canada

John E. Roemer, Department of Economics, University of California at Davis

Cecilia Rouse, Department of Economics, Princeton University, and National Bureau of Economic Research

Amartya Sen, Trinity College, Cambridge, UK

Richard Startz, Department of Economics, University of Washington

Edward Vytlacil, Department of Economics, University of Chicago

John Robert Warren, Department of Sociology, University of Wisconsin–
  Madison, and Center for Demography and Ecology

Christopher Winship, Department of Sociology, Harvard University

Introduction

KENNETH ARROW, SAMUEL BOWLES, AND
STEVEN DURLAUF

PROGRAMS to assure a modicum of economic security for the poor and to guarantee equality of opportunity for all have faltered in recent years; egalitarian initiatives from progressive taxation to support for single parents have come under attack and many redistributive programs are now less widely supported among the U.S. public than a decade or two ago.

Among the reasons for this reversal, we believe, is the public's growing division concerning the requirements of justice. Americans continue to support equality of opportunity as a goal, and the U.S. public remains deeply committed to helping those in need. In 1991 those who were "willing to pay higher taxes" both to "reduce poverty" and more specifically to "provide job training and public service jobs for people on welfare so that they can get off welfare" outnumbered those "unwilling" to support these activities by a two-to-one margin (Weaver et al. 1995). Almost three-quarters of those surveyed agreed (most of them "completely") with the statement, "The government should guarantee every citizen enough to eat and a place to sleep." Many, however, think that current policies to pursue these objectives are either ineffective or unfair. Americans appear to be profoundly divided on how to define equality of opportunity and bewildered by contradictory claims about how any of the competing conceptions might be advanced through social policy. Three sources of the demoralization of the egalitarian project in the United States are notable.

The first is moral. The concept of fairness—in the everyday sense of a level playing field—though strongly endorsed in the abstract, does not enjoy a consensus on what it entails; as a result the concept fails to provide much guidance in the formulation and promotion of egalitarian efforts. Even so basic a concept as equality of educational opportunity eludes definition, with proposals ranging from securing the absence of overt discrimination based on race or gender to the far more ambitious goal of eliminating race, gender, and class differences in educational outcomes. Many are disappointed by the apparently limited ability of conventional meritocratic policies to overcome the legacies of past discrimination. Not surprisingly, then, competing conceptions of meritocracy are advanced—that pay and privilege should be awarded solely on the basis of merit, however defined—along with other possibly more egalitarian principles.

A century ago the desirability of at least some redistribution from the rich to the less well off was thought by its advocates to be so transparent that it scarcely required justification. The appeal of this egalitarian ethic relied on the implicit identification of the "poor" with hardworking, low-wage workers, a group of people who in the public mind were at once numerous (perhaps the majority), the least well off, economically productive, and impeded by socially contrived barriers to their advancement (Cohen 1995, pp. 152–158).

But the system of income transfers that evolved in the United States after the Great Depression eschewed the logic that work at low pay established a claim on society's resources (though the workings of the social security system, as distinct from its explicit justification, did implement a version of this egalitarian logic). Rather, as Theda Skocpol (1992) has pointed out, it was the social contribution of "mothers and veterans" that was seen as most demanding of social reciprocity. And with the passage of time—accelerated by an unpopular war and a rapid change in family structure—even these claims now command less consensus.

Thus, today many of the least well off are not regarded as productive in any respect, and widespread understandings of their actions now serve more often to disqualify than to entitle them to a larger share of the social product. Rather, the "poor" appear to be a distinct minority facing few readily identified social exclusions from advancement. In many people's opinion it is the poor, not the rich, who are social parasites, the more benign version of which opinion adds that the poor lack the ability to be productive (Bowles and Gintis 1999).

"Ability" can be a powerful claim on society's resources. More than 90 percent of Americans surveyed in the 1970s, when asked to describe a "fair economic system," favored "people with more ability would earn higher salaries" over "all people would earn about the same" (McClosky and Zaller 1984). If mounting inequalities in earnings can be attributed to a growing market scarcity of skill or an increase in the rate of return to ability, the widening gaps in living standards command less concern and may even be seen as a benign signal that the poor should smarten up (if they can) or pay the price.

The egalitarian project is unraveling for a second reason: shifts in public knowledge of the causes of inequality have exacerbated the problem of "the deservingness of the poor." Poverty and inequality were once thought to be the effect of systemic impediments such as discrimination and class bias in schooling and employment. But with the television images of a southern governor barring the schoolhouse door to exclude black children fading, and with privileged access by the rich to elite higher education on the wane, poverty and inequality now invite either cultural or genetic explanations. These accounts appear to resonate with the U.S. public today in a way they did not in the past, when the economic disadvantages of racial minorities and the poor could be readily explained by widely acknowledged forms of discrimination. But the eclipse of the most dramatic forms of overt discrimination, coupled with phenomena such as the educational success of some Asians and extensive media coverage of crime, drug use, and other social pathologies in low-income communities, has shifted public perceptions toward attributing full responsibility to the poor for their condition.

The third contribution to the demise of egalitarianism concerns public policy. The shift in public understandings of the causes of inequality underlies an increasingly widely held view that our current levels of inequality—whether reprehensible or not—are simply immune to public-policy intervention, whether in the form of employment training or expanded educational opportunity. Thus, for example, the much-touted hypothesis that cognitive abilities are in important measure inherited is falsely thought to imply that the knowledge capacities of people are immune to societal influences such as enriched education. Many who believe that deficiencies of "cultural capital" impede the economic advancement of the poor argue that the scope for public policy in the expansion of economic opportunity is severely limited. That these pessimists ignore many social interventions that might enhance the cultural capital of the poor—from adequate schooling, to home ownership, to subsidies for job creation—apparently does not detract from the superficial persuasiveness of their quiescent position. Belief in the efficacy of education in particular may also have been eroded both by massive public exposure to the unscientific claims of genetic determinism and by an unfounded conviction that government programs are ineffective in general.

The result is a dismal prognosis of immutable inequality. Two specters of intractable inequality now haunt the public imagination. One vision, more prevalent in Europe than in the United States, is the "three thirds" hypothesis: future generations will be sorted into three groups of roughly equal size—a privileged professional and technical elite, a blue-collar working class, and the warehoused population of those unable to find jobs or even incapable of productive employment.

The other image, reminiscent of Michael Young's *Rise of Meritocracy* (1958), is of a hereditary cognitive elite whose position is secured by the possession of advanced mental skills and passed on from generation to generation through the genetic inheritance of these skills. According to this view, any attempt to attenuate this stratification by mental ability—inhibiting employers' and educators' use of cognitive test scores to screen workers and prospective students, for example—will be costly in efficiency terms.

All three of these aspects of the assault on egalitarianism—public understandings about the requirements of justice, the sources of unequal economic and social standing, and the efficacy of governmental programs—have been the subject of extensive and deep scholarly inquiry. In the pages that follow we have assembled recent contributions to scholarship in this area by leading scholars in their respective fields. We have sought answers to the following questions:

First, *what kind of justification of economic inequality does reward according to merit provide, and are market rewards thus justified? If merit is underdefined, what should be equalized?* Answering this first group of questions requires answers to two additional groups of questions.

Second, *what determines the distribution of economic reward, and in particular what relationship does economic reward bear to various individual characteristics that might be termed merit, as well as to other characteristics unrelated to merit, such as race?*

And third, *what determines the degree of intergenerational mobility and to what extent do the mechanisms accounting for the substantial persistence across generations in economic and social status accord with meritocratic principles?*

Because of the important role of inherited or "immutable" abilities in recent discussions of meritocracy we also sought answers to the following:

Fourth, *what role is played by genetic inheritance as opposed to social influences in the distribution of economically relevant abilities and in the process of intergenerational transmission of economic status?*

And fifth, *to what extent can social policy alter the distribution of economic reward, the degree of intergenerational status persistence, and particularly the low earnings of the least well off?*

The chapters that follow provide ample material for addressing these questions.

The chapters by Amartya Sen and John Roemer challenge widely held views of meritocracy. Amartya Sen points out that merit is essentially underdefined, and when appropriately defined it is necessarily a normative concept, one that expresses views on what kind of society one would hold to be just and good. Sen points out that it is natural in an economic approach to endorse the view that it is the consequences of actions that are to be deemed worthy of merit (rather than the actions per se). But if this is the case, and if an aversion to inequality is among our notions of what is just and good in a society, then the consequences of one's actions for egalitarian objectives must inform our definition of merit.

John Roemer contrasts merit- (or nondiscrimination-) based views of justice with "level playing field" conceptions and develops and defends a strong version of equality of opportunity as a preferable version of the latter. According to the equality of opportunity paradigm, opportunities must be equalized "before the competition starts," after which individuals are on their own. The key features of any practical approach then are to determine what it means to level the playing field "before the competition starts," and to determine after what point in life individuals are fully responsible for the advantages they attain. Roemer's chapter provides answers to these questions and also presents the results of a striking empirical investigation of the redistribution of educational resources between whites and African Americans in the United States that his concept of justice would require.

Two chapters then take up the question of IQ. James Flynn documents substantial trends in IQ test scores over time (the so-called Flynn effect) and cautions against the view that the cognitive abilities measured by the tests are immutable. He finds little evidence of the emergence of a class-stratified meritocracy.

Marcus Feldman, Sarah Otto, and Freddy Christiansen, adopting the quantitative approach to the study of gene-culture coevolution pioneered by Feldman and Cavalli-Sforza, critically review the literature on heritability. They provide new estimates of the heritability of IQ that are based not solely on twins but on diverse sets of relatives. They conclude that heritability has been considerably overestimated in studies restricted to twins and observe that heritability of a trait need not be closely related to the susceptibility of the trait to influence through changed environment.

The next five chapters explore the relationship between schooling and subsequent earnings. Orley Ashenfelter and Cecilia Rouse review recent studies addressed specifically to the causal impact of schooling on earnings. Using data from educational differences within families (including between identical twins) as well as those making use of exogenous determinants of schooling attainment, they find strong evidence that education raises earnings and that the correlation of earnings and schooling does not arise due to the covariation of schooling and earnings with omitted variables such as family background or genotypic influences on ability. Especially important, they find that the economic benefits of additional schooling are as strong among those of low scholastic ability (as measured by the Armed Forces Qualification Test [AFQT] score) as among those with higher scores. Children from less well off families also benefit from schooling at least as much as those from more advantaged homes. Schooling thus appears to be a powerful intervention to raise earnings of the least well off.

Samuel Bowles and Herbert Gintis then take up the apparent tension between Ashenfelter and Rouse's results (that schooling raises earnings) and the common econometric finding that measures of cognitive performance are poor predictors of economic success. They question the view that the economic returns to schooling are explained by the contribution of schools to cognitive functioning, showing that most of the return to schooling must arise from other sources. They then show how individual traits that are not skills at all—attributes such as a high marginal utility of income, or trustworthiness—might contribute to earnings by attenuating incentive problems in the workplace. Their conjecture is that schooling may contribute to earnings substantially by contributing to these "incentive-enhancing preferences."

Sanders Korenman and Christopher Winship review the empirical estimates in Richard Herrnstein and Charles Murray's *The Bell Curve*, and find that parental family background is at least as important, and may be much more important, than the AFQT score in determining economic success.

Moreover, like Ashenfelter and Rouse, they find substantial effects of additional schooling even in models with extensive controls for family background and AFQT. They conclude that the economic importance of the abilities measured on cognitive tests is frequently overestimated.

Robert Hauser, John Robert Warren, Min-Hsiung Huang, and Wendy Carter review the evidence from four rich data sets on the impact of schooling, family background, and cognitive scores on occupational success. The substantial effect of schooling on occupational attainment is a robust finding from all the data sets, and the fact that this effect remains substantial even among those with the same cognitive scores suggests that, as in the model of Bowles and Gintis, schooling may affect occupational success by avenues unrelated to its contribution to cognitive functioning. Hauser and his co-authors caution against identifying merit solely with cognitive abilities, noting that schooling attainment is also a plausible indicator of "merit."

The last chapter specifically on schooling, by John Cawley, James Heckman, Lance Lochner, and Edward Vytlacil, explores the relationship between cognitive skill, schooling, post-schooling investments in training, and earnings. They show that the frequent use of samples of younger workers may lead to an underestimate of the importance of cognitive skills as a determinant of lifetime earnings. They also demonstrate that most previous estimates of the rising trend in the return to cognitive skill are not robust once implausible estimating assumptions are rejected.

Three chapters on policy issues highlight both the broad scope for governmental interventions to enhance equality of opportunity and the importance of policy design in minimizing the costs of the interventions and avoiding unintended negative effects. Shelly Lundberg and Richard Startz provide a survey of the role of race, and particularly black-white differences, in the structure of inequality in the United States. They show that race is important in the processes both of human capital accumulation and of valuation of human capital by employers, and that the social—rather than individual—nature of both processes generates inefficiencies that may be addressed by public policy. Moreover, these same processes typically generate multiple long-run, sustainable outcomes in labor markets, some of which are unambiguously normatively preferred to others. Strong temporary interventions may thus lead to substantial welfare improvements where weaker permanent measures would fail.

Glenn Loury's chapter identifies a set of cases in which quota-like interventions on behalf of a disadvantaged group may result in reduced incentives for skill acquisition among the group, and thus could exacerbate group differences. Like Lundberg and Startz, Loury urges that the micro-level problems of individual incentives be addressed in policy design.

Roland Bénabou develops a unified approach for addressing the optimal degree of redistribution when a society values both equality of opportunity and average living standards. Because Bénabou's model incorporates imperfections in markets for loans and insurance, a major result is that policies to enhance equality of opportunity—such as reallocating educational funds toward the poor—tend to raise the rate of economic growth. By contrast, policies to implement greater equality of outcome reduce work incentives and reduce total output. Bénabou's approach, like that of Lundberg and Startz, illustrates the value of identifying market failures that may be attenuated by policies that enhance equality of opportunity, thus supporting an equality-efficiency *complementarity* rather than *trade-off*.

We will not attempt a conclusion from these diverse contributions, except to note a broad consensus that important violations of equality of opportunity exist, that many of these could be attenuated by social policies ranging from greater educational opportunity to anti-discrimination measures, that for some of these interventions the costs would be minimal and might be offset by long term gains in aggregate productivity, and that the problem of policy design to achieve these objectives requires attention to the incentive structures of all the relevant actors and the possibility of unintended negative consequences when the full range of impacts is considered.

References

Bowles, Samuel, and Herbert Gintis. 1999. "Reciprocity, Self Interest, and the Welfare State." *Nordic Journal of Political Economy* (forthcoming).

Cohen, G. 1995. *Self Ownership, Freedom, and Equality.* Cambridge: Cambridge University Press.

McClosky, Herbert, and John Zaller. 1984. *The American Ethos: Public Attitudes toward Capitalism and Democracy.* Cambridge, MA: Harvard University Press.

Skocpol, Theda. 1992. *Protecting Soldiers and Mothers: The Political Origins of Social Policy in the U.S.* Cambridge, MA: Harvard University Press.

Weaver, R. Kent, Robert Y. Shapiro, and Lawrence R. Jacobs. 1995. "The Polls—Trends: Welfare." *Public Opinion Quarterly* 59: 606–627.

Young, Michael. 1958. *The Rise of Meritocracy, 1870–2033.* London: Thames and Hudson.

MERITOCRACY AND ECONOMIC INEQUALITY

Part One ———————————————————————

MERIT, REWARD, AND OPPORTUNITY

One

Merit and Justice

AMARTYA SEN

Justitia and *Justitium*

I have been asked to write on "Justice in Meritocratic Environments." The idea of meritocracy may have many virtues, but clarity is not one of them. The lack of clarity may relate to the fact, as I shall presently argue, that the concept of "merit" is deeply contingent on our views of a good society. Indeed, the notion of merit is fundamentally derivative, and thus cannot but be qualified and contingent. There is some elementary tension between (1) the inclination to see merit in fixed and absolute terms, and (2) the ultimately *instrumental* character of merit—its dependence on the concept of "the good" in the relevant society.

This basic contrast is made more intense by the tendency, in practice, to characterize "merit" in inflexible forms reflecting values and priorities of the past, often in sharp conflict with conceptions that would be needed for seeing merit in the context of contemporary objectives and concerns. Some of the major difficulties with "meritocracy" arise, I would argue, from this internal conflict *within* the concept of "merit" itself.

When I received the invitation to write on justice in meritocracies, I was reminded of an amusing letter I had received a couple of years earlier from W. V. O. Quine (addressed jointly to John Rawls and me, dated December 17, 1992):

> I got thinking about the word *justice*, alongside *solstice*. Clearly, the latter, *solstitium*, is *sol* + a reduced *stit* from *stat-*, thus "solar standstill"; so I wondered about *justitium*: originally a legal standstill? I checked in Meillet, and he bore me out. Odd! It meant a court vacation.
>
> Checking further, I found that *justitia* is unrelated to *justitium*. *Justitia* is *just(um)* + *-itia*, thus "just-ness," quite as it should be, whereas *justitium* is *jus* + *stitium*.

I shall argue that meritocracy, and more generally the practice of rewarding merit, is essentially underdefined, and we cannot be sure about its content—and thus about the claims regarding its "justice"—until some further specifications are made (concerning, in particular, the objectives to be pursued, in terms of which merit is to be, ultimately, judged). The merit of actions—and (derivatively) that of persons performing actions—cannot be judged independent of the way we understand the nature of a good (or an acceptable) society. There is, thus, something of *justitium* or "standstill" in our understanding of merit, which involves at least a temporary "stay" (if not quite a "court vacation"). Indeed, examining the nature of this "standstill," which is ethically and politically illuminating, may be a better way of understanding the place of meritocracy in modern society than seeing it as a part of some categorical *justitia* that demands our compliance.

Merits and Theories of Justice

The general idea of merit must be conditional on what we consider good activities (or to see it in more deontological terms, right actions). The promotion of goodness, or compliance with rightness, would have much to commend it, and in this basic sense the encouragement of merit would have a clear rationale. But given the contingent nature of what we take to be good or right, there would inevitably be alternative views regarding (1) the precise *content* of merit, and (2) its exact *force* vis-à-vis other normative concerns in terms of which the success of a society may be judged. This problem would be present even without the difficulties raised by rigid and inflexible conceptions of what is to be seen as "merit" (an issue to which I shall turn later on).

This is not to deny that any particular comprehensive theory of justice will contain within its specifications the relevant parameters in terms of which the content and force of merit-based rewards can be judged. For example, John Rawls's (1958; 1971) classic theory of "justice as fairness," which has been overwhelmingly the most influential proposal in contemporary political philosophy, does provide enough structure and specification to allow us immediately to judge the demands of merits and meritocracy.[1] Yet the Rawlsian substantive theory of justice involves a particular compromise between conflicting concerns: formalized in his "two principles of justice," including the priority of liberty and the significance of efficiency and equity in the achievement and distribution of individual advantages. Many who have been much influenced by Rawls (including this author) are more at peace with the importance of these general concerns than they are with the specific compromise arrived at in Rawlsian theory.

There are, in particular, (1) different ways of recognizing the prior impor-

---

[1] On this, see Rawls (1971 and 1993). Rawls can, within the structure of his theory of justice as fairness, arrive at clear conclusions on this subject. He argues, for example (Rawls 1971, p. 107): "Thus a meritocratic society is a danger for the other interpretations of the principles of justice but not for the democratic conception. For, as we have just seen, the difference principle transforms the aims of society in fundamental respects."

tance of liberty, (2) distinct "spaces" in which efficiency and equity can be judged, and (3) dissimilar ways of balancing the two types of concerns.[2] It is indeed hard to expect a reasoned unanimity on the exact lines of any particular compromise between these concerns, given the depth of these demands. Further, it is not obvious that even in an imagined "original position" (with primordial equality) a consensus of reasoning would emerge to settle this issue adequately.[3]

The absence of a general agreement on a precise resolution (or on an exact formula) that balances the forces of the discordant concerns against each other does not, however, make it useless to analyze the role of meritocracy or to examine the nature of its conflict with the demands of other aspects of justice. Since I have argued in favor of "incomplete" theories of justice elsewhere (particularly in Sen 1970 and 1992), I am less uneasy with a "standstill" than a more determined or a more resourceful theorist of justice (or of welfare economics) would be.

Merits, Actions, and Incentives

The term *meritocracy* seems to have been invented by Michael Young in his influential book *The Rise of Meritocracy, 1870–2033* (Young 1958). Young himself was deeply critical of the development he identified, and meritocracy as a formalized arrangement has not, in general, received good press.[4] The *Fontana Dictionary of Modern Thought* (1988, p. 521) presents the following uncharming definition:

> A word coined by Michael Young (*The Rise of Meritocracy*, 1958) for government by those regarded as possessing merit; merit is equated with intelligence-plus-effort, its possessors are identified at an early age and selected for an appropriate intensive education, and there is an obsession with quantification, test-scoring, and qualifications. Egalitarians often apply the word to any elitist system of education or government, without necessarily attributing to it the particularly grisly features or ultimately self-destroying character of Young's apocalyptic vision.

[2] I have discussed possible variations from the Rawlsian system in Sen (1970, 1980, and 1992). Other proposals can be seen in Arneson (1989), Cohen (1989), Dworkin (1981), Roemer (1985 and 1994), Van Parijs (1995), and Walzer (1983), among other contributions.

[3] The lack of complete decidability in the Rawlsian "original position" was one of the two main theses presented in a paper that I jointly authored with Gary Runciman, "Games, Justice and the General Will" (Runciman and Sen 1965). The other thesis of that essay concerned the usefulness of game theory in clarifying Rousseau's concepts of "social contract" and "general will," and Rawls's ideas of the "original position" and "justice as fairness."

[4] The term *merit-monger*, the use of which is traced to 1552 by The *Oxford English Dictionary*, is described by the *OED*—not surprisingly—as "contemptuous."

I tend to share some of the suspicion of meritocratic systems to which such descriptions relate (more on this later), but when characterized in these frightening terms, it hardly seems possible that any reasonable society today would encourage or tolerate "the rise of meritocracy," and yet that is exactly what Michael Young claims has occurred. Meritocracy may rightly deserve condemnation, but to define it in such thoroughly revolting terms makes it hard to understand how it can appeal to anyone and why it may have an expanding role in modern society.[5] We have to do more groundwork first to understand what it is that gives meritocracy its appeal *within* its own rationale, and only after that can we examine whether that appeal can survive scrutiny.

In fact, meritocracy is just an extension of a general system of rewarding merit, and elements of such a system clearly have been present in one form or another throughout human history. There are, it can be argued, at least two different ways of seeing merit and systems of rewarding it.[6]

1. *Incentives:* Actions may be rewarded for the good they do, and a system of remunerating the activities that generate good consequences would, it is presumed, tend to produce a better society. The rationale of incentive structures may be more complex than this simple statement suggests, but the idea of merits in this *instrumental* perspective relates to the motivation of producing better results. In this view, actions are meritorious in a derivative and contingent way, depending on the good they do, and more particularly the good that can be brought about by rewarding them.

2. *Action propriety:* Actions may be judged by their propriety—not by their results—and they may be rewarded according to the quality of such actions, judged in a result-independent way. Much use has been made of this approach to merit, and parts of deontological ethics separate out right conduct—for praise and emulation—independent of the goodness of the consequences generated.

In one form or another both these approaches have been invoked in past discussions of merit, but it is fair to say that the incentives approach is the dominant one now in economics, at least in theory (even though the language used in practice often betrays interest in the other categories—more on which presently). Although the praiseworthiness of "proper" actions is

---

[5] I am, of course, aware that definitions constructed by the respective "enemies" provide many of the contemporary battlegrounds in cultural studies and social sciences (for example, "modernism" is discussed largely in terms specified by postmodernists, "subjectivism" is often examined in the way objectivists see it, and so on).

[6] The rewards can be material and financial, but there are other rewards, too, including *praise* and what Adam Smith called *approbation*—though some would no doubt find such rewards rather cheap and empty.

not denied in economic reasoning, the economic justification of rewarding merit tends to be grounded in consequences.[7] Adam Smith (1776 and 1790) made this distinction forcefully and proceeded to provide one of the first systematic analyses of the use of incentive systems as they operate naturally in societies and how they can be further sharpened. The distinction between the propriety and merit of an action is described by Smith (1790, II.i.1–2, p. 67) in the following way:

> There is another set of qualities ascribed to the actions and conduct of mankind, distinct from their propriety and impropriety, their decency or ungracefulness, and which are the objects of a distinct species of approbation. These are Merit and Demerit, the qualities of deserving reward, and of deserving punishment. . . . [u]pon the beneficial or hurtful effects which the affection proposes and tends to produce, depends the merit or demerit, the good or ill desert of the action to which it gives occasion

I shall concentrate in this chapter on the view of merit in terms of results and incentives. It is, in fact, virtually the only grounded and defended theory that can be found in the contemporary economic literature (shared by welfare economics, social choice theory, game theory, and implementation theory).[8]

Indeed, the practice of rewarding good (or right) deeds for their incentive effects cannot but be an integral part of any well-functioning society.[9] No matter what we think of the demands of "meritocracy" as it is usually defined, we can scarcely dispense with incentive systems altogether. The art of developing an incentive system lies in delineating the content of merit in such a way that it helps to generate valued consequences.

Merit Rewarding as a System

The derivative character of merit leads us to the central question as to what the "valued consequences" are and how the success and failure of a society are to be judged. Once an instrumental view of merit is accepted, there is no

---

[7] A related aspect of normative economics is its relentlessly consequentialist form, and in this respect it goes well beyond Adam Smith's position. I have argued elsewhere (particularly in Sen 1982 and 1985) both (1) for broadening the limits of consequential analysis (in particular through departures from the utilitarian way of judging consequences), and (2) for recognizing the extensive reach of consequential ethics in this broadened form (undercutting some of the arguments for the necessity of a deontological ethics). Seeing merits in terms of incentive systems fits well into a broadly consequentialist framework.

[8] See, however, the broader concerns discussed by Sugden (1981), along with the incentive-oriented view.

[9] There are *merit-rewarding arrangements* in all "incentive-compatible" systems, though the rewarding of merit can coexist with incentive incompatibility as well.

escape from the contingent nature of its content, related to the characterization of a good—or an acceptable—society and the criteria in terms of which assessments are to be made.

If, for example, the conceptualization of a good society includes the absence of serious economic inequalities, then in the characterization of instrumental goodness, including the assessment of what counts as merit, note would have to be taken of the propensity of putative merit to lessen—or generate—economic inequality. In this case, the rewarding of merit cannot be done independent of its distributive consequences.[10]

In India shortly after independence, a system of preference for lower-caste candidates in the civil service was introduced in the newly formulated constitution of the Republic of India, reserving a certain proportion of places for them minimally, although recruitment in general was governed by examination. The argument defending this preference system was partly based on some notion of fairness to the candidates (given the educational and social handicap typically experienced by lower-caste candidates), but, more important, it was argued that the reduction of inequality in the society at large depended on breaking the effective monopoly of upper-caste civil servants. The upper-caste bias in the distribution of justice and in the allocation of governmental help could be changed only by having civil servants from less privileged backgrounds.[11] This latter argument is an "efficiency reason"— efficiency in pursuit of a distribution-inclusive social goal.

Even though the typical "objective functions" that are implicitly invoked in most countries to define and assess what is to count as merit tend to be indifferent to (or negligent of) distributive aspects of outcomes, there is no necessity to accept that ad hoc characterization. This is not a matter of a "natural order" of "merit" that is independent of our value system. The dependent nature of merit and its reward has to be more fully understood to see the nature and reach of merit-based systems.

This dependence is the main reason behind the "standstill" that has to be overcome. There are also, however, other tensions that arise within the general approach of merit-based rewards. There is, in particular, a tension of moral psychology within the incentive-based rationale of rewarding merits, arising from its instrumental nature. Actions are rewarded for what they help to bring about, but the rewarding is not valued in itself. Insofar as the rewards handed out could have been used for some purpose that is valued in itself, it would obviously have made sense—*given other things*—to use them for that purpose. But equally obviously this very thought denies the productive role of the incentives, and thus the "side use" is not entertainable

---

[10] On the integration of distributive concerns in assessing states of affairs and social arrangements, see Atkinson (1983).

[11] A similar argument was used to reserve, for a specified period, a certain proportion of seats in the Indian parliament for lower-caste candidates.

in practice. The psychological tension that it creates arises from the necessity of accepting some assignments that are not themselves valued (and may, in fact, be revoltingly unequal and unattractive), which are contingently justified by the actions of the recipients and the effects that these actions have on the rest of the society (for example, on aggregate outputs and incomes).[12]

There is some tension also in the feature that the extent of inequality that an incentive-based system has to tolerate would depend crucially on what motivates people to act in one way rather than another. Various proposals for the development of cooperative values have been considered in this context.[13]

The instrumental nature of incentive systems makes the justification for payments turn pervasively on the actual effects of different payments on behavior and choices. To consider a rather unattractive example of an incentive argument, in deciding how much to pay a blackmailer, the payment that would be justified would depend on what would induce him or her to give up those compromising documents. It would be in the blackmailer's interest to pretend that nothing short of a very vast sum would be acceptable, and it would be for the payer to judge whether he or she is bluffing.

In the normal working of an economy, of course, we do not encounter cases on this level of directness, and also competition—when present—limits what an individual operator can demand and expect to get. But there is often an element of unclarity in deciding on the incentive effects of changes in reward systems, for example in deciding on the likely effects of reducing remarkably high payments to top executives that have now become standard and are typically defended on incentive grounds.[14] There are also interesting incentive questions to be sorted out in predicting the likely results of raising the regulational minimum wage for employees (potentially influencing the profitability and employment decisions of firms).

Debates on these subjects have tended to be quite intense in recent years.[15]

---

[12] Some radical critiques of a functioning capitalist economy, with its manifest inequalities, relate to this tension; it provides grounds for powerful egalitarian rhetoric and condemnation of inequality even when the economic reasoning remains incomplete. Arguments of this kind have to be distinguished from other radical critiques that see the real incentive effects as quite different from what is claimed on their behalf by the beneficiaries—or "apologists"—of the system.

[13] When Marx (1875), following a line of socialist thinking, considered the case for "from each according to his ability to each according to his need," he noted the unfeasibility of this option, because of incentive problems, even when socialism would be established. He settled, thus, for an incentive system of payment according to the value of work "at the early stages of socialism," but also expressed his hope for an evolution of human motivation in the long run such that need-based distribution could become practicable without being, then, derailed by incentive problems.

[14] For an important critical scrutiny of the issues related to high payments to executives and professionals in contemporary America, see Bok (1993).

[15] For example, the unorthodox findings of Card and Krueger (1995) on the predicted consequences of minimum wage variations have been subjected to remarkably intense attacks in some business publications.

This is not surprising since incentive arguments of different kinds provide the intellectual backing for many prevailing practices as well as proposals for change. These arguments draw a good deal of their immediate significance from the tension under discussion. Since rewards to merit in the form of incentive requirements are not valued in themselves, there is a tenacious rationale for discussing the possibility of reducing their demands in favor of social objectives that may be valued *in themselves* (including reduction of economic inequality, insofar as it is generally favored in the society in question), so long as this can be done without greater harm through the actual—as opposed to imagined—effects on incentives. The lack of intrinsic status of merit-rewards in an incentive system makes that complex *instrumental* connection central to economic debates on policies and strategies.

Meritocracy and Additional Features

So far I have been discussing the nature and implications of rewarding merit, particularly given the dependence of merit on social criteria of success. The approach of what may be called meritocracy, however, tends to take a less "parametric" view of the determinants of merit and frequently sees it as *given* characteristics that deserve rewards. The definition of meritocracy, quoted earlier from The *Fontana Dictionary of Modern Thought* (1988), somewhat exaggerated the "extremism" of the chosen views of merit and its reward, but it drew attention to the fact that the idea of "meritocracy" must be seen as something quite a bit more demanding than the rewarding of merit according to some agreed criteria of social success.

There would seem to be at least three substantial departures from the kind of general system of rewarding meritorious actions that I have been considering in the preceding discussion.

1. *Personification and genetics:* In the incentive approach to merit, it is characteristic of *actions*, not of people as such. But conventional notions of "meritocracy" often attach the label of merit to *people* rather than actions. A person with standardly recognized "talents" (even something as nebulous as "intelligence") can, then, be seen as a meritorious person even if he or she were not to use the "talents" to perform acts with good consequences or laudable propriety. This "personal quality" of merits sometimes gets invoked even in a largely incentive-oriented system of economic reasoning, with which the "personal quality" view is basically in conflict.

Some people are seen as being just more meritorious than others, and may indeed have been born more talented. In some versions of personification, the inborn talents are seen not only as being variable between one person and another (for which there may be considerable evidence), but also as distributed according to some other readily distinguishable characteristic, such as skin color or the size of the nose (for which the evidence seems very problematic, to say the least).[16] When used in this form, personification can encourage meritocratic acceptance of—rather than resistance to—inequalities of achievement (often along racial and ethnic groupings), which are present in many contemporary societies.

2. *Deserts and entitlement:* An incentive argument is entirely "instrumental" and does not lead to any notion of intrinsic "desert." If paying a person more induces him or her to produce more desirable results, then an incentive argument may exist for that person's pay being greater. This is an instrumental and contingent justification (related to results)—it does not assert that the person intrinsically "deserves" to get more. To return to an illustration used earlier, an incentive argument may well exist even for paying a blackmailer some money to induce him or her to hand over some compromising material, but that incentive argument is not the same as accepting that the blackmailer "deserves" to get that money because of the blackmailer's intrinsic virtue.

In a meritocratic system, however, this distinction gets blurred, and the established and fixed nature of the system of rewards may generate the implicit—sometimes even explicit—belief that the rewards are "owed" by the society to the meritorious persons. As Michael Walzer (1983, p. 136) points out,

> *Desert* implies a very strict sort of entitlement, such that the title precedes and determines the selection, while *qualification* is a much looser idea. A prize, for example, can be deserved because it already belongs to the person who has given the best performance; it only remains to identify that person. Prize committees are like juries in that they look backward and aim at an objective decision.

When this idea of desert is combined with rewarding "talents" as such— indeed, even the *possession* of talents (rather than the *production* of desirable results with them)—the connection with the incentive rationale of meritocracies is fairly comprehensively severed.

3. *Distribution independence:* A system of rewarding of merits may well generate inequalities of well-being and of other advantages. But, as was argued earlier, much would depend on the nature of the consequences that are sought, on the basis of which merits are to be characterized. If the results desired have a strong distributive component, with a preference for equality, then in assessing merits (through judging the generated results, including its distributive aspects), concerns about distribution and inequality would enter the evaluation.

Since distributive concerns would come in only inter alia in these accountings, an incentive system of rewarding merits may still generate much in-

---

[16] A caste system often derives its rationale from beliefs regarding the distribution of talent. Such beliefs are, of course, a standard part of the "intellectual" background of the practice of racism.

equality. Nevertheless, there would then be something *within* that consequential system of evaluation that would work, to a varying extent, against generating more inequality.

In most versions of modern meritocracy, however, the selected objectives tend to be almost exclusively oriented toward aggregate achievements (without any preference against inequality), and sometimes the objectives chosen are even biased (often implicitly) toward the interests of more fortunate groups (favoring the outcomes that are more preferred by "talented" and "successful" sections of the population). This can reinforce and augment the tendency toward inequality that might be present *even with* an objective function that, inter alia, attaches some weight to lower inequality levels.

None of these three additional features of meritocracy is necessary for a general system of rewarding merits on incentive grounds. What are often taken to be "meritocratic" demands have moved, in many ways, so far away from their incentive-based justification that they can scarcely be defended on the classic incentive grounds. These ad hoc additions call for close scrutiny, especially given the hold they have on popular discussions—and sometimes even professional deliberations—on this subject.

Concluding Remarks

Although I shall not try to summarize this chapter, I shall comment on a few of the issues that have emerged in the preceding analysis.

First, the rewarding of merit and the very concept of merit itself depend on the way we see a good society and the criteria we invoke to assess the successes and failures of societies. The "incentive view" of merit competes with the view of merit based on "action propriety," but it is the incentive approach that tends, with good reason, to receive attention in contemporary justificatory discussions.

Second, the incentive view of merit is underdefined, since it is dependent on the preferred view of a good society. The theory of merit, thus, needs to draw on other normative theories. The rewarding of merit is, to adapt a Kantian distinction, a "hypothetical imperative" that is dependent on the way we judge the success of a society; it does not involve a "categorical imperative" on what should in any case be done.

Third, the contingent nature of merit also indicates that its relationship with economic inequality would depend very much on whether an aversion to economic inequality is included in the objective function of the society. If it is included, then merit for reward would have to be judged in an inequality-sensitive way. Despite the inclusion of inequality aversion among the criteria for judging a society, however, merit-based rewards may, in fact, generate considerable inequality, since there are other criteria as well (or other aspects of the combined objective function). The presence of inequality and other drawbacks can lead to some psychological tension, especially since the rewarding of merit is not directly valued under the incentive approach.

Fourth, even though the incentive-based argument for rewarding merit tends to be, in principle, accepted as the main justification for such a reward system, some of the particular interpretations that go with the championing of merit-rewards are unnecessary and, in some cases, inconsistent with the incentive approach. The common additional features include: (1) confounding merit of *actions* with that of *persons* (and possibly of groups of people), (2) overlooking the *instrumental* nature of the incentive argument and seeing the rewards of merit as intrinsic *entitlements or deserts*, and (3) ad hoc exclusion of *distributional* concerns from the objective function in terms of which merit is characterized.

Each of these departures makes meritocracies more prone to generate economic inequality, but they are in no sense part of the basic incentive approach to rewarding merit. Perhaps the most fundamental problem with the conventional understanding of "meritocracy" is the distance that has grown between "meritocracy" (thus conceived) and the foundational idea of rewarding merit.

References

Arneson, R. 1989. "Equality and Equality of Opportunity for Welfare." *Philosophical Studies* 56: 74–94.

Atkinson, A. B. 1983. *Social Justice and Public Policy.* Brighton: Wheatsheaf; and Cambridge, MA: MIT Press.

Bok, Derek. 1993. *The Cost of Talent. How Executives and Professionals Are Paid and How It Affects America.* New York: Free Press.

Card, David, and Alan Krueger. 1995. *Myth and Measurement: The New Economics of the Minimum Wage.* Princeton, NJ: Princeton University Press.

Cohen, G. A. 1989. "On the Currency of Egalitarian Justice." *Ethics* 99: 906–944.

Dworkin, Ronald. 1981. "What Is Equality? Part 1: Equality of Welfare" and "What Is Equality? Part 2: Equality of Resources." *Philosophy and Public Affairs* 10: 85–246, 293–345.

Marx, Karl. 1875. *Critique of the Gotha Program.* English translation, New York: International Publishers.

Rawls, John. 1958. "Justice as Fairness." *Philosophical Review* 67: 164–194.

———. 1971. *A Theory of Justice.* Cambridge, MA: Harvard University Press.

———. 1993. *Political Liberalism.* New York: Columbia University Press.

Roemer, John. 1985. "Equality of Talent." *Economics and Philosophy*, 1: 151–187.

———. 1994. *Egalitarian Perspectives: Essays in Philosophical Economics.* Cambridge: Cambridge University Press.

Runciman, Gary, and Amartya Sen. 1965. "Games, Justice and the General Will." *Mind* 74 (October): 554–562.

Sen, Amartya. 1970. *Collective Choice and Social Welfare.* San Francisco: Holden-Day. Republished, Amsterdam: North Holland, 1979.

———. 1980. "Equality of What?" In *Tanner Lectures on Human Values,* ed. S. McMurrin, pp. 197–220. Cambridge: Cambridge University Press; and Salt Lake City: University of Utah Press.

———. 1982. "Rights and Agency." *Philosophy and Public Affairs* 11: 3–39.

———. 1985. "Well-being, Agency and Freedom: The Dewey Lectures 1984." *Journal of Philosophy* 82: 169–224.

———. 1992. *Inequality Reexamined.* Oxford: Clarendon Press; and Cambridge, MA: Harvard University Press.

Smith, Adam. 1776. *An Inquiry into the Nature and Causes of the Wealth of Nations.* Republished, Oxford: Clarendon Press, 1976.

———. 1790. *The Theory of Moral Sentiments.* Revised edition, republished, Oxford: Clarendon Press, 1975.

Sugden, Robert. 1981. *The Political Economy of Public Choice.* Oxford: Martin Robertson.

Van Parijs, Philippe. 1995. *Real Freedom for All.* Oxford: Clarendon Press.

Walzer, Michael. 1983. *Spheres of Justice.* New York: Basic Books.

Young, Michael. 1958. *The Rise of Meritocracy, 1870–2033.* London: Thames and Hudson.

Two

Equality of Opportunity*

JOHN E. ROEMER

I

Two conceptions of equality of opportunity are prevalent today in Western democracies. The first says that society should do what it can to "level the playing field" among individuals who compete for positions, or among individuals during their periods of formation, so that all those with relevant potential will eventually be admissible to pools of candidates competing for positions. The second conception, which I call the nondiscrimination or merit principle, holds that in the competition for positions in society, all individuals who possess the attributes relevant for the performance of the duties of the position in question should be included in the pool of eligible candidates, and that an individual's possible occupancy of the position should be judged only with respect to those relevant attributes. An instance of the first principle is the belief that compensatory education should be provided for children from disadvantaged social backgrounds so that a larger fraction of them will acquire skills required later on to compete for jobs against persons with more advantaged childhoods. An instance of the second principle is the belief that race or sex, as such, should not count for or against a person's eligibility for a position, when race or sex is an irrelevant attribute insofar as the performance of the duties of the position is concerned.

The typical application of the level-the-playing-field principle goes farther than the nondiscrimination principle. It might, for example, say that equal opportunity requires that educational expenditures per pupil in public schools be equalized in a state or country. Were such equalization not to have been implemented, then nondiscrimination alone, in the competition for jobs, would not constitute the provision of equal opportunity, for earlier on the playing field was not leveled, if children from rich school districts had access to better education than children from poor school districts. Indeed, equalizing per pupil expenditures may not go far enough in leveling the playing field in such cases. If an educated child is the output forthcoming from applying a certain technology to a bundle of inputs or resources, some

* Parts of this essay are taken from my book (Roemer 1998). I thank my collaborator Julian Betts for permission to report some of our joint work in this chapter.

of which are beyond the influence of schools (for example, the child's genes, family, and neighborhood) and some of which can be supplied by the school district (for example, teachers, schools, books), then leveling the playing field might be thought to require compensating those with inferior bundles of the first kind of resource with an extra dose of the second kind.

Among the citizenry of any advanced democracy we find individuals who hold a spectrum of views concerning what is required for equal opportunity, from the nondiscrimination view at one pole to pervasive social provision to correct for all manner of disadvantage at the other. Common to all these views, however, is the precept that the equal opportunity principle at some point holds the individual accountable for the achievement of the advantage in question, whether that advantage be a level of educational achievement, health, employment status, income, or the economist's utility or welfare. Thus, there is in the notion of equality of opportunity a "before" and an "after": before the competition starts opportunities must be equalized, by social intervention if need be, but after it begins individuals are on their own. The different views of equal opportunity can be categorized according to where they place the starting gate that marks the point after which individuals are on their own.

In this chapter I attempt to propose exactly how the playing field should be leveled once we have decided where to place the starting gate. I will eventually propose an algorithm that will enable a society (or a social planner) to translate any view about where the starting gate should be into a social policy that will implement a degree of equal opportunity consonant with that view. If my algorithm is accepted as reasonable, then the political debate about what equality of opportunity requires can be refined from a debate about social policy to one about the proper realm of individual accountability. For once that realm has been agreed upon, then a specific equal opportunity policy will follow more or less automatically from application of my proposed algorithm.

My aim is pluralistic in the sense that I shall provide a tool that can be used to calculate an equal opportunity policy consonant with any of a spectrum of views of individual accountability. It is pluralistic in another sense as well. People with many different conceptions of what distributive justice consists in all endorse equality of opportunity. I do not intend here to advocate a particular conception of distributive justice. People who hold various theories of distributive justice advocate the provision of equal opportunity not only in different degrees (that is, with different conceptions of accountability) but also in different spheres of social life. I hope that persons from many points of the political spectrum will be able to use my proposal without committing themselves to a more pervasive egalitarianism than they generally hold.

II

As the nondiscrimination principle is well known, my task here is to articulate carefully the "level playing field" view of equal opportunity.

What in the backgrounds of the individuals in question corresponds to the mounds and troughs in the playing field metaphor that should be leveled off? I propose that these are the differential circumstances of individuals, for which we believe they should not be held accountable, that affect their ability to achieve or have access to the kind of advantage that is being sought. To be concrete, consider the access to a good life that is facilitated by education. Our society considers education a sufficiently important input into the good life that it views the social provision of a decent education to all individuals as mandatory. Indeed, guaranteeing equal opportunity might seem to require providing equal amounts of educational resources for all individuals, and this goal has been achieved to varying extents in different countries and states. In the United States education has been, historically, funded by municipalities, and this engenders unequal schools for municipalities with unequal tax bases. In California there is a law requiring the state to fund local public schools so that an equal amount is spent on each student in the state. The landmark *Brown* decision (U.S. Supreme Court, 1954) provided that equal education for blacks and whites required that schools be integrated: the previous "separate but equal" policy was, it was ruled, an oxymoron. But in the United States, even were public educational financing to be equalized per capita, educational funding would not be equalized because of the existence of private schools. In the Nordic countries, by contrast, private schooling is for all practical purposes unavailable.

Guaranteeing equal per capita financing of education is, however, not sufficient to provide equal educational achievement, since different children are able to use educational resources (teachers, books, school buildings) with different degrees of effectiveness or efficiency. To take an extreme case, mentally retarded children require substantially more resources than normal children to reach a similar level of functioning, or at least a level that we find acceptable. That we provide more educational resources for such children shows that we do not think that equal opportunity for the good life, insofar as the educational dimension is relevant, is achieved by providing equal educational resources per capita: we believe that more resources should be provided to some types of children if those children are unable to process the resources as effectively as others. When is it the case that different types of children are unable to process resources with equal effectiveness, and when is it the case that, although able to process them equally effectively, they do not by virtue of choice?

We must distinguish between the *circumstances* beyond a child's control that influence her ability to process educational resources, and her acts of autonomous volition and *effort*. Equalizing opportunity for educational achievement requires distributing educational resources in such a way that lower *abilities* of children to turn resources into educational achievement are compensated for (I take ability to be determined by circumstances beyond the control of the individual). Differential achievements due to the application of autonomous volition or effort, however, should not be "leveled" or compensated for by an equal opportunity policy.

Thus, I am defining the "ability" of a child to transform resources into educational achievement as the propensity she has to effect that transformation by virtue of the influence of circumstances beyond her control, which— let us say, for the moment—include her genes, her family background, her culture, and, more generally, her social milieu. But two children with the same relevant circumstances, and hence the same ability, may achieve different levels of education by virtue of the differential application of effort. One extreme metaphysical view is that circumstances determine everything, so there is no room left for autonomous effort: if this were true, then we would say that what appears to be differential effort is in fact fully determined by differential circumstances. This case, called the deterministic one, is just one possibility. The general case is that educational achievement is determined jointly by circumstances and freely chosen effort, and equality of opportunity requires compensating persons for the differences in their circumstances insofar as those differences affect educational achievement, but not compensating them for the consequences of the differential application of effort. Since most people believe that such a thing as freely chosen effort exists, they endorse the second view.

Suppose—a tall order—that we knew exactly what circumstances jointly determined a child's ability to process school resources into educational achievement. Suppose further that the circumstances of a child could be characterized as the value of a certain vector with, say, n components. Suppose, for simplicity, that this vector takes on a small, finite number of values in the population, considerably fewer than the number of individuals. Then we could partition the population of children in question into a set of *types*, where a type consists of all individuals whose value of this vector is approximately the same. By definition of ability and type, all individuals in a given type have the same ability to transform resources into educational achievement. By supposition, there are, on average, a fairly large number of individuals across types, since the number of types is small compared to the number of individuals. Suppose further that there is a large number of individuals in each type.

I construct the equal opportunity policy as follows. Consider a distribution of the educational resources in which, within each type, each individual receives the same amount of resources. (There will generally be, however, different per capita amounts of the resource for different types.) We will observe a *distribution* of effort levels in each type, leading to differential educational achievements within each type. (I am here assuming that effort is one-dimensional and measurable.) Note that this distribution of effort is itself a *characteristic of the type*, not of any individual. *Where* on that distribution an individual sits is, however, due to his choice of effort, for by construction, individuals of the same type are identical with respect to circumstances.

I propose that the equal opportunity policy must equalize, in some average sense yet to be defined, the educational achievements of all types, but not equalize the achievements of individuals within types, which differ according to effort expended. Thus, equality of opportunity requires compensating individuals for their differential circumstances, but not for their differential efforts, holding ability (the consequence of circumstance) constant.

Alternatively phrased, the equal opportunity policy should make it the case that an individual's expected level of achievement of the outcome in question is a function only of his effort, and not of his circumstances.

By definition, any difference in achievement, once types have been defined, is viewed as following from the differential application of effort, or, as I also say, of different autonomous choices that individuals make. I view the different choices that individuals within a type make as relevantly autonomous in the sense of not being explained by circumstances (since circumstances are the same within a type). It is not immediately clear, however, how to compare the difference in efforts made by individuals of different types: for those effort differences are in part due to there being different *distributions* of effort across types.

I have no way of discovering exactly what aspects of a person's environment are beyond her control and affect her relevant behavior in a way that relieves her of personal accountability for that behavior. In actual practice, the society in question would decide, through some political process, what it wishes to deem "circumstances." Two kinds of disagreement would surface in that political discussion: first, concerning what aspects of a person's behavior really lie beyond his control, and hence should be attributed to circumstance, and second, whether to level the playing field partially or fully. I will return to these issues below.

Pursuing the education example, one might advocate a set of circumstances comprising income and education levels of the parents, race, and IQ.[1] Let us suppose that society chose this set of circumstances, which could be characterized as a vector with three components. The last component, IQ,

---

[1] One might, however, argue that IQ is affected by past effort and therefore is not an appropriate dimension of circumstance.

would not be represented by a continuous value but perhaps by five intervals—thus, the first component could take on five values. Similarly, each component could take on a (small) finite number of values. This would define a finite number of types; each type, in a nation with millions of children, would contain a large number of individuals, large enough to be able to speak of continuous distributions of effort and educational achievement within types.

The process of arriving at the set of circumstances used to characterize type would be a contentious one, as I have said, in which different political, psychological, biological, and social views and theories would be debated. The choice of the set of circumstances, however, would not be determined only by different views in the above senses, but by the practicalities of gathering information. For instance, many might agree that an important circumstantial variable influencing the child's ability to process educational resources is the love the parents express for her. It is, however, neither feasible nor, perhaps, appropriate (because invasive of privacy) to collect such information. Thus, the circumstances should be easily observable and nonmanipulable characteristics of individuals.

Clearly, the larger the set of circumstances and the more finely we measure differences in components of circumstance, the more types there will be. Some compromise must be struck that will keep the number of types down to a manageable level.

In what average sense should social policy attempt to equalize achievements of the advantage in question across types? Consider the problem of allocating educational resources to equalize opportunities, among the nation's children, for the attainment of future earning capacity. Once the amount of the education budget has been decided upon by the political process, the problem for the Department of Education, in my model, is to decide how that budget should be distributed among the various types of child. Imagine a particular distribution of that budget that assigns a certain amount of educational finance to each type, so that all children of the same type get the same amount but the per capita expenditures vary for different types. There would ensue a certain distribution of effort within each type: let us take, hypothetically, the measure of effort as the number of years of school attended by the individual.

Now the *distribution* of effort, as I said, is itself a characteristic of the type, not of any individual. That some types display inferior distributions of effort than other types is due not to individuals, but to the circumstances that characterize the types in question. For the purpose of comparing the effort expended by individuals in different types, we need an intertype comparable effort measure that factors out, so to speak, the "goodness" or "badness" of the distribution of effort itself. I propose that such a measure is the *centile* of the effort distribution of his type at which an individual is located. For example, I propose to say that two individuals, each at the thirtieth centile of their type distributions of effort, have tried equally hard.

What is the idea behind choosing the centile of the effort distribution as the type-neutral measure of effort? It is that in judging how hard a person has tried, it is only fair to judge him against others with similar circumstances. If there were a small number of individuals in a type, then the centile measure would not be so compelling, but with thousands, or hundreds of thousands, of individuals in each type, the distribution of effort within the type can be thought of as a fact of nature. The centile then provides a reliable measure of how hard the person has tried relative to those of her type. But since the measure is entirely relative (that is, not defined in terms of any absolute units of effort), it is as well compelling as a measure of relative effort expenditures across types.

The ideal of the equal opportunity policy is to allocate educational resources to render it so that how well a person eventually does in the acquisition of the outcome in question reflects only his effort, not his circumstances. Since I have identified the centile of the effort distribution as the appropriate intertype-comparable measure of effort, the policy I propose is that which renders the outcomes—in this case, future earning capacity—as equal as possible for all those individuals, across types, who sit at the same centile of their effort distributions. Within each type, however, there may well be large differences of future earning capacity, as effort varies.[2]

III

Let me now describe how my collaborator Julian Betts and I are applying this theory to compute what educational finance policy would be required to equalize opportunities for earning capacity between blacks and whites in the United States today. The calculation I will report does not aim to equalize opportunities quite generally among children with different circumstances: in this calculation, we will consider only the effect of one circumstance, namely race, on future earning capacity. I must add that we are in the process of carrying out an extensive set of calculations in which we will use the socioeconomic status of the family the child comes from, in addition to race, as a relevant circumstance.

To employ the theory, we need to know how effort and educational expenditures affect future wages of individuals, by type. Once we have econometric estimates of these relationships, we can compute how educational expenditures should be distributed in order that our equal opportunity (EOp) objective be realized—to make it the case that as far as possible the effect of

[2] The exact mathematical algorithm for computing the equal opportunity policy is presented and studied at some length in Roemer 1998.

one's circumstances on the outcome is neutralized, but not the effect of one's effort. There are some technical issues of exactly what such equalization requires, for discussion of which the reader is referred to the literature noted.

Fortunately, in the United States we have longitudinal data sets from which such data can be extracted. Because educational financing has been so unequal across school districts in our country, we have a good natural experiment from which we can estimate the response of future earning capacity to differential educational inputs. We employ the National Longitudinal Study of Young Men (NLSYM).

To carry out the equal opportunity calculation, we require a measure of effort of individuals. We have taken a conservative approach, by deriving effort implicitly from the data, as follows. We partition our sample into types, and then into subgroups within each type, where a subgroup consists of all members of the type who attended secondary schools spending the same amount per capita. (These secondary school expenditures are available in the NLSYM data set.) Within each subgroup, we observe a distribution of wages at age thirty. We attribute that distribution entirely to differential effort. Thus, we define a person's effort as consisting of all those things (which, in reality, include luck and family connections) that lead to having a higher wage at age thirty, holding constant type and educational expenditures. Since this modeling choice attributes more to effort than in fact should be so attributed, our equal opportunity policy will be less radical (i.e., compensatory) than otherwise.

Betts and I calculate that to equalize opportunity for future earning capacity between black and white males, we would have to spend approximately ten times as much on each black student as on each white student. There are some reasons not to put enormous faith in this precise number: to wit, our econometric estimates of the effect of school expenditures on wages must be extrapolated beyond the domain of observed data points at these levels of expenditure for blacks. What we can comfortably assert is that given the current educational production functions, we would have to expend *much* more on the education of blacks than on the education of whites to compensate the former for the economic disadvantage associated with growing up black in the United States.

Table 2.1 presents the exact results.[3] The first line of the table says that if the educational budget in the United States were $2,500 per student in 1990 dollars,[4] then equalizing opportunity for future wage earnings would require spending $12,001 on each black student in public school and $1,204 on each white student. If the educational budget were funded at $3,950 per capita, then

---

[3] A full report of our method and results is contained in Betts and Roemer 1998.

[4] This is approximately the real expenditures in U.S. secondary schools during the mid 1960s, when much of the cohort of the NLSYM, from which our data come, were in secondary school.

TABLE 2.1
Equal Opportunity Educational Expenditures

Per Capita Resource	X_{black}	X_{white}	$\dfrac{W_{EOp}}{W_{ER}}$
$2,500	$12,001	$1,204	0.976
3,950	14,538	2,506	0.974

the second line of the table reports the required expenditures on black and white students. At this higher level of expenditure, the ratio of EOp-required black to white expenditure is less than in the first line of the table.

The reason for these large differentials in EOp-mandated spending on the two types of child is that the observed elasticity of future wages with respect to educational spending is very small, a fact that has been noted extensively in the literature. Consequently, to increase the expected wages of a type, large educational expenditures are required. The econometric estimates we have made of these elasticities take the current modes of spending educational resources as given—we have simply used the observed statistical relationship between spending in the secondary school the student attended with his wages at age thirty, a relationship we can compute from the data in the NLSYM. In point of fact, were our nation to embark upon a program to equalize opportunities for earning capacity, we would not simply increase funding of schools as they are, but would doubtless invent new programs—along the lines, for instance, of Head Start—whose effectiveness might be considerably greater. Were this so, then the funds required for equalizing opportunities for future earning capacity between blacks and whites would be less than what our estimates stipulate.

I turn now to the issue of "efficiency." One need hardly remark that it is commonly held that the social cost of achieving equality is a loss in total output, or income. This equality-efficiency trade-off is manifest here in the following way. If we allocate a given educational budget disproportionately to disadvantaged types, then total output of society will suffer in the future, for the economic mechanism gives more "bang per buck" if we channel educational resources into students who can more efficiently convert them into future earning power—and those students come from predominantly advantaged types. To pursue this issue with regard to the type-partition I have been discussing, into black and white students, we should compute how the total wage bill of the country would change were we to allocate educational expenditures according to table 2.1's prescription. In the last column of that table we report the ratio of the total wage bill of the United States were the EOp policy to be implemented to the total wage bill were the "equal resource" policy implemented, in which exactly the same amount is spent on every student. For a national budget of $2,500 per capita, that ratio is 97.6 percent. Thus, the "efficiency cost" of the EOp policy is about 2.4 percent, using the equal resource policy as the benchmark. This is perhaps surprisingly small, given the large differential on educational spending by type postulated in the table. The explanation is two-fold: first, as noted earlier, the elasticity of wages with respect to educational expenditures is small, and second, blacks—the disadvantaged type here—comprise only 12 percent of the U.S. population. In South Africa, an EOp policy would be much more costly.

The estimate of 2.4 percent may even be an overestimate of the cost of implementing EOp, because a workforce in which skills are less differentiated than at present may be a more productive workforce. That is to say, there may be positive externalities in production attendant to reducing the skewness in the distribution of skills in the workforce.

Finally, a remark is appropriate on the sparse delineation of circumstances in the computation I have presented—that a person's circumstances are summarized by his race. Earlier I mentioned that a much longer list of circumstances might be employed to partition the relevant population into types, including perhaps IQ and measures of the socioeconomic status of the person's parents. The choice only of race as a circumstance means that we are attributing all differences in eventual earning capacity other than those directly correlated with race as aspects of "effort." Implicitly, we are holding individuals responsible for the effects of all those other dimensions of circumstance on future wages. To the extent that low socioeconomic status or low IQ is correlated with race, that will be picked up in our econometric estimates, but we take no explicit account of those other circumstances. Therefore, our recommended EOp policy is more *conservative* than it would be if we explicitly counted IQ, or socioeconomic status of parents, as a dimension of type. To be precise, if we took the partition of the {Black, White} type partition that would be associated with introducing socioeconomic status (SES) of parents as another dimension of type, then the "Black Low SES status" type would receive more than $12,001 per capita, and the "White High SES status" type would receive less than $1,204 per capita in educational resources at the EOp policy.[5]

In choosing the sole dimension of type to be race, we are taking a relatively conservative position—only that a person's race should not affect her opportunity for future earning capacity. Herrnstein and Murray (1994) would disagree, for efficiency reasons: they maintain that spending too much on black students would be too costly for society. But we have shown that the efficiency costs of a race-based EOp policy are quite small, arguably worth the benefit of equalizing opportunities.

---

[5] The reader is referred to Betts and Roemer 1998 for details.

Our argument, moreover, need never address the question of the heritability of IQ.[6] To advocate the implementation of equal opportunity for the acquisition of wage-earning capacity, one need only agree that, ethically speaking, it is desirable that a person's eventual wage-earning capacity be a function only of all the elements of effort that he or she has expended in youth, here defined as that period in which one prepares for the period of employment. Against that view, one can—correctly, I think—mount the attack that efficiency considerations should count as well. At some point, sacrifices in the size of the pie may legitimately cause us to limit the equalization of opportunity. The question whether IQ, or some more complex measure of native talent, is differentially or identically distributed in different racial groups itself has no independent bearing on the question, once the ethic of equal opportunity has been endorsed *and* the efficiency costs have been shown to be small.

Against the claim of the last sentence, one might say that the *mere possession* of a higher dose of native talent *entitles* the bearer to greater income, independent of her having worked harder to earn it. Such a view is incompatible with the philosophy of equal opportunity and, indeed, with contemporary democratic sentiments.

Suppose the American citizenry were won over to the idea of implementing the equal opportunity policy here discussed. How would we implement it? This, again, is a topic whose scope is beyond the present chapter. Let us simply observe that many methods are in principle possible, from vouchers, to special educational programs targeted to different types, to funding public schools differentially based on the distribution of types within the school.

IV

Until now, I have discussed one application of the equal opportunity algorithm, to educational spending in public schools used as an instrument to equalize opportunity for future earning capacity. I now turn to my final topic, the scope of equal opportunity policy.

Should the equal opportunity principle be applied to admit a certain number of short players, who try very hard, to professional basketball teams? Being short is, after all, a circumstance beyond one's control. Should individuals who fail the medical boards in surgery nevertheless be licensed as surgeons if they tried hard, and come from disadvantaged backgrounds? The equal opportunity principle, if applied, would answer both questions affir-

---

[6] Other chapters in this book argue that no statistical evidence exists showing that intelligence is differentially distributed in different racial groups. Although I find these arguments persuasive, my point here is that the outcome of this scientific debate is unimportant for evaluating the desirability of equal opportunity policy.

matively. But I would not advocate applying the principle in these cases. What, then, is the *scope* of the equal opportunity principle?

The EOp principle counts as an objective only the advantage accruing to the individuals competing for resources (education, income, jobs), whereas the nondiscrimination or merit principle, which I mentioned at the beginning, is concerned not only with exercising a degree of fairness to those competitors, but also with the welfare of consumers of the product those individuals will produce. Thus, basketball players produce a game consumed by spectators and surgeons produce appendectomies consumed by patients. If we apply the EOp principle to the licensing of surgeons, then we are assigning primary weight to the fulfillment of aspirations of would-be surgeons; if we apply the non-discrimination principle, we are assigning primary weight to the fulfillment of the lives of patients. In general, of course, one must be concerned with the welfare or advantage accruing both to those who aspire to positions and to those whom they serve. It is by limiting the scope and extent of EOp policies that one addresses the welfare of those who are served.

I must say that I do not think we can definitively decide the proper scope of the EOp principle without adopting a theory of distributive justice for the community in question. Until now, my purpose has been to describe what equality of opportunity consists in once three decisions have been made: that we shall apply the EOp principle to the situation in question (scope), that the circumstances defining type have been determined (one aspect of extent), and that the amount of resource society shall devote to equalizing oppor-tunities in the situation at hand has been established (another aspect of ex-tent). To establish what that amount should be requires a theory of distribu-tive justice for the community as a whole, for society must somehow trade off the consumption of the present generation of adults with the educational level of its children—if education is the issue—and hence, the degree of fulfillment of the next period's adults.

I have indicated that we can adjust the extent that opportunities are equal-ized by adjusting the amount of resources allocated to the task. A second way of adjusting that extent is to limit the set of circumstances. Reconsider the example of education, where I suggested that IQ be an element of cir-cumstance. Including IQ would require us, under the equal opportunity pol-icy, to invest substantial resources in low-IQ children, and correspondingly reduce the resources invested in high-IQ children, in an effort to raise the former's wage-earning capacity to the level of that capacity for high-IQ chil-dren. This might well entail a substantial loss in total output for the society in the next period, when those children become adults and join the labor force (here, assume that a worker's wage is an accurate measure of the social value of output she produces). It is clear that this social cost, in the form of the shrinking of the pie to be consumed by society, could be reduced by deleting IQ from the set of circumstances. Doing so would limit the extent to which we equalize opportunities: it is a decision to level the playing field only partially, rather than fully. The general principle here is that values other than equal opportunity, such as the size and quality of society's consumption pie, may induce us to limit the extent to which we equalize opportunity. As I noted earlier, this principle is often called the equality-efficiency trade-off, a terminology I dislike because it is not the case that social efficiency should be equated with the size of the consumption pie. Other things matter in judging how well a society's institutions serve its citizens.

Political liberals, who are usually concerned with equality, will generally argue for including many characteristics of a person's environment in the list of circumstances, and political conservatives, who are generally concerned mainly with the size of the pie, will argue for including few characteristics in that list.

Returning to the issue of the proper scope of EOp policy: my aim, as I have said, is pluralist in the sense that I do not wish to argue for a particular theory of distributive justice, but instead to describe what I think equality of opportunity entails, so that holders of various theories of justice may apply it in the cases where their theory prescribes it. Given what I have said above, I therefore cannot prescribe, in a rigorous way, what the scope of EOp should be. Nevertheless, I will propose a rule of thumb for delineating the spheres of the EOp principle and the nondiscrimination principle that I think is politically realistic in contemporary societies.

I propose that the EOp principle be applied when the advantage in question is the acquisition of an attribute required to compete for a position (a job or career), but that the nondiscrimination principle be applied in the competition for jobs and careers.

Let me elaborate. Having a medical education is required to compete for certain positions. I advocate applying the EOp principle for admission to medical schools. But becoming a surgeon eventually requires competing for a position: I would apply the nondiscrimination principle in licensing and hiring surgeons. Disadvantaged individuals who try hard but fail the surgery boards would not be licensed, under this rule, nor would a hospital be obligated to hire surgeons who lack the standard attributes.

According to this cut, I would not apply the EOp principle in recruiting professional basketball players but I would apply it in the recruitment of high school basketball players, perhaps even college basketball players, for these amateur teams are, in part, training individuals to compete for jobs and careers, either as professional basketball players, or, more likely, as coaches or other athletic personnel. I say my proposal is a rule of thumb because one could argue that the main function of amateur teams is not to train their players but to entertain the public, and entertainment is enhanced by recruiting the best players. A community theory of justice is needed to adjudicate this question.

There are two generic criticisms that can, I think, be levied against my proposal. The "right-wing" criticism is that my proposal gives too much scope to the EOp principle and not enough to the nondiscrimination principle, and the "left-wing" criticism is that it gives too much scope to the nondiscrimination principle and not enough to the EOp principle. I shall consider these criticisms in turn.

What I have called the right-wing criticism is based on the view that application of the EOp principle engenders social inefficiency. It challenges the attempt to distinguish between the formation of general attributes necessary for competing for positions and the actual competition for positions. If we spend a lot on educating individuals from disadvantaged backgrounds, we will spend correspondingly less on educating highly talented individuals from advantaged backgrounds, and consequently will have fewer people able to take important positions in society that require high levels of talent and training. Applying the EOp principle in medical school admissions will lead to having fewer successful candidates at the surgery boards; if society requires a fixed number of surgeons, the EOp principle, if applied here, would lead to lowering the standards for passing the surgery boards, thereby reducing the general quality of surgery. Indeed, at every level of education or training, the EOp principle would squander social resources, leading to the diminution of the pool of well-trained and highly talented individuals that the economy needs to grow and society needs to provide a basket of high-quality goods and services. Society will have met its obligation to equalize opportunities if it provides equal amounts of the educational resource to all individuals through secondary schooling; after that, the competition for positions for further training should be governed by the nondiscrimination principle.

The left-wing critique says that society owes more to disadvantaged individuals than my cut between the two kinds of situation would provide. Consider the case of surgeons. It is so important to have members of certain socially disadvantaged types represented in the surgery profession that we should have lower standards on the surgery boards for such types. Only by having members of these types ascend to the surgery profession will young people from them begin to form aspirations that will lead them to train themselves for a medical career (the role model effect). Granted, this would reduce the quality of surgery that some patients would receive, but patients should view this reduction as the partial repayment of a debt that society owes its disadvantaged types, recalling that members of those types are, by definition, disadvantaged by virtue of circumstances for which society says they should not be held accountable.

I said that my proposal for the scope of the EOp principle is intended as consistent with what I think a broad section of citizens in many advanced industrial democracies would advocate. Specifically, I think that their judgment would be, first, that the social cost of filling positions with relatively incompetent individuals is greater than the benefit accruing to those individuals from holding those positions, and second, that the benefits to disadvantaged individuals from education and training, and the eventual social benefits from education and training of the disadvantaged, are greater than the immediate social costs of forgone opportunities incurred by applying the EOp principle in such situations.

My basis for this evaluation of the views of these citizenries is in part the American experience with affirmative action policy: to be precise, with one specific feature of that experience. Affirmative action policy, as everyone knows, is under attack in the United States, both in its application in the competition for jobs and in admissions to universities and programs of higher education. There is, however, an important difference in the nature of the attack on affirmative action in these two applications. With regard to the competition for positions, the attack maintains that the most competent candidate should win the job competition, but with regard to university admissions, it maintains that race is not a good measure of disadvantage. Even Ward Connerly, the University of California regent who spearheaded the successful campaign to end affirmative action admissions policies in the University of California system, says that he supports preferential admissions for students from families of low socioeconomic status. Thus, the attack on the equal opportunity policy in university admissions focuses not on the application of the principle, but on the delineation of the set of circumstances.

By contrast, the critique of affirmative action in job competition focuses on the principle itself, arguing, in the language used here, that the non-discrimination principle is the one to apply. Once we have the language of equal opportunity that I have introduced here, it is clear that these two criticisms of affirmative action policy are very different: insofar as education and training are concerned, the *principle* of leveling the playing field is not called into question, whereas with respect to filling jobs, it is.

V

I have illustrated the equal opportunity algorithm with the example of the allocation of educational finance, an application that falls within what I consider to be the proper jurisdiction of level-the-playing-field policy. Other applications that I am pursuing in current research are the use of a nation's health budget to equalize opportunities for quality-adjusted life expectancy and the use of progressive income taxation to equalize opportunities for income. In each case, to apply the equal opportunity algorithm, four decisions have to be made: what the *outcome* or *objective* is (wage-earning capacity, life expectancy), what constitutes the relevant *circumstances*, what constitutes the relevant measure of *effort*, and what the *policy instrument* will be (an allocation of educational funding, a schedule of insurance premiums, or expenditures on disease treatments). In each of these decisions there are options, and the one chosen will depend not only on political and philosophical considerations, but also on the availability of data.

Some will doubtless object that the proposal here offered is utopian. Isn't someone who talks about spending ten times as much on black education as on white education oblivious to current political reality? In social science, I advocate the view that one must know what the ethically desirable policy is before compromising for the sake of political reality. Let us not mix ethics and political pragmatism, but rather remain clear on the distinction between what is right and what compromises are necessary, because our societies have not yet fully embraced what is right.

References

Betts, Julian, and J. E. Roemer. 1998. "Equalizing Opportunity through Educational Finance Reform." University of California at Davis Working Paper.
Herrnstein, Richard, and C. Murray. 1994. *The Bell Curve.* New York: Free Press.
Roemer, John E. 1998. *Equality of Opportunity.* Cambridge, MA: Harvard University Press.

Part Two ———————————————————————

THE CAUSES AND CONSEQUENCES
OF "INTELLIGENCE"

Three

IQ Trends over Time: Intelligence, Race, and Meritocracy

JAMES R. FLYNN

IQ TRENDS divide into two kinds. First, we can focus on a particular group and measure whether it has made IQ gains over time. Here we find the so-called "Flynn effect": at least throughout the industrialized world, each generation outscores the previous generation on IQ tests often by huge margins. Second, we can compare two groups to see if the IQ gap between them is altering over time. For example, black and white Americans, or upper- and lower-class children, might be gaining at different rates. If so, the IQ gap between them would expand or contract from one time or another. Clearly the best way to determine this is to ignore the general phenomenon of gains over time and measure between-group gaps at regular intervals.

The first kind of trend has implications for the theory of intelligence and for practical issues such as classifying people as mentally retarded. The first and second taken together have implications for black and white Americans, particularly whether the IQ gap between black and white is genetic or environmental in origin. The second kind of trend, when focused on class, falsifies the meritocracy thesis as presented in Herrnstein and Murray's *Bell Curve* (1994), which may give pleasure by banishing pessimism. However, the same data reveal interaction between ethnicity and class that few will welcome.

IQ Tests and IQ Gains

Those who endorse IQ tests as measures of intelligence have begun to coalesce around a particular theory, which I call the Spearman-Jensen theory of intelligence. Its concept of intelligence is g, or the general intelligence factor, which is derived by factor analysis. It is a kind of supercorrelation coefficient that measures the tendency of the same people to do better, or worse, across a wide range of mental test items, ranging from completing patterns, rotating shapes, recognizing verbal analogies, and seeing similarities and differences, to vocabulary, general information, and arithmetic (Flynn 1987b).

A particular IQ test, Raven's Progressive Matrices, plays a crucial role.

According to the theory, it settles a fundamental question: whether there is some one intelligence factor, a single ability rather than a collection of diverse abilities, that allows a person to do well on such a diversity of mental tasks. Raven's measures g, the tendency to do well, almost perfectly and its content is surprisingly simple: all you have to do is find the missing part of a complex pattern by perceiving what is relevant to the pattern and dismissing what is irrelevant. The ability measured by Raven's and similar tests is more properly called fluid g, or fluid intelligence, because it represents the mind's ability to solve problems at the moment. Other tests, such as the vocabulary or arithmetic subtests of the Wechsler Tests, are said to measure crystallized g, or crystallized intelligence, the kind of knowledge an acute mind normally tends to acquire over time.

The Spearman-Jensen theory has had much success in attempting to show that IQ tests deserve to be called measures of intelligence. However, this record of success has recently been broken by the phenomenon of massive IQ gains over time, that is, the phenomenon of each generation outscoring the previous generation on IQ tests. We now have data for twenty industrialized nations and there is not a single exception. They include the advanced nations of Western Europe and virtually all English-speaking nations. The examples of urban Brazil and Israel tempt us to include all nations of European culture, and the examples of urban China and Japan tempt us to include all those that have adopted European technology. Recent data show that IQ gains in Britain began no later than the last decade of the nineteenth century, at a time when, paradoxically, IQ tests did not exist. The time between the advent of industrialization and the beginning of IQ gains is probably short and the two may well coincide (Flynn 1987a; Flynn 1994; Raven, Raven, and Court 1993).

Recent IQ gains, those covering the last sixty years, reveal a pattern. They are largest on the tests that are supposed to be the purest measure of intelligence, Raven's and other tests of fluid g. The very best data, primarily military tests of comprehensive samples of young men, show Belgium, the Netherlands, and Israel gaining at a rate of twenty points over a generation (thirty years), while Norway, Sweden, and Denmark have gained at a rate of about ten points (Emanuelsson and Svensson 1990; Flynn 1987a, pp. 172–174; Flynn 1998a; Teasdale and Owen 1989). These data suggest an average gain of about fifteen points (or one standard deviation) per generation. The next best data tend to put Britain, Australia, and Canada, nations similar in culture, at twelve to sixteen points per generation (Flynn 1987a, pp. 176 and 180; Raven, Raven, and Court 1993, graph G2). The British estimate is based on adults; samples of schoolchildren give much lower rates. Weak data show wide-ranging results for France, the (pre-unification) Germanies, Northern Ireland, China, Brazil, and New Zealand.

Wechsler performance scale gains among schoolchildren show much the same range of results as the culture-reduced tests they resemble: only the weaker data give gains greater than twenty points over a generation or less than nine points (Flynn 1987a, pp. 185–186). Although tests like Raven's have generated much adult data, the Wechsler tests offer very little. There is no obvious tendency for gains to diminish with age, but recent Japanese data, from a small sample, suggest caution. Japanese schoolchildren have doubled the rate of gain of white American children, about twenty points compared to nine, while Japanese and U.S. adults show similar rates (Hattori, personal communication, November 30, 1991).

Verbal IQ gains vary from almost nil to twenty points per generation, with nine as a rough median, and some of this is adult data from military testing. Among the eleven countries that allow a comparison, there is not one in which verbal gains match the gains on Raven's-type, performance, or non-verbal tests. Often the ratios run against verbal gains by two or three to one. Where vocabulary gains can be distinguished from verbal gains in general, they rarely match them. Despite sizeable IQ gains in Scotland and Northern Ireland, there have been no vocabulary gains. British adults of all ages gained twenty-seven points over fifty years on Raven's, but gained only six points over forty-five years on the Mill Hill Vocabulary Scale (Flynn 1987a, pp. 185–186; Flynn 1990, p. 47; Lynn 1990, p. 139; Raven, Raven, and Court 1993, graphs G2 and G6; Raven, Raven, and Court 1994, table MHV3).

Intelligence and IQ Gains

I believe that most IQ gains are simply too massive to be equated with intelligence gains. As figure 3.1 shows, the Dutch gained twenty-one IQ points on Raven's in a single generation (thirty years). You can take your choice between putting the earlier generation at a mean IQ of 79 (in terms of 1982 norms) or putting the later generation at 121 (in terms of 1952 norms). Has the average person in the Netherlands ever really been near mental retardation or near giftedness? The Netherlands, like all the rest of our twenty nations, shows no evidence of an epidemic of enhanced intelligence, no reports of a renaissance of creative genius, no reports by teachers that gifted students fill their classrooms. Indeed, there has been a decrease rather than an increase in things such as inventions patented, and educators find that academic achievement gains are limited or nonexistent (Flynn 1987a).

Vincent (1993, p. 62) argues that intelligence has escalated because we can cope with the complexity of the modern world, whereas "our grandparents, because of a lack of environmental stimulation, were simply not bright enough as a group to have run the modern world." No doubt our grandparents, raised without video recorders, word processors, and computer

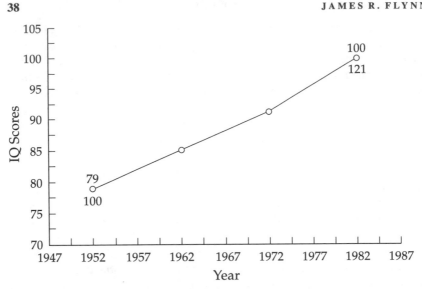

Figure 3.1. The Netherlands and Raven's Progressive Matrices: Dutch males gain twenty-one IQ points from 1952 to 1982. *Source:* Table 1 of Flynn 1987a, p. 172.

games, would (and do) find it difficult to cope if plunged into the modern world. But do we call this new ability our generation has developed "enhanced intelligence" or "acquired learning"? The only way I know to settle this is to focus on something shared by both our world and the world of our grandparents: playing sports with fairly complicated rules. This stratagem supplies us with a rough-and-ready concept of intelligence that I will call "understanding-baseball intelligence." It is derived from an account Arthur Jensen gives to illustrate the limitations of a subject with a Wechsler IQ of seventy-five. Despite the fact that the man in question volunteered baseball as his chief interest and attended or viewed games frequently, he was vague about the rules, did not know how many players comprised a team, could not name the teams his home team played, and could not name any of the most famous players (Jensen 1981, p. 65).

In 1942 J. C. Raven standardized Raven's Progressive Matrices. For ages twenty to thirty, he selected soldiers in army camps whose education matched that of British males at the time. For older ages, he tested large samples from a private firm and a government department, a department a majority of whose employees joined as youths and remained until retirement. They gave him a curve of performance from one age cohort to another and he grafted that curve onto his military sample, thereby deriving norms covering all ages (Foulds and Raven 1948; J. C. Raven 1941). In 1992 John Raven restandardized Raven's on a representative sample of the adult population of Dumfries in Scotland, selected as typical of an area whose norms matched those of Britain as a whole (J. Raven 1981, p. RS1.25). John Raven then took the test scores of all of these subjects, those aged twenty-five to sixty-five tested in 1942 and those aged twenty-five to sixty-five tested in 1992, and plotted them by birth date. This gave him scores for those born from 1877 to the 1970s (Raven, Raven, and Court 1993, graph G2).

The birth date method of estimating trends over time assumes that performance is constant between maturity and old age, that is, Raven has assumed that the sixty-five-year-olds tested in 1942 would have received much the same scores if they had been tested as twenty-year-olds in 1897. Raven is convinced that this is roughly true, but I suspect that age depressed their performance significantly. Another source of error is that although Raven's was administered without a time limit to both the 1942 and 1992 standardization samples, the later sample completed the test at leisure between visits to their homes. Raven and Gudjonsson have debated whether this inflated scores, but comparative data, plus data from a short test each subject completed under supervision, suggest that if score inflation occurred, it was primarily among the top 10 percent, not extending below the fiftieth percentile (Raven 1995). Therefore, I will use the fifth percentile from 1992 to compare the two standardization samples.

Figure 3.2 shows that the bottom 90 percent of Britons born in 1877 fall below the fifth percentile of those born in 1967, which is to say below an IQ of 75. We must not forget our reservations about the birth date method and different testing procedures. Nonetheless, it will be difficult to defend any estimate that puts less than 70 percent of late nineteenth-century Britons below an IQ of 75, when scored on current norms. In order to identify IQ gains with understanding-baseball intelligence, we would have to assume that even if it became their chief interest, 70 percent of Britons could not understand cricket in 1897. The military data, which are the very best available, pose the same kind of problem. Can we assume that in 1952 almost 40 percent of Dutch males lacked the capacity to understand soccer, their favorite national sport?

Tests such as Raven's are supposed to be able to make intelligence comparisons across diverse groups, including races, nations, and ethnic groups. A few years ago Jensen claimed that we could compare the intelligence of chickens with that of dogs, with that of primates, with that of humans, with that of extraterrestrials. He envisaged a chain of tests running from the detour problem through oddity problems, through Raven's, to presumably a form of Raven's adapted to extraterrestrials, which would measure intelligence not only between all human groups but also between species (Jensen 1980, pp. 247–251, 646–648). Today we know that Raven's cannot compare the Dutch of 1982 with the Dutch of 1972 for intelligence. The evolution of Dutch society during a single decade may well cover less cultural distance than the cultural distance that separates black and white Americans, or Chi-

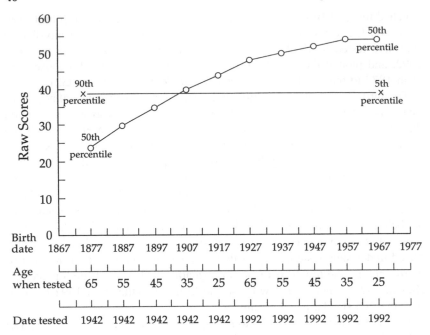

Figure 3.2. Britain and Raven's Progressive Matrices: The bottom 90 percent born in 1877 fall within the bottom 5 percent born in 1967 (IQ 75 or below). *Source:* Adapted from graph G2 of Raven, Raven, and Court 1993.

nese and white Americans, and so forth. Until we know what has gone amiss we should be cautious about equating group IQ differences with intelligence differences.

Mental Retardation and IQ Gains

Raven's has pride of place within the Spearman-Jensen theory of intelligence but psychologists usually use Wechsler and Stanford-Binet tests, tests that measure a mix of fluid and crystallized intelligence. American gains on these tests are well documented, although comparison of the WISC-III (1989) (Wechsler Intelligence Scale for Children-Third Edition) and the WAIS-III (1995) standarization samples give varying rates since 1972. There is no doubt, however, that America has recorded substantial gains all the way from 1918 to the present. Every study from the interwar era shows large gains, and these results are supported by a comparison of performance on the Stanford-Binet by soldiers in 1918 with the standardization sample of 1932 (Flynn 1984b; Flynn 1993; Flynn 1998b; Terman and Merrill 1937, p. 50; Weschler 1992, p. 198; Yerkes, 1921, pp. 654, 789). American gains on

Wechsler-Binet tests are the best data to illustrate the practical implications of IQ gains over time. These are very many, but I will single out an example of great human significance: using IQ tests to attach labels such as "mentally retarded" or "learning disabled" to students.

Figure 3.3 shows that white Americans gained twenty-five IQ points on Wechsler-Binet tests between 1918 and 1995. These gains reveal that IQ tests have targeted radically different groups for mental retardation over time, that psychologists in the field were not monitoring the validity of the IQ criterion suggested for mental retardation, and that all IQ criteria are arbitrary in the sense that no one has ever accumulated a body of evidence in favor of any particular IQ score.

Since 1945 the dominant criterion of mental retardation has been an IQ of 70 or below, which is two *SD*s below the population mean of 100. The American Association on Mental Deficiency believes that both impaired adaptive behavior and impaired intellectual functioning should be considered in classifying people as mentally retarded, but the suggested operational criterion of the latter is low IQ. Wechsler manuals published as recently as 1992 quote the Association as leaving the criterion of 70 unaltered (Wechsler 1992, p. 8). The criterion was adopted on the assumption that it had real-world significance: it was supposed to isolate the bottom 2.27 percent of the biologically normal population.

If the sampling was impeccable, a test score of 70 may have isolated the bottom 2.27 percent the day the test was normed. But immediately American gains on Wechsler tests would begin to erode that percentage. Sometimes these gains were slightly greater for those below 70 than for those with average IQs. For example, between 1947–1948, when the WISC (Wechsler Intelligence Scale for Children) was normed, and 1972, when the WISC-R (Wechsler Intelligence Scale for Children-Revised) was normed, children at that level gained 8.25 IQ points (Flynn 1985, p. 240). Every year more and more low-IQ children climbed above a score of 70; indeed, by 1972 only the bottom 0.54 percent would have been eligible to qualify as mentally retarded. Then in 1974 the WISC-R with its recent norms was published, and overnight the percentage of those eligible dramatically escalated. At that point, new IQ gains began to erode the percentage eligible all over again. In 1989 the WISC-III was normed on a new, higher-performing sample. We lack the data needed for a precise estimate of how much, at the level of mental retardation, IQ gains had raised IQ scores by that date. A small sample from the WISC-III manual suggests a value of nine points (Wechsler 1992, p. 211), which is larger than expected and sampling error may be a factor. However, using nine points, if an IQ of 70 isolated 2.27 percent in 1972, it was isolating only 0.47 percent in 1989. Then the WISC-III was published, and overnight there was another leap back to a higher percentage.

That is the hidden history of using IQ tests to classify Americans as men-

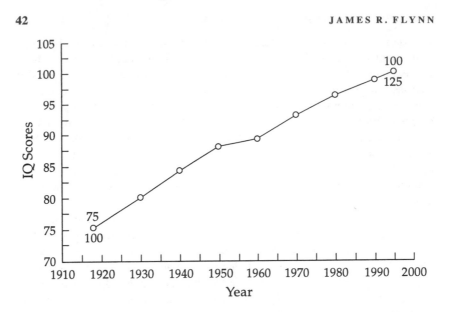

Figure 3.3. Americans and Wechsler-Binet Tests: Whites gain twenty-five IQ points from 1918 to 1995. *Source:* Adapted with permission from graph (p. 14) of Horgan 1995. The graph has been revised and extended to accommodate the WAIS-III standardization sample. *Notes on tests and samples* (see text for further detail): (1) Gains from 1918 to 1932 are based on Stanford-Binet data only. The rate shown is a minimum estimate and miscellaneous studies using a variety of tests show that gains may have been higher. (2) Gains from 1932 to 1972 are based on both Wechsler and Stanford-Binet standardization samples. (3) Gains from 1972 to 1995 are based on Wechsler standardization samples only.

tally retarded. A standard that is supposed to do the job of isolating the bottom 2.27 percent of the biologically normal population may do so briefly; then over twenty years it gradually lets most of them escape; then it dramatically snaps back to targeting the bottom 2.27 percent; then the twenty-year cycle starts all over again. This is what has really been going on for the last sixty years.

The other half of the hidden history concerns how clinical psychologists reacted during these cycles. As far as I can determine, no clinical or school psychologist using the WISC over the relevant twenty-five years noticed that its criterion of mental retardation became more lenient over time. Until the data on IQ gains over time appeared, no one using the WISC-R over the relevant seventeen years complained that it had begun to classify only a fragment of the biologically normal population as mentally retarded. No doubt they relied primarily on their observations of whether a subject showed impaired behavior that seemed the result of a cognitive deficit. But that is the body of evidence that is supposed to provide external validity for the IQ criterion of mental retardation. If they were perfectly content with IQ criteria that ranged all the way from 70 down to 61 (scored against current norms), there can hardly be an accumulated body of clinical evidence that favors any particular IQ score.

Beginning in 1944 Wechsler (1944, pp. 36–38) claimed he had clinical evidence for the norms of that day. If so, all subsequent Wechsler manuals were in error when they claimed validity for later and different norms. Wechsler gives no citations for his evidence and I cannot find a body of evidence cited in any Wechsler manual to this day. The obvious conclusion is that no evidence for the external validity of an IQ criterion for mental retardation has ever existed. Psychologists in the field should forget IQ scores and use their clinical judgment as their sole criterion. If they suspect that impaired behavior is due to a cognitive deficit, they should follow Jensen's example: if a subject claims baseball as a favorite sport, they should have a chat and see whether or not he or she has grasped the concept of a double play.

A postscript: sometimes psychologists use diagnostic criteria that consist of a profile of test scores. For example, the WISC-III manual says that children should be screened for learning disabilities or reading disorders if they tend to do badly on four Wechsler subtests: Arithmetic, Information, Coding, and Digit Span (Wechsler 1992, pp. 212–213). They call this an AICD profile, and a partial AICD profile is present when children get scores on three of these four subtests that are lower than their score on any of the seven remaining subtests (Mazes and Symbol Search are excluded). The manual also contains a table that reveals score gains on various subtests between 1972, when the WISC-R was normed, and 1989, when the WISC-III was normed (Wechsler 1992, p. 198). During that period, the three subtests showing the lowest gains are without exception AICD profile subtests: Information at −0.3 scaled score points (a loss), Digit Span at +0.1, and Arithmetic at +0.3. As for the remaining subtests, all but one show gains that are two to six times as great (+0.6 to +1.9).

In sum, if the WISC-III standardization sample had taken the WISC-R test, differential IQ gains over time on the various subtests would have had this effect: a general tendency to exhibit a partial AICD profile, that is, lower scores on Arithmetic, Information, and Digit Span than on any other subtest. Suspicion of learning disability and reading disorders would have been rife in a sample selected to be typical of American children in general. The same pattern of differential gains may not be occurring at the present time, of course, but that shows how intractable the problem is. If we could predict the gains, we could allow for them, but since trends over time follow no immutable law, we can only guess. IQ scores have no better case to diagnose learning disability than they do to diagnose mental retardation.

Race and IQ

When groups are separated by significant cultural distance, we have expressed reservations about whether IQ differences should be identified with intelligence differences. Setting aside these reservations, how viable is an environmental explanation of the fifteen-point IQ gap between American whites and American blacks? IQ gains over time cannot contribute direct evidence as to causal factors, but they can help us evaluate analyses that prejudice us for or against an environmental explanation. I refer to Jensen (1972, 1973a, 1973b) and his use of high estimates of the heritability of IQ within both the black and white American populations and low estimates of the potency of between-family environmental factors. Others in this volume will challenge Jensen's estimates; I will take them as given and challenge their relevance.

Jensen hypothesizes that the environmental factors that affect IQ differences within both the black and white populations are also the principal factors that cause the racial IQ gap. This means that blacks can be treated as a subgroup or sample of the white population and an environmental hypothesis can be tested as follows: if purely environmental factors selected out a subgroup of the white population, how many SDs of environmental deficiency would be necessary to account for a one SD IQ deficit? Since correlations measure failure to regress to the mean, all we need is the correlation between between-family environment and IQ. A plausible value is 0.35, based on Jensen's estimate of 12 percent of IQ variance explained by between-family environment (the square root of 0.12 equals 0.35). Therefore, the average black environment would have to be 2.86 SDs below the quality of the average white environment (2.86 times 0.35 equals 1.00 SD IQ deficit), which is to say that the average black environment would have to be inferior to that enjoyed by 99.79 percent of white Americans. Can anyone maintain that such a thing is plausible?

Jensen's analysis is mathematically elegant, but IQ gains over time show that something has gone wrong. The literature on heritability of IQ is not comprehensive; however, it suggests similar values for America, Britain, Denmark, and so forth, and no dramatic changes over the last two generations. Yet all of these nations have been making massive IQ gains over time, which means that high heritability estimates within groups do not forbid environmental explanations of large IQ gaps between groups. Take the Dutch of 1962 as one group and the Dutch of 1982 as another group: they were separated by an IQ gap of fifteen points, or one SD (see figure 3.1). The explanation of that IQ gap must be entirely environmental; no one argues for a trend toward better genes, indeed, the usual case is for dysgenic trends. Either there is something wrong with the present methodology of calculating heritability estimates and they are much lower than assumed, or high heritability estimates are compatible with environmental factors of enormous potency, factors that operate between groups despite being largely absent within groups. Moreover, this scenario holds even when the two groups are separated by a cultural distance that looks quite modest. Once again: given a highly homogeneous society like the Netherlands, few would believe that the cultural distance between two groups born twenty years apart is greater than the cultural distance between American whites and American blacks.

IQ gains over time can make a further contribution. It appears that black Americans have enjoyed a slightly higher rate of gain than white Americans (Herrnstein and Murray 1994, pp. 276, 292). This implies that since 1945 blacks have gained at an average rate of more than 0.300 points per year, and gained a total of 16 points over fifty years. So the blacks of 1995 should have matched the mean IQ of the whites of 1945. And this puts an entirely different perspective on the viability of an environmental hypothesis. It drags the environmental difference such a hypothesis assumes down out of the stratosphere and allows us to put dates on it. All we need to assume is that the average black environment of 1995 matches the quality of the average white environment of 1945. Many will find that plausible enough to keep an open mind about the causes of the black-white IQ gap.

The Bell Curve and Meritocracy

The Bell Curve shifts our attention from nations and races to classes. Herrnstein and Murray have revived the meritocracy thesis, which posits that genes for IQ are becoming more highly correlated with class. However, their presentation of the thesis must not obscure an important distinction, namely, there are really two meritocracy theses, which assume different social dynamics and possess different levels of significance. I will call the first the "social mobility" meritocracy thesis because the dynamic that correlates genes with class is social mobility in the absence of inequality and privilege. It has potentially universal applicability because it could occur in all societies, whether ethnically homogeneous or ethnically diverse; and it is of enormous ideological significance because it strikes at the very heart of humane-egalitarian ideals. I will call the second the "ethnic mix" meritocracy thesis because its dynamic is simply the growth of an ethnic group characterized by both below-average IQ and inferior social status. As for its significance, the implication that genes for IQ are becoming more highly correlated with class is much weaker. Further, it poses no direct threat to humane-egalitarian ideals, although it creates social problems any decent society would wish to address.

The second thesis has not been formulated hitherto, which is hardly surprising because it is an ad hoc hypothesis arising out of the data presented herein. I will postpone analysis until it arises naturally out of the data. As for Herrnstein and Murray, their focus on the first thesis is quite explicit. They say that a meritocracy would occur even within an ethnically homogeneous white America, with black and Hispanic America set aside. Although the first thesis has a long history, they present it with unusual force and amplifying detail.

Herrnstein and Murray (1994, pp. 105, 109, 510) argue as follows: (1) If differences in mental abilities are inherited, and (2) if success requires those abilities, and (3) if earnings and prestige depend on success, then (4) social standing (which reflects earnings and prestige) will be based to some extent on inherited differences between people. They imagine a United States that has magically made good on "the contemporary ideal of equality." First, every child has equal environmental quality insofar as environment affects intelligence. Second, each person can go as far as talent and hard work can take him (or her), with neither social background nor lack of money barring the way. I think this—the abolition of environmental inequality, at least in its worst forms, and the abolition of privilege—is a fair statement of an ideal many of us hold: the humane-egalitarian ideal.

Herrnstein and Murray (1994, pp. 91, 105–115, 509–520) believe that the humane-egalitarian ideal has been realized in practice to a significant degree. The irony is that insofar as it is realized, America approaches a kind of caste society egalitarians would loathe. If environmental inequality is diminished, intelligence differences between individuals increasingly reflect genetic differences. If privilege is diminished, intelligence or IQ becomes an enhanced factor in social mobility, so that upper-class occupations become filled by the bright and lower-class occupations by the not bright. Genes for intelligence become more and more segregated by class. There is an elite class with good genes for IQ whose children tend to replicate their parents' high status because of luck in life's lottery, that is, because they inherit their parents' good genes. There is a large underclass with bad genes for IQ whose children suffer from cognitive disadvantage at birth and find it difficult to escape low status. In other words, the meritocracy thesis strikes at the very heart of the humane-egalitarian ideal because that ideal is revealed to be counterproductive in practice. The abolition of inequality and privilege produces a class-equals-caste society with high status the inheritance of a few, dependency and low status the inheritance of many. How little this vision will appeal will vary from person to person, but it is safe to say that countless idealistic men and women did not lay down their lives for this.

Herrnstein and Murray (1994, pp. 551, 113–115, 178, 520) hold out no hope for the long term. Cognitive partitioning cannot be stopped because the forces driving it cannot be stopped. They are less clear about how far toward meritocracy those forces have taken us thus far. Sometimes they focus on the success of the top 5 percent of the IQ curve, a phenomenon that could leave the mainstream of American society largely untouched. Sometimes they refer to a large underclass with roots in the "illegitimacy revolution" that began in 1960. At other times they claim that the underclass is not yet a conflagration but something likely to ignite over the next few decades. These comments have the look of ambiguity but their overall analysis does not, in my opinion, leave much room for such. Rather it generates a prediction precise enough to be tested.

Herrnstein and Murray (1994, pp. 29–61, 111–113, 509–511) believe that the first half of our century made considerable progress in equalizing environments, beginning in 1900, the year in which primary-school education became nearly universal. Since 1920 the proportion of people getting university degrees has increased from just over 2 percent to about 32 percent. The 1950s were a watershed, not only because of the escalation of the number attending universities but also because privilege was virtually eliminated even at elite universities. By 1960 Harvard students were no longer the northeastern socioeconomic elite but had become the brightest and best drawn from all over America. The universities collectively began to sort students for ability and became a cognitive hierarchy ranging from second-rate state institutions, through the typical top state university, through elite institutions ranging from Colby to Harvard. Since 1960 cognitive partitioning has steadily increased to startling proportions.

The abolition of privilege within the university community was accompanied by a decline of privilege in occupations, driven partially by the expansion of cognitively demanding professions and partially by the demand for university credentials as prerequisites for entry. The social segregation of people by intelligence during education began to dominate their entire life span. Beginning as early as 1940, this social segregation probably led to increased assortative mating. Bright were more likely to marry bright, encouraging cognitive partitioning in terms of the occupational status of the family. Herrnstein and Murray (1994, p. 101) go so far as to state that "most people at present are stuck near where their parents were on the income distribution in part because IQ . . . passes on sufficiently from one generation to the next to constrain economic mobility." By age eighteen, meritocratic factors have sorted out the emerging generation.

In sum, by 1960 potent meritocratic mechanisms were in place; the cohort that turned eighteen that year felt their effects, and those who have turned eighteen since that time should show those effects to a steadily escalating degree. This brings us to the white members of the WISC-III standardization sample. The sample was selected and tested in 1989 and the children were aged from six to sixteen years. White Americans bear children primarily between the ages of fifteen and forty-five with a median age of thirty (Herrnstein and Murray 1994, pp. 216, 351–352). These data imply that 85 percent of the six-year-olds had parents who turned eighteen in 1960 or after, with the proportion steadily falling to 50 percent for the sixteen-year-olds, which gives a minimum of 65 percent for all ages collectively. Recall what a trend toward meritocracy means. The more meritocracy, the more good genes for IQ go to high-status occupations, the more bad genes to low-status occupations. The genes are passed on from parent to child, so the more meritocracy, the more of an IQ gap between upper- and lower-class children. If Herrnstein and Murray are correct, the gap between upper- and lower-class children should show a visible jump when we compare the WISC-III sample to earlier samples. Meritocracy has generated a prediction precise enough to be verified or falsified.

The Relevant Data

Fortunately, the standardization of Stanford-Binet and Wechsler IQ tests in 1932, 1947–1948, 1972, 1985, and 1989 gives us the data we need to trace trends over time. The dates refer to the years in which the standardization samples were selected and tested, not the years in which test manuals or technical reports were published. The relevant data are: the percentage of American homes in various occupational categories ranked in a hierarchy from the professions down to the least valued; and the mean IQ of the children being raised in those homes, that is, the mean IQ of children from professional homes, from white-collar homes, and so forth. Sometimes the testing organizations did not have up-to-date data for the percentages in various occupational categories: the 1932 Stanford-Binet used the 1930 census, so I merely made small adjustments to better match their sample, which was white American-born; the 1948 WISC used the 1940 census, so I supplied 1950 data; the 1985 Stanford-Binet used the 1980 census, so I supplied data from 1985 (U.S. Bureau of the Census 1930, vol. 2, table 3; U.S. Bureau of the Census 1950, vol. 2, part 1, table 159; U.S. Bureau of the Census 1994, tables 637 and 665, pp. 407 and 429).

The overall mean of every sample was put at an IQ of 100. The raw data showed deviations from that value because of a number of factors. First, sometimes the parents who report their occupations are slightly elite. Second, when you multiply the occupational means by the percentages, up-to-date percentages cause a slight deviation. Third, white samples must all be normed on whites only, putting the white mean at 100 and the SD at 15. This was the convention through 1948 because in those days only whites were tested. The scores of white members of later samples including all races have been translated from all-races norms to white-only norms. Finally, there are the nonwhite samples. I kept these scores within the context of all-races norms because their main use was to estimate the effect the presence of nonwhites had on all-races scores. However, their overall means were also put at an IQ of 100. For all samples, a mean of 100 was achieved simply by taking the overall deviation from that value and adding it to, or subtracting it from, each occupational mean.

This account of the manipulation of the data is to satisfy experts that the obvious tasks have been done. Those not expert may suspect sleight of hand. Therefore, I wish to stress that the manipulation has had no effect on the differences between mean IQs for the various occupational categories, or on the correlations between mean IQs and occupational status. Its sole purpose is to make IQ values across data sets comparable, that is, make them all values normed on a mean of 100 with an appropriate *SD* set at 15. It is analogous to taking temperatures, some of which are Fahrenheit and some of which are Centigrade, and making them comparable by translating from one to the other. The arithmetic is more complex but the rationale is not.

Comparability across data sets also requires comparable occupational hierarchies, and this task is not so straightforward. Occupational categories and the pecking order of occupations have altered somewhat over the years. Elsewhere the 1932 categories have been equated with those that were constant between 1948 and 1972 (Flynn 1984a). The latter were: (1) professionals; (2) managers, officials, proprietors, clerical workers, and salespeople; (3) craftsmen and foremen; (4) operatives, service workers, farmers, and farm managers, and (5) laborers, farm laborers, and farm foremen. By the time of the 1985 Stanford-Binet and the 1989 WISC-III, managers had moved up to join professionals, much enlarging the top category. The second category had become technical workers, salespeople, and administrative support workers. The third category still included craftsmen (precision production, craft, repair), but what few farmers remained and service workers (particularly among whites) had become a more elite group, moving up from category 4 to category 3. The fourth category still had operatives but now included laborers as well. Or more precisely, I moved laborers up because a new bottom or fifth category had emerged, namely, homemakers.

To maximize comparability, I have adhered to one principle: every hierarchy has been constructed by ranking occupational categories in terms of the mean IQs of the children whose parents filled those categories. For example, the children of white service workers and farmers today show a three-point IQ advantage over the children of operatives and laborers, and therefore service workers and farmers were moved upward. Homemakers were made the bottom category simply because their children had the lowest mean IQ. This principle not only maximizes comparability, it also gives the meritocracy thesis its best chance. It is logically possible that the occupational status hierarchy and the children's IQ hierarchy would not be the same. I have equated them by definition. The Psychological Corporation created a peculiar problem by changing its method of classifying homes. For

the WISC and WISC-R, they used the male's occupation in all two-parent
homes. For the 1989 WISC-III, after ensuring their sample was representative against census data, they selected whichever partner, whether male or
female, had the higher occupational status. The top category, already en-
larged to about 30 percent for white Americans by the addition of managers
to professionals, rose to about 40 percent, which is to say that in 10 percent
of white American homes, a women is either a professional or a manager
although her partner is neither.

The altered method of the WISC-III should not handicap the meritocracy
thesis unless it is argued that when a female betters her partner, merit counts
for less than when a male does so. Social scientists who find life too dull or
too lacking in controversy are invited to step forward. The altered method
does mean that, using the numbers of earlier occupational categories, some
homes from categories 2 to 5 have joined category 1, and some homes from
3 to 5 have joined category 2. I have tried to remind the reader of this by
giving WISC-III categories composite numbers like 1/2, 2/3, and so forth. It
must be remembered that WISC-III category 5 is the new one of homemakers. This is absent in the 1985 Stanford-Binet system so its data end at
category 4, a catchall for everyone below skilled-worker status. Those who
wish to check out detail should consult the relevant publications (Kaufman and Doppelt 1976; Terman and Merrill 1937, pp. 12, 14, 48; Terman
and Merrill 1973, p. 339; Thorndike, Hagen, and Sattler 1986, pp. 16, 22,
34–35). The WISC-III occupational data have not been published, and come
courtesy of The Psychological Corporation, copyright 1994, all rights
reserved.

The data are presented in three tables that share a common format and
rationale. Even when occupational status categories remained the same over
time, the proportions in them altered; for example, the percentage of white
professionals doubled between 1948 and 1972. As a category becomes less
elite, the mean IQ of the children must fall. Therefore, when comparing, say,
the professions between 1948 and 1972, the best guide is not the actual mean
IQs of professional children from those two years. Rather it is the correlations for those two years: correlations that relate the mean IQ of the children
in a given category to the elite (or nonelite) status of that category in terms
of the percentiles it covers.

For example, in 1932 professionals were a highly elite group, covering
only the top 3.59 percent of the population. If there had been a perfect
correlation between parental occupational status and child's IQ, the children
would have been the top 3.59 percent of the IQ curve. This gives a *predicted*
mean of 132.99. The *actual* mean IQ of professional children was 112.63
(after scores were converted to deviation IQs with *SD* at 15 and mean at 100
and adjusted as described). Since the Pearson-product-moment correlation is
a measure of failure to regress to the mean, you get an estimate of it by

simple division: 12.63 divided by 32.99 gives 0.383 as the correlation. Those unfamiliar with this method should recall that it was how Galton himself originally formulated the notion of a "co-relation" between two variables. Preliminaries done, what story do the data tell?

Social Mobility and IQ

Table 3.1 covers white Americans from 1932 to 1989. Some of the occupational status categories have correlations marked with a question mark because the predicted value is too close to the population mean to get a plausible measure of regression. The more reliable correlations show no tendency to increase. However, the best measures of trends over time are at the foot of the table. Using algebra plus the relevant category correlations, it is possible to derive mean IQs for children whose parents were in the top third, the middle third, and the bottom third in terms of occupational status. I shall call these the upper, middle, and lower classes. Particularly significant is the difference between the mean IQs of upper- and lower-class children, which I shall call the class IQ gap.

Table 3.1 shows that between 1932 and 1948 the class IQ gap for white American children fell from 12.57 points to 10.61 points. White American data are the relevant data to test the first (social mobility) meritocracy thesis, but I do not believe that a downward trend beginning as early as 1932 should count against it. Both the proponents and opponents of the first thesis might say that such a trend was a common expectation. If I understand Herrnstein and Murray, the post-1960 meritocratic era has been characterized by relatively stable environmental differences (much reduced from earlier times) and the retreat of privilege, whereas from the Great Depression to the end of World War II, the period from 1932 to 1948, the reverse was true: a considerable equalization of environments and little abolition of privilege. If people were trapped in their various classes without enhanced social mobility, and if environmental differences between the classes were declining, then a smaller class IQ gap would result.

However, table 3.1 also shows that from 1948 to 1972 to 1989, the class IQ gap for white American children was remarkably constant. That constancy does count against the first meritocracy thesis. As we have seen, the 1972 children were too young for their parents to have been much affected by the class stratification of genes for IQ supposed to have begun in the meritocratic era, whereas fully 65 percent of the 1989 children had parents who should have been affected. As for the size of the class IQ gap, from World War II to the present it has been essentially ten points, with a variation of little more than half a point. The pattern is a mean IQ of 105 for upper-class, 100 for middle-class, and 95 for lower-class children. There is

TABLE 3.1

White Americans, 1932 to 1989. Mean IQ of children and parental occupational status; class differences; correlations

Sample	Occupational Status	Percentage	Predicted Mean	Actual Mean	Correlations
SB 1932	1	3.59	132.99	112.63	0.383
	2	23.59	116.08	105.57	0.346
	3	30.50	102.93	102.03	0.692 ?
	4	25.41	91.77	94.42	0.678 ?
	5	16.91	77.64	94.29	0.255
WISC	1	7.93	127.93	109.05	0.324
1947–48	2	25.50	112.72	104.45	0.350
	3	19.90	102.53	100.05	0.020 ?
	4	35.70	91.18	96.95	0.346
	5	10.97	74.35	92.95	0.275
WISC-R	1	15.50	123.07	107.70	0.334
1972	2	28.00	108.31	102.05	0.247
	3	23.90	97.92	98.78	0.587 ?
	4	27.60	86.03	96.35	0.261
	5	5.00	69.03	90.57	0.304
WISC-III	1/2	40.52	114.35	104.43	0.309
1989	2/3	21.24	99.56	99.63	0.841 ?
	3/4	19.15	91.44	97.99	0.235
	4	13.68	82.20	94.22	0.325
	5	5.41	69.56	89.99	0.329

		1932	1948	1972	1989
Mean IQ:	top third	106.28	105.55	104.97	105.05
	middle third	100.01	99.51	99.55	99.91
	bottom third	93.71	94.94	95.48	95.04
Difference:	top/middle	6.27	6.04	5.42	5.14
	top/bottom	12.57	10.61	9.49	10.01
Regression correlations		0.384	0.324	0.290	0.306
Correlation ratios		0.353	0.300	0.289	0.289

Note: See text for discussion of occupational status categories and why correlations marked with a question mark are suspect. Text identifies top, middle, and bottom thirds with upper, middle, and lower classes.

no tendency for the upper class to take off. Indeed, the gap between upper- and middle-class children (top and middle thirds) has steadily decreased over time.

Table 3.1 also gives overall correlations between children's IQ and parental occupational status, and these add confirmation. The regression correlations are a product of dividing the actual class IQ gap by the predicted gap. The predicted gap is always 32.72 points. This is the difference between the top and bottom thirds of the IQ curve, the difference dictated by a perfect correlation between occupational status and child's IQ. These correlations are analogous to the Pearson, and since 1948 they have varied only slightly around a value of 0.300. Finally, table 3.1 gives correlation ratios because calculating a Pearson in the conventional way on this kind of data can be merely a test of linearity. The correlation ratios show even greater stability. Concerning the effect of social mobility on stratifying genes for IQ within white America, the most parsimonious conclusion is this: nothing, nothing, absolutely nothing has happened.

Ethnic Mix and IQ

Table 3.2 covers Americans of all races. It shows that between 1972 (pre-meritocratic) and later years (post-meritocratic), the class IQ gap was either stable or rose slightly, depending on what data you choose to emphasize. The value in 1972 was 11.64 points. The 1985 Stanford-Binet shows stability; the 1989 WISC-III shows a rise of 1.21 points; pooling the 1985 and 1989 data shows a very small rise of 0.39 points. The correlations at the foot of the table tally as usual. Those marked with an asterisk were boosted by 0.015. This was to compensate for the fact that the correlation ratio gives an underestimate when it is applied to data with less than five cells.

The rationale for pooling is that the current Stanford-Binet and Wechsler tests measure much the same thing. The correlation between Stanford-Binet composite IQ and Wechsler full-scale IQ is 0.85. At least that is the value given by averaging the Stanford-Binet's correlations with the WPPSI (Wechsler Preschool and Primary Scale of Intelligence), the WAIS-R (Wechsler Adult Intelligence Scale-Revised), and the WISC-R (Thorndike, Hagen, and Sattler 1986, pp. 62, 64, 66). The correlation between the WISC-III and the same trio of Wechsler tests averages at 0.87 (Wechsler 1992, pp. 198, 200, 202). Moreover, in order to get children whose parents were clearly affected by the meritocratic era, my analysis of the 1985 Stanford-Binet covers ages two to eleven years. Their birth dates correspond almost perfectly with the 1989 WISC-III children, who were aged six to sixteen and tested four years later. Therefore, the pooled data are called "POOLED 1989" on the fiction that they refer to children aged six to sixteen all tested in that year.

TABLE 3.2
Americans of All Races, 1972 to 1989. Mean IQ of children and parental
occupational status; class differences; correlations

Sample	Occupational Status	Percentage	Predicted Mean	Actual Mean	Correlations
WISC-R	1	14.60	123.52	108.26	0.351
1972	2	26.60	109.04	103.26	0.361
	3	22.80	99.01	99.66	0.343
	4	29.70	87.36	95.96	0.320
	5	6.30	70.53	87.36	0.429
SB 1985	1	23.98	119.44	107.80	0.401
	2	29.93	104.33	100.70	0.162 ?
	3	30.63	92.21	95.83	0.535
	4/5	15.46	76.92	94.80	0.225
WISC-III	1/2	34.56	116.00	106.09	0.380
1989	2/3	19.55	102.16	101.38	0.637 ?
	3/4	20.15	94.48	98.26	0.316
	4	16.93	85.57	93.61	0.443
	5	8.81	72.79	89.35	0.392
POOLED	1	28.20	117.97	106.97	0.388
1989	2	25.79	103.44	100.90	0.262
	3	26.45	93.15	96.56	0.502
	4/5	19.56	78.82	93.42	0.311

		1972	1985	1989W	1989P
Mean IQ:	top third	105.80	106.00	106.21	106.20
	middle third	100.04	99.44	100.43	99.63
	bottom third	94.16	94.56	93.36	94.17
Difference:	top/middle	5.76	6.56	5.82	6.57
	top/bottom	11.64	11.44	12.85	12.03
Regression correlations		0.356	0.350	0.393	0.368
Correlation ratios		0.351	0.343*	0.369	0.352*

Note: See text for discussion of occupational status categories, why correlations marked with
a question mark are suspect, and how correlations marked with an asterisk were calculated. Text
identifies top, middle, and bottom thirds with upper, middle, and lower classes.

The 1985 Stanford-Binet classified parental occupations in the usual way.
The 1989 WISC-III used the new method of classifying two-partner homes,
that is, selecting whichever partner had the higher occupational status.
Therefore, whereas the 1989 Wechsler data gave women a chance to raise
occupational status in all two-parent homes, the 1989 pooled data give

women that chance in only about 40 percent of two-parent homes. However, once again, there is no reason to think that this innovation whatever its sweep, introduces an anti-meritocratic bias. Since IQs are norm referenced, the subjects pooled had to be the weighted subjects of the standardization samples rather than actual children tested.

The total number of pooled subjects from the two samples is 5,460, of which 3,281 are Stanford-Binet and 2,179 WISC-III. This gives 1,820 subjects each in the top and bottom thirds. Treating stratified samples as if they were random samples raises a host of questions, but doing so allows us to estimate the effect of sample size on reliability. Given these numbers, the pooled data show that in 1989 the class gap for American children of all races was twelve IQ points, plus or minus one point.

Table 3.3 lays bare the dynamics of the possible rise of 0.39 to 1.21 points in the class IQ gap for all-races America. It shows what happens when you merge nonwhite Americans with white Americans to get data for all races. Such a merger increases the class IQ gap of ten points for white children by an additional two or three points for all races of children. This is an automatic effect having nothing to do with social mobility, that is, it does not show that social mobility in America is higher within all races than within whites only. It arises simply from adding an ethnic minority to an ethnic majority when the former has a lower mean IQ and is concentrated in lower-status occupations. The paucity of lower-IQ subjects in the top third of occupations results in only a slight lowering of the mean IQ there. The concentration of lower-IQ subjects in the bottom third results in a substantial lowering of the mean there. Therefore, the IQ gap between children in the top and bottom thirds increases. Not only does this have nothing to do with social mobility within all races, it has nothing to do with social mobility within the nonwhites added. When the 1972 WISC-R added 15 percent nonwhites— largely blacks in those days—the class IQ gap jumped by two points despite the fact that the IQ gap within the nonwhites was very small. When later data sets added almost 30 percent nonwhites—blacks plus large Hispanic and significant Asian components—the class IQ gap jumped by almost three points. The later data do show a nonwhite class IQ gap that is sizable. But the significant thing to note is that *both* the nonwhite gap *and* the white gap are less than the all-races gap.

The lesson is clear: the class IQ gap for all races can fluctuate purely because of changes in the ethnic mix. Even within the nonwhite population taken in isolation, we cannot measure a trend toward social mobility because of the steadily increasing Asian component. As a minority among nonwhites with a higher mean IQ and a concentration in the higher-status professions, they must increase the nonwhite class IQ gap. They simply boost the mean of the top third much more than they do the mean of the bottom third. I suspect that merit among nonwhites does count for more today than

TABLE 3.3

Nonwhite Americans, 1972 and 1989. Data showing that merging white and nonwhite (into all races) automatically increases class differences

Sample	Occupational Status	Percentage	Predicted Mean	Actual Mean	Correlations
WISC-R	1	7.90	127.96	103.26	0.117
1972	2	14.80	115.62	104.33	0.277
	3	14.20	108.01	100.43	0.054
	4	46.90	95.78	100.01	−0.002 ?
	5	16.20	77.29	94.04	0.262

Regression correlation 0.172; Correlation ratio 0.204

Sample	Occupational Status	Percentage	Predicted Mean	Actual Mean	Correlations
WISC-III	1/2	20.34	120.85	107.78	0.373
1989	2/3	15.53	108.78	104.09	0.466
	3/4	22.52	101.09	99.65	−0.321 ?
	4	24.69	91.63	95.71	0.513
	5	16.92	77.63	93.62	0.285

Regression correlation 0.374; Correlation ratio 0.342

	WISC-R 1972	SB 1985	WISC-III 1989	POOLED 1989
Nonwhite percentage of all races	15.00	27.19	29.55	28.13
Nonwhite IQ deficit (below white)	15.80	13.06	11.17	11.96
Nonwhite IQ gap between top and bottom thirds	5.64	—	12.24	—
White IQ gap top/bottom thirds	9.49	(8.60)	10.01	(9.19)
All races IQ gap top/bottom thirds	11.64	11.44	12.85	12.03
Increase from white to all races	2.15	(2.84)	2.84	(2.84)

Note: See text for discussion of occupational status categories and why correlations marked with a question mark are suspect. The values in parentheses are rough estimates, as discussed in the text.

it did in 1972. At that time, nonwhites were assigned occupational status almost randomly, indeed, the correlation was no more than 0.200. But thanks to the Asians, the size of the trend from that time to the present cannot be estimated.

Two Kinds of Meritocracy

In accord with our distinction between two kinds of meritocratic theses, I will distinguish two kinds of meritocratic trends: (1) toward a class-stratified meritocracy, purportedly caused by social mobility as environmental inequality and privilege decline, and (2) toward an ethnic-group meritocracy, caused by a shift in the relative size of ethnic groups within a hierarchy in which group IQ rankings match occupational rankings.

The second trend is probably occurring in America, thanks to greater natural increase and immigration of blacks and Hispanics compared to whites. It is as if America were an all-white country that annexed an adjoining black and Hispanic country, whose people were concentrated at the bottom of the occupational hierarchy and whose mean IQ matched white Americans at that level. Overnight America would become more of the second kind of meritocracy, but this would have nothing to do with stratification of genes by class within white America. Whether the new all-races America was stratifying genes by class would depend on whether you thought the IQ gap between whites and other races was genetic in origin. That IQ differences between individuals within white America have a strong genetic component is widely conceded; whether there is a genetic component in between-race IQ differences is contested. The future of this kind of trend in America will be determined by whether blacks and Hispanics increase or diminish as a proportion of the American population, whether they close the IQ gap with whites, and whether their occupational status improves despite the same IQ gap. The latter could come about from affirmative action or because IQ differences between groups are less potent predictors of achievement than IQ differences between individuals. Chinese Americans, Japanese Americans, and perhaps Filipino Americans are cases of achievement beyond IQ (Flynn 1991).

However important the second kind of trend, it lacks the universal application and ideological significance of the first kind of trend, that charted by Herrnstein and Murray. If their thesis is valid, every nation, even those without much ethnic diversity—Ireland, Norway, Sweden, Denmark, Finland, Japan, Korea—must face the fact that as they abolish environmental inequality and privilege they will evolve toward an unpalatable class stratification of genes for talent. Therefore, a final marshalling of the evidence and further analysis are in order.

We return to trends within white America and to table 3.3 as a supplement to table 3.1. Table 3.3 gives what the 1985 Stanford-Binet and the 1989 pooled data would show if we could isolate their white subjects. These values are based on the fact that their percentages of nonwhite subjects, and the IQ deficit of those subjects compared to whites, are similar to the percentage and deficit for the WISC-III. The 1989 pooled data yield a class IQ gap for white children of only 9.19 points. This is a rough estimate, of course, but it is overwhelmingly probable that the pooled data would give a value of no more than 10 points. It includes 3,924 white subjects, with 1,308 each in the top and bottom thirds. The most judicious conclusion is that the class IQ gap for white American children today is holding steady at 10 points, plus or minus 1.15 points.

This ten-point class IQ gap looks almost as if it were writ in the stars. It is as if white America has struck some sort of equilibrium, that is, has attained just about as much class-stratified meritocracy as it can easily accommodate. Herrnstein and Murray can argue that the meritocratic era dawned only thirty-five years ago and that the next thirty-five years will show its effects. The sample sizes from 1989 could easily conceal a one-point trend in the class IQ gap. Clearly, we will all look forward to the next standardization of the Stanford-Binet and the WISC, we hope not later than the year 2004, for more data. That data may well falsify the prediction generated by the Herrnstein-Murray thesis, at least for our time and place, beyond a reasonable doubt.

But would even overwhelming falsification be accorded any significance? The obvious answer is that it would leave the central contention of the social mobility meritocracy thesis untouched. That contention is that if the humane-egalitarian quest of abolishing inequality and privilege is successful, it will result in class stratification of genes for talent, of which IQ is a marker. If such stratification has not occurred, the quest has simply been unsuccessful. Moreover, Herrnstein and Murray claim that a meritocratic future is inevitable. This means that the human-egalitarian ideal has been given a reprieve both temporary and humiliating. It is a poor ideal that must pray for eternal failure in order to avoid unwelcome consequences.

Elsewhere I have argued that the trend toward a class-stratified meritocracy is not inevitable, indeed, that the scenario assumed is both psychologically and sociologically incoherent (Flynn 1996). Here I will only pose a few questions. First, equalization of environments requires massive redistribution of wealth: how far can equalization go unless Americans adopt far less materialistic and elitist values than at present? Second, assume Americans do undergo such a sea change: would this not alter a class system based on money and prestige beyond recognition? Third, equalization of environments means allocating a decent life to everyone without regard to merit: how then can an immiserated underclass possibly emerge? Fourth, assume everyone does have the guarantee of a decent life: would not many people of talent settle for that, thus weakening the correlation between high status and talent? All in all, whatever dark spirits slumber in the depths of equality, we have a right to demand a sighting before a class-stratified meritocracy is numbered among them.

Summary

As Ulric Neisser has said, IQ trends over time should encourage social scientists to be reticent about their opinions in a wide range of areas (Horgan 1995). Measuring intelligence and developing an adequate theory of intelligence is more difficult than we thought. The role of IQ tests in labeling people as mentally retarded, learning disabled, and so forth is suspect. When groups are separated by significant cultural distance, we should be cautious about identifying group IQ differences with group intelligence differences. High heritability estimates within groups do not forbid environmental explanations of IQ differences between groups; indeed, an environmental explanation of the IQ gap between American whites and American blacks rests on plausible assumptions. America's changing ethnic mix poses a growing problem of below-average IQ groups concentrated in low-status occupations. However, the apocalyptic vision of human-egalitarian ideals entailing an unpalatable class stratification of genes for talent may well be an illusion.

References

Emanuelsson, I., and A. Svensson. 1990. "Changes in Intelligence over a Quarter of a Century." *Scandinavian Journal of Educational Research* 34: 171–187.

Flynn, J. R. 1984a. "Banishing the Spectre of Meritocracy." *Bulletin of the British Psychological Society* 37: 256–259.

———. 1984b. "The Mean IQ of Americans: Massive Gains 1932 to 1978." *Psychological Bulletin* 95: 29–51.

———. 1985. "Wechsler Intelligence Tests: Do We Really Have a Criterion of Mental Retardation?" *American Journal of Mental Deficiency* 90: 236–244.

———. 1987a. "Massive IQ Gains in 14 Nations: What IQ Tests Really Measure." *Psychological Bulletin* 101: 171–191.

———. 1987b. "The Ontology of Intelligence." In *Measurement, Realism, and Objectivity*, ed. J. Forge, pp. 1–40. Dordrecht, The Netherlands: Reidel.

———. 1990. "Massive IQ Gains on the Scottish WISC: Evidence against Brand et al.'s Hypothesis." *Irish Journal of Psychology* 11: 41–51.

———. 1991. *Asian Americans: Achievement beyond IQ*. Hillsdale, NJ: Erlbaum.

———. 1993. "Skodak and Skeels: The Inflated Mother-Child IQ Gap." *Intelligence* 17: 557–561.

———. 1994. "IQ Gains over Time." In *The Encyclopedia of Human Intelligence*, ed. R. J. Sternberg, pp. 617–623. New York: Macmillan.

———. 1996. "Group Differences: Is the Good Society Impossible?" *Journal of Biosocial Science* 28: 573–585.

———. 1998a. "Israeli Military IQ Tests: Gender Differences Small; IQ Gains Large." *Journal of Biosocial Science* 30: 541–553.

———. 1998b. "WAIS-III and WISC-III: IQ Gains in the US from 1972 to 1995; How to Compensate for Obsolete Norms." *Perceptual and Motor Skills* 86: 1231–1239.

Foulds, G. A., and J. C. Raven. 1948. "Normal Changes in the Mental Abilities of Adults as Age Advances." *Journal of Mental Science* 94: 133–142.

Herrnstein, R. J., and C. Murray. 1994. *The Bell Curve: Intelligence and Class Structure in American Life*. New York: Free Press.

Horgan, J. 1995. "Get Smart, Take a Test: A Long-Term Rise in IQ Scores Baffles Experts." *Scientific American* (November): 10–11.

Jensen, A. R. 1972. *Genetics and Education*. New York: Harper & Row.
———. 1973a. *Educability and Group Differences*. New York: Harper & Row.
———. 1973b. *Educational Differences*. London: Methuen.
———. 1980. *Bias in Mental Testing*. London: Methuen.
———. 1981. *Straight Talks about Mental Tests*. New York: Free Press.
Kaufman, A. S., and J. E. Doppelt. 1976. "Analysis of WISC-R Standardization Data in Terms of Stratification Variables." *Child Development* 47: 165–171.
Lynn, R. 1990. "Differential Rates of Secular Increase of Fine Major Primary Abilities." *Social Biology* 38: 137–141.
Raven, J. 1981. *Manual for Raven's Progressive Matrices and Mill Hill Vocabulary Scales, Research Supplement no. 1*. London: H. K. Lewis.
———. 1995. "Methodological Problems with the 1992 Standardisation of the SPM: A Response." *Personality and Individual Differences* 18: 443–445.
Raven, J., J. C. Raven, and J. H. Court. 1993. *Manual for Raven's Progressive Matrices and Vocabulary Scales*, section 1. Oxford: Oxford Psychologists Press.
———. 1994. *Manual for Raven's Progressive Matrices and Vocabulary Scales*, section 5A. Oxford: Oxford Psychologists Press.
Raven, J. C. 1941. "Standardization of Progressive Matrices." *British Journal of Medical Psychology* 19: 137–150.
Teasdale, T. W., and D. R. Owen. 1989. "Continued Secular Increases in Intelligence and a Stable Prevalence of High Intelligence Levels." *Intelligence* 13: 255–262.
Terman, L. M., and M. A. Merrill. 1937. *Measuring Intelligence*. London: Harrap.
———. 1973. *Stanford-Binet Intelligence Scale 1973 Norms Edition*. Boston: Houghton Mifflin.
Thorndike, R. L., E. P. Hagen, and R. L. Sattler. 1986. *Technical Manual: Stanford-Binet Intelligence Scale, Fourth Edition*. Chicago: Riverside.
U.S. Bureau of the Census. 1930. *Fifteenth Census of the United States: 1930—Population*, vol. 2. Washington, DC: U.S. Government Printing Office.
———. 1950. *Seventeenth Census of the United States: 1950—Population*, vol. 2, part 1. Washington, DC: U.S. Government Printing Office.
———. 1994. *Statistical Abstract of the United States*, 114th edition. Washington, DC: U.S. Government Printing Office.
Vincent, K. R. 1993. "On the Perfectibility of the Human Species: Evidence Using Fixed Reference Groups." *Texas Counseling Association Journal* 22: 60–64.
Wechsler, D. 1944. *The Measurement of Adult Intelligence*. 3rd ed. Baltimore: Williams & Wilkins.
Yerkes, R. M. 1921. *Psychological Examining in the United States Army*. Vol. 15 of *Memoirs of the National Academy of Sciences*. Washington, DC: Government Printing Office.

Four

Genes, Culture, and Inequality*

MARCUS W. FELDMAN, SARAH P. OTTO, AND FREDDY B. CHRISTIANSEN

"MEN ARE NOT BORN GOOD OR EVIL"
"It is impossible for man to be endowed by nature from his very birth with either virtue or vice, just as it is impossible that he should be born skilled by nature in any particular art. It is possible, however, that through natural causes he may from birth be so constituted as to have a predilection for a particular virtue or vice, so that he will more readily practice it than any other. For instance, a man whose natural constitution inclines toward dryness, whose brain-matter is clear and not overloaded with fluids, finds it much easier to learn, remember, and understand things than the phlegmatic man whose brain is encumbered with a great deal of humidity. But if one who inclines constitutionally toward a certain excellence is left entirely without instruction, and if his faculties are not stimulated, he will undoubtedly remain ignorant. On the other hand, if one by nature is dull and phlegmatic, possessing an abundance of humidity, is instructed and enlightened, he will, though of course with difficulty, gradually succeed in acquiring knowledge and understanding.

"In exactly the same way, he whose blood is especially warm has the requisite quality to become a brave man. But another whose heart is colder than it should be, is naturally inclined toward cowardice and fear, so that if he should be encouraged to be a coward, he would easily become one. If, however, it be desired to make a brave man of him, he can without doubt become one, providing he receive the proper training which would require, of course, great exertion.

"I have entered into this subject so that thou mayest not believe the absurd ideas of astrologers, who falsely assert that the constellation at the time of one's birth determines whether one is to be virtuous or vicious, the individual being thus necessarily compelled to follow out a certain line of conduct."

(Moses Maimonides (1135–1204), Comm. Mishna, Eight Chapters VIII, *from* The Wisdom of Israel, *ed. Lewis Brown, 1948)*

* Research supported in part by NIH grant GM28016, a grant from the Canadian NSERC, and grant 94-0163-1 from the Danish Natural Science Council.

"We used to think that our fate was in our stars. Now we know, in
large part, that our fate is in our genes."

(James D. Watson, quoted by John Horgan, Scientific American, *June
1993)*

1. Introduction

In 1969 Jensen wrote that it was a "not unreasonable hypothesis that genetic
factors are strongly implicated in the average Negro-White intelligence difference" (Jensen 1969). As a result, he argued, there was little point in intervening to reduce this average difference. His argument was based on the
high heritability (80 percent was his estimate) of IQ. It was largely in response to this extremely hereditarian explanation of inequality in educational
achievement that Cavalli-Sforza and Feldman (1973a) initiated the quantitative study of gene-culture coevolution.

This research program had two main objectives. The first was to establish
an evolutionary dynamic basis for the proper computation of statistics that
are commonly used to measure familial aggregation. The second was to develop an analog to the extremely well studied field of evolutionary population genetics that would apply to population variability in culturally transmitted traits (Cavalli-Sforza and Feldman 1973; Cavalli-Sforza and Feldman
1981).

The reaction of population geneticists to these endeavors was, on the
whole, favorable. From anthropologists and other social scientists, on the
other hand, there was almost no response for about ten years.[1] Recent treatments, however, appear to have addressed in some detail the issues that we
first raised in the early 1970s (Durham 1991; Laland 1993).

This chapter will be partly historical and partly expository. Since many of
the issues that were relevant in our early studies of gene-culture interaction
have resurfaced as a consequence of the publicity surrounding Herrnstein
and Murray's attack (1994) on the feasibility of societal intervention to rem-
edy socioeconomic inequality, we shall discuss the concept of heritability
and the evolution of its magnitude over the past twenty-seven years. The
most detailed analyses of the heritability of IQ, those that use thousands of
related individuals rather than the tens of twins studied in the papers cited by
Herrnstein and Murray, are not cited in most of the psychological literature.
This literature, with its focus almost exclusively on twins, produces estimates substantially higher than studies with more diverse sets of relatives
that allow more detailed estimation of culturally transmitted components. In

---

[1] For example, the historian Carl Degler (1991), while citing several authors who actually
used ideas developed by Cavalli-Sforza and Feldman, fails to cite the original sources.

fact, cultural and genetic heritability estimates are virtually the same for IQ when more complete models are used. We discuss some properties of these models as well as the relevance of measured heritability to inferences about the process of natural selection.

Following this more or less classical analysis, we will formulate a general approach to the joint evolutionary dynamics of genes and culture and show how such mathematical models are relevant to the problems of familial aggregation. We conclude with a review of a recent example of how culturally transmitted human prejudice about a biologically determined trait, namely, the sex of an offspring, can influence a population-level variable, the sex ratio. This example pertains to cultural and socioeconomic inequality of the sexes.

2. The Origins of "Heritability"

The clear distinction between genetic and environmental variation was drawn by W. Johannsen (1903; 1909) early in this century, and the principles of genetic analysis of metric characters were well developed when the word "heritability" first appeared in a book by J. L. Lush (1937) in an analysis of breeding for agricultural improvement. A character with trait value P (for phenotype) is considered, and its variance V_P is divided into two parts, usually written V_G and V_E, where V_G, in the words of Lush, is "that part of the variance caused by the heredity that different individuals have" and V_E is "that part of the variance caused by the differences in the environments under which different individuals develop." The heritability of the trait, H^2, is given by the variance ratio

$$H^2 = \frac{V_G}{V_P} = \frac{V_G}{V_G + V_E}.$$

It is absolutely clear that Johannsen and Lush intended the distinction between the genetic and the environmental variance to apply to the controlled environments possible in animal or plant breeding or experimentation, so that *by design* correlations between genotype and environment are absent.

R. A. Fisher (1918) partitioned V_G into components that represented the effects of alleles (V_A) and how alleles and genes interacted with each other (V_D and V_I). Suffice it to say here that the heritability measure introduced by Lush only represents the fraction of additive genetic variance V_A, and if this fraction is high, artificial selection will be easy. This fraction of the total phenotypic variance due to additive genetic variance is now called narrow-sense heritability and is most important to animal and plant breeders. The narrow-sense heritability, which we will denote here by h^2, is

$$h^2 = \frac{V_A}{V_P} = \frac{V_A}{(V_A + V_D + V_I) + V_E} \ .$$

This heritability is closely related to the hereditary value used by Johannsen, which is simply the parent-offspring regression of trait values. Heritability in this sense is simply an index of amenability of the character to artificial selection. The above broad-sense heritability, H^2, includes all other genetic effects, and if genotype $\times$ environmental interactions occur, these will also be included. The broad-sense heritability seems to have its major use in human behavioral genetics.

A slightly different approach to the etiology of complex traits was introduced by Wright (1931). He developed path analysis to specify the transmission and various sources of influence on a trait and transmission of these influences. As is common in heritability studies, Wright also assumed that genotype $\times$ environmental interactions were absent in his analysis of Burks' data on mental development in humans, even though such interactions could not in reality be eliminated.

In fact, the term *heritability* applied to human behavior seems to have been first used by Jensen (1969) in his discussion of the "genetics" of IQ. It must be stressed that both definitions, narrow and broad, say little about the underlying biology and are purely statistical constructs. As such, heritability is sensitive to the statistical model that produces it. The best source for more on the genetics of continuously varying traits under artificial selection and how heritability is useful in that context is Falconer's book (Falconer and Mackay 1996).

3. The "Evolution" of the Heritability of IQ

It is fair to say that prior to 1974 the accepted estimate, published in many textbooks of human or behavioral genetics, for the heritability of IQ was 80 percent. Following the introduction of cultural transmission into the picture (Cavalli-Sforza and Feldman 1973a), Morton's group in Hawaii embarked on a major effort to use path analysis to estimate the genetically transmitted, culturally transmitted, and nontransmitted environmental components of variability in IQ. In 1976 Rao et al. published an article modestly titled, "Resolution of Cultural and Biological Inheritance by Path Analysis" (Rao, Morton, and Yee 1976). Their estimate of the genetic heritability of IQ (i.e., h^2) was 67 percent. They also obtained an estimate of 9.4 percent for a transmitted environmental component, with 10.1 percent as the genotype $\times$ environment covariance. Nontransmitted environment accounted for 13.5 percent of the variance in this analysis.

Soon after this study by Morton's group, we were fortunate to have Arthur

Goldberger visit the Center for Advanced Studies in the Behavioral Sciences at Stanford, and we benefitted greatly from discussions with him on the formulation of models that included cultural transmission and various modes of assortative mating (Cavalli-Sforza and Feldman 1978; Feldman and Cavalli-Sforza 1979; Goldberger 1978a and 1978b). These discussions and the resulting publications played an important role in the subsequent analyses by the Washington University group (Cloninger, Rice, and Reich 1979), who analysed all the published U.S. IQ data and estimated the genetic heritability of IQ to be 32.6 percent, the cultural heritability to be 27.2 percent, the covariance between cultural and genetic factors to be 9.3 percent, and the contribution from nontransmitted environmental effects to be 30.1 percent. A new feature of this treatment was an estimate of 1.0 for the nontransmitted environmental contribution from MZ (monozygotic) twins, with 0.35 the corresponding value for DZ (dizygotic) twins.

One of the interesting consequences of the study by Cloninger, Rice, and Reich (1979) was that it stimulated Morton's group to reassess their previous "resolution." Rao, Morton, Lalouel, and Lew (1982) then produced two estimates, depending on the assumptions about assortative mating: one of 31 percent for genetic and 42 percent for cultural heritability and another of 44 percent for genetic and 33 percent for cultural heritability. They do not cite their own earlier 1976 study.

The two studies just described, those of Cloninger et al. and Rao et al., are undoubtedly the most detailed published path analyses of IQ. Yet the numbers they report have not penetrated *psychological* literature. For example, Jensen (1989) claimed that "the overall average of the best estimates we have for the broad-sense heritability of IQ is between 0.60 and 0.70." In 1992 Sandra Scarr, then president of the Society for Research in Child Development, said that the estimates of heritability lay between 40 and 70 percent; on the basis of "a considerable amount of data from families and twins, the heritability . . . is about 50%" (Scarr 1992). And relying on information by psychologists R. Plomin and J. C. Loehlin, Deborah Franklin wrote in a 1989 *New York Times* article that "genes are 50 to 70 percent responsible for an individual's IQ" (Franklin 1989). The reporter's use of the word "responsible" here is important; it conveys to the uninformed reader a relationship between the statistical value of the heritability and the extent of individual genetic causation that is quite erroneous.

Much publicity has surrounded the twins reared apart reported by Bouchard over the past several years. As part of the Human Genome issue of *Science* magazine, Bouchard et al. (1990) reported on fifty-six pairs of twins reared apart and, using the correlation in IQ between these pairs, produced an estimate of 70 percent for the heritability of IQ. In that paper neither the Cloninger et al. nor the Rao et al. estimates were cited, but an earlier paper in *Science* by Bouchard and McGue (1981) was. In that study, the authors summarized 111 studies of familial resemblance in measured intelligence, although they did not produce an estimate of heritability. Nevertheless, in 1990 Bouchard et al. were prepared to offer the estimate of 70 percent, based on fifty-six pairs of twins reared apart, as superior to earlier, lower estimates based on thousands of families.

It is worth concluding this historical review with the following excerpt from Herrnstein and Murray (1994, p. 105): "In fact IQ is substantially heritable . . . [and] the genetic component of IQ is unlikely to be smaller than 40 percent or higher than 80 percent. . . . For purposes of this discussion, we will adopt a middling estimate of 60 percent heritability, which, by extension, means that IQ is about 40 percent a matter of environment. The balance of the evidence suggests that 60 percent may err on the low side." It is not surprising that in neither Bouchard's work nor in Herrnstein and Murray's book are the 1979 paper of Cloninger et al. and the 1982 paper of Rao et al. cited.

4. Some Formal Linear Models of Transmission

One of the major conclusions to come from our recent work on cultural inheritance is that heritability estimates are extremely sensitive to the underlying model that one invokes for the development and inheritance of a trait. To illustrate this point, we outline a set of models that we have used to estimate transmission parameters for IQ and personality traits. A word of warning: although these and other models used to estimate heritability often seem quite complex, they still fail to capture many of the potential sources of influence on human behavioral traits. Therefore, all estimates of heritability, including ours, must be treated with circumspection.

The phenotypic value of an individual, denoted by the variable P, is represented as a deviation from the mean in the population so that its expectation may be set to zero, $E(P) = 0$ (by subtracting the population mean value of the trait from the individual values). Also, the variance of the phenotypic variable is normalized to unity, $\text{Var}(P) = 1$ (by using the population standard deviation of the trait as the unit of measurement). The effect of the genotype of the individual on its phenotype is denoted by the variable A, with $E(A) = 0$. The environmental contribution to an individual's phenotype will be divided into two parts: an effect influenced by cultural transmission, B, and a nontransmitted environmental effect, E, dependent only on the particular environmental experiences of the individual, with $E(B) = E(E) = 0$. All variables are assumed to be normally distributed and any collection of variables follows a multidimensional Gaussian distribution. In addition, the variances of the variables are all normalized to unity, $\text{Var}(A) = \text{Var}(B) = \text{Var}(E) = 1$, and we use the parameters h, b, and e to describe the strength of the influence of genes, cultural environment, and nontransmitted environment, respectively, on the phenotype of an individual. The phenotype is then specified as a linear combination of the normalized genotypic and environmental deviations:

$$P = hA + bB + eE. \tag{4.1}$$

The genetic (A) and environmental (B and E) deviations (the "latent" variables) are measured in such a way that the parameters h, b, and e are positive and each is bounded by 0 and 1. In general, a covariance w will exist between the genotypic deviation and the cultural deviation of the individual, $w = \mathrm{Cov}(A, B)$, but we assume that all transmissible components are independent of the nontransmitted environmental component, that is, $\mathrm{Cov}(E, A) = \mathrm{Cov}(E, B) = 0$. The phenotypic variance is therefore

$$\mathrm{Var}(P) = h^2 + b^2 + e^2 + 2hbw, \tag{4.2}$$

and, since $\mathrm{Var}(P) = 1$, the strength of the nontransmitted environmental effects (e) must satisfy

$$e = \sqrt{1 - h^2 - b^2 - 2hbw}. \tag{4.3}$$

The principal parameters of the model, h and b, depend on the nature of the variation in the population. In a genetically homogeneous population, h would be zero because genes are unimportant to the observed *variation* within the population. When the genotype and cultural type do not covary ($w = 0$), we have $h^2 + b^2 + e^2 = 1$ and h^2, b^2, and e^2 may be interpreted as the fractions of the variance due to genotypic, culturally transmitted, and nontransmitted environmental variation, respectively. In studies of quantitative inheritance in which correlations between relatives are analyzed, h^2 is the *genetic heritability* of the studied character.

The above description depends on the state of the population at a specific point in time. The population changes over time, and, in particular, changes in variance components must be specified in a dynamically consistent manner to obtain a completely rigorous model (Cavalli-Sforza and Feldman 1973a and 1978; Feldman and Cavalli-Sforza 1979; Goldberger 1978a and 1978b). Here we make the assumption that the population has reached an *equilibrium* so that h, b, and w reflect stable characteristics of the population. This assumption entails that w must be specified as a function of h and b.

4.1 Genetic Transmission

The genotypic variation in the population is assumed to be stable over time and to originate in allelic variability at a large number of loci not subject to selection. We assume a fully additive genetic model where the genotypic effect is determined by summing the effects of each allele at each locus.[2] The mean genotypic value of an offspring is then simply the average of the parental genotypic values:

$$E(G_O | G_M, G_F) = \frac{G_M + G_F}{2}.$$

where the subscripts O, M, and F are used to denote the offspring, maternal, and paternal deviations of the relevant variable, here the genotypic value, G. An extension of this analysis would include effects of dominance, epistasis, and genotype-environment interaction (Falconer and Mackay 1996). The assumption of genetic equilibrium entails that the variance in the offspring generation equals the variance in the parental generation, so $\text{Var}(G_O) = \text{Var}(G_M) = \text{Var}(G_F) = V_G$, say. Assuming that the genotypic values of the parents are independent, we can write

$$G_O = \frac{G_M + G_F}{2} + D, \tag{4.4}$$

where D describes the deviation due to Mendelian segregation, so $E(D) = 0$, $\text{Cov}(D, G_M) = 0$, and $\text{Cov}(D, G_F) = 0$. For the genotypic variance to remain constant over time with value V_G, equation (4.4) implies that $\text{Var}(D) = \frac{1}{2}V_G$. In terms of the normalized genotypic variable $A = G/\sqrt{V_G}$ in (4.1) we have

$$A_O = \frac{1}{2} A_M + \frac{1}{2} A_F + \sigma S, \tag{4.5}$$

where $S = D/\sqrt{\frac{1}{2}V_G}$ with $E(S) = 0$, $\text{Var}(S) = 1$, and $\sigma = 1/\sqrt{2}$.

Now consider the effect of a correlation r_{AA} between the genotypic values of parents. This correlation will be positive when the parents are related or when there is assortative mating with respect to the quantitative trait. Assuming that the segregation variance, V_D, remains the same regardless of the value of r_{AA}, a genetic correlation between mates augments the genotypic variance. Using equation (4.4), we see that

$$\text{Var}(G_O) = \frac{1}{4}\text{Var}(G_M) + \frac{1}{4}\text{Var}(G_F) + \frac{1}{2}r_{AA}\sqrt{\text{Var}(G_M)\text{Var}(G_F)} + V_D,$$

which entails that $V_G = 2V_D(1 - r_{AA})$ at equilibrium.

---

[2] This assumption is commonly applied to simplify the analysis of quantitative characters. It entails that $V_D = V_I = 0$, and therefore that $H^2 = h^2$.

4.2 Cultural Transmission

Whereas Mendelian laws of inheritance may be used to justify assumptions about the transmission of genes that affect a continuous trait, no such laws exist for cultural transmission. Rather, the dynamics of cultural transmission will vary depending on the nature of the character under study (Cavalli-Sforza and Feldman 1973b and 1981). Here we will limit our attention to vertical transmission, where only parents contribute to the transmissible environmental component of an individual as described by the variable B. Two models that differ in how parents influence the cultural values of their offspring will be examined: an indirect model in which only the cultural values of the parents have an influence $(B \to B)$ and a direct model in which the phenotypes of the parents determine the offspring's cultural value $(P \to B)$.

4.2a INDIRECT CULTURAL TRANSMISSION

The variable B refers to a latent factor that can be transmitted culturally from generation to generation and that may include factors such as wealth, education, and residence. This transmission occurs with some error (or "cultural segregation") described by S_C with $E(S_C) = 0$ and $\text{Var}(S_C) = 1$. That is, we assume a transmission equation for culture similar to equation (4.5) for genes,

$$B_O = \beta_I(B_M + B_F) + \delta S_C, \tag{4.6}$$

where β_I describes the fidelity with which family environment is transmitted and δ measures the degree of transmission error. The normalization of the variables produces $\delta = \sqrt{1 - 2\beta_I^2(1 + r_{BB})}$, where r_{BB} is the correlation between the cultural value of mates; $r_{BB} = \text{Cov}(B_M, B_F)$.

4.2b DIRECT CULTURAL TRANSMISSION

In this case, the variable B describes the cultural experiences of an offspring, but is not itself transmitted. Instead, the cultural value of an offspring B_O is influenced by its parents' phenotypic values and therefore by *all* of the determinants of parental phenotype. The maternal and paternal influences are equal and the cultural transmission occurs with some error, so the cultural value of an offspring is given by:

$$B_O = \beta_D(P_M + P_F) + \delta S_C, \tag{4.7}$$

where S_C is a normalized variable describing the random error in the cultural transmission. The correlation between the phenotypic values of mates is $m = \text{Cov}(P_M, P_F)$, and since all the variables have unit variance,

$\delta = \sqrt{1 - 2\beta_D^2(1 + m)}$. When cultural transmission is perfectly faithful, that is, $\delta = 0$, then β_D equals $1/\sqrt{2(1 + m)}$, and if there is error in transmission, that is, $\delta > 0$, then β_D is less than $1/\sqrt{2(1 + m)}$.

4.3 Assortative Mating

Empirical studies on human behavioral traits have often revealed strong patterns of nonrandom mating. One of the most common forms is assortative mating, which is a departure from random mating in which similar individuals mate with each other more frequently than would occur at random. Such assortment may be caused by conscious mate choice or by the ways in which humans meet one another. We consider two types of assortative mating on linear models of quantitative inheritance: the *phenotypic homogamy* model, where assortment is based on the phenotype of individuals, and the *social homogamy* model, where assortment occurs because individuals belong to the same social group.

4.3a PHENOTYPIC HOMOGAMY

The simplest model assumes that assortment is based on phenotype and this assortment creates a correlation $m = \text{Cov}(P_M, P_F)$ between the phenotypic values of mated pairs. That is, phenotypic homogamy occurs when individuals tend to choose mates that have similar trait values.

The model of phenotypic assortment that we consider is equivalent to what Goldberger (1978a) calls "Fisher's model" of assortative mating. Here any correlation between the latent variables A_F, B_F, and E_F in the female and latent variables A_M, B_M, and E_M in the male arise only because of their respective correlations with P_F and P_M. That is, we assume that G_M given P_M, written $(G_M \mid P_M)$, is independent of $(G_F \mid P_F)$; $(B_M \mid P_M)$ is independent of $(B_F \mid P_F)$; and $(E_M \mid P_M)$ is independent of $(E_F \mid P_F)$. These assumptions allow us to derive all of the correlations between the latent variables A_M, B_M, and E_M of the mother and A_F, B_F, and E_F of the father as a matrix Θ:

$$\Theta = m \begin{pmatrix} (h + bw)^2 & (h + bw)(b + hw) & (h + bw)e \\ (h + bw)(b + hw) & (b + hw)^2 & (b + hw)e \\ (h + bw)e & (b + hw)e & e^2 \end{pmatrix}, \quad (4.8)$$

where $m = \text{Cov}(P_M, P_F)$.

4.3b SOCIAL HOMOGAMY

Nonrandom mating can also result from assortment on the basis of the cultural value or the genotype of an individual. Assortment may occur on the basis of social class, residence, school, church, job, social activities, or race. To the extent that mating occurs among individuals within a group and to the extent that groups differ in their composition with respect to cultural and genetic variables, group membership will produce a correlation between the cultural and genotypic values of mates that will lead, indirectly, to a correlation between the phenotypes of spouses.

Although groups may differ in their genetic and cultural composition, it is assumed that the distribution of nontransmissible environmental experiences is *independent* of the grouping. Specifically, any and all experiences that depend on group membership will be transmissible to the extent that group membership is inherited, and these experiences would be included in the cultural value summarized by the variable B. Therefore, specific environmental experiences summarized in E, which by definition are not transmitted from generation to generation, cannot depend on grouping. Thus, assortment that occurs on the basis of grouping may be specified by the correlation coefficients r_{AA}, r_{AB}, and r_{BB} between the variables A and B of mated pairs, while correlations that involve the specific environmental values of mates, that is, r_{AE}, r_{BE}, and r_{EE}, will all be zero:

$$\Theta = \begin{pmatrix} r_{AA} & r_{AB} & 0 \\ r_{AB} & r_{BB} & 0 \\ 0 & 0 & 0 \end{pmatrix}. \tag{4.9}$$

This formulation follows that of Goldberger (1978a) and Rao, Morton, and Yee (1976).

4.4 Correlations among Relatives

Using the theory developed in this section, it is possible to compute expected correlations between relatives of any degree (Otto, Feldman, and Christiansen 1994). Otto, Feldman, and Christiansen focus on three models that incorporate different assumptions about cultural transmission and assortative mating as described in table 4.1. These models are each used to compute any familial correlation, $r^{(i)}$, as a function of the transmission and mating parameters. These expected correlations are compared to observations using Fisher's z transform and written z_{exp}^i. From a set of observed correlations among relatives, the corresponding observed transformed values are $z_{obs}^{(i)}$. We estimate the parameters by minimizing the quantity

$$\text{SSD} = \sum_{i=1}^{N} (n_i - 3) \left(z_{obs}^{(i)} - z_{exp}^{(i)} \right)^2 \tag{4.10}$$

whose distribution approximates $\chi^2_{N - p}$, where n_i is the number of observations used to compute the ith correlation, N is the number of correlations,

72 FELDMAN, OTTO, AND CHRISTIANSEN

TABLE 4.1
Three Linear Models of Inheritance

Model	Cultural Transmission	Homogamy
"IP"	Indirect	Phenotypic
"DP"	Direct	Phenotypic
"IS"	Indirect	Social

and p is the number of parameters estimated (see Goldberger 1978a and 1978b).

5. Some Results

Here we give two sets of results, one for IQ and one for some personality traits. Many more details may be found in Otto, Feldman, and Christiansen (1994). For IQ, our parameter estimates are very close to those obtained by Cloninger, Rice, and Reich (1979). In all of our expected correlations we have included parameters c_s, c_{hs}, c_{dz}, and c_{mz}, which specify the correlations between the nontransmitted environmental contribution to the phenotype between sibs, halfsibs, DZ twins, and MZ twins, respectively. As will become obvious, these turn out to be important.

5.1 IQ

Bouchard and McGue (1981) summarized several published studies that reported familial correlations for the intelligence quotient, IQ. Their mean values for the correlations between relatives are given in table 4.2. These mean correlations are weighted averages of correlations from 111 studies on IQ variation. Table 4.3 records the parameter values that best fit these observed correlations for the three models of table 4.1. Ninety-five percent confidence limits for the estimates of heritability are also given in table 4.3 for each model. The heritability estimate is highest for the IS Model (indirect transmission, social homogamy), followed by the IP Model (indirect transmission, phenotypic homogamy), and the estimate is lowest for the DP Model (direct transmission, phenotypic homogamy). As the χ^2 values show, however, none of the models adequately fits the data.

The two phenotypic homogamy models give very similar estimates for heritability, although these differ somewhat from the estimate in the IS Model. The DP Model and the IS Model even give non-overlapping estimates for heritability. This is not unexpected. Parameter estimates should depend on the model used, and there is no theoretical reason not to expect

TABLE 4.2
Familial Correlations in IQ

Relationship	Symbol	Number of Pairs	Correlation
MZ Twins (Together)	MZT	4672	0.86
MZ Apart	MZA	65	0.72
DZ Twins (Together)	DZT	5546	0.60
Sibs (Together)	SST	26473	0.47
Sibs Apart	SSA	203	0.24
Adopted/Natural Sibs	SAN	345	0.29
Adopted/Adopted Sibs	SAA	369	0.34
Half Sibs	HSS	200	0.31
Offspring–Parent	OPT	8433	0.42
Offspring–Midparent	OMT	992	0.50
Midoffspring–Midparent	MMT	410	0.72
Offspring Parent Apart	OPA	814	0.22
Foster Offspring–Parent	FOP	1497	0.19
Foster Offspring–Midparent	FOM	758	0.24
Cousins	CZ1	1176	0.15
Spouses	m	3817	0.33

Source: Bouchard and McGue (1981)

different models to give non-overlapping estimates of heritability. The essential question, to which we do not have an answer, is which of many possible models best reflects the transmission of IQ. Since heritability estimates are sensitive to the model used, heritability estimated from imperfect models such as these may tell us little about the heritability estimated from a more accurate model. We can give a 95 percent confidence interval for h^2 using a particular model, but we cannot give a measure of confidence in the model itself.

Note that the estimates for c_{MZ} and c_{DZ} are high, while these parameters are assumed to be zero in even the most detailed twin studies. They suggest that "twinship" itself is a special relationship and that estimates based on twins that ignore this specialness should be viewed with circumspection. Similar values for c_{MZ} and c_{DZ} were found by Cloninger, Rice, and Reich (1979) and by Rao, Morton, Lalouel, and Lew (1982). From these high estimates one might be tempted to infer that twins construct environments for themselves that differ qualitatively from those of other sibs. The details are, of course, a subject for further psychological study and not a matter of statistics. Table 4.4 shows that when data for twins are removed from the data set of table 4.2, the resulting estimates of h^2 change very little. It is clear that estimates of 60 percent for the genetic heritability of IQ are just too high to fit the full spectrum of data available. It is doubtful that an eight-hundred-page book on IQ, cognitive ability, race, and inequality would have been

TABLE 4.3
The Best-Fitting Parameter Sets for the Data Reviewed by Bouchard and McGue (1981) on Familial Aggregation of IQ

	IP Model	DP Model	IS Model
h	0.57	0.54	0.65
b	0.52	—	0.52
β	0.47	—	0.35
$b\beta$	*0.25*	0.14	*0.18*
m	0.32	0.33	*0.32*
e	*0.58*	*0.72*	*0.53*
w	*0.11*	—	*0.04*
γ	*0.63*	*0.67*	*0.67*
r_{aa}	*0.13*	—	0.01
r_{ab}	*0.12*	—	*0.08*
r_{bb}	*0.11*	—	1.00
c_s	0.24	0.22	0.37
c_{hs}	0.22	0.17	0.09
c_{dz}	0.64	0.47	0.82
c_{mz}	0.98	0.73	1.00
χ^2	41.85	48.75	35.80
df	8	9	7
h^2	0.33	0.29	0.42

Note: The estimates of the basic parameters in the three models are shown in roman type and the derived values are shown in *italic* type. Estimates of values not applicable for a particular model are indicated by a bar. The 95 percent confidence limits for the estimates of heritability for each model are as follows:
IP Model: $0.28 < h^2 < 0.38$
DP Model: $0.25 < h^2 < 0.35$
IS Model: $0.35 < h^2 < 0.48$

TABLE 4.4
Heritability Estimates with Certain Subsets of the Data from Table 4.2 Removed

	Data		
	All	No Twins	No Raised-Apart
IP Model	0.33	0.32	0.31
DP Model	0.29	0.27	0.27
IS Model	0.42	0.23	0.35

Note: "No twins" data means that r_{MZT}, r_{MZA}, and r_{DZT} are removed from table 4.2. "No raised-apart" data means that r_{MZA}, r_{SSA}, and r_{OPA} are removed from table 4.2.

taken seriously if the premise had been a 33 percent genetic heritability for IQ, with a very similar number for cultural heritability.

5.2 Personality

Bouchard (1994) reviews recent twin studies purporting to study the genetic basis of human personality traits such as extraversion and neuroticism. His conclusion from his own data is that "the most parsimonious fit to the Minnesota [twin] data is a simple additive genetic model . . . with an estimate of genetic influence of 46%." He goes on in the next paragraph to state, "The similarity we see in personality between biological relatives is almost entirely genetic in origin."

We have reexamined the large set of data published by Eaves, Eysenk, and Martin (1989) on familial aggregation for three personality traits: psychoticism, extraversion, and neuroticism (two of which were in Bouchard's list). The data of Eaves, Eysenik, and Martin are presented in table 4.5. Our estimates of h^2 for the three models of section 4, as well as the estimates by Eaves, Eysenik, and Martin are given in table 4.6. Details are given in Otto, Feldman, and Christiansen (1994), but suffice it to say that the correlations c_{MZ} and c_{DZ} again turn out to be important. It would take a large imagination to infer from either our estimates or those of Eaves, Eysenik, and Martin that the correlations are "almost entirely" due to genetics.

TABLE 4.5
Familial Correlations in Three Synthetic Personality Characters

		Correlation		
Relationship	Number	Psychoticism	Extraversion	Neuroticism
MZ Twins	297	0.438	0.507	0.459
DZ Twins	231	0.257	0.160	0.081
Spouses	155	0.273	0.036	0.063
Parent—Offspring	533	0.125	0.207	0.117
Siblings	409	0.160	0.246	0.044
Grandparent—Offspring	45	−0.016	0.043	0.199
Aunt/Uncle—Nephew	302	0.016	0.127	0.042
Cousins	104	0.008	0.093	0.052
Second Cousins	23	−0.214	0.178	−0.293
Foster Parent—Offspring	208	0.001	−0.022	0.068
Foster Siblings	52	0.016	−0.115	0.232

Source: Eaves, Eysenik, and Martin (1989)

TABLE 4.6
Heritability Estimates for the Data of Eaves, Eysenik, and Martin

	Psychoticism	Extraversion	Neuroticism
$h^{2\dagger}$	0.22	0.45	0.00
$h^2_{broad}{}^\dagger$	0.46	0.52	0.42
h^2(IP Model)††	0.16	0.40	0.00
h^2(DP Model)††	0.16	0.40	0.04
h^2(IS Model)††	0.17	0.36	0.00

[†]Heritability estimates provided by Eaves, Eysenik, and Martin (1989).

[††]These estimates are from the models with sib, dz, and mz environmental correlations included.

6. A Mistaken Evolutionary Interpretation

Bouchard (1994) attempts to remind us of "our links to the biological world and our evolutionary history" by focusing our attention on "the core problem of the genetics of personality—the function of the variation." In his mind, the purpose of this variation is "undoubtedly rooted in the fact that humans have adapted to life in face-to-face groups (sociality)." In other words, the traits that he has studied, for example, extraversion and neuroticism, have been under natural selection, which has left its mark in the current measurable variation. This reasoning contains a classic error whose explication is grounded in the fundamentals of population genetics, in fact, in Fisher's Fundamental Theorem of Natural Selection (Fisher 1930). The theorem states that the rate of change in the mean fitness is equal to the additive genetic variance in fitness. Thus, if a trait truly had an effect on fitness (i.e., if the degree of adaptation did depend on the trait value), then the additive genetic variance would be dissipated by natural selection. Eventually we would be left only with nonadditive genetic variance, genotype by environment interaction, and cultural or environmental variability. You cannot have it both ways: high additive genetic variance means not very important to natural selection, whereas low additive genetic variance means not very interesting to Bouchard. It is worth recalling what Darwin says in *The Descent of Man* (1871, p. 249): "The variability of all the characteristic differences between the races . . . indicates that these differences cannot be of much importance; for had they been important, they would long ago have been either fixed and preserved, or eliminated."

In short, the prediction to be drawn from the premise that IQ or behavioral traits were selectively important in our ancestors is that there should be little additive genetic variability remaining for these traits among modern humans.

7. A Final Remark on Heritability

For most of the human traits that we have investigated, the cultural heritability is not significantly different from the genetic heritability. In many twin studies, cultural transmission is not included and no allowance is made for the specialness of the twin relationship. Without including these influences, estimates of heritability are about double those reported here. In *The Bell Curve* (1994), Herrnstein and Murray fail to mention the extreme sensitivity of estimates of heritability to the inclusion of such factors as cultural transmission. They also fail to cite the most comprehensive studies, which are based on thousands of families and more complex (if still imperfect) models, each of which gives substantially lower estimates for heritability than are cited by Herrnstein and Murray. Even if heritability actually provided information about gene action (which it does not), the uncertainties in its estimation would be enough to invalidate its inclusion in policy deliberations.

More important, heritability tells us nothing about the effectiveness of different social policies on a trait. In population biology, those interested in understanding how important environment is in the development of a trait have abandoned the use of heritability in favor of the concept of a reaction norm. A reaction norm is simply a graph indicating the phenotypic value for a given genotype in a series of different environments. These graphs may be quite different for different genotypes: in one environment the variability among genotypes may be high, while in another it may be low. Heritability does not describe this dependence of variability on the environment. It cannot tell us which environmental factors are most favorable for the development of, say, IQ. It cannot tell us how we may structure the learning experience of different individuals so that each may maximize his or her potential in whichever directions may be important to that person. Those who would advocate that high heritability means low plasticity to environmental change ignore the basic fact that heritability in one set of environments tells us nothing about means or variances in another environment.

The Bell Curve (Herrnstein and Murray 1994), with its thesis that in the process of forming a meritocracy the importance of genes has increased and will continue to do so, reiterates the fundamentally racist propositions of the Jensen-Shockley era nearly thirty years ago. It is yet another attempt to release us from any obligation to search for and supply those conditions that may enhance the lives of each member of our society. Not only does its thesis rest on estimates of heritability that are inexcusably high, but it fails to acknowledge the fact that heritability has no bearing on socioeconomic inequality and what to do about it.

8. Discrete Valued Traits and Gene-Culture Dynamics

Our understanding of the etiology of human behavioral traits is limited, at best, and hampers the development of truly appropriate models. To better understand what heritability does and does not say about genetic transmission, we have developed a simple genetic-cultural model. Actual transmission parameters can then be compared to inferences made from familial correlations. In this model, the cultural variation is dichotomous and the genetic variation is due to a single diploid locus. In a sense this approach, which we originated in 1976 (Feldman and Cavalli-Sforza 1976), tries to move closer to the mechanistic causative level than is possible using the statistical approach of the previous sections. We shall concentrate here on vertical cultural transmission, although we have written elsewhere (Cavalli-Sforza and Feldman 1973b and 1981) about cultural transmission of information from individuals other than parents.

The approach taken here may be regarded as an alternative to the widely used sociobiological theory of inclusive fitness maximization often used by animal behaviorists (and some anthropologists) to explain observed behaviors, which is based essentially on assumptions about evolution at a single gene locus under Hardy-Weinberg constraints. Before we move on to more general models, it is instructive to see how vertical cultural transmission can overcome natural selection; it therefore offers an alternative to kin selection for the evolution of disadvantageous traits. Suppose that a behavior exists in two forms labeled 1 and 2 in frequencies u and $1 - u$ at some time t. If these mate at random, and if an offspring becomes type 1 when at least one of its parents is type 1, we can write a mating table (see table 4.7).

If type 1 suffers a fitness loss s relative to type 2, then in the next generation we have

$$u' = \frac{[u^2 + 2u(1 - u)](1 - s)}{[u^2 + 2u(1 - u)](1 - s) + (1 - u)^2}. \qquad (8.1)$$

TABLE 4.7
Dichotomous Trait Mating Table

Mating	Mating Frequency	Offspring	
		1	*2*
1 × 1	u^2	1	0
1 × 2	$u(1 - u)$	1	0
2 × 1	$u(1 - u)$	1	0
2 × 2	$(1 - u)^2$	0	1
Fitness		$1 - s$	1

It is clear from this dynamic that type 1 will remain in the population even if it suffers up to 50 percent viability loss, whereas it would be eliminated in the face of any viability loss with Mendelian inheritance.

This trivial example illustrates that the rules of evolution under cultural transmission may be very different from the genetic rules of evolution. It also draws attention to the dynamic aspect of this gene-culture theory that distinguishes it from statistical models.

9. A General One-Gene, Two-Trait Model

Suppose that there are three genotypes AA, Aa, aa to which we assign the numbers 1, 2, and 3, respectively, and two phenotypes denoted by the subscripts 1 and 2 (Feldman and Cavalli-Sforza 1976). The six *phenotypes* are then AA_1, Aa_1, aa_1, AA_2, Aa_2, and aa_2. The simultaneous transmission of genotype and phenotype is described by the array of probabilities $\{\beta_{ghi,lmn}\}$ where $\beta_{ghi,lmn}$ is the probability that a mating between a mother of genotype g and phenotype l and a father of genotype h and phenotype m produces an offspring of phenotype n given that the offspring's genotype is $i(g, h, i = 1, 2, 3,; l, m, n = 1, 2)$. With two phenotypes the subscript n can be deleted since $\beta_{ghi,lmn} = 1 - \beta_{ghi,lm1}$. There are then sixty possibly distinct parameters that describe the dependence of transmission on both genotype and phenotype.

9.1 Reverse Statistics: A Bilinear Model

Suppose that parental phenotype and a child's genotype both have a direct influence on a child's phenotype, but that parental genotype only acts indirectly through these other influences. In this case, the sixty transmission parameters may be reduced to a mere five. The entries in table 4.8 are the probabilities that the respective parent-child combinations result in a child of phenotype 1.

TABLE 4.8
Transmission Model

Parental Mating	Offspring Genotype		
	AA	Aa	aa
1×1	$2\eta + 2\alpha + \beta$	$2\eta + \sigma\alpha + \beta$	$2\eta + \beta$
2×1	$\tau\eta + 2\alpha + \beta$	$\tau\eta + \sigma\alpha + \beta$	$\tau\eta + \beta$
2×2	$2\alpha + \beta$	$\sigma\alpha + \beta$	β

Here β is a baseline rate of transmission that plays no role in the analysis and could be set to zero, α is the usual additive contribution of allele A to the probability that a child has phenotype 1, with σ the amount of genetic dominance. The parameter η measures the importance of cultural transmission, with τ a measure of the "cultural dominance" of trait 1.

In addition to these transmission parameters, we postulate a probability m of assortative mating. The idea is then to explore the parameter space of the transmission rates and m, bring the resulting dynamical system to equilibrium, and examine the statistical properties of this equilibrium, namely, correlations between relatives. We are then in a position to compare the input parameters, which are truly gene- and culture-action rates, with statistics that are frequently interpreted as genetic and environmental effects.

The results of this analysis are in Feldman, Christiansen, and Otto (1994). Two points are worth highlighting here. First, none of the measures of heritability tested provided a good estimate for the actual heritability (V_A/V_P) in all cases examined. In fact, some measures often gave estimates greater than one. Heritability based on the difference betwen monozygotic and dizygotic twins was, however, less sensitive to the relative importance of genetic and cultural transmission rates (α and η) than was a measure based on the parent-offspring correlation. The latter provided large overestimates of genetic heritability when η was large relative to α. The second point concerns the gene frequency, often left out of discussions of heritability because it is never known for any quantitative trait. For a given set of transmission parameters, heritability (V_A/V_P) varied tremendously with gene frequency, especially with dominant genes. Consequently, a single value of heritability (say, 30 percent) is compatible with a number of different combinations of parameters, for instance with $\alpha = 0.2$, $\eta = 0.2$, $m = 0.5$ or with $\alpha = 0.4$, $\eta = 0$, and $m = 0.0$ or 0.5, depending on the gene frequency. In other words, the usual measure of heritabiity as a variance ratio is not very informative about the underlying transmission mechanism.

10. An Even-Handed Approach to Handedness

Models that incorporate culture can be used to study human evolution as well as human inheritance. We have used cultural-genetic models to study the evolution of several traits, including handedness and sex ratio, which we will briefly discuss. These studies illustrate the potential importance of cultural change as well as genetic change in human evolution.

About 90 percent of humans are right-handed, with the rest either left-handed or ambidextrous. Most of the widely cited models for the determina-

tion of handedness assume a genetic basis to both handedness and its putative biological basis, hemispheric asymmetry. Genetic models would predict
some concordance for handedness among MZ twins and that MZ twins
would be more alike than DZ twins. In practice, however, there appears to
be no association in handedness between MZ twins.

None of the most cited models incorporate cultural influences on handedness, although most authors admit to the potential importance of culture.
Indeed, in mice it has been shown that exposure to a biased environment can
cause strong bias in handedness (pawedness, actually). An exclusively environmental or cultural model, however, has the difficulty of explaining how
right-handedness came to be common in all societies. We should remember
that through much of human history left-handers have been treated badly,
assigned to insane asylums or jails and generally regarded as stupid at best
and criminal at worst.

We have recently used a model very similar to that of the previous section
to fit the known familial data on handedness. Table 4.9 shows the transmission model used in our analysis with the entries giving the probability that
the given offspring in the given family is right-handed (Laland, Kumm, Van
Horn, and Feldman 1995).

We first established that unless there is selection in favor of the hetero-
zygote DC, the population will fix on DD. With DD fixed (i.e., no genetic
variation), using all seventeen published studies of right- and left-handed
parents and offspring, as well as fourteen studies on MZ and DZ twins, the
maximum likelihood estimates are $\hat{\alpha} = 0.148, \hat{\beta} = 0.012, \hat{\rho} = 0.267$. There
is good fit to all except one of the thirty-one studies. In other words, a model
of purely cultural variation in transmission fits the familial data better than
any model so far suggested. Obviously, more sophisticated genetic models,
with threshold effects and the like, might do better, and we cannot claim that
our model is "right." It is curious, nevertheless, that an "abiological" model
cannot be rejected for what has usually been regarded as a biological
distinction.

TABLE 4.9
Handedness Transmission

Parental Mating	Offspring Genotype		
	DD	DC	CC
Right × right	$\frac{1}{2} + \rho + \alpha$	$\frac{1}{2} + h_{1\rho} + \alpha$	$\frac{1}{2} + \alpha$
Right × left	$\frac{1}{2} + \rho + \beta$	$\frac{1}{2} + h_{1\rho} + \beta$	$\frac{1}{2} + \beta$
Left × left	$\frac{1}{2} + \rho - \alpha$	$\frac{1}{2} + h_{1\rho} - \alpha$	$\frac{1}{2} - \alpha$

11. Genes, Prejudice, and the Sex Ratio

Infanticide has been observed in virtually all known societies and is still frequent in many preindustrial communities (Dickemann 1975; Williamson 1978). The killing may not be direct: other behaviors such as neglect, abandonment, excessive punishment, and underinvestment can have the same effect (Hrdy and Hausfater 1984; Johansson 1984). Where direct or deferred infanticide is sex-biased, the bias is almost always against females. With the advent of amniocentesis, sonography, and fetoscopy, fetal sex can be predicted and female-biased abortion is becoming increasingly common. What effect will this have on the sex ratio?

Besides addressing this question in demographic terms (Tuljapurkar, Nan Li, and Feldman 1995), we have formulated it as a problem involving transmission of genes that affect the sex of their carriers and the vertical transmission from parent to child of a prejudice against having female children.

R. A. Fisher (1930) was the first to make a quantitative prediction (although he did it verbally) on the sex ratio. He argued that if males were more common than females, the latter will be much sought after and some males will not mate. Thus, any parents who carry genes that bias their offspring toward being female will on average have more grandoffspring. The result will be a tendency toward an even sex ratio. This purely genetic argument can be made mathematical (Eshel and Feldman 1982a and 1982b), although there are well-understood situations in which it should fail (Hamilton 1967; Uyenoyama and Bengtsson 1979).

In our recent work we have combined the transmission of sex-determining genes with parent-to-offspring transmission of prejudice against daughters. At the population level, genetic variation affects the ratio of male to female fetuses conceived, the primary sex ratio, because of its effect on the brood composition of every mating. In addition, the beliefs and activities of parents that are culturally transmitted to their offspring may result in a postconception modification of the primary sex ratio and alter it to a secondary sex ratio. Each individual in the population is defined by its sex, its genotype, and its status with respect to prejudice. Individuals who are inclined to adjust the sex ratio among their offspring are called "biased" and those who are not so inclined are "unbiased." If we consider a single diallelic locus, there are then six phenogenotypes of each sex: A_1A_1, A_1A_2, A_2A_2; biased, unbiased.

A detailed analysis of the evolutionary dynamics of the twelve phenogenotype frequencies has been carried out under different demographic assumptions as to whether lost offspring are replaced (Kumm, Laland, and Feldman 1994; Laland, Kumm, and Feldman 1995).

Among the more interesting findings from this analysis is the importance of the sex of the dominant cultural transmitter in the parents. Thus, if the father is more important than the mother in transmitting a bias against daughters, the bias against female offspring will spread. This is likely to be the case in patrilineal societies where, anthropologists inform us, female infanticide is more common than in matrilineal societies. The interaction between genotypic and cultural transmission gives rise to very complicated dynamics, which may result in male- or female-biased population sex ratios. The important point is that with specific knowledge from a given community, predictions are possible. This knowledge will usually require careful survey work (Li Shuzhuo and Feldman 1996), which can, in turn, suggest leverage points for the alteration of prejudices, which might in turn result in greater equity.

Our work on the sex ratio suggests that other areas of gene-culture interaction, perhaps concerning food preferences and related biological reactions, may be profitably examined in a similar framework. These might be simple examples of more important and more cryptic norms or values whose transmission may be horizontal as well as vertical.

Acknowledgment

The authors are grateful to Professors Arthur Goldberger and Samuel Bowles for their comments on the manuscript.

References

Bouchard, T. J., Jr. 1994. "Genes, Environment, and Personality." *Science* 264: 1700–1701.

Bouchard, T. J., Jr., D. T. Lykken, M. McGue, N. L. Segal, and A. Tellegan. 1990 "Sources of Human Psychological Differences: The Minnesota Study of Twins Reared Apart." *Science* 250: 223–228.

Bouchard, T. J., Jr., and M. McGue. 1981. "Familial Studies of Intelligence." *Science* 212: 1055–1059.

Burks, B. S. 1928. "The Relative Influence of Nature and Nurture upon Mental Development: A Comparative Study of Foster Parent–Foster Child Resemblance and True Parent–True Child Resemblances." In *Twenty-seventh Yearbook of the National Society for the Study of Education*, part 1, pp. 219–316. Bloomington, IL: Public School.

Cavalli-Sforza, L. L., and M. W. Feldman. 1973a. "Cultural versus Biological Inheritance: Phenotypic Transmission from Parents to Children (A Theory of the Effect of Parental Phenotypes on Children's Phenotypes)." *Amer. J. Hum. Gen.* 25: 618–637.

———. 1973b. "Models for Cultural Inheritance: I. Group Mean and Within Group Variation." *Theor. Pop. Biol.* 4: 42–55.

Cavalli-Sforza, L. L., and M. W. Feldman. 1978. "Dynamics and Statistics of Traits under the Influence of Cultural Transmission." In *Genetic Epidemiology*, ed. N. E. Morton and C. S. Chung, pp. 133–144. New York: Academic Press.

———. 1981. *Cultural Transmission and Evolution*. Princeton, NJ: Princeton University Press.

Cloninger, C., J. Rice, and T. Reich. 1979. "Multifactorial Inheritance with Cultural Transmission and Assortative Mating: II. A General Model of Combined Polygenic and Cultural Inheritance." *Amer. J. Hum. Gen.* 31: 176–198.

Darwin, C. 1871. *The Descent of Man, and Selection in Relation to Sex*. London: J. Murray.

Degler, C. 1991. *In Search of Human Nature*. Oxford: Oxford University Press.

Dickemann, M. 1975. "Demographic Consequences of Infanticide in Man." *Ann. Rev. Ecol. System.* 6: 107–137.

Durham, W. H. 1991. *Coevolution, Genes, Culture, and Human Diversity*. Stanford, CA: Stanford University Press.

Eaves, L. J., H. J. Eysenik, and N. G. Martin. 1989. *Genes, Culture, and Personality*. San Diego: Academic Press.

Eshel, I., and M. W. Feldman. 1982a. "On Evolutionary Genetic Stability of the Sex Ratio." *Theor. Pop. Biol.* 21: 430–439.

———. 1982b. "On the Evolution of Sex Determination and the Sex Ratio in Haplodiploid Populations." *Theor. Pop. Biol.* 21: 440–450.

Falconer, D. S., and T. F. C. Mackay. 1996. *Introduction to Quantitative Genetics*. 4th ed. Harlow, UK: Longman Scientific and Technical.

Feldman, M. W., and L. L. Cavalli-Sforza. 1976. "Cultural and Biological Evolutionary Processes: Selection for a Trait under Complex Transmission." *Theor. Pop. Biol.* 9: 238–259.

———. 1979. "Aspects of Variance and Covariance Analysis with Cultural Inheritance." *Theor. Pop. Biol.* 15: 276–307.

Feldman, M. W., F. B. Christiansen, and S. P. Otto. 1994. "Statistics of Discrete Valued Traits under Vertical Transmission." Stanford University, Morrison Institute Working Paper no. 65.

Fisher, R. A. 1918. "The Correlation between Relatives on the Supposition of Mendelian Inheritance." *Trans. Roy. Soc. Edinburgh* 52: 399–433.

———. 1930. *The Genetical Theory of Natural Selection*. Reprinted 1958, New York: Dover.

Franklin, D. 1989. "What a Child Is Given." *New York Times Magazine*, September 3, p. 36.

Goldberger, A. S. 1978a. *Models and Methods in the IQ Debate: Part I*, revised. Madison: Social Systems Research Institute, University of Wisconsin.

———. 1978b. "Pitfalls in the Resolution of IQ Inheritance." In *Genetic Epidemiology*, ed. N. E. Morton and C. S. Chung, pp. 195–215. New York: Academic Press.

Hamilton, W. D. 1967. "Extraordinary Sex Ratios." *Science* 156: 477–488.

Hernnstein, R. J., and C. Murray. 1994. *The Bell Curve*. New York: Free Press.

Hrdy, S. B., and G. Hausfater. 1984. "Comparative and Evolutionary Perspectives on Infanticide: Introduction and Overview." In *Infanticide: Comparative and Evolutionary Perspectives*, ed. G. Hausfater and S. B. Hrdy, pp. xiii–xxxv. Hawthorne: Aldine.

Jensen, A. R. 1969. "How Much Can We Boost IQ and Scholastic Achievement?" *Harvard Educational Review* 39, no. 1: 1–123.

———. 1989. "Raising IQ without Increasing Intelligence?" *Developmental Review* 9: 234–258.

Johannsen, W. 1903. *Über Erblichkeit in Populationen und in reinen Linien*. Jena: Gustav Fisher.

———. 1909. *Elemente der exacten Erblichkeitslehre*. Jena: Gustav Fisher.

Johansson, S. R. 1984. "Deferred Infanticide: Excess Female Mortality during Childhood." In *Infanticide: Comparative and Evolutionary Perspectives*, ed. G. Hausfater and S. B. Hrdy, pp. 463–485. Hawthorne: Aldine.

Kumm, J., K. N. Laland, and M. W. Feldman. 1994. "Gene-Culture Coevolution and Sex Ratios: The Effects of Infanticide, Sex-Selective Abortion, Sex Selection, and Sex-Biased Parental Investment on the Evolution of Sex Ratios." *Theor. Pop. Biol.* 46: 249–278.

Laland, K. N. 1993. "The Mathematical Modelling of Human Culture and Its Implications for Psychology and the Human Sciences." *British J. Psychology* 84: 145–169.

Laland, K. N., J. Kumm, and M. W. Feldman. 1995. "Gene-Culture Coevolutionary Theory." *Current Anthropology* 36: 131–156.

Laland, K. N., J. Kumm, J. D. Van Horn, and M. W. Feldman. 1995. "A Gene-Culture Model of Human Handedness." *Behavior Genetics* 25: 433–445.

Li Shuzhuo and M. W. Feldman. 1996. "Sex Differentials in Infant and Child Mortality in China: Levels, Trends, and Variations." [In Chinese.] *Chinese Population Science* 1, no. 52: 7–21.

Lush, J. L. 1937. *Animal Breeding Plans*. Ames: Iowa State University Press.

Otto, S. P., M. W. Feldman, and F. B. Christiansen. 1994. "Genetic and Cultural Transmission of Continuous Traits." Stanford University, Morrison Institute Working Paper no. 64.

Rao, D. C., N. E. Morton, J. M. Lalouel, and R. Lew. 1982. "Path Analysis under Generalized Assortative Mating: II. American I.Q." *Genetical Research, Cambridge* 39: 187–198.

Rao, D. C., N. E. Morton, and S. Yee. 1976. "Resolution of Cultural and Biological Inheritance by Path Analysis." *Amer. J. Hum. Gen.* 28: 228–242.

Scarr, S. 1992. "Developmental Theories for the 1990s: Development and Individual Differences." *Child Development* 63: 1–19.

Tuljapurkar, S., Nan Li, and M. W. Feldman. 1995. "High Sex Ratios in China's Future." *Science* 267: 874–876.

Uyenoyama, M. K., and B.. Bengtsson. 1979. "Towards a Genetic Theory for the Evolution of the Sex Ratio." *Genetics* 93: 721–736.

Williamson, L. 1978. "Infanticide: An Anthropological Analysis." In *Infanticide and the Value of Life*, ed. M. Kohl, pp. 61–75. Buffalo: Prometheus Books.

Wright, S. 1931. "Statistical Methods in Biology." *J. Amer. Statistical Assoc.* 26 (supp.): 155–163.

Part Three

SCHOOLING AND ECONOMIC OPPORTUNITY

Five

Schooling, Intelligence, and Income in America*

ORLEY ASHENFELTER AND CECILIA ROUSE

ONE OF THE best-documented relationships in economics is the link between education and income: more highly educated people have higher incomes. Advocates argue that education provides skills, or human capital, that raises an individual's productivity. Because productivity is reflected in income, education is thus a key determinant of social mobility. Critics argue that the documented relationship is not causal. Education does not generate higher incomes; instead, individuals with higher ability receive more education and more income. In this view education and income are positively correlated because they share a common foundation, individual ability.

The debate about the income-schooling relationship has taken on greater urgency as income inequality in the United States has steadily increased during the 1980s and 1990s. Advocates support educational programs and urge low-income workers to remain in school in the belief that the gap between rich and poor arises from a lack of skills among the poor. Others believe the gap between rich and poor arises because poor individuals do not benefit as much from additional education as do the rich. According to this view, increasing support for educational programs for the disadvantaged will have no effect on the overall income distribution.

This chapter reviews the evidence on the relationship between education and income. We focus on recent studies that have attempted to determine the causal effect of education on income by either comparing income and education differences within families or using exogenous determinants of schooling in what are sometimes called "natural experiments." In addition, we assess the potential for education to reduce income disparities by presenting evidence on the return to education for people of differing family backgrounds and measured ability.

The results of all these studies are surprisingly consistent: they indicate

* Prepared for the conference on meritocracy and inequality at the University of Wisconsin at Madison, December 1–3, 1995. We thank our colleagues for helpful conversations, and Barbara Wolfe and participants at the conference on meritocracy and inequality for insightful comments. We also thank Stephanie Abundo for expert research assistance. Rouse thanks the Mellon Foundation, the National Academy of Education, and the NAE Spencer Postdoctoral Fellowship Program for financial support. All errors are ours.

that the return to schooling is not caused by an omitted correlation between ability and schooling. Moreover, we find no evidence that the return to schooling differs significantly by family background or by the measured ability of the student.

1. Schooling and Income: The Simple Relationship

The basic relationship between income and education is shown in figure 5.1, which graphs the average of the logarithm of hourly earnings by the number of completed years of schooling using the Current Population Survey (CPS).[1] The slope is fairly flat for those who did not complete a high school education, approximately 13 percent of the working population. On the other hand, the relationship is much stronger for the 87 percent with higher levels of educational attainment. For example, in 1990 and 1991 high school graduates earned 18 percent more than high school dropouts with eleven years of schooling. Similarly, those who had completed one year of college earned 8 percent more than high school graduates. Despite what is sometimes claimed, figure 5.1 indicates no tendency for the effect of schooling on earnings to be associated solely with the years in which degrees are awarded. Apparently it is more than the award of a degree that is associated with greater earnings.

It is conventional to summarize the overall relationship between schooling and income by regressing the (natural) logarithm of the hourly wage on years of (completed) education controlling for explanatory variables such as experience, sex, race, and region of the country (Mincer 1974). The coefficient on the education variable is interpreted as the percentage increase in the hourly wage associated with one additional year of schooling, and is referred to as the "return to schooling."[2]

Figure 5.2 graphs the estimated (cross-section) return to education for each of the years from 1979 through 1995.[3] The figure shows the tremen-

[1] The data in figure 5.1 are from the 1990 and 1991 merged outgoing rotation group files of the CPS. (These were the last years in which "years of schooling" were reported.) The sample included employed individuals aged eighteen to sixty-seven years old who earned at least $1.00 per hour (in 1996 dollars) and excluded the self-employed. All means were weighted using the earnings weight.

[2] Although labor economists refer to it as the "return to schooling," it is actually just the average percentage difference in mean earnings for each additional year of schooling. As Mincer (1974) shows, if forgone earnings are the only cost of school attendance this is the private rate of return to the investment in a year of schooling. A more detailed calculation of the "return" would incorporate the tuition costs of schooling, as well.

[3] The data in figure 5.2 are from the 1979–1996 merged outgoing rotation group files of the CPS. The samples included employed individuals aged eighteen to sixty-seven years old who usually work full-time (more than thirty-four hours per week) and earned at least one-half of the minimum wage; they excluded the self-employed. All estimates were weighted using the earnings weight and represent three-year moving averages.

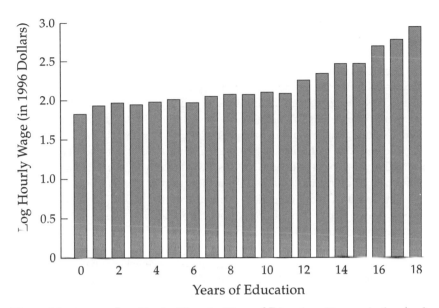

Figure 5.1. Average Log Hourly Wage by Years of Education. *Source:* Authors' calculations using the 1990 and 1991 merged outgoing rotation group files of the Current Population Survey.

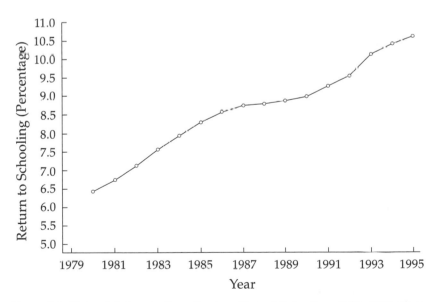

Figure 5.2. Rate of Return to Investing in a Year of Schooling, 1980–1995 (three-year moving average). *Source:* Authors' calculations using the 1979–1996 merged outgoing rotation group files of the Current Population Survey.

dous increase in the value of schooling in the labor market that took place throughout the 1980s and early 1990s. The return to an additional year of schooling in 1979 was 6.2 percent; in 1995 it had grown to 10.5 percent. This increase in the return to schooling is well documented and is a primary source of the increasing income inequality in the United States.[4]

But does the estimated return to schooling reflect the causal effect of schooling on earnings? A nagging concern is that higher-ability people get more schooling and would earn higher wages and salaries even if they had not received the additional schooling. In this case, the schooling-income connection may be a mirage; it is just a symptom of the fact that higher-ability people command a premium for their (innate) skills in the labor market. The result is that regression estimates of the return to schooling are upward biased due to "family background" or "ability" bias.

In the past decade several methods have been designed and implemented in order to determine whether the schooling-income connection is causal. Before we turn to a discussion of those analyses, we ask a separate question: What would be the ideal, definitive study? That is, if there were no limitations on our resources, how would we ideally test whether schooling causes higher wages and salaries? Understanding the basis for an ideal empirical test of the hypothesis that schooling boosts income makes it far easier to understand the other tests that have been proposed.

2. Schooling and Income: The Ideal Experiment

In principle, the only way to determine definitively whether schooling causes higher incomes is to perform an experiment. In such an experiment, different groups of students would be randomly assigned to different educational levels without regard to their ability or general background. Years later we would compare the incomes of these students. On average the only differences among the students would be the level of their schooling. Contrasts of the earnings of the various groups would, with a large enough sample, provide an entirely credible estimate of the causal effect of schooling on earnings.

Of course, the experiment just described has not been performed, and likely will not be performed in the near future. Some people would object that it would be morally objectionable to deny a potentially valuable education to those who might otherwise have obtained it.[5] As a result, researchers

---

[4] However, there has also been tremendous growth in within-education income inequality, leading researchers to attribute the bulk of the growth to an increase in the demand for "unobservable skills." Just what these "unobservable skills" represent and why the demand for them has changed is a matter of debate.

[5] One way to address this objection is to make sure that no one is denied access. For example, in many developing countries inadequate finances make it impossible to educate all students

must look elsewhere for convincing nonexperimental evidence. Two broad approaches have been taken to address the problem of ability bias. The first compares the wages of workers who have similar genetic and family backgrounds but differ in educational levels. A systematic correlation between the educational differences and income differences of such workers is evidence of the link between income and schooling that cannot be a result of common family backgrounds. The second approach looks for a determinant of education that is not also a determinant of incomes (so-called "natural experiments").

3. Schooling and Income: Intrafamily Comparisons

In recent years the availability of new data has made it possible to use sibling pairs to construct new estimates of the return to schooling. Although much of the emphasis in the most recent literature is on careful adjustment of the estimates for problems of measurement error, the methods used are similar to those used by Gorseline (1932), Chamberlain and Griliches (1975, 1977), Corcoran, Jencks, and Olneck (1976), Olneck (1977), and Behrman, Hrubec, Taubman, and Wales (1980).[6]

3.1 Father and Son Comparisons

To see how the use of within-family correlations can identify a causal relationship between schooling and income, consider first the case of fathers and sons. Raised in the same extended family and sharing many similar genetic endowments, fathers and sons are expected to perform far more similarly in the labor market than randomly selected worker pairs. If the father's background and genetic endowments are inherited by the son, then the father and son should have similar earnings if they have similar educational backgrounds. On the other hand, we would expect that if a father is better educated than his son, he would earn a higher wage than his son only if schooling is a causal determinant of earnings.[7]

Ashenfelter and Zimmerman (1997) matched data on fathers and sons for a period in the 1980s using the National Longitudinal Surveys of Youth and Older Men. Using these data, they computed the relationship of the schooling differences to income differences between fathers and sons. Figure 5.3 is

---

who wish to attend secondary schools. If students were admitted to secondary schools in part on a randomized basis, it would be possible to perform a credible experiment that would not be objectionable. When people must be denied access to educational opportunities in any case, why not use a randomized allocation system so that we may learn from their experiences?

[6] See especially Griliches (1979) for an insightful review of these studies.

[7] A more formal derivation of the empirical framework is outlined in the technical analysis appendix to this chapter.

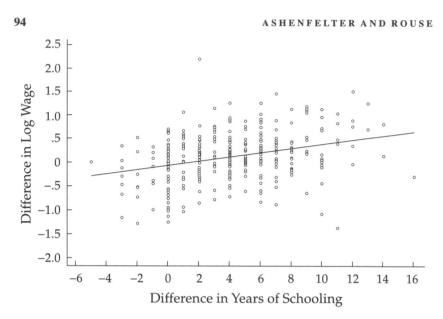

Figure 5.3. Father and Son Schooling and Income Differences. *Source:* Ashenfelter
and Zimmerman (1997).

a scatter diagram from their paper that shows this relationship. On the vertical axis is a measure (in ratio or logarithmic scale) of the difference between
the hourly wage rate of each father and his son. On the horizontal axis is the
difference between the years of schooling of the father and his son. Each
point on the diagram represents one father-son pair; there are 332 such pairs
in the National Longitudinal Survey.

As one would expect in an economy where the average schooling level
has been growing, fathers have about four fewer years of schooling than
sons. As one would also expect in a society that has imperfect generational
mobility, fathers with higher education levels tend to have sons with higher
education levels. (The correlation coefficient is about 0.4.) This suggests that
family background bias leads to overestimates of the causal effect of schooling on income. That is, the simple correlation between the income and
schooling of the sons may be the result of the fact that better-educated sons
also have better-connected fathers. If this were the only reason for the correlation between the income and schooling of sons, however, we would also
find that the correlation between the difference in the father's and son's
education levels and the difference in the father's and son's incomes is
negligible.

As figure 5.3 indicates, however, this cannot be the entire story. The diagram reveals that there still remains a substantial correlation between the
difference in the education levels of fathers and their sons and the difference

in their incomes. The slope of the best-fitting line in these data indicates that a one-year difference in the education levels of father and son translates into about a 5 percent difference in wage rates. This implies that estimated returns to schooling are not simply a result of the fact that sons with more schooling have fathers with more schooling, too.

3.2 Sibling Comparisons

Ashenfelter and Zimmerman (1997) and Altonji and Dunn (1996) also implement a within-family estimator of the return to schooling based on sisters and brothers using the National Longitudinal Survey (NLS) and the Panel Study of Income Dynamics (PSID). Table 5.1 summarizes their results. As it indicates, an additional year of schooling is associated with a 3.7 to 6.3 percent increase in earnings depending on the study and the group analyzed.[8]

TABLE 5.1
Summary of the Estimated Return to Schooling from Sibling Studies

Data	Comparison	Estimated Return to Schooling		
		Overall	Within-Family	Difference
NLS (1981)[a]	Brothers	5.9%	4.8%	1.1%
		(1.4)	(1.8)	
NLS (1982–1984)[b]	Brothers	4.7%	3.7%	1.0%
		(0.5)	(1.2)	
PSID (1982–1984)[b]	Brothers	6.2%	4.6%	1.6%
		(0.2)	(0.5)	
NLS (1982–1984)[b]	Sisters	7.4%	6.3%	1.1%
		(0.4)	(1.0)	
PSID (1982–1984)[b]	Sisters	7.2%	4.2%	3.0%
		(0.2)	(0.5)	

Note: The dependent variable is log hourly wages. Estimated standard errors are in parentheses. The NLS is the National Longitudinal Survey. The PSID is the Panel Study of Income Dynamics.

[a]*Source:* Ashenfelter and Zimmerman (1997)

[b]*Source:* Altonji and Dunn (1996). These estimated returns to schooling are evaluated for individuals with no labor-market experience.

[8] The estimated returns to schooling reported by Altonji and Dunn (1996) are evaluated for an individual with zero labor market experience in order to include the standard errors in the table. The comparable estimates, from both data sets, of the return to schooling for those with the panel mean experience (adjusted for family background) are about 6.6 percent for men and about 7.2 percent for women.

For comparison, table 5.1 also provides estimates of the effect of an additional year of schooling on earnings when we ignore the sibling connections. A comparison of the estimates in columns 1 and 2, which is contained in column 3, indicates the extent to which family background bias contaminates the observed correlation between schooling and earnings. As table 5.1 indicates, the simple regression estimates are upward biased by between 15 and 42 percent. Although part of the correlation between income and schooling may be due to family background characteristics, the intrafamily correlation between income and schooling indicates that most of the relationship between income and schooling is due to something else.

Finally, it has been shown that the presence of measurement error in the schooling data introduces a downward bias in the within-family estimates of the effect of an additional year of schooling on earnings (Griliches 1977). Ashenfelter and Zimmerman (1997) find that the within-family estimate of the return to schooling is downward biased by 25 to 40 percent due to measurement error. Thus, the estimates in table 5.1 almost certainly overstate the extent to which ability or family background is responsible for the observed correlation between schooling and earnings among siblings. Most adjustments for measurement error imply that the upward bias in returns to schooling caused by omitted ability factors is about the same size as the downward bias due to measurement error. Thus, the simpler regression estimates of returns to schooling may well be the most accurate.

3.3 Identical Twins Comparisons

Although ordinary siblings share family backgrounds and some genetic factors, they may still have considerable differences in genetic ability. If the "genetically superior" sibling obtains more schooling, then the schooling/ income correlation within families may simply be a result of the fact that the more able sibling has spent more time in school. One way to resolve this question is to compare the earnings and schooling of identical twins. Identical (monozygotic—one-egg) twins are formed when a single, fertilized egg divides. It is generally believed that the division of a fertilized egg occurs at random. Thus, identical twins have identical genetic endowments. As with the other family comparisons, a simple test of whether genetic ability causes the schooling/income correlation can be made by comparing the incomes of identical twins with different schooling levels. If better-educated twins earn more, the correlation between income and schooling cannot be a result of genetic differences, for among identical twins there are none.

For the past four years, we have collected new data on twins in order to study the role of genetic endowments in the determination of income. To do this at reasonable cost, we have interviewed twins who have assembled for the National Twins Festival in Twinsburg, Ohio. We administered a survey similar to the Current Population Survey to about one thousand twins in a brief, but intensive, three-day period. The data we have collected provide a unique and rich opportunity to test whether the correlation between income and schooling that we observe among twins is a result of genetic endowments. These data are probably the closest it is possible to come to an experiment in which schooling is assigned randomly with respect to genetic endowments.

Our main findings are displayed in figure 5.4 and table 5.2. Figure 5.4 is a scatter diagram in which each point represents a single pair of twins. The vertical axis represents the difference (in ratio terms) between the incomes of identical twins, and the horizontal axis represents the difference between the schooling levels of the twins. As one would expect, the diagram indicates (by the concentration of observations at zero on the horizontal axis) that in the most typical case the twins have the same education level. The diagram also makes clear that there is a considerable correlation between income differences and schooling differences. In these data, the better-educated twin earns about 8 percent more for each extra year he (or she) attains compared to his (or her) twin.

More detail is contained in table 5.2. The second column of the table provides the estimated effect of schooling on earnings within twin-pairs. As

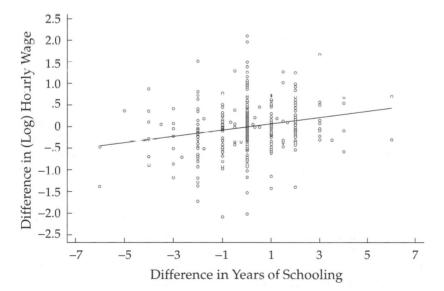

Figure 5.4. Intrapair Return to Schooling, Identical Twins. *Source:* Princeton Twins Survey, 1991–1993.

TABLE 5.2

Estimated Return to Schooling Using Identical Twins

Data (Year of Wages)	Return to Schooling		
	Overall	Within-Twin	
		OLS	IV
NAS-NRC (1973)[a]	7.6%	3.1%	NA
	(0.4)	(0.7)	
NAS-NRC (1973)[a,b]	9.4%	3.5%	5.0%
	(1.1)	(0.4)	(2.9)
Minnesota (1980)[b]	5.5%	4.1%	NA
	(0.2)	(0.4)	
Australia (1980–1982, 1989)[c]	6.4%	2.5%	4.5%
	(0.2)	(0.5)	(0.9)
Princeton (1991)[d]	8.7%	11.2%	13.2%
	(1.5)	(2.3)	(2.8)
Princeton (1991–1993)[e]	10.6%	7.8%	9.9%
	(0.9)	(1.7)	(2.1)

Note: Standard errors are in parentheses.

[a]Source: Behrman, Rosenzweig, and Taubman (1994)—men only. NAS-NRC is the National Academy of Sciences-National Research Council. The dependent variable is the logarithm of annual earnings.

[b]Based on the subset of twins for which at least one child each of both twins reported their father's schooling.

[c]Source: Miller, Mulvey, and Martin (1995)—men and women. The dependent variable is the logarithm of annual earnings.

[d]Source: Ashenfelter and Krueger (1994)—men and women. The dependent variable is logarithm hourly wages.

[e]Source: Ashenfelter and Rouse (1998)—men and women. The dependent variable is logarithm hourly wages.

the table indicates, a one-year schooling difference between twins is associated with about an 8 percent greater wage for the more highly educated twin.

Table 5.2 also provides the estimate of the effect of an additional year of schooling on earnings when we ignore the twin connections. A comparison of the estimates in columns 1 and 2 indicates the extent to which genetic endowments contaminate the observed correlation between schooling and earnings. As the table indicates, ability bias accounts for about 25 percent of the simple estimate of the effect of schooling on income. Again, although some part of the correlation between income and schooling may be due to family background or genetic endowments, the intratwin correlation between income and schooling indicates that most of the relationship between income and schooling must be due to something else.

In order to validate the data on the education level of each twin, we separated the twins during our interviews and asked each twin about his (or her) own education level as well as the education level of his (or her) twin. We can, therefore, correct for measurement error by instrumenting for the difference in the twins' own reports of their schooling levels using the difference in the twin-reported schooling levels as an instrumental variable (assuming that the twins' reports of each other's schooling levels are uncorrelated). The estimated effect of a year of schooling on wages allowing for measurement error is about 10 percent, as reported in the third column of table 5.2. Failure to account for measurement error in schooling in within-twin comparisons apparently leads to about a 30 percent downward bias in the estimate of the effect of schooling on earnings.

Table 5.2 also contains data from three other studies of twins, one of which uses data from Australia.[9] Although the magnitude of the estimated return to schooling varies because of the widely different time periods covered, each of these studies indicates a significant correlation between schooling level and earnings within twin pairs. When adjustments for measurement error are possible, the resulting estimates typically differ insignificantly from the simpler regression estimates of the return to schooling.

4. Schooling and Income: Instrumental Variables

4.1 Instrumental Variables Estimates of the Return to Schooling

The evidence from the studies of intrafamily differences in education and their correlation with intrafamily differences in income strongly supports the view that additional schooling is responsible for increases in worker earnings. Despite the consistency of this evidence, none of it represents the equivalent of an ideal experiment. In the past few years, several researchers have attempted to find so-called natural experiments that would provide the kind of information that an ideal experiment would provide. To do this they have attempted to locate exogenous events that might be expected to alter the schooling decisions of some people but would not be expected to independently alter their income.

The basic idea used in the application of this method is straightforward. Suppose that we knew of an event that would increase a group's schooling level. Suppose further that we were certain that this event would not have any direct effect on the group's earnings. We would then estimate the effect of schooling on income in two steps: In the first step we would estimate the effect of the event on the schooling level of the group. In the next step we would measure the effect of the same event on the earnings level of the

---

[9] Both the Australian and Minnesotan data use income imputed from detailed occupational categories as the dependent variable.

group. If we find that the income of the group has increased, then we can be sure that education was the cause of the income increase since we were certain that the event had no *direct* effect on income. The ratio of the income increase caused by the event to the schooling increase caused by the event is a straightforward estimate of the causal effect of an additional year of schooling on income. This instrumental variables (IV) estimator uses the "exogenous" event as the instrumental variable.

To see how this estimation strategy works, consider the paper by Angrist and Krueger (1991). Angrist and Krueger note that there is a relationship between the quarter in which an individual is born and the mean level of schooling that the individual attains. Angrist and Krueger argue that compulsory schooling laws are a natural explanation for why individuals born in the first quarter of the year attain less schooling than individuals born later in the year. They observe that school districts typically require that students turn age six by January first of the year they enter school. Thus, students born early in the (calendar) year enter school at an older age. Since compulsory schooling laws permit students to drop out as soon as they attain age sixteen, students born early in the year may drop out of school with fewer years of school completed than those born later in the year. Quarter of birth is a suitable instrumental variable so long as we assume that any difference in the wages of those born in different quarters is a result only of the differences in their schooling.

Angrist and Krueger find that workers born in the first quarter of the year typically average about one-tenth of a year less schooling than workers that are born in the other three quarters of the year. These same workers also generally earn about 1 percent less per week than other workers. The accident of being born in the first quarter of the year is, therefore, associated with a lower schooling level and a lower earnings level. The implied return to schooling is about 10 percent per additional year of education attained.

Table 5.3 contains a summary of the results of several studies that have used the instrumental variables approach to measure the effect of a year of schooling on income. As table 5.3 indicates, there have been various applications of this method. Table 5.3 also indicates that all of these studies have found significant effects of schooling on earnings.

In two studies that use similar instruments, Kane and Rouse (1993) use the distance that a high school student lives from the nearest two- and four-year colleges and Card (1993) uses whether an individual grew up near an accredited four-year college as instruments. Kane and Rouse's regression estimate of the return to schooling is about 8 percent; on the other hand, their instrumental variables estimate suggests a return of about 9 percent. Similarly, Card's instrumental variables estimate of the return to schooling is about 10 percent, an increase from the ordinary regression estimate of 7.3 percent. Finally, Butcher and Case (1994) have found that the presence of

TABLE 5.3
Summary of the Estimated Effect of an Additional Year of Schooling on Wages
from "Natural Experiments"

Study	Source of "Natural Experiment"	Estimated Return to Schooling	
		OLS	IV
Angrist and Krueger (1991)	Compulsory schooling laws	6.3%	8.1%[a]
		(0.0)	(1.1)
Butcher and Case (1994)	Sibling sex composition	9.1%	18.5%
		(0.8)	(1.1)
Kane and Rouse (1993)	Proximity to nearest college	8.0%	9.1%
		(0.5)	(3.3)
Card (1993)	Presence of a nearby college	7.3%	9.7%
		(0.4)	(0.5)
Behrman, Rosenzweig, and Taubman (1994)[b]	Birth weight	4.1%	4.0%
		(0.4)	(0.5)

Note: Estimated standard errors are in parentheses.

[a]This IV estimate differs from that in the text because it is for a more recent cohort and includes other covariates.

[b]A within-twin estimate of the return to schooling using both identical and fraternal twins. The OLS estimate in the table is for identical twins; the coefficient estimate for fraternal twins is 4.3% with a standard error of 0.4.

sisters in a family tends to depress the schooling and earnings of women born into these same families. Although one can only speculate about the reasons why the presence of sisters results in lower schooling levels for women, their implied (instrumental variables) estimate of the effect of a year of schooling on the earnings of women is 19 percent.

All of these estimates indicate that the instrumental variables estimate of the return to schooling is at least as large as that implied by conventional procedures. What might explain these results? These instrumental variables estimates of the return to school may simply reflect the fact that if one views schooling as an investment, then those who undertake the investment must expect to receive a positive net return on their investment (Becker 1967). Individuals will stay in school until the marginal benefit of the additional schooling equals the marginal discount rate (which may be a function of factors such as the cost of funds). As a result, the group of individuals with lower levels of schooling will be composed of individuals for whom the marginal benefit was low (e.g., individuals with low ability) or for whom the marginal discount rate was high (e.g., individuals from disadvantaged families). Now consider the events (instruments) that have been employed. Compulsory schooling laws will only have an effect on the education level of those who would otherwise have dropped out of school. Similarly, the presence of a nearby college will have its largest effect on the schooling of those for whom transportation costs could prove prohibitive. Both such "exogenous" events are likely to have a disproportionate effect on the schooling of individuals with high marginal discount rates, particularly those from disadvantaged families.[10] Thus, the instrumental variables estimate of the return to schooling will reflect the marginal benefit of schooling for a group with high marginal discount rates, which could well exceed the average return in the population estimated using OLS.[11]

Of course, the extent to which these estimates are credible depends on your willingness to believe that the event used to identify the effect of schooling on income has no direct effect on income. Different observers will have different opinions about this issue, and may even disagree about each example. Taken together, however, they consistently provide evidence that schooling is a causal determinant of earnings.[12]

4.2 Using Instrumental Variables to Evaluate Twins Studies

Behrman, Rosenzweig, and Taubman (1994) use the instrumental variables approach to assess the validity of twins studies. Skeptics of twins studies often ask, "If identical twins are so identical, why did one twin receive more schooling?" The concern is that if identical twins do differ in their abilities, then the within-twin estimate of the return to schooling will be biased upward by ability bias (Neumark 1994). Unfortunately, because identical twins are generally raised in identical family environments it is nearly impossible to assess the importance of this critique.

Behrman, Rosenzweig, and Taubman (1994) have assembled data on twins based on the Minnesota Twins Registry that allows them to attempt to assess the extent to which the within-twin estimate of the return to schooling is upward biased.[13] Since the registry records the twins' birth weights, the authors use birth weight as the exogenous event that determines schooling, but

---

[10] The mechanism by which the Butcher and Case (1994) instrument would disproportionately affect the disadvantaged is unclear.

[11] This explanation is developed in Card (1995) and Lang (1993).

[12] One criticism that has been raised about a few of the papers using instrumental variables is that the event used as the "natural experiment" is not highly enough correlated with schooling to produce an estimate of the return to schooling that is less biased than the OLS estimate (Bound, Jaeger, and Baker 1995). Although this is potentially an important problem, the events used in all of the studies cited above are strongly enough correlated with schooling that they probably do reduce the bias from using OLS. (See, in particular, Angrist and Krueger 1995.)

[13] The registry contains the birth records on all twins born in Minnesota from 1936 to 1955 (approximately 10,400 pairs) with additional family background and individual characteristics information on about 8,400 surviving intact pairs. These data have been recently supplemented with survey information on occupation, education, and martial and fertility histories.

does not influence later earnings. An infant's birth weight is affected by his or her environment in the womb and, after the egg splits, identical twins are exposed to different environments. They argue that birth weight has also been shown to affect a child's early mental and physical development, which affects schooling but not later earnings. As shown in table 5.3, Behrman, Rosenzweig, and Taubman estimate a return of about 4 percent, whether or not they use birth weight as an instrumental variable. The estimate would rise to about 5.7 percent if corrected for measurement error.[14] Thus, they find no evidence that the within-twin estimate of the return to schooling is upward biased.

5. Ethnic and Socioeconomic Differences in the Economic Value of Schooling

A second argument advanced by critics of educational programs aimed at low-achieving students is that such programs will not reduce skill *differences*. These critics argue that although educational programs may raise the average skill level, they will not reduce the disparity of skills because the bright students will benefit more from the schooling than the below-average students. Thus, they argue, the "interaction" between education and student characteristics leads to a widening of the skill, and therefore income, distribution.

This assertion has important implications for education policy. According to economic theory, policy makers concerned about efficiency should focus on educational expenditures that have the greatest net benefits for society. More precisely, society should allocate educational resources until the net (marginal) benefit of the last dollar spent on each program is equalized. An implication of this principle is that if high-ability students benefit more from educational expenditures than do low-ability students, then governments should construct educational policy that emphasizes gifted programs.[15] In the case of the United States, there may be a case for the government to redistribute education dollars away from compensatory education and toward "gifted and talented" programs until the value of the last dollar spent on gifted programs equals the value of the last dollar spent on special or compensatory education programs.

[14] The estimate of the return to schooling is from our table 5.2; the estimate that the within-twin return to schooling is attenuated by 30 percent is from table 5.3. We also note that Behrman, Rosenzweig, and Taubman (1994) do not have actual wages. Rather, they use the average income of the respondent's occupation as their measure of income.

[15] Of course, even if brighter students do benefit the most from schooling, distributional concerns may lead policy makers to emphasize compensatory education programs over gifted programs.

While the economic principle is fairly clear, it rests on the assumption that brighter and more advantaged students benefit more from schooling than their lower-achieving and more disadvantaged classmates. In this section we test the assertion that bright and advantaged students benefit most from schooling by examining the value of education in the labor market for different groups of individuals.[16]

5.1 Racial and Ethnic Differences in the Return to Schooling

We begin by comparing the return to education across racial and ethnic groups. Figure 5.5 graphs the economic value of an additional year of schooling by race and ethnicity, separately for women and men, using the 1990 U.S. Census.[17] The income measure is yearly earnings. The returns to schooling are based on separate regressions by race and ethnic group.[18]

As figure 5.5 indicates, there is remarkably little variability in the estimates of the return to schooling by race or sex group. For example, white females earn an additional 13 percent per year of schooling compared to African-American females, who earn a return of 13.3 percent. Native American women benefit the most from schooling in the labor market. For men, there is even less variation in the return to schooling by race and ethnicity. White, Hispanic, African-American, and Native American males earn between 10.1 and 10.8 percent more for each additional year of schooling. The exception are Asian/Pacific males, who earn an additional 13 percent per year of additional schooling. Overall, however, these differences are too small to be economically meaningful, particularly since we have not accounted for other potentially important factors, such as discrimination in the labor market.[19]

---

[16] Earlier estimates of the returns to schooling by ability group and social class by Wolfle and Smith (1956), Weisbrod and Karpoff (1968), Hause (1972), Hauser (1973), Taubman and Wales (1973), and Jencks et al. (1979) produced inconclusive results. This no doubt reflects, in part, the greater demands on the data required by attempts to stratify by measures of ability or family background.

[17] The data in figure 5.5 are from the 5 percent sample of the U.S. Census. We included individuals aged eighteen to sixty-five who were born in the United States, worked at least one week in the previous year, and earned at least one-half of the minimum wage.

[18] We defined "Hispanics" as all those who identified their ethnicity as "Hispanic"; "Native American" includes Eskimos and Aleuts. The regressions controlled for a quadratic in experience, whether the individual was ever married, and eight division dummies, and were weighted using the census weight.

[19] We find greater variation in the returns to schooling across the racial and ethnic groups if we use a measure of weekly earnings rather than annual earnings. The difference is accounted for by the fact that for minority groups the association between schooling and weeks worked is stronger than for whites. Whether this means that schooling leads to more stable jobs (so that the number of weeks worked is exogenous) or that schooling changes individuals' labor supply

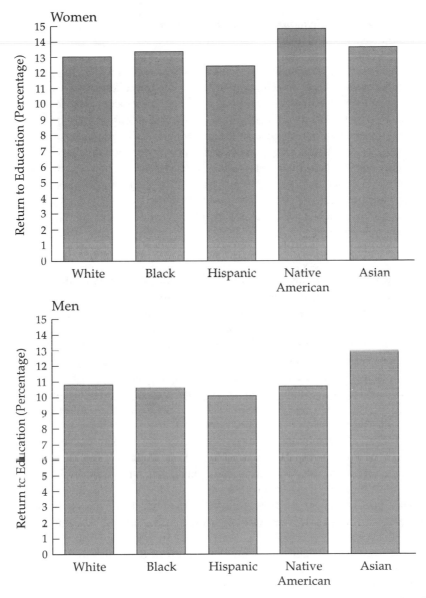

Figure 5.5. The Return to Education by Sex and Race/Ethnicity. *Source:* Authors' calculations using the 1990 U.S. Census.

decisions (so that the number of weeks worked in endogenous) is an empirical question. Ashenfelter and Ham (1979) develop an empirical test to assess the relative importance of these two hypotheses.

5.2 The Value of Schooling by Family Background
and Measured Ability

The data from the National Longitudinal Survey of Youth (NLSY) permit us
to examine the value of schooling by socioeconomic status and measured
ability. The NLSY began surveying 12,686 individuals, aged fourteen to
twenty-two, from across the nation in 1979. These same individuals have
been reinterviewed every year since then. The NLSY data are unique because they have a rich set of variables from which to construct measures of
socioeconomic status and measured ability. In the base year, individuals
were asked about their parents' educational attainment, income, occupation,
and about amenities in the home. Since then, the survey has collected data
on each individual's marital status, fertility, educational attainment, and labor
market outcomes.[20]

In addition, in 1980 most survey participants were administered the
ASVAB (Armed Services Vocational Aptitude Battery), a basic skills test,
from which it is possible to construct an Armed Forces Qualification Test
(AFQT) score. Herrnstein and Murray (1994) argue that the AFQT has many
of the properties of an IQ test: the scores do not just reflect specific knowledge that has been learned in school; rather they reflect more general factors
of "intelligence." Neal and Johnson (1996) argue the contrary, that AFQT
scores increase with years of schooling and therefore are not a good measure
of IQ. Others, such as Rodgers and Spriggs (1996), argue that the AFQT is a
racially biased test. Although researchers disagree about the determinants of
AFQT scores, most would agree that they reflect *some* information about the
skills that individuals possess at the time of the test.

We estimate the return to schooling by family background and ability
group by regressing the logarithm of the hourly wage on years of schooling,
parents' education or AFQT test score interacted with years of schooling,
and other regressors. An estimate of how the return to schooling varies by
family background or measured ability is obtained from the coefficient on
the years of schooling interacted with either the parents' education or the
AFQT test score.[21]

The top panel of table 5.4 shows the return to education by the parents'
average education level. We report on the value for four levels of parental
schooling: an average level less than twelve years (i.e., no high school diploma), an average level equal to a high school diploma, an average level
between thirteen to fifteen years (i.e., some college, but no bachelor's degree), and an average level of at least sixteen years of schooling (i.e., at least

---

[20] The data appendix describes how we construct our NLSY sample.

[21] The technical analysis appendix derives our specification.

TABLE 5.4
The Return to Education by Parents' Education Level and AFQT Quartile

	Average of Parents' Education Level			
	Less than High School	High School Graduate	Some College	College Graduate
Return to Education	6.7% (0.5)	4.8% (0.6)	5.6% (0.9)	4.9% (0.7)
	AFQT Quartile			
	First	Second	Third	Fourth
Return to Education	5.1% (0.7)	6.8% (0.8)	5.3% (0.6)	5.3% (0.6)

Source: Authors' calculations using the NLSY.

Note: The dependent variable is log hourly wages. Estimated standard errors are in parentheses. See appendix tables A5.1 and A5.2 for the actual regression coefficients and other regressors.

a bachelor's degree). The graph suggests a higher economic value to schooling for individuals who come from low socioeconomic backgrounds, although the differences are slight. Those whose parents have not attended college have a return of 5–7 percent. On the other hand, those whose parents have attended college earn a return of about 5 percent. Although these differences are statistically indistinguishable, if we were to take them at face value we would conclude that those students whose parents have lower levels of schooling actually benefit slightly *more* from schooling than those from more advantaged backgrounds.

We consider whether "brighter" students benefit more from additional schooling than "low-achieving" students by using the AFQT score as a measure of achievement or "ability." The return to schooling by the AFQT quartile of the individual is displayed in the bottom panel of table 5.4. We find that the return to schooling is unrelated to AFQT quartile.[22] Those with test scores in the bottom two quartiles receive a return on their education of about 5–7 percent compared to those with test scores in the top quartiles, who have a return of 5.3 percent. Figure 5.6 graphs the return to schooling by the AFQT decile of the individual. As before, it is apparent that the return to schooling is essentially unrelated to ability as measured by test scores.

[22] Blackburn and Neumark (1993) find that those with higher AFQT scores have a higher return to schooling. However, they do not adjust their AFQT scores for the education level of the individual at the time of the test as we do (see our data appendix).

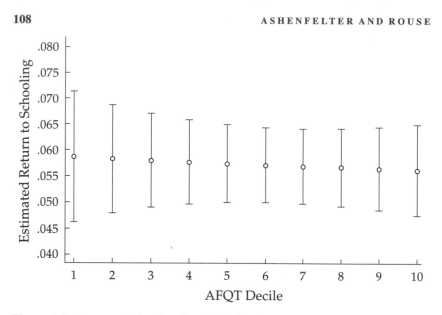

Figure 5.6. Return to Schooling by AFQT Decile (point estimate and confidence interval). *Source:* Authors' calculations using the 1993 wave of the National Longitudinal Survey of Youth (NLSY).

5.3 The Value of Schooling by Family Background Using Siblings

Given the controversy regarding the validity of the AFQT as an accurate measure of "innate ability," perhaps a more convincing way to address the issue of innate ability is to analyze returns to schooling using intrafamily variation in education and income. If the value of schooling increases with family background or innate ability, then we should observe higher estimated returns to schooling for siblings and twins with higher socioeconomic backgrounds or higher levels of ability.

Altonji and Dunn (1996) analyze the NLS and PSID to estimate the return to schooling by IQ and family background. They do so by estimating first-differenced equations that include an interaction between the difference in the siblings' schooling levels and the measure of ability or family background. The coefficient on the interaction term indicates the extent to which the return to schooling varies by measured ability. A summary of their estimated interaction terms is presented in table 5.5.

For men, Altonji and Dunn estimate that a one standard deviation increase in IQ increases the return to schooling by 0.82 percentage points.[23] However, the estimate is not statistically significant. A one-year increase in parental

[23] The estimates of the overall return to schooling are in our table 5.1.

TABLE 5.5
The Within-Sibling Return to Education by IQ and Family Background

| | BROTHERS | |
Data	*Measure of Ability/ Family Background*	*Estimated* Additional *Return to Schooling*
NLS	IQ	0.82%[a] (0.93)
NLS	Father's education	0.51%[b] (0.20)
NLS	Mother's education	0.81%[b] (0.28)
PSID	Father's education	0.09%[b] (0.12)
PSID	Mother's education	0.33%[b] (0.15)
	SISTERS	
Data	*Measure of Ability/ Family Background*	*Estimated* Additional *Return to Schooling*
NLS	IQ	1.46%[a] (0.74)
NLS	Father's education	−0.04%[b] (0.17)
NLS	Mother's education	0.58%[b] (0.21)
PSID	Father's education	−0.11%[b] (0.13)
PSID	Mother's education	−0.17%[b] (0.18)

Source: Altonji and Dunn (1996).

Note: The dependent variable is log hourly wage. Estimated standard errors are in parentheses.

[a]The coefficient is the percentage-point change in the return to schooling for a one-standard-deviation increase in the IQ score.

[b]The coefficient is the percentage-point change in the return to schooling for a one-year increase in father's or mother's education.

education increases the estimated return between 0.09 and 0.81 percentage points, and three out of four of the estimates are statistically significant. For women, however, the results are much less consistent, as three out of five of them are negative (and insignificant). Overall, these results provide little consistent evidence that more advantaged individuals enjoy a higher return to schooling. In addition, because siblings do not necessarily have identical genetic endowments, these estimates may be upward biased.

5.4 The Value of Schooling by Family Background Using Identical Twins

In Ashenfelter and Rouse (1998) we report analyses of the extent to which the within-family return to schooling varies by family background among individuals with identical genetic endowments using a sample of identical twins. We do so by interacting measures of family background with the difference in the twins' schooling levels, as did Altonji and Dunn (1996). Table 5.6 shows the value of an additional year of schooling by measures of the family backgrounds of the twins. In the top panel we measure family background as the average of the parents' years of schooling. In the bottom panel we construct an index of family background using parental education, number of siblings, and parents' occupations. Because the number of individuals upon which the analysis is based is much smaller than in the NLSY, we use only three levels of family background.

The results in the top panel suggest slight variation in the economic value of additional schooling. Those whose parents have an average level of schooling that is less than a high school diploma earn approximately 6.2 percent more for each additional year of schooling, compared to a return of 14.4 percent for those whose parents have a high school diploma (and no college), and 9.8 percent for those whose parents attended college. These differences are not statistically significant, however. The results in the bottom panel tell a similar story. In fact, one could conclude that individuals from

TABLE 5.6
The Within-Twin Return to Education by Family Background (Identical Twins)

	Average of Parents' Education Level		
	Less than High School	High School Graduate	At Least Some College
Return to Education	6.2%	14.4%	9.8%
	(3.4)	(3.5)	(4.4)
	Family Background Index[a]		
	Low	Medium	High
Return to Education	6.9%	16.3%	6.1%
	(3.2)	(3.7)	(4.3)

Source: Ashenfelter and Rouse (1995).

Note: The dependent variable is log hourly wages. Estimated standard errors are in parentheses. These regressions are estimated by instrumental variables to allow for measurement error.

[a] The "Family Background Index" is a weighted average of parents' education and occupations, and number of siblings. "Low," "Medium," and "High" family indexes are the bottom, middle, and top thirds of the index distribution.

families in the middle (not the upper end) of the socioeconomic distribution receive the highest return to schooling.

6. Conclusion

Herrnstein and Murray (1994) write, "In short, the school is not a promising place to try to raise intelligence or to reduce intellectual differences" (p. 414). The evidence presented in this chapter shows that, on the contrary, the school *is* a promising place to increase the skills and incomes of individuals. As a result, educational policies have the potential to decrease existing, and growing, inequalities in income.

Herrnstein and Murray also qualify their statement, "given the constraints on school budgets and the state of educational science." Again, we disagree. Discussions about policy are discussions about possibly changing these constraints. A lack of resources is one problem that has plagued the attempts of public-sector training programs to significantly increase the incomes of participants (LaLonde 1995). If we really want to make educational programs effective, we must become much more serious about investing in them. Similarly, there is a great deal more to be learned about the role of education in the determination of income. For example, we know relatively little about how the quality of education determines earnings. This is an area where the experimental method can be used extensively to study the role of class size and other educational innovations on learning.

Appendixes

Technical Analysis

To derive our econometric framework, write a standard log wage equation as

$$y_{1i} = F_i + bS_{1i} + dX_i + \epsilon_{1i} \qquad (1)$$

and

$$y_{2i} = F_i + bS_{2i} + dX_i + \epsilon_{2i} \qquad (2)$$

where y_{1i} and y_{2i} are the logarithms of the wage rates of the sons and fathers (or any other two family members), S_{1i} and S_{2i} are the schooling levels of the sons and fathers (or, more generally, all attributes that vary within families), X_i are other observable determinants of wages that vary across families, but not within families (such as race), and ϵ_{1i} and ϵ_{2i} are unobservable individual components. F_i is assumed to be either an observed family or individual component (in the cross-sectional analysis) or an unobserved family or genetic component (in the within-family analysis) that is correlated with observed schooling levels. As a result, if either equation (1) or (2) is estimated by OLS without controlling for family background, the estimate of the coefficient, b, will reflect not only the causal effect of schooling on wages, but the effect of family background (or ability) as well. In the cross-section analysis, one can simply control for family background or "ability" using measures of parents' education or test scores. In the sibling analysis, one can difference equations (1) and (2) to eliminate the family effect, obtaining the (unbiased) within-family (or fixed-effects) estimator,

$$y_{2i} - y_{1i} = b[(S_{2i} - S_{1i})] + \epsilon_{2i} - \epsilon_{1i}. \tag{3}$$

In order to test whether the returns to schooling vary by family background, one can estimate an equation with an interaction term between the family members' schooling difference and their family background. The estimating equation is obtained by assuming that the return to schooling, b_i, varies by family and is a function of the family's unobserved "ability," A_i,

$$b_i = b_0 + b_1 A_i . \tag{4}$$

The parameter, b_1, reflects the extent to which the return to schooling varies by the "ability" or "learning environment" across families. If some families have higher levels of innate "ability" or more enriching learning environments for their children, and if this background allows the children to benefit more from schooling, then b_1 should be positive. If we permit family background to influence the family effect we have

$$A_i = \gamma_2 F_i \tag{5}$$

where F_i represents measures such as parents' education or measured ability. The corresponding reduced-form and fixed-effects equations are,

$$\begin{aligned} y_{1i} &= b_0 S_{1i} + \gamma_2 F_i + b_1 \gamma_2 F_i S_{1i} + dX_i + \epsilon_{1i'} \\ y_{2i} &= b_0 S_{2i} + \gamma_2 F_i + b_1 \gamma_2 F_i S_{2i} + dX_i + \epsilon_{2i'} \end{aligned} \tag{6}$$

and,

$$y_{2i} - y_{1i} = b_0 [S_{2i} - S_{1i}] + b_1 \gamma_2 F_i (S_{2i} - S_{1i}) + \epsilon_{2i'} - \epsilon_{1i'}. \tag{7}$$

Data: The National Longitudinal Survey of Youth (NLSY)

The NLSY data are from the 1993 wave. In constructing our sample we drop members of the military subsample, the self-employed, those missing information on education in 1993, those enrolled in school in 1993, and those earning less than two dollars per hour. We use an average of the hourly wages in 1993 and 1992 if both are available, and one if only one is available. We drop those with no valid wage. Wages are converted to 1994 dollars using the implicit price deflator for personal consumption expenditures. The tenure variable is the number of weeks worked at the first or second job. The Armed Forces Qualification Test (AFQT) score is computed as a linear combination of the word knowledge, arithmetic reasoning, paragraph comprehension, and mathematics knowledge subtests of the Armed Services Vocational Aptitude Battery (ASVAB).

In order to test whether the return to schooling varies by the AFQT of the individual, we estimate a specification based on equation (6) in the technical analysis appendix. That is, we include total completed schooling S_{Ti}, an unobservable family (or ability) component, F_i, and an interaction between the two:

$$y_i = \delta F_i + \beta S_{Ti} + \gamma S_{Ti} F_i + \epsilon_i. \tag{8}$$

The problem in the NLSY is that the AFQT was administered when the individuals were different ages and had completed differing years of education. To incorporate this fact into our framework, we assume that the AFQT score, T_i, is a function of F_i, and schooling at the time of the test, S_{Bi}:

$$T_i = F_i + bS_{Bi} + e_i \tag{9}$$

which can be rewritten as,

$$F_i = T_i - bS_{Bi} - e_i \tag{10}$$

Substituting equation (10) into equation (8) results in our basic specification,

$$y_i = \beta S_{Ti} - (\delta b)S_{Bi} + \gamma S_{Ti}T_i - (\gamma b)S_{Ti}S_{Bi} + \delta T_i - v_i \tag{11}$$

where the error term $\mu_i = \delta e_i + \gamma S_i e_i - \epsilon_i$. Thus, to control for schooling at the time of the test, we include the level effect of this previous schooling and an interaction of the previous schooling with the total level of schooling in 1993. We also include a quartic in age.

The AFQT quartiles are calculated using the weighted distribution of scores (using the ASVAB weight). The distribution across the AFQT quartiles is:

	AFQT Quartile			
	First	Second	Third	Fourth
Percentage of Sample	42.1	24.1	18.3	15.4

The distribution is not even because the NLSY oversamples (as part of the supplementary sample) the disadvantaged.

We average the parents' education if both are available and use only one if only one is available. We also include a dummy variable indicating that both parents' education levels are missing.

	Average of Parents' Education Levels				
	Less than High School	Equal to High School	Some College	At Least College Degree	Missing Both Parents' Education
Percentage of Sample	47.1	29.0	14.3	5.8	3.8

TABLE A5.1
OLS Estimates of the Return to Schooling and by Family Background
Using the NLSY

	Overall Return to Schooling	Return to Schooling by Parents' Education
Education in 1993	0.057	0.050
	(0.004)	(0.006)
Education*Parents' educ = High School		0.017
		(0.007)
Education*Parents' educ = Some College		−0.001
		(0.008)
Education*Parents' educ = College+		0.006
		(0.011)
Parents' education = High School		−0.166
		(0.091)
Parents' education = Some College		0.133
		(0.110)
Parents' education = College+		−0.0002
		(0.164)
Parents' education (Years) ÷ 10	0.092	
	(0.026)	
AFQT score ÷ 10	0.033	0.033
	(0.003)	(0.003)
Education in 1980	0.043	0.044
	(0.006)	(0.006)
R^2	0.296	0.298

Note: There are 6,748 observations. Estimated standard errors are in parentheses. Other regressors included a dummy indicating whether both parents' education levels were missing, a quartic in age in 1979, a dummy variable indicating if the grade in 1980 is missing, a dummy indicating whether the individual was part of the supplementary sample, sex, race, an urban dummy and whether the urban status is missing, three region dummies, and a constant. The regressions were weighted using the 1993 sample weight.

TABLE A5.2

OLS Estimates of the Return to Schooling by AFQT Using the NLSY

	Return to Schooling by AFQT Quartile	Return to Schooling by Linear AFQT
Education in 1993	0.022	0.030
	(0.012)	(0.012)
Education*AFQT, 2nd quartile	0.015	
	(0.010)	
Education*AFQT, 3rd quartile	−0.001	
	(0.010)	
Education*AFQT, 4th quartile	−0.004	
	(0.010)	
AFQT, 2nd quartile	−0.081	
	(0.128)	
AFQT, 3rd quartile	0.228	
	(0.124)	
AFQT, 4th quartile	0.339	
	(0.136)	
Education*AFQT ÷ 1000		−0.032
		(0.109)
Parents' education (Years) ÷ 10	0.077	0.093
	(0.026)	(0.026)
AFQT score ÷ 10		0.038
		(0.015)
Education in 1980	0.003	0.007
	(0.019)	(0.019)
Education in 1993*Education in 1980	0.003	0.003
	(0.001)	(0.001)
R^2	0.299	0.296

Note: There are 6,748 observations. Estimated standard errors are in parentheses. Other regressors included a dummy indicating whether both parents' education levels were missing, a quartic in age in 1979, a dummy variable indicating if the grade in 1980 is missing, a dummy indicating whether the individual was part of the supplementary sample, sex, race, an urban dummy and whether the urban status is missing, three region dummies, and a constant. The regressions were weighted using the 1993 sample weight.

References

Altonji, Joseph, and Thomas Dunn. 1996. "The Effects of Family Characteristics on the Return to Education." *Review of Economics and Statistics* 78: 692–704.

Angrist, Joshua D., and Alan B. Krueger. 1991. "Does Compulsory Schooling Affect Schooling and Earnings?" *Quarterly Journal of Economics* 106: 979–1014.

———. 1995. "Split-Sample Instrumental Variables Estimates of the Return to Schooling." *Journal of Business and Economics Statistics* 13: 225–235.

Ashenfelter, Orley, and John Ham. 1979. "Education, Unemployment, and Earnings." *Journal of Political Economy* 87: S99–S116.

Ashenfelter, Orley, and Alan Krueger. 1994. "Estimating the Returns to Schooling Using a New Sample of Twins." *American Economic Review* 84: 1157–1173.

Ashenfelter, Orley, and Cecilia Rouse. 1998. "Income, Schooling, and Ability: Evidence from a New Sample of Twins." *Quarterly Journal of Economics* 113: 253–284.

———. 1995. "Income, Schooling, and Ability: Evidence from a New Sample of Twins." Princeton University mimeo.

Ashenfelter, Orley, and David Zimmerman. 1997. "Estimates of the Return to Schooling from Sibling Data: Fathers, Sons, and Brothers." *Review of Economics and Statistics* 79: 1–9.

Becker, Gary S. 1967. *Human Capital and the Personal Distribution of Income.* Ann Arbor: University of Michigan Press.

Behrman, Jere R., Z. Hrubec, Paul Taubman, and Terence J. Wales. 1980. *Socioeconomic Success: A Study of the Effects of Genetic Endowments, Family Environment, and Schooling.* Amsterdam: North-Holland.

Behrman, Jere R., Mark R. Rosenzweig, and Paul Taubman. 1980."Endowments and the Allocation of Schooling in the Family and in the Marriage Market: The Twins Experiment." *Journal of Political Economy* 102: 1131–1174.

Blackburn, McKinley L., and David Neumark. 1993. "Omitted-Ability Bias and the Increase in the Return to Schooling." *Journal of Labor Economics* 11: 521–544.

Bound, John, David Jaeger, and Regina Baker. 1995. "Problems with Instrumental Variables Estimation When the Correlation between the Instruments and the Endogenous Explanatory Variable Is Weak." *Journal of the American Statistical Association* 90: 443–450.

Butcher, Kristin F., and Anne Case. 1994. "The Effect of Sibling Sex Composition on Women's Education and Earnings." *Quarterly Journal of Economics* 109: 531–563.

Card, David. 1993. "Using Geographic Variation in College Proximity to Estimate the Return to Schooling." National Bureau of Economic Research Working Paper no. 4483, October.

———. 1995. "Earnings, Schooling, and Ability Revisited." In *Research in Labor Economics*, ed. Solomon Polachek, pp. 23–48. Greenwich, CT: JAI Press.

Chamberlain, Gary, and Zvi Griliches. 1975. "Unobservables with a Variance-Components Structure: Ability, Schooling and the Economic Success of Brothers." *International Economic Review* 16: 422–449.

———. 1977. "More on Brothers." In *Kinometrics: Determinants of Socio-economic Success within and between Families*, ed. Paul Taubman, pp. 97–124. Amsterdam: North-Holland.

Corcoran, Mary, Christopher Jencks, and Michael Olneck. 1976. "The Effects of Family Background on Earnings." *American Economic Review* 66: 430–435.

Gorseline, D. W. 1932. *The Effect of Schooling upon Income.* Bloomington: Indiana University Press.

Griliches, Zvi. 1977. "Estimating the Returns to Schooling: Some Econometric Problems." *Econometrica* 45: 1–22.

———. 1979. "Sibling Models and Data in Economics: Beginnings of a Survey." *Journal of Political Economy* 87: S37–S64.

Hause, John C. 1972. "Earnings Profiles: Ability and Schooling." *Journal of Political Economy* 80: S109–S138.

Hauser, Robert M. 1973. "Socioeconomic Background and Differential Returns to Education." in *Does College Matter? Some Evidence on the Impacts of Higher Education*, pp. 129–145. New York: Academic Press.

Herrnstein, Richard J., and Charles Murray. 1994. *The Bell Curve: Intelligence and Class Structure in American Life*. New York: Free Press.

Jencks, Christopher, Susan Bartlett, Mary Corcoran, et al. 1979. *Who Gets Ahead? The Determinants of Economic Success in America*. New York: Basic Books.

Kane, Thomas J., and Cecilia E. Rouse. 1993. "Labor Market Returns to Two- and Four-Year Colleges: Is a Credit a Credit and Do Degrees Matter?" Princeton University Industrial Relations Section Working Paper no. 311, January.

LaLonde, Robert. 1995. "The Promise of Public Sector–Sponsored Training Programs." *Journal of Economic Perspectives* 9: 149–168.

Lang, Kevin. 1993. "Ability Bias, Discount Rate Bias, and the Return to Education." Boston University Economics Department mimeo.

Miller, Paul, Charles Mulvey, and Nick Martin. 1995. "What Do Twins Studies Reveal About the Economic Returns to Education? A Comparison of Australian and U.S. Findings." *American Economic Review* 85: 586–599.

Mincer, Jacob. 1974. *Schooling, Experience, and Earnings*. New York: Columbia University Press.

Neal, Derek A., and William A. Johnson. 1996. "The Role of Premarket Factors in Black-White Wage Differences." *Journal of Political Economy* 104: 869–895.

Neumark, David. 1994. "Biases in Twin Estimates of the Return to Schooling: A Note on Recent Research." National Bureau of Economics Research Technical Working Paper no. 158.

Olneck, Michael R. 1977. "On the Use of Sibling Data to Estimate the Effects of Family Background, Cognitive Skills, and Schooling: Results from the Kalamazoo Brothers Study." In *Kinometrics: Determinants of Socio-economic Success Within and Between Families*, ed. Paul Taubman, pp. 125–167. Amsterdam: North-Holland.

Rodgers, William M., and William E. Spriggs. 1996. "What Does AFQT Really Measure: Race, Wages, Schooling and the AFQT Score." *The Review of Black Political Economy* 24: 13–46.

Taubman, Paul J., and Terence J. Wales. 1973. "Higher Education, Mental Ability, and Screening." *Journal of Political Economy* 81: 28–55.

Weisbrod, Burton A., and Peter Karpoff. 1968. "Monetary Returns to College Education, Student Ability, and College Quality." *Review of Economics and Statistics* 50: 491–497.

Wolfle, Dael, and Joseph G. Smith. 1956. "The Occupational Value of Education for Superior High-School Graduates." *Journal of Higher Education* 27: 201–212, 232.

Six

Does Schooling Raise Earnings by Making People Smarter?*

SAMUEL BOWLES AND HERBERT GINTIS

SCHOOLING raises individuals' scores on cognitive tests. It also raises individual earnings. What is the connection between these two facts?

Many have interpreted the substantial economic returns to schooling as evidence for the importance of cognitive skills as a determinant of individual earnings. But skill enhancement is not the only way schooling affects earnings. We shall argue that schooling raises wages and output per hour of labor in part by transforming individuals in ways that are profitable for employers but are not the sort of "skills" that appear as arguments in a production function. We do not question that schools also produce such skills and that these skills are important in production, but if we are correct, skill enhancement explains only part of the contribution of schooling to individual earnings.[1]

Instead, we argue, schooling also raises earnings by its effects on individuals' norms and preferences, making the prospective worker more attractive to the employer by attenuating problems of work incentives and labor discipline. Schooling, we will show, may contribute to what we term *incentive-enhancing preferences*. If we are right, explanations of recent empirical trends in the economics of education and of inequality that rely solely on a shift in demand away from unskilled and toward skilled labor are likely to provide misleading guides to public policy.

The availability of data on individuals' cognitive performance scores on dozens of test instruments appears to have crowded out other reasonable hypotheses concerning less copiously measured individual attributes. Two

* This chapter draws on the more technically complete presentation in Bowles and Gintis (1998b) and data analysis in Bowles and Gintis (1998a). We are grateful to Roland Bénabou, Steven Durlauf, James Heckman, Charles Manski, Cecilia Rouse, and seminar participants at the University of Wisconsin, Yale University, and MIT for comments, to Melissa Osborne for research assistance, and to the MacArthur Foundation for financial support.

[1] Schooling may affect earnings by other avenues as well, for example by enhancing the individual's ability to respond flexibly to disequilibrium situations associated with rapid change (Schultz 1975 and Rosenzweig 1995, for example) or by fostering productivity-enhancing neighborhood effects in the production or diffusion of social capital. We address these disequilibrium returns or social capital explanations in Bowles and Gintis (1998a).

examples of the importance of the latter are the following. The first is from a recent survey of 3,000 employers conducted by the U.S. Census Bureau in collaboration with the Department of Education (Bureau of the Census 1998), which asked, "When you consider hiring a new nonsupervisory or production worker, how important are the following in your decision to hire?" Employers ranked "industry-based skill credentials" at 3.2 on a scale of 1 (unimportant) to 5 (very important), with "years of schooling" at 2.9, "score on tests given by employer" and "academic performance" both at 2.5. By far the most important was "attitude," ranked 4.6, followed by "communication skills" (4.2).

The second example is from the far more detailed Employers' Manpower and Skills Practices Survey of 1,693 British employers reported in Green, Machin, and Wilkenson (1998). Of the somewhat more than a third of the establishments reporting a "skill shortage," personnel managers identified the recruitment problem as "lack of technical skills" in 43 percent of the cases, but "poor attitude, motivation, or personality" in a remarkable 62 percent of the cases. Poor attitude was by far the most important reason given for the recruitment difficulty. The importance of motivation relative to technical skill was even greater in the full sample.

Both examples illustrate a possible bias: we tend to refer to "skill shortages" when we mean any difficulty in recruiting or retaining suitable employees. Among economists, at least, other more conceptual biases are at work, the main one being the presumption that anything rewarded in a competitive labor market must be a skill. Our chapter is addressed to this second bias, which, if we are correct, acquires its plausibility by default, there being no widely accepted model of why individual traits that are *not* skills might be rewarded in a competitive labor market equilibrium.

We begin by introducing evidence that the measured skills produced by schooling explain only part (rarely more than half) of the contribution of schooling to earnings. We then address the following puzzle: why might employers pay more for employees exhibiting personal traits other than productive skills? We show that paying more for nonskill traits is readily motivated in a model of the principal-agent relationship between employer and employee. The reason is that where contracts are incomplete, characteristics of the parties to an exchange affect the level and distribution of gains from trade, even when these characteristics are not attributes of the goods and services being transacted. Incentive-enhancing preferences are an example of these individual characteristics, and may thus account for some of the contribution of schooling to higher earnings. The evidence and model we present illustrate a flaw in the commonplace equation of higher earnings with "superior skill."

1. Why Do the Educated Earn More?

There is no longer any doubt that those with more schooling earn more at least in substantial measure *because* they are educated, and not solely because schooling covaries with ability, parental social status, and other traits rewarded in the labor market.[2] While schooling may also perform a credentialing function, the magnitude of the resulting diploma effects, where these have been identified, represents only a small proportion of the statistical association between years of schooling and earnings.[3]

Because schooling increases earnings and imparts skills, many have supposed that the acquisition of skills is the mechanism whereby schooling increases earnings. Why would employers pay the education premium? Tacitly accepting this argument, economists tend to equate differences in levels of schooling with skill differences.[4]

Yet it has proven remarkably difficult to give an adequate account of the skills that schools produce and to document their reward in labor markets. The most straightforward approach is to ask what schools teach and to consider the economic returns to the resulting curricular outcomes. It is simple to identify individual characteristics that are acquired through instruction and that also appear to raise earnings. But these characteristics typically explain only a small fraction of the observed economic return to schooling. Thus the economic contribution of the curricular content of schooling has proven elusive. Altonji (1995), for example, found that additional years of science, math, and foreign language in high school contribute to subsequent earnings, but that the value of courses taken in an additional year of high school is far less than the value of an additional year of high school.[5] Moreover, those school programs most deliberately designed to contribute to occupational skill enhancement—vocational programs—appear to have limited success.[6]

A more promising approach might be to define skills broadly as generic cognitive capacities, and to explore the contribution of schools to labor-market success via their teaching of the kinds of mental capacities required in employment. The most direct test of the proposition that the contribution

---

[2] See Card (1998) for a survey of recent studies of the returns to schooling in the United States.

[3] Hechman, Layne-Farrar, and Dodd (1995), for example, identify statistically significant credentialing effects, but the economic return to years of schooling per se remains substantial even after accounting for these effects.

[4] See, for example, Juhn, Murphy, and Pierce (1993) and Katz and Murphy (1992).

[5] These results control for family background, aptitude, and participation in an academic program and are invariant to the use of OLS, OLS fixed effects, or instrumental variable estimation.

[6] For instance, Altonji (1995) finds, both for OLS and instrumental variables estimates, lower than average returns to vocational programs.

of schooling to the development of skills accounts for the effect of schooling on earnings is to ask if earnings covary with years of schooling in populations that are homogeneous with respect to level of skill. A positive answer in a well-specified model suggests that schools contribute to earnings by means other than their contribution to skills.

An approximation of this test is available: we can compare two estimated regression coefficients for a years-of-schooling variable, one in an equation in which a measure of cognitive skill also appears and another in which the measure is absent. An approximation of this test is available. Suppose that the income-generating structure for a given demographic group is

$$\ln(w) = \beta_0 + \beta_s s + \beta_c c + \beta_b b + \epsilon \qquad (1)$$

where w, s, b, and c measure earnings, schooling, parental socioeconomic background, and cognitive skill level, and ϵ measures stochastic influences on earnings uncorrelated with the other explanatory variables. Most estimates lack measures of cognitive skill and hence estimate

$$\ln(w) = \beta_0' + \beta_s' s + \beta_b' b + \epsilon' \qquad (2)$$

with ϵ' representing the stochastic influences as above plus the influences of cognitive skill operating independently of demographic grouping, socioeconomic background, and schooling. We can compare two estimated regression coefficients for a years-of-schooling variable, one in an equation like (1) in which a measure of cognitive skill also appears (β_s) and another like (2) in which the cognitive measure is absent (β_s'). Subject to a number of estimation biases that we address in another paper (Bowles and Gintis 1998a), available from the authors upon request, the ratio of the first to the second, which we write as

$$\alpha = \frac{\beta_s}{\beta_s'}, \qquad (3)$$

is a measure of the contribution of what we call *incentive-enhancing preferences* to the estimated return to schooling (Gintis 1971). If schooling affected earnings solely through its contribution to skills (assuming these to be adequately measured by the test scores used), α would be zero, because the regression coefficient of years of schooling would fall to zero once the skill level of the individual is accounted for, there being (by hypothesis) no contribution of schooling to earnings beyond its effect on skills. By contrast, if the contribution of schooling to skills explained none of schooling's contribution to earnings, α would be unity. This is illustrated in figure 6.1.

We have been able to locate twenty-five studies allowing fifty-eight estimates of the relationship between the coefficient of schooling and income with and without a direct measure of cognitive skills, and thus an estimate of

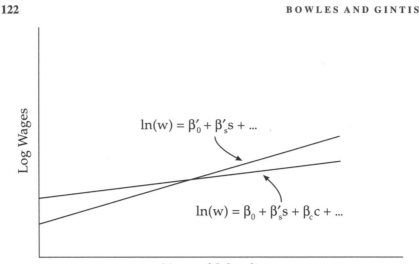

Figure 6.1. Estimating the Incentive-Enhancing Preferences in the Returns to Schooling. Years of schooling is s, $\ln(w)$ is the natural logarithm of the wage, and cognitive
performance is measured by the variable c. Our measure of the portion of the returns
to schooling that cannot be explained by cognitive performance is $\alpha = \beta_s / \beta'_s$.

α (these studies are available from the authors).[7] Methods of estimation differ, of course, and the demographic groups covered and the years for which
the data apply vary considerably. We have surveyed these studies and selected what we considered to be the best-specified estimates in each study.
For example, we favored estimates using measurement error correction and
instrumental variables estimation or other techniques to take account of endogeneity of the explanatory variables. We have included all studies available to us.

The mean value of α in our studies is 0.82, meaning that introducing a
measure of cognitive performance into an equation using educational attainment to predict income reduces the coefficient of years of education by an
average of 18 percent. This suggests that a substantial portion of the returns
to schooling are generated by effects or correlates of schooling substantially
unrelated to the skills measured on the available tests. In figure 6.2 we present these data, along with the year(s) to which the earnings data pertain.[8]

[7] We have found an additional five studies, allowing an additional six estimates, where the
dependent variable is a measure of occupational status rather than earnings: Bajema (1968),
Conlisk (1971), Duncan (1968), Sewell, Haller, and Ohlendorf (1970), and Porter (1974). The
mean value of α in these studies is 0.89, and the lowest is 0.81. These results are not reported in
figure 6.2.

[8] In a regression using categorical variables to take account of the demographic groups stud-

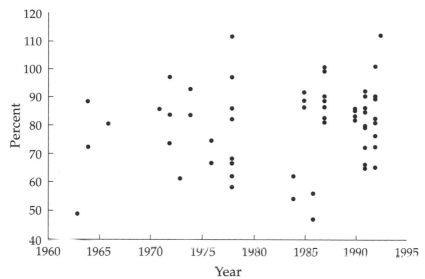

Figure 6.2. The Component (%) of the Private Return to Schooling That Is Unrelated to Cognitive Performance: A Summary of Fifty-Eight Estimates from Twenty-Five Studies

A single study, Huang (1997), uses the same cognitive test as well as earnings and schooling measures over a long period of time and thus allows an assessment of the secular movement of α. Huang presents estimates, based on the General Social Survey, of the returns to three levels of schooling among eight demographic groups using appropriate measures of family background as copredictors of the logarithm of earnings. Confining ourselves to the thirty-three cases where the estimated return to schooling is positive and significant at the 10 percent level, the mean estimates of α are: 0.85 for 1974–1982, 0.90 for 1984–1989, and 0.95 for 1990–1994. There appears to be no tendency for the skills component in the returns to schooling to increase over time.

These data do not indicate the unimportance of skills as an influence on earnings or, more narrowly, on the returns to schooling. However, they do suggest that a major portion of the effect of schooling on earnings operates in ways independent of any contribution of schooling to cognitive functioning.[9] Rather, we will suggest, schooling contributes to earnings in part by

ied, the estimated positive time trend is small and statistically insignificant; there is inadequate evidence to sustain the conclusion that the role of skills in the contribution of schooling to earnings has increased over the past three decades.

[9] There is additional evidence that skill demands at work explain at least some of the returns to schooling. Alan Krueger (1993) found that increased use of computers explained a third to a

fostering the development of individual traits that contribute to labor discipline and hence are valuable to employers, given the informational asymme-
tries between employer as principal and employee as agent and the resulting
incompleteness of the employment contract.

2. Endogenous Enforcement of the Employment Contract

In the following pages we develop this interpretation of the economic returns
to schooling, addressing two questions. First, how might schooling contribute to earnings independent of its contribution to skill? Second, is the postu-
lated answer to this question consistent with competitive equilibrium if employers have complete information about the characteristics of employees?

Sociological accounts frequently stress the motivational aspects of the
contribution of schooling to the economy, often under the heading of "socialization for work."[10] The reason that an employer would be more willing to
pay a premium for the services of a "well-socialized" employee than a shop-
per would be to pay a higher price for the fruit of a "well-socialized" grocer
is that the employment relationship is generally contractually incomplete.[11]
A costlessly enforceable promise of a wage is exchanged not for costlessly
enforceable labor services but rather for the employees' agreement to accept

---

half of the increased returns to schooling during the 1980s. However, Krueger's data do not
indicate that the economic return to schooling derives substantially from the covariance of the
level of schooling and the extent of computer use at work: the estimated coefficient of years of
schooling in Krueger's main sample when estimated without the computer use variables in the
equation is reduced when the equation is estimated including a variable measuring computer use
at work, but by only 9 percent for his 1984 sample and 13 percent for his 1989 sample.
Moreover, Raphael and Toseland (1995) found that the estimated effect of schooling on log
wages is reduced by only one-fifth when the extent of on-the-job use of eight distinct skills
(including use of mathematics and use of computers) is measured and included in the estimating
equation. Farkas, England, Vicknair, and Kilbourne (1997) found that including a measure of
the skill demands of the respondent's job in a log wage equation reduced the estimated return to
schooling by an average of 26 percent for six estimated equations involving male and female
whites, Mexican Americans, and African Americans (age, experience, mother's education, and
rural residence were included in the equation). These data concern the United States alone, and
we do not draw any inference from them about the returns to schooling in other economies. We
suspect, and there is some evidence (Boissière, Knight, and Sabot 1985), that in societies where
schooling is more limited in its scope, the skill component in the returns to schooling may be
considerably larger than in the United States. However, according to Moll (1995), in a sample
of black workers in South Africa, the value of α for returns to primary schooling is 0.73, for
secondary schooling it is 0.67, and for higher education the value is 0.92. These are well within
the range of estimates presented in figure 6.2.

   [10] See Parsons (1959) and Dreeben (1967).

   [11] It is interesting to note that the theory of social exchange (Blau 1964) on which the soci-
ologists' account of schooling as influencing individual preference structures is readily based, is
recognizable to an economist as a theory of incomplete contracts.

the employer's authority during the hours of work. This authority is then used to secure the flow of labor services that, when combined with other productive inputs, produces output. The employer's payment of a wage superior to the employee's next best alternative, coupled with the threat of termination of the contract, constitutes an essential part of the necessarily endogenous enforcement of the employer's objectives in the exchange.

In such a model, which we will formalize presently, employers choose to pay for nonskill aspects of individuals that assist in the exercise of the employer's authority. Examples of such profitable individual traits are a predisposition to truth telling, identification with the objectives of the firm's owners and managers as opposed to the objectives of coworkers or customers, a high marginal utility of income, a low disutility of effort, and a low rate of time preference—an orientation toward the future rather than the present. We call these *incentive-enhancing preferences.*

Just as the employer's valuation of productive skills of employees will depend on the product mix and production functions in use, the valuation of incentive-enhancing preferences will vary with the nature of the endogenous enforcement problem. Where monitoring is impossible, for example, the importance of truth telling might be heightened. Where one employee is expected to monitor other employees, behavioral traits, demographic markers, or costly-to-acquire credentials contributing to the legitimacy of the exercise of authority might be highly valued by employers.

By developing incentive-enhancing preferences in individuals and thus attenuating the costs of endogenous enforcement of the labor contract, schooling may have economic effects similar to, and perhaps complementary to, work norms and other shared values that often prove individually or collectively useful when individuals interact in the absence of complete contracting.

But do schools produce incentive-enhancing preferences? We know of only one study that has attempted to provide an answer. This study is not a satisfactory basis for generalization, but it is nonetheless worth reviewing. The study asked whether schools reward students who exhibit the specific personality traits valued by employers in the workplace. If true, we might reasonably infer that schools foster the development of these traits and that the economic return to schooling might represent payments to individuals with these traits.

In an investigation conducted during the early 1970s, Richard Edwards (1976) used a peer-rated set of personality measures of members of work groups in both private and public employment to predict supervisor ratings of these employees. In a parallel investigation with a distinct sample, Peter Meyer (Bowles, Gintis, and Meyer 1975) used the same peer-rated personality variables to predict grade-point averages of students in a high school controlling for SAT (verbal and math) and IQ scores. Edwards found that being judged by their peers as "perseverant," "dependable," "consistent," "punctual," "tactful," "identifies with work," and "empathizes with orders" was positively correlated with supervisor ratings, whereas those judged to be "creative" and "independent" were ranked poorly by supervisors. Meyer found virtually identical results for the high school students in his grading study; independent of the student's skill level, schools reward with higher grades the same traits that Edwards found to predict favorable supervisor ratings. The simple correlations between grade-point average and the twelve identified personality traits are barely distinguishable from the analogous correlations in Edwards's study of employees.[12] Teachers and employers in these samples reward the same personality traits.

We would like to know, of course, if schools produce the traits they reward, and if traits valued by supervisors are rewarded by enhanced pay.[13] But the juxtaposition of the Edwards and Meyer data is suggestive that the incomplete contracts model of the employment relationship coupled with the incentive-enhancing preferences account of schooling may provide insights into the nature of the contribution of schooling to individual earnings.

As thus far developed, however, the incomplete contracts model is an insufficient basis for an analysis of the private returns to schooling. First, none of the relevant principal agent models has been formulated in a way that would allow schooling to affect the process of endogenous enforcement. Second, it is not clear in the above account why enhanced schooling in an entire population would raise rather than lower equilibrium wages, since if schooling renders employees more susceptible to the exercise of authority by the employer, it is counterintuitive to think that this disciplining effect would result in wage increases. An appropriate model thus remains to be developed.

3. Incentive-Enhancing Preferences

Suppose the amount of labor services an employee supplies to a firm is the product of two terms: the number of hours h worked and the employee's effort level e, where $0 \leq e \leq 1$. We assume the employer can contract for hours h, but effort e is not verifiable and hence cannot be determined by contractual agreement. However, the employer has an imperfect measure of

---

[12] These results are reported in Bowles, Gintis, and Meyer (1975). For the ten personality traits common to both studies, the simple correlations with grade-point average explain 96 percent of the variance in the simple correlations of these traits with supervisor ratings.

[13] See Jencks (1979) for a survey and analysis of the role of noncognitive personality traits in earnings and occupational status achievement. Jencks provides evidence for the economic importance of such traits, but supports few inferences about the role of schooling in their production.

e that indicates with probability $p(e)$ that the employee has "shirked," where $p' < 0$ and $p'' \leq 0$.

We will model the employer-employee relationship as an infinitely repeated game in which the employer hires a team of h employees, each of whom works for one hour and is paid a wage w at the end of the period. An employee discovered shirking is dismissed and replaced by a new employee (identical to the one replaced), also at the end of the period. The employer as first mover chooses h and w to maximize profits, in the knowledge that a higher wage may induce the employee to supply more effort, since the cost of job loss increases with the wage. The employee then chooses effort e to maximize the present value of expected utility. We call this a *contingent renewal* model of the employment relationship.[14]

Our model of incentive-enhancing preferences depends on the effects of education on the employee's best response function $e = e(w,z)$, which shows the level of effort e chosen by an employee faced with a wage rate w and fallback position z, defined as the expected present value of utility for a dismissed agent. One may think of z as depending on the availability of income-replacing transfers such as unemployment benefits, the expected duration of a spell of unemployment, and the expected stream of utility in the employee's subsequent employment. We abstract from reputation effects and so represent z as exogenous to the employer and employee in their choices of w and e. We will see presently, however, that exogenous variation in the level of schooling will affect firm employment levels and will thus plausibly influence the expected duration of employment and hence the level of z.

Suppose the employee has the utility function $u(w,e)$, which is smooth, strictly increasing, and concave in the wage w, and strictly decreasing in effort e. If the discount rate is ρ, then the present value $v(e)$ of having the job is given by

$$v(e) = \frac{u(w,e) + (1 - p(e))v(e) + p(e)z}{1 + \rho},$$

assuming (without loss of generality) that the utility accrues at the end of the period. This simplifies to

$$v(e) = \frac{u(w,e) - \rho z}{\rho + p(e)} + z. \tag{4}$$

This equation has a simple interpretation: the value v of the job equals the value z of the fallback plus the stream of net returns $u(w,e) - \rho z$ discounted by ρ plus the probability of dismissal $p(e)$. The employee then chooses effort

---

[14] Contingent renewal models of this type are analyzed in Gintis (1976), Shapiro and Stiglitz (1984), Bowles (1985), Gintis and Ishikawa (1987), and Bowles and Gintis (1993).

e to maximize $v(e)$. This gives rise to an employee best response function
$e = e(w,z)$, which is increasing in w.[15] Using a subscripted variable to represent its partial derivative with respect to the subscript, the employee's first-order condition can be written

$$v_e = \frac{1}{\rho + p} [u_e - (v - z)p'] = 0, \tag{5}$$

which implies

$$u_e = (v - z)p';$$

that is, the marginal disutility of effort must equal the cost of job loss times the marginal effect of increased effort on the probability of job loss. Equation (5) defines the employee's best response function $e(w,z)$. As expected, the best response function is increasing in w and decreasing in z.[16]

We say a parameter a is *incentive-enhancing* if along the employee's best response function, an increase in a increases the marginal effect of effort e on the present value v of having a job, that is, if $v_{ea} > 0$. We call such a preference "incentive-enhancing" because, differentiating the first-order condition $v_e = 0$ from which the employee's best response function is derived, we get

$$\frac{de}{da} = -\frac{v_{ea}}{v_{ee}},$$

and $v_{ee} < 0$ by the second-order condition, so an increase in a shifts up the best response function $e(w,z)$. Thus an increase in incentive-enhancing preferences will lead an employee to work harder, holding all else constant.

Here are two examples of incentive-enhancing preferences. The argument in the remainder of this section is a summary of the theorems presented in Bowles and Gintis (1998b). First, it is easy to see that a reduction in the individual's rate of time preference—that is, a greater orientation toward the future—is an incentive-enhancing preference because it raises the importance, in the individual's evaluations, of the prospect of retaining the job in the future and thus in avoiding any behavior that might result in termination. This may be confirmed by differentiating (5) with respect to ρ using (4).

Second, suppose $u = u(w,e,a)$, where $u_a > 0$, and $u_{ea} \geq 0$ (i.e., an increase in a increases utility derived from the job and does not increase the marginal disutility of effort). Then from (5), $v_{ea} > 0$ and a is incentive-

[15] The longer version of this paper, Bowles and Gintis (1998b), available on request, proves this and other mathematical results asserted but not demonstrated below.

[16] Actually, $e_w > 0$ holds globally only if $u_{ew} \geq 0$. Under more general conditions, the employee best response function will be inverted u-shaped as a function of w. But necessarily $e_w > 0$ in the neighborhood of a firm's profit-maximizing equilibrium.

enhancing. If $u_{ea} > 0$, a enhances incentives by reducing the marginal disutility of effort, while if $u_{ea} > 0$, a is incentive-enhancing because it increases the desirability of holding the job, as might occur through an increase in the marginal utility of income or the social stigma of being without work.

For an example of an incentive-enhancing parameter that lowers the disutility of effort, consider the utility function

$$u(w,e,a) = w - \frac{1 - a}{1 - e}. \tag{6}$$

Suppose also $p(e) = 1 - e$, so full shirking ($e = 0$) ensures dismissal, and zero shirking ($e = 1$) precludes dismissal. The first-order condition (5) then implies the employee best response function

$$e(w,z) = 1 - \tilde{a} - \sqrt{\tilde{a}^2 + \rho\tilde{a}}, \tag{7}$$

where $\tilde{a} = (1 - a)/(w - \rho z)$. This employee best response function is shown in figure 6.3.

The parameter a is clearly incentive-enhancing in this case because from (6) we see that u_a, $u_{ae} > 0$, which implies $de/da > 0$. The utility function (6) represents a as a reduction in the disutility of labor, but transforming (6) by dividing the right-hand side by the constant $1 - a$ yields an equivalent representation where a increases the average and marginal utility of income.

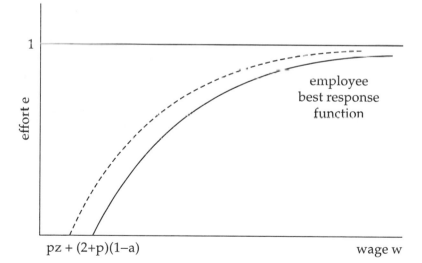

Figure 6.3. The Employee's Best Response Function. The dashed line indicates the effect of an incentive-enhancing change in preferences for the utility function (6).

4. Schooling and Earnings

Suppose that schools produce both skills c and incentive-enhancing preferences a. We can then write the quantity of effective labor embodied in an hour of work as $(1 + \gamma c)e(w,z,a)$ where $\gamma \geq 0$ is a measure of the importance of skills in the production process, $\gamma = 0$ implying the unimportance of skills. Suppose the firm has revenue function $q(\cdot)$, with $q' > 0$ and $q'' < 0$. Normalizing the price of output at unity, we can write the firm's net profit as

$$\pi = q((1 + \gamma c)e(w)h) - wh. \tag{8}$$

The first-order conditions for profit maximization are

$$\pi_h = (1 + \gamma c)q'e - w = 0 \tag{9}$$

$$\pi_w = (1 + \gamma c)q'he' - h = 0, \tag{10}$$

from which the well-known Solow condition follows:

$$e_w = \frac{e}{w} \tag{11}$$

profit maximization leads employers to equate the average and marginal returns to varying the wage. This equilibrium condition is illustrated in figure 6.4, which shows that the equilibrium (w^*,e^*) is located at the tangency between the employee best response function and the firm's minimum isocost line $e = w/\mu$, where μ is the cost-minimizing wage/effort ratio.[17] As (9) shows, the firm then chooses the number of hours h of labor to satisfy the standard condition that the wage equals the value of the marginal product of an hour of labor given the effort level e, determined by (11).

An important comparative static result that we use below is that an increase in the employee's reservation position z unambiguously raises both the firm's optimal wage offer and the cost of obtaining effort. Figure 6.5 illustrates the effect of increasing z, leading to a move from equilibrium (w^*,e^*) to (w_+^*, e_+^*).

What are the effects of changes in the levels of skills c and incentive-enhancing preferences a? Consider a shift from preferences described by a to $a^+ > a$.

An increase in incentive-enhancing preferences shifts up the marginal product of labor function and makes labor more profitable to hire at each wage rate, and hence generates an increased demand for labor at each wage.

---

[17] Several authors, most notably Carmichael (1985), have suggested that since the employee receives a rent from this relationship, the employer could extract a one-time fee in exchange for hiring an employee. Adding this to the model would not change our results and would complicate the exposition. Hence we abstract from up-front fees in this chapter.

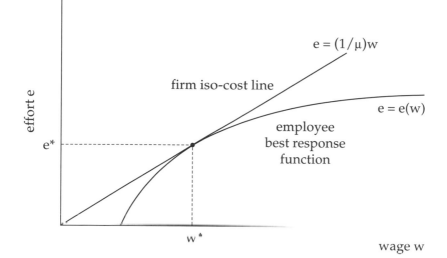

Figure 6.4. Equilibrium Wage and Effort Levels for the Firm. The Solow condition (11) (profit maximization) obtains at the equilibrium (w^*, e^*), as does condition (11) for the employee's optimal provision of effort.

An increase in the demand for labor reduces the expected duration of a spell of unemployment, and hence raises the fallback position of employees. This induces the firm to raise its profit-maximizing wage offer. In effect, the incompleteness of the labor contract provides a reason why changes in the incentive-enhancing preferences of the employee may raise equilibrium

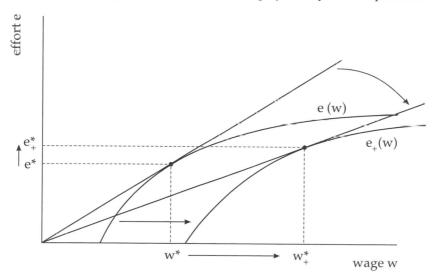

Figure 6.5. The Effect of an Increase in the Employee Fallback

wages even if these traits have no bearing on the production process per se
and hence cannot be deemed "skills" in the common sense of the term.

These comparative static results are illustrated in the figures that follow.
From figures 6.3 and 6.4 it is obvious that incentive-enhancing preferences
lower the cost of hiring labor. We also assume all markets are competitive,
so a *zero-profit condition* holds. Because the profit rate varies monotonically
and inversely with μ, the zero-profit condition uniquely determines a value
of μ consistent with competitive equilibrium. Given a and c for the labor
force as a whole, the demand for labor adjusts the equilibrium fallback position z^* so that equilibrium profits $\pi^*(z^*) = 0$, where $\pi^*(z)$ is (8), using the
employee and firm equilibrium values of $e(z)$, $w(z)$, and $h(z)$. The zero-profit
condition implies that an increase in incentive-enhancing preferences a or
skill-enhancing human capital c leads to a rise in the equilibrium value z^* of
the employee's fallback. An increase in the competitively determined wage
rate follows. As a result we can conclude that, given utility function (6), in
market equilibrium, an incentive-enhancing increase in a or the discount
factor, $\delta = 1/(1 + \rho)$, or a skill-enhancing increase in c n the part of employees, leads to an increase in the wage rate w. This conclusion is illustrated in figure 6.6. The direct effect of an increase in a on the firm, holding
the fallback z constant, is to shift the employee's best response function
upward (the dashed line) and hence to decrease the firm's cost of effort μ.
However, this raises the profit rate, violating the zero-profit condition. Since
μ^* remains unchanged in equilibrium, the whole best response function must
shift to the right until it is once again tangent to the firm's original iso-cost
line. This can only occur through an increase in the fallback z occasioned by
the increased demand for labor. This is depicted at point R in figure 6.6.

Figure 6.6 also makes it clear that a heterogeneous labor force, some with
preferences a and others with a^+ (but otherwise identical), would be paid
wages w_{old} and w_{new}, respectively, in competitive equilibrium, assuming that
some of each were hired.

Notice that in the "new" equilibrium output per worker-hour is also higher
(because $e_{new} > e_{old}$) so the incentive-enhancing preference change has
raised the productivity of labor hours (but not of labor effort).

5. Conclusion

Why, then, do the educated earn more? A part of the answer is doubtless
captured by the conventional wisdom; schools teach skills that are scarce in
equilibrium because they are limited in supply because they are costly to
acquire. But the evidence does not support the argument that the cognitive
and other skills that have been measured exhaust the mechanisms by which
schooling affects wages and labor productivity. If the educated are more

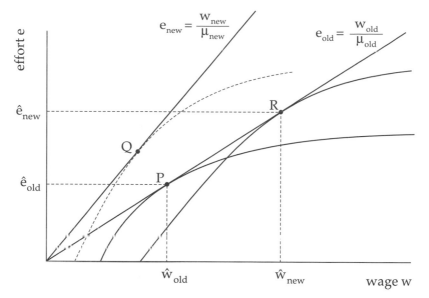

Figure 6.6. The Partial and General Equilibrium Effects of Raising the Level of Incentive-Enhancing Preferences on Wages and Effort. The improvement in incentives initially shifts upwards the employee best response function, yielding a partial equilibrium at Q, inducing an improvement in the fallback position of the employee, displacing the best response function to the right, until the general equilibrium outcome R is obtained.

skilled in ways not captured by the tests commonly used, we may have underestimated this aspect of the contribution of schooling to earnings. But more likely, we think, is our initial response to the question: additional schooling enhances the labor-market value of individuals in ways other than enhanced skills. We have shown that with incomplete contracts governing the employment relationship, the relevant earnings-enhancing effects of schooling will not be confined to skills in the conventional sense, but may be incentive-enhancing preferences that, by attenuating the costs of endogenous contract enforcement, are valuable to the employer. Like skills, efficiency-enhancing preferences are scarce in equilibrium because they are costly to acquire.

These effects of schooling work by altering the behavioral response of the employee to the employer's incentives and sanctions, rather than by altering a skill that affects the technical specification of labor as a factor of production. This influence on the employee's behavioral response is easily modeled as a reduction in the disutility of labor, but schooling could plausibly affect employees' behavior in other ways as well. In a companion paper (Bowles and Gintis 1996) we have modeled the effect of schooling on the employee's rate of time preference and the influence of this on labor market outcomes. Alternatively one could represent schooling's effect as a change in the employee's behavioral response to the authority relationship implied by the assignment of control rights and monitoring to the employer.

What can one say of the welfare implications of this analysis of the economic returns to schooling? The answer is: very little, the reason being that plausible effects of schooling operate by changing behavioral responses of employees to incentives, sanctions, and authority and these are most conveniently analyzed as changes in the employee's utility function. To assess these changes requires an evaluation of the implied preference changes themselves. Even an apparently innocuous change—a reduction in the disutility of effort—cannot be evaluated simply, as the same results could have been generated assuming that schools increase the shame of job loss or the social stigma of being unemployed. Although these changes are behaviorally equivalent in our model, they appear to be at odds normatively.

It is common to attribute *any* trait rewarded in a competitive labor market to an underlying "skill," and hence to superior "merit." The conclusion that the earnings distribution is consonant with the meritocratic principle readily follows. Our results cast doubt on this interpretation. It is, of course, true that skills and many dimensions of incentive-enhancing preferences, such as a low rate of time preference, trustworthiness, and willingness to work hard (a low disutility of labor), are widely considered meritorious. However, other aspects of incentive-enhancing preferences, such as a high marginal utility of income, or a highly competitive attitude toward fellow employees, do not readily fall under the heading of merit. In any case, incentive-enhancing preferences have little in common with the characteristics purportedly rewarded in the "meritocratic society," such as IQ.

Our conclusion is that because schools both impart skills and transform preferences, their effects cannot be evaluated in a framework that assumes exogenously determined preference orderings. Even in an idealized economy, in which all prices accurately reflect social costs and benefits, then, the standard welfare analysis of the returns to schooling might be misleading. This does not mean, of course, that schooling cannot be evaluated or that conventional evaluations overstate the value of education. Among the skills and incentive-enhancing preferences fostered by schooling, some, perhaps most, are highly valued either intrinsically or instrumentally by large numbers of people. These valuations by parents, students, and others are a reasonable datum for normative evaluation of schooling, but they are obviously insufficient.

References

Altonji, Joseph G. 1995. "The Effects of High School Curriculum on Education and Labor Market Outcomes." *Journal of Human Resources* (summer): 410–438.

Bajema, C. J. 1968. "A Note on the Interrelations among Intellectual Ability, Education Attainment, and Occupational Achievement: A Follow-Up Study of a Male Kalamazoo Public School Population." *Sociology of Education* 41, no. 3 (summer): 317–319.

Blau, Peter. 1964. *Exchange and Power in Social Life*. New York: John Wiley.

Boissière, M., J. B. Knight, and R. H. Sabot. 1985. "Earnings, Schooling, Ability, and Cognitive Skills." *American Economic Review* 75, no. 5 (December): 1016–1030.

Bowles, Samuel. 1985. "The Production Process in a Competitive Economy: Walrasian, Neo-Hobbesian, and Marxian Models." *American Economic Review* 75, no. 1 (March): 16–36.

Bowles, Samuel, and Herbert Gintis. 1993. "The Revenge of Homo Economicus: Contested Exchange and the Revival of Political Economy." *Journal of Economic Perspectives* (winter): 83–102.

———. 1996. "Time Preference, Labor Discipline and Earnings: Explaining the Economic Return to Education." Unpublished paper, University of Massachusetts.

———. 1998a. "The Determinants of Individual Earnings: Skills, Preferences, and Schooling." Unpublished paper, University of Massachusetts.

———. 1998b. "Incentive Enhancing Preferences." Unpublished paper, University of Massachusetts.

Bowles, Samuel, Herbert Gintis, and Peter Meyer. 1975. "The Long Shadow of Work: Education, the Family, and the Reproduction of the Social Division of Labor." *Insurgent Sociologist* 5, no. 4: 3–24.

Bureau of the Census. 1998. "First Findings from the EQW National Employer Survey." EQW Catalog no. RE01.

Card, David. 1998. "The Causal Effect of Education on Earnings." University of California, Berkeley, Center for Labor Economics, Working Paper no. 2.

Carmichael, H. Lorne. 1985. "Can Unemployment Be Involuntary? The Supervision Perspective." *American Economic Review* 75: 1213–1214.

Conlisk, John. 1971. "A Bit of Evidence on the Income-Education-Ability Interaction." *Journal of Human Resources* 6, no. 3 (summer): 358–362.

Dreeben, Robert. 1967. *On What Is Learned in School*. Reading, MA: Addison-Wesley.

Duncan, Otis Dudley. 1968. "Ability and Achievement." *Eugenics Quarterly* 15, no. 1 (March): 1–11.

Edwards, Richard C. 1976. "Personal Traits and 'Success' in Schooling and Work." *Educational and Psychological Measurement* 37: 125–138.

Farkas, George, Paula England, Keven Vicknair, and Barbara Stanek Kilbourne. 1997. "Cognitive Skill, Skill Demands of Jobs, and Earnings among Young European American, African American, and Mexican American Workers." *Social Forces* 75, no. 3 (March): 913–940.

Gintis, Herbert. 1971. "Education, Technology, and the Characteristics of Worker Productivity." *American Economic Review* 61, no. 2: 266–279.

———. 1976. "The Nature of the Labor Exchange and the Theory of Capitalist Production." *Review of Radical Political Economics* 8, no. 2 (summer): 36–54.

Gintis, Herbert, and Tsuneo Ishikawa. 1987. "Wages, Work Discipline, and Unemployment." *Journal of Japanese and International Economies* 1: 195–228.

Green, Francis, Stephen Machin, and David Wilkenson. 1998. "The Meaning and

Determinants of Skill Shortages." *Oxford Bulletin of Economics and Statistics* 60. no. 2 (May): 165–188.

Heckman, James, Anne Layne-Farrar, and Petra Dodd. 1995. "Does Measured School Quality Really Matter? An Examination of the Earnings-Quality Relationship." Unpublished paper, University of Chicago and American Bar Foundation.

Huang, Min-Hsiung. 1997. Personal communication. University of Wisconsin, Madison.

Jencks, Christopher. 1979. *Who Gets Ahead?* New York: Basic Books.

Juhn, Chinhui, Kevin Murphy, and Brooks Pierce. 1993. "Wage Inequality and the Rise in Returns to Skill." *Journal of Political Economy* 101: 410–442.

Katz, Lawrence, and Kevin Murphy. 1992. "Changes in Relative Wages, 1963–1987: Supply and Demand Factors." *Quarterly Journal of Economics* 107, no. 1: 35–78.

Krueger, Alan. 1993. "How Computers Have Changed the Wage Structure." *Quarterly Journal of Economics* 108, no. 1: 33–60.

Moll, Peter. 1995. "Primary Schooling, Cognitive Skills and Wages in South Africa." Unpublished paper.

Parsons, Talcott. 1959. "The School Class as a Social System." *Harvard Educational Review* 29: 297–318.

Porter, James N. 1974. "Race, Socialization, and Mobility in Education and Early Occupational Attainment." *American Sociological Review* 39 (June): 303–316.

Raphael, Steven, and Dennis Toseland. 1995. "Skills, Skill Breadth, and Wage Determination." Unpublished paper, University of California, Berkeley.

Rosenzweig, Mark R. 1995. "Why Are There Returns to Schooling, Household Savings and Human Investment in Development?" *American Economics Association Papers and Proceedings* 85, no. 2 (May): 153–158.

Schultz, T. W. 1975. "The Value of the Ability to Deal with Disequilibria." *Journal of Economic Literature* 13: 872–876.

Sewell, William H., Archibald P. Haller, and George W. Ohlendorf. 1970. "The Education and Early Occupational Status Achievement Process." *American Sociological Review* 35, no. 6 (December): 1014–1027.

Shapiro, Carl, and Joseph Stiglitz. 1984. "Unemployment as a Worker Discipline Device." *American Economic Review* 74, no. 3 (June): 433–444.

Seven

A Reanalysis of *The Bell Curve*: Intelligence, Family Background, and Schooling*

SANDERS KORENMAN AND CHRISTOPHER WINSHIP

SINCE ITS PUBLICATION at the beginning of October 1994, *The Bell Curve* by the late Richard Herrnstein and Charles Murray has been discussed in more than one thousand articles in the public and academic press. Initial commentary focused primarily on the book's treatment of race. The majority of these essays were negative, with many denouncing the book as racist. More recent reviews (e.g., Heckman 1995; Hunt 1995; Goldberger and Manski 1995) have focused on the disjunction between the evidence presented and the strong conclusions drawn by the authors.

Herrnstein and Murray argue in *The Bell Curve* that intelligence is the most important determinant of social and economic success in present-day America. They support this conclusion with statistical analyses that suggest that a youth's intelligence (measured at ages fifteen to twenty-three by the Armed Forces Qualifications Test [AFQT]) is considerably more important than his or her parents' social and economic status (SES) in determining social and economic status in adulthood, the well-being of a woman's children, and the avoidance of antisocial behaviors. In their analyses, the effect of AFQT score is more than twice as large as the effect of parents' SES in predicting whether, at ages twenty-five to thirty-two, someone (1) is poor, (2) dropped out of high school, (3) is unemployed, (4) had a child out of wedlock, (5) had been on welfare, (6) had a low-birth-weight baby, or (7) had a child with low IQ scores.[1] In this chapter, we reanalyze Herrnstein and

* We gratefully acknowledge the financial support of the Russell Sage Foundation. We thank Charles Murray for providing a copy of the data used in *The Bell Curve* and for answering numerous questions about the analyses therein. We thank John Bound, Christopher Jencks, Larry Katz, Charles Murray, Doug Staiger and seminar participants at the NBER, the Harris School of Public Policy Studies at University of Chicago, RAND Corporation, UC Santa Barbara, University of Minnesota, and the University of Wisconsin, Madison, for their suggestions. We are responsible for any errors. An earlier version of this paper appeared as NBER Working Paper no. 5230, August 1995.

[1] See also Goldberger and Manski 1995, pp. 765–766, for a succinct summary of Herrnstein and Murray's conclusions regarding the importance of AFQT score relative to parents' SES.

Murray's data in order to assess whether their principal conclusions are warranted.

Our analyses address three questions. The first two are related to whether Herrnstein and Murray's estimates of the effects of AFQT score and parents' SES are biased by measurement error (especially in parents' SES) or by unmeasured or omitted parental SES or other family background characteristics. The third involves their treatment of schooling.

(1) Is Herrnstein and Murray's index of parents' socioeconomic status adequate for isolating the effects of AFQT score on economic and social success in adulthood? Ideally, in order to isolate the effects of AFQT on adult outcomes, one would like to hold constant—with perfect measures— all aspects of family background that influence both adult outcomes and AFQT scores. Herrnstein and Murray employ a narrowly conceived and poorly measured index of parental SES. As Heckman (1995) notes:

> The statistical methods used by Herrnstein and Murray are vulnerable to measurement error. It would be incredible if 15 to 23 years of environmental influences, including the nurturing of parents, the resources they spent on a child, their cultural environment, their interactions with their children and the influence of the larger community on the children could be summarized by a single measure of education, occupation and family income in one year. If environment is poorly measured but affects the test score—and there is solid evidence of environmental impacts on test scores—the Murray and Herrnstein finding that IQ has a stronger impact on socioeconomic outcomes than measured environment may simply arise from the poor quality of their measure of the environment. Their measure of IQ proxies the mismeasured environmental variable. (p. 21)

In the first part of our analysis we use comparisons of siblings in order to control more completely and broadly for differences in family background characteristics that may influence AFQT scores and adult outcomes. We estimate the effects of AFQT score net of family background by relating differences between siblings in adult outcomes to differences in their AFQT scores (controlling for age and gender). In effect, a youth's sibling(s) acts as his or her "control group." Incredible as it may seem, our sibling analyses suggest that, even though Herrnstein and Murray's parental SES index is poorly measured, it appears to be adequate for producing unbiased estimates of the effects of *AFQT score* on socioeconomic outcomes.

(2) Is Herrnstein and Murray's measure of parents' socioeconomic status adequate for estimating the effects of either parental SES or family socioeconomic background more broadly conceived on social and economic success in adulthood? Here there are two problems. (1) Random measurement error in the parental SES index will bias downward the estimated effects of parental SES. (2) Herrnstein and Murray's index of parents' SES may fail to capture important components of parents' SES and other environmental in-

fluences shared by family members (such as neighborhood and school characteristics). Regarding the first point, because Herrnstein and Murray's index of parental SES is highly correlated (0.55) with AFQT score, and because, as we shall see, parental SES is less reliably measured than is AFQT score, Herrnstein and Murray's estimates may substantially understate the effects of parents' SES and overstate the effects of AFQT score on adult outcomes. This is the classical errors-in-variables problem, and the potential for bias is easily demonstrated for a subset of Herrnstein and Murray's adult outcomes that are continuous (as opposed to binary) variables. For these outcomes, we adjust estimates for measurement error using a range of values for the reliability of AFQT score and parents' SES. We find evidence of substantial downward bias in their estimates of the effects of parents' SES.

Next, we investigate more directly the consequences of Herrnstein and Murray's narrow conceptualization of parents' SES. As reviewers have noted, Herrnstein and Murray's index of parental SES covers an important but limited range of socioeconomic attributes of the parental family. For example, Goldberger and Manski (1995, pp. 768–769) remark: "In practice they simply take it for granted that their SES index—a rather ad hoc concoction of information on parental attributes—adequately captures the socioeconomic environment within which a child grows up. This single variable carries the burden of expressing all aspects of the child's upbringing from family structure to sibling relationships to neighborhood characteristics."[2]

We find evidence that Herrnstein and Murray's index of parents' SES produces substantially misleading estimates of the effects of parental family socioeconomic status on social and economic outcomes of youths. Herrnstein and Murray's index of parents' SES fails to capture components of socioeconomic family background that are demonstrably important determinants of adult outcomes. We illustrate this point in two ways that together form upper and lower bounds for the effects of family socioeconomic background.

To obtain lower-bound estimates we first add to Herrnstein and Murray's models a variety of socioeconomic family background controls including indicators of parental family arrangement (e.g., single-parent family, stepparent) at age fourteen, family structure (e.g., number of siblings), urban/rural residence at age fourteen, as well as other aspects of the home environment at age fourteen. We combine the effects of Herrnstein and Murray's parental SES index with the effects of this richer set of socioeconomic background controls to form a single standardized composite effect of family socioeconomic background. The composite effect is dramatically larger than the effect of parental SES alone, and is sometimes larger than the effect of

---

[2] A similar point is raised by Fischer et al. (1996). They also emphasize the importance of race and gender in the determination of social and economic status in adulthood.

AFQT score. Nonetheless, these composite effects are lower bounds for the effects of family socioeconomic background because they are based on the necessarily limited set of imperfectly measured family background characteristics available in the National Longitudinal Study of Youth.

Our upper-bound estimates of the effects of family socioeconomic background are based on analyses of siblings. These estimates are upper bounds because they are derived under the assumption that anything common to siblings other than AFQT score, age, and gender is attributable to family background. These residual effects of family background are far larger than Herrnstein and Murray's estimated effects of parental SES, and are at times two to four times as large as the effects of AFQT score.

(3) Are Herrnstein and Murray's estimates of the effects of AFQT score sensitive to their treatment of education? Does schooling have an effect on different outcomes, controlling for AFQT score? For a variety of reasons, Herrnstein and Murray were reluctant to include education controls in their models of various outcomes (pp. 124–125). Herrnstein and Murray do estimate their models for educationally homogenous subsamples (i.e., high school graduates; college graduates). Nonetheless, it is difficult to get a sense from their analyses either of the sensitivity of the effects of AFQT to the inclusion of education controls, or, perhaps more important, of the size of the schooling effects, controlling for AFQT score. It may be important to examine more carefully the role of education, however, given the potential for public policy to change educational attainment and thus, possibly, individual outcomes.

In our analyses we find that for many outcomes the effects of AFQT are substantially reduced by the inclusion of education controls. Furthermore, for many outcomes the standardized effect of schooling is larger than the effect of AFQT. This suggests that even if Herrnstein and Murray are correct that AFQT is largely immutable and unaffected by schooling, attempts to raise educational attainment may nonetheless be important, due to its positive partial effect on a variety of social and economic outcomes.

Outline of *The Bell Curve*

The Bell Curve is divided into four sections. In part one Herrnstein and Murray argue that America is becoming increasingly dominated by a cognitive elite. They discuss the increasing selectivity of elite universities and colleges and the rising educational credentials of top managers. In part two they present an extensive set of original analyses aimed at demonstrating that intelligence is the principal determinant of a variety of social and economic outcomes. We are concerned with this portion of the book. The third section examines previous work on racial differences in intelligence and presents new analyses of the importance of AFQT score as a determinant of different outcomes across racial/ethnic groups. The final section of the book discusses a variety of policy issues, most notably affirmative action.

Much of *The Bell Curve* reviews and interprets the analyses and data of others. The exceptions are the chapters in section II, and chapters 14 and 16 of section III, in which Herrnstein and Murray present original analyses of the National Longitudinal Survey of Youth.

The analysis methods used by Herrnstein and Murray are those commonly employed in the social sciences, and their approach to the data is straightforward and clearly explained.[3] As noted, Herrnstein and Murray's principal conclusion is that for all racial and ethnic groups and across a variety of social and economic outcomes, an individual's AFQT score is a more important determinant than is the social and economic status of his parents.

Methods and Data

The original analyses in *The Bell Curve* all use the Department of Labor's National Longitudinal Survey of Youth (NLSY). The NLSY is an ongoing longitudinal study of approximately 12,000 youths aged fourteen to twenty-one as of January 1, 1979 (Center for Human Resource Research 1994).

In section one of their book, Herrnstein and Murray restrict their analyses to whites. In chapter 14 and appendix 6 they repeat these analyses for blacks and Latinos. In our analyses, we estimate models for the entire sample and enter controls for race, ethnicity, and sex. Most of the time we have done so to ensure that we had the largest sample possible. As explained below, sample size becomes an important concern in analyses of sibling differences. We have also repeated the analyses for black, Latino, and white subsamples for continuous outcomes (income, wages, and years of schooling) where sample sizes are sufficient to permit analysis of sibling differences. The results of these analyses, which we present in appendix A, parallel those for the full sample.

Table 7.1 provides a description of the outcome variables and samples from *The Bell Curve* that we have used in our analysis. Our approach to the analysis is to use Herrnstein and Murray's data (supplied to us by Murray) and estimate models analogous to their models. We then report alternative estimates based on different assumptions or modeling strategies. Because we present some models that include controls for years of schooling completed

---

[3] They use linear and logit regression, and estimate the effects of AFQT score and parental SES on different outcomes when age is controlled. In models for some outcomes they include one additional control variable or restrict the analysis sample as a way to "control" for one important characteristic (e.g., they study a sample of poor mothers in their analyses of welfare use; see pp. 122–125 for a description of their modeling strategy).

TABLE 7.1

Unweighted Sample Means, (SDs), [Analysis Sample Sizes], and Descriptions of
Analysis Variables

	Mean (SD) [Obs]	Descriptions of Variables and Sample
Family income (1990$) in 1989	34,345 (27,080) 7,977	Total net family income in 1989, 1990 dollars. Excludes persons not working because of school in 1989 or 1990.
In poverty in 1989	0.15 (0.36) 7,977	Total net family income below U.S. Census poverty line. Excludes persons not working because of school in 1989 or 1990.
Annual earnings (1990$) in 1989	24,225 (16,083) 4,974	Year-round workers
Years of schooling completed 1990 (z-score)	−0.1 (1.0) 9,885	
HS dropout	0.18 (0.39) 8,718	Did not get a HS diploma, including those who later earned a GED
BA degree	0.18 (0.38) 9,588	Obtained a bachelor's degree or higher. Excludes persons enrolled as undergraduates in 1990.
High-IQ occupation	0.04 (0.20) 7,944	Excludes persons enrolled in college or graduate school in 1990
Out of LF 1+ mos. in 1989, men	0.15 (0.36) 4,144	
Unemployed 1+ mos. in 1989, men	0.10 (0.30) 3,225	Excludes persons not working because of school in 1989 or 1990
Married by age 30	0.72 (0.45) 4,221	Excludes persons under 30 at 1990 interview (H&M exclude age as a control)
Divorced, first 5 years of marriage	0.20 (0.40) 4,684	
Middle-class values index	0.37 (0.48) 7,692	Men: HS grad + in LF full year + never in jail + married to first wife; Women: HS grad + no out-

(*table continues*)

TABLE 7.1 (*continued*)

	Mean (SD) [Obs]	Descriptions of Variables and Sample
		of-wedlock births + never in jail + married to first husband. Excludes single persons who met other conditions and men who were disabled or enrolled in school.
Ever interviewed in jail, men	0.07 (0.25) 4,809	
CHILD OUTCOMES, FIRSTBORN CHILDREN		
"Illegitimate" (out-of-wedlock) birth	0.36 (0.48) 3,448	
Early AFDC use	0.24 (0.43) 2,683	Mothers poor in year prior to birth
Mother smoked during pregnancy	0.30 (0.46) 3,333	
Low birth weight	0.06 (0.24) 3,325	Below 5.5 pounds. Excludes LBW-premature babies whose weight was appropriate for gestational age.
Ever in foster or relative care?	0.05 (0.23) 3,475	Ever lived in foster care or with nonparental relatives
CHILD OUTCOMES, ALL CHILDREN[a]		
HOME score (percentiles)	46.2 (25.9) 6,711	Home Observation for Measurement of the Environment (short form). Test year and age of child entered as controls.
Motor and social development index (percentiles)	51.1 (26.7) 4,246	Children aged 0–4. Test year and age of child entered as controls.
PPVT (standardized score)	85.9 (20.7) 4,707	Peabody Picture Vocabulary Test. Receptive vocabulary for standard American English. Test year and age of child entered as controls.

(table continues)

TABLE 7.1 (*continued*)

	Mean (SD) [Obs]	Descriptions of Variables and Sample
PPVT, 6+ year-olds (standardized score)	87.5 (16.9) 1,784	Sample restricted to children age 6 years and over.
Behavior problems index (standardized score)	107.5 (13.2) 4,645	Children aged 4–12. Maternal reports of behavior problems. Test year and age of child entered as controls. Higher score indicates more problems.

Source: Herrnstein and Murray 1994, p. 646 and elsewhere.

Note: In addition to sample restrictions listed in the table, all samples are restricted to observations with non-missing values for: AFQT score, parents' SES score, age, and 1990 education.

[a]If an assessment (or test score) is available for a given child in more than one year (1986, 1988, or 1990), then the outcome is the average (across years) of the assessments for that child.

as of 1990, we have restricted the samples to respondents who have valid information on Herrnstein and Murray's (standardized) schooling attainment variable. This restriction results in the loss of about 1 percent of the sample.

In 1980 the ASVAB (Armed Services Vocational Aptitude Battery) was administered to nearly the entire sample so that the Department of Defense could renorm the tests based on a national population. The AFQT score Herrnstein and Murray use as their measure of IQ is a weighted average of four of the ten components of the ASVAB. They provide arguments and evidence that their measure is one of the best available for general intelligence. We leave discussion and evaluation of this claim to future work in which we intend to take up issues of endogenous determination of AFQT scores (see also Neal and Johnson 1995; Rogers and Spriggs 1995; Hunt 1995; Winship and Korenman 1997 and forthcoming).

The components of AFQT with their factor loadings are (Herrnstein and Murray 1994, p. 583): Word Knowledge (.87), Paragraph Comprehension (.81), Arithmetic Reasoning (.87), and Mathematical Knowledge (.82). Herrnstein and Murray do not discuss whether, net of their measure, other components of the ASVAB might affect the different adult outcomes. For example, Heckman (1995) notes that the numerical operations component is a strong predictor of labor-market outcomes. Although the construction and interpretation of the AFQT score is an important issue, it is one that we do not explore.

Herrnstein and Murray's measure of parental social and economic status is a combination of the respondent's father's and mother's education, occupation of parents or other adults in the household (the highest revised Duncan

Index score among the two parents or adults), and the natural log of income of the parental family (the average of available years, 1978 and 1979, for youths who report income of the parental household). The components of SES are each standardized to have variance one. A simple average of the available standardized measures is taken in order to create the SES index. The index is standardized to have variance one.

Omitted Variable Bias in the Effects of AFQT Score: Family Fixed-Effect Estimates

Many aspects of the family socioeconomic environment could conceivably be included in Herrnstein and Murray's models because they may influence AFQT score at age fifteen to twenty-three and adult outcomes, and may not be captured adequately by the parental SES index. For example, growing up in a single-parent family has been linked to a variety of social and economic disadvantages (e.g., Murray 1984; Garfinkel and McLanahan 1986). The effects of IQ score estimated by Herrnstein and Murray may be exaggerated (biased upward) by omitted variables. One approach to this problem is to attempt to measure and include in the models additional family background variables. We pursue this strategy below.[4]

Our initial approach is to carry out analyses of siblings. We compare the effect on various outcomes of differences in AFQT scores between siblings. In the case of continuous outcomes (dependent variables), fixed-effect analysis amounts to entering a dummy variable for each family of origin. For dichotomous (binary) outcomes, we estimate fixed-effect logit models for the oldest pair of siblings from each baseline household. The estimation of fixed-effects logit models necessarily involves a substantial reduction in sample sizes because only sibling pairs that have different values for an outcome (e.g., one graduated from high school and the other did not) contribute to the likelihood function (Chamberlain 1980).

The fixed-effect analyses correct for bias due to both measurement error in the parental SES index and omitted family characteristics (i.e., characteristics that are common to siblings). This is a broad notion of family background that includes, for example, characteristics of the neighborhood and the surrounding geographic area (Griliches 1979). The advantage of this

---

[4] Herrnstein and Murray (1994, p. 123) argue that adding a variety of additional family background variables may be problematic if these variables are "intervening" variables (i.e., endogenous) in the relationship between AFQT score and the outcomes they studied. However, we add variables that describe in more detail the socioeconomic status of the family. A youth's intelligence presumably does not determine the number of siblings he or she has, or the marital status of his or her parents. More important, the effects of AFQT score are not sensitive to the inclusion of additional family background controls in the models, even though the coefficients of the family background variables are often significant.

method is that, to the extent that siblings share identical family backgrounds, the fixed-effect approach provides a way of fully controlling (without measurement error) all aspects of family background. The assumption that siblings have identical family backgrounds is most reasonable when they are close in age.

Table 7.2 presents OLS and logit estimates along with fixed-effects estimates for twenty-six outcomes studied by Herrnstein and Murray. For each outcome, we present models that both include and exclude education controls. In this section of the chapter, we discuss results of models that exclude education controls, and we postpone discussion of models that include education controls to a later section of the chapter.[5]

In the first three columns of the table we present cross-section results for the full sample. These are analogous to (and are very similar to) the models presented by Herrnstein and Murray in *The Bell Curve*. In the fourth through sixth columns we repeat the cross-section analyses for the pooled subsample of siblings in the NLSY. The purpose of these analyses is to gauge the representativeness of the siblings subsample that we use for analyses of sibling differences. In general, cross-section results for the sibling subsample are similar to those for the full sample. As a result, we can be confident that differences we might find between cross-section and fixed-effects estimates are not an artifact of the use of a different sample (the sibling subsample of NLSY respondents).

In the final two columns of the table we present results from family fixed-effect (sibling difference) analyses. With a few exceptions, the fixed-effects estimates for AFQT are remarkably similar to the standard OLS and logit estimates. The exceptions, where the effect of AFQT is reduced, are family

---

[5] Our treatment of the outcomes for children of NLSY sample women requires additional explanation. Our analyses of outcomes for firstborn children are analogous to Herrnstein and Murray's. However, in our analyses of outcomes for samples that (potentially) include multiple children per woman, we study continuous versions of the binary outcomes studied by Herrnstein and Murray. For example, Herrnstein and Murray study a binary variable that indicates whether or not a child's PPVT score was in the bottom decile for his/her age, whereas we study the (continuous) standardized and age-adjusted PPVT score. The PPVT-R (revised) measures receptive vocabulary for Standard American English for children age three and older. It consists of 175 vocabulary items. Children point to one of four pictures that best describes a word's meaning. The normal percentile score is based on a national norm. The PPVT-R has been found highly correlated with other childhood intelligence tests such as Weschler and Binet, and with subsequent achievement in school (Baker and Mott 1989). Qualitatively, our cross-section results are the same as theirs—higher maternal AFQT score is associated with higher child test score, controlling for parents' SES (i.e., maternal grandparents' SES). The use of continuous outcomes greatly facilitates family fixed-effects analysis and enables us to use all available scores for all children of women included in a given analysis. For tests or assessments that were administered at more than one age for a given child, we average the assessment scores available for each child, and we average the child's ages at assessment. We adjust standard errors for nonindependence among child siblings and among first cousins (i.e., children whose mothers are sisters).

TABLE 7.2

Estimated Effects from Models of Socioeconomic Status and Child Development, All Races Combined

	OLS or Logit Coefficients (SEs)							
	Full Sample[a]			Siblings XSEC[a]			Siblings FE[b]	
	zAFQT	zSES	zED	zAFQT	zSES	zED	zAFQT	zED
Family income	6,975	4,580		7,296	4,487		5,558	
(1990$) in 1989	(354)	(324)		(622)	(577)		(975)	
	4,134	3,627	4,612	4,607	3,717	4,422	3,610	4,305
	(421)	(330)	(379)	(733)	(575)	(699)	(1044)	(963)
Number of obs.		7,977			3,316		3,316	
In poverty in 1989	−0.95	−0.33		−0.99	−0.31		−0.78	
	(.05)	(.04)		(.08)	(.07)		(.17)	
	−0.67	−0.25	0.50	−0.68	−0.23	−0.59	−0.60	−0.48
	(.06)	(.04)	(.05)	(.09)	(.07)	(.09)	(.18)	(.17)
Number of obs.		7,977			2,926		284	
Annual earnings	4,866	1,531		5,548	1,169		5,317	
(1990$), YR work-	(270)	(246)		(603)	(459)		(852)	
ers, in 1989	3,040	910	3,092	3,879	803	2,667	4,023	2,341
	(291)	(240)	(300)	(617)	(451)	(592)	(821)	(856)
Number of obs.		4,974			1,579		1,579	
Yrs. schooling com-	0.62	0.20		0.59	0.18		0.45	
pleted (z-score)	(.01)	(.01)		(.02)	(.02)		(.02)	
Number of obs.		9,885			4,758		4,578	
HS dropout	−1.82	−0.48		−1.75	−0.48		−1.63	
	(.06)	(.04)		(.10)	(.07)		(.26)	
Number of obs.		8,739			3,468		263	
BA degree	1.76	0.70		1.76	0.66		1.87	
	(.06)	(.05)		(.09)	(.08)		(.23)	
Number of obs.		9,588			3,884		309	
High-IQ occ.	1.36	0.39		1.39	0.45		1.72	
	(.08)	(.07)		(.14)	(.11)		(.43)	
	0.78	0.14	1.12	0.83	0.23	1.07	1.15	0.92
	(.09)	(.07)	(.08)	(.17)	(.10)	(.15)	(.50)	(.37)
Number of obs.		7,944			2,946		94	
Out of LF 1+ mos.	−0.39	−0.02		−0.34	−0.17		−0.30	
in 1989, men	(.06)	(.05)		(.10)	(.11)		(.19)	
	−0.33	−0.01	−0.10	−0.23	−0.13	−0.19	−0.18	−0.26
	(.06)	(.06)	(.06)	(.12)	(.11)	(.12)	(.22)	(.25)
Number of obs.		4,144			1,096		132	
Unemployed 1+	−0.44	−0.09		−0.52	−0.02		−0.47	
mos. in 1989, men	(.07)	(.07)		(.14)	(.15)		(.29)	

(*table continues*)

TABLE 7.2 (*continued*)

	OLS or Logit Coefficients (SEs)							
	Full Sample[a]			Siblings XSEC[a]			Siblings FE[b]	
	zAFQT	zSES	zED	zAFQT	zSES	zED	zAFQT	zED
	−0.33	−0.05	−0.19	−0.44	0.01	−0.15	−0.35	−0.23
	(.08)	(.07)	(.09)	(.16)	(.16)	(.19)	(.32)	(.29)
Number of obs.		3,225			720		65	
Married by age 30	−0.04	−0.07		0.13	−0.10		0.20	
	(.05)	(.04)		(.11)	(.10)		(.18)	
	0.24	.01	−0.42	0.27	−0.07	−0.24	0.39	−0.33
	(.06)	(.04)	(.05)	(.14)	(.10)	(.12)	(.24)	(.21)
Number of obs.		4,221			664		136	
Divorced, first 5	−0.22	0.18		−0.26	0.28		−0.53	
years of marriage	(.05)	(.05)		(.12)	(.10)		(.21)	
	−0.19	0.19	−0.05	−0.22	0.29	−0.08	−0.47	−0.11
	(.06)	(.05)	(.05)	(.13)	(.11)	(.13)	(.24)	(.24)
Number of obs.		4,684			1,046		159	
Middle class values	0.75	0.23		0.84	0.20		0.67	
index	(.04)	(.03)		(.07)	(.06)		(.13)	
	0.27	0.09	0.87	0.28	0.06	1.02	0.31	0.77
	(.04)	(.04)	(.04)	(.08)	(.06)	(.08)	(.14)	(.15)
Number of obs.		7,692			2,652		430	
Ever interviewed in	−0.91	−0.06		−0.94	0.16		−0.91	
jail, men	(.08)	(.07)		(.13)	(.13)		(.26)	
	−0.76	−0.01	−0.29	−0.76	0.21	−0.32	−0.82	−0.16
	(.09)	(.07)	(.07)	(.15)	(.14)	(.14)	(.33)	(.31)
Number of obs.		4,809			1,422		72	
CHILD OUTCOMES, FIRSTBORN CHILDREN								
"Illegitimate" (out-	−0.46	−0.22		−0.65	−0.02		−0.10	
of-wedlock) birth	(.06)	(.05)		(.18)	(.15)		(.36)	
	−0.31	−0.19	−0.22	−0.54	0.01	−0.19	−0.06	−0.19
	(.08)	(.06)	(.06)	(0.20)	(.15)	(.16)	(.40)	(.38)
Number of obs.		3,448			658		91	
Early AFDC use	−0.54	−0.19		−0.77	−0.13		−0.84	
	(.08)	(.06)		(.18)	(.15)		(.33)	
	−0.38	−0.15	−0.28	−0.62	−0.11	−0.30	−0.72	−0.34
	(.09)	(.06)	(.08)	(.19)	(.15)	(.18)	(.35)	(.37)
Number of obs.		2,683			510		75	
Mother smoked	−0.52	−0.01		−0.94	0.29		−0.90	
during pregnancy	(.06)	(.05)		(.16)	(.14)		(.31)	
	−0.17	0.11	−0.64	−0.53	0.44	−0.90	−0.49	−0.86
	(.07)	(.05)	(.06)	(.18)	(.14)	(.20)	(.34)	(.41)
Number of obs.		3,333			624		85	

(*table continues*)

TABLE 7.2 (*continued*)

	OLS or Logit Coefficients (SEs)							
	Full Sample[a]			Siblings XSEC[a]			Siblings FE[b]	
	zAFQT	zSES	zED	zAFQT	zSES	zED	zAFQT	zED
Low birth weight	−0.35	−0.08		−0.26	−.13		0.46	
	(0.10)	(.09)		(.23)	(.22)		(.53)	
	−0.35	−0.08	−0.00	−0.23	−0.12	−0.06	0.70	−.36
	(.13)	(.09)	(.10)	(.24)	(.22)	(.22)	(.74)	(.71)
Number of obs.		3,325			598		37	
Ever in foster or	−0.42	−0.22		−0.71	0.15		−0.84	
relative care?	(.10)	(.09)		(.26)	(.23)		(.50)	
	−0.27	−0.23	−0.24	−0.69	0.16	−0.04	−0.54	−0.65
	(.13)	(.07)	(.11)	(.28)	(.23)	(.25)	(.56)	(.44)
Number of obs.		3,475			662		39	
CHILD OUTCOMES, ALL CHILDREN[c]								
HOME score	6.9	4.4		9.2	3.9		3.6	
(percentiles)	(0.5)	(0.5)		(1.2)	(1.0)		(1.3)	
	4.2	3.7	4.8	6.1	3.0	6.3	2.7	2.5
	(0.6)	(0.5)	(0.6)	(1.4)	(1.0)	(1.4)	(1.3)	(1.3)
Number of obs.		6,711			1,342		1,342	
Motor & social de-	2.2	1.9		2.8	1.1		−1.1	
velopment index	(0.6)	(0.5)		(1.3)	(1.3)		(1.9)	
(percentiles)	1.1	1.6	2.0	1.3	0.7	2.8	−2.0	2.9
	(0.8)	(0.5)	(0.7)	(1.6)	(1.2)	(1.7)	(1.9)	(2.2)
Number of obs.		4,101			819		819	
PPVT (standardized	6.8	3.7		5.8	4.0		0.88	
score)	(0.5)	(0.4)		(1.2)	(1.0)		(1.4)	
	5.2	3.3	3.1	5.2	3.7	1.4	1.4	−2.1
	(0.6)	(0.4)	(0.5)	(1.4)	(1.1)	(1.4)	(1.6)	(1.6)
Number of obs.		4,607			794		794	
PPVT, 6+ year	6.8	2.6		9.0	2.3		6.8	
olds (standardized	(0.6)	(0.5)		(1.9)	(1.7)		(2.2)	
score)	5.1	2.1	3.1	8.4	2.1	0.9	8.3	−3.3
	(0.7)	(0.5)	(0.7)	(2.1)	(1.7)	(1.8)	(2.5)	(2.7)
Number of obs.		1,784			139		139	
Behavior problems	−1.6	−0.5		−2.2	0.2		−1.4	
index (standardized	(0.4)	(0.3)		(0.8)	(0.8)		(1.2)	
score; higher =	−1.4	−0.5	−0.4	−1.8	0.4	−1.0	−0.9	−1.8
more problems)	(0.4)	(0.3)	(0.4)	(0.9)	(0.8)	(1.0)	(1.2)	(1.1)
Number of obs.		4,101			819		819	

Notes: See table 7.1 for a description of dependent variables and samples.

XSEC: cross-section; FE: fixed-effects; YR: year-round; PPVT: Peabody Picture Vocabulary Test; HOME: Home Observation for Measurement of the Environment (short form).

(*table continues*)

income ($7,296 in column 4, versus $5,558 in column 7), poverty ($-.99$ versus $-.78$), years of school completed (.59 versus .45), out-of-wedlock birth ($-.65$ versus $-.10$), HOME (Home Observation for Measurement of the Environment) score (9.2 versus 3.6), motor and social development (2.8 versus -1.1), PPVT (Peabody Picture Vocabulary Test) score (5.8 versus 0.8), PPVT for children older than six (9.0 versus 6.8), and the Behavior Problems Index (-2.2 versus -1.4). Much of reduction in the size of the effects of AFQT most likely reflects the exacerbation of attenuation bias (due to measurement error) when data are differenced as compared to when they are entered in levels. For example, adjusting for measurement error bias in fixed-effects estimates raises the estimated effects of AFQT score from 5,558 to 6,558 for family income, and from 5,317 to 6,228 for annual earnings (see appendix C; see also section on measurement error, below). However, it is unlikely that attenuation bias alone could explain the reduction in the AFQT effects in several of the outcomes for children.[6]

The fixed-effect estimator is a powerful method of controlling for family background in that it captures all components that are common to siblings. It

TABLE 7.2 (*continued*)

[a]Models contain controls for age (z-score) and, where appropriate, dummy variables for gender, race/ethnicity (3 dummy variables), year and child's age at the time of assessment. Standard errors are corrected for non-independence of observations among youths from the same baseline household. Thus, unlike Herrnstein and Murray, we combine races and control for race (and gender) of youth, and we do not use sampling weights.

[b]Sibling fixed-effects models for continuous dependent variables (outcomes) are sibling differences estimated by including in the models a dummy variable for each family of origin. For dichotomous outcomes, samples used to conduct sibling cross-section and fixed-effects analyses are restricted to the oldest sibling pair in each household for which necessary data are available. The number of observations that enter fixed-effects logit analyses is relatively small because a sibling pair enters the likelihood function only if outcome values differ (e.g., one graduated from high school and one did not).

[c]Models for "all children" are based on average (across years) of values of outcomes and control variables for children who were assessed in more than one year. In fixed-effects models for children (i.e., first-cousin differences), standard errors are corrected for non-independence of observations among (child) siblings.

[6] Appendix A presents results from analyses of education, wages, and income for subsamples of blacks, Latinos, and whites. The estimates are broadly consistent with those reported in table 8.2 for the full sample. However, figures in the table indicate greater family background heterogeneity bias for blacks than whites (i.e., fixed-effects estimates are smaller relative to cross-section estimates for blacks). However, bias from measurement error (attenuation bias) is greater in fixed-effects analyses than in cross-section analyses, and is probably more severe for blacks in the sample. The reliability of differences in test scores is equal to $(R - C)/(1 - C)$, where R is the reliability of the test score and C is the intrafamily correlation in test scores. The intrafamily correlation in AFQT is higher for whites than blacks in the sample, and therefore, given R, the reliability is lower for blacks. When we corrected the fixed-effects estimates for reliability of AFQT score using a value of 0.95 for R and values of C that vary by race, there was no longer any evidence of greater heterogeneity bias for blacks. We do not present these results because a proper reliability correction would require separate estimates of R for blacks, whites, and Latinos. We are not aware of the existence of such estimates.

is surprising that for many outcomes the fixed-effect estimates for AFQT are similar to the standard estimates. However, Herrnstein and Murray's measure of SES is highly loaded on father's and mother's education. A reasonable conjecture is that parents' education might capture well the component of family background most highly correlated with AFQT and thus serve as an adequate control for family background in estimating the effects of AFQT. If so, the fixed-effect estimates of AFQT would not differ greatly from the standard estimates. The one set of outcomes where the fixed-effect estimates of AFQT are substantially smaller than the cross-section estimates is for outcomes involving children. Here AFQT may be proxying other dimensions of the home environment.

Biases in the Effects of Herrnstein and Murray's Index of Parents' SES: Measurement Error

Above we noted that Herrnstein and Murray's parental SES index and the AFQT score are highly correlated. As a result, separating the effects of these two variables may be difficult and is likely to be sensitive to model specification and other assumptions.

AFQT score is potentially more comprehensive than their SES measure. First, the AFQT score is based on four separate tests, each of which is composed of a large number of questions, whereas SES is based on only the answers to four questions about parental status. Furthermore, Murray (personal communication) reports that the reliability of their four component measure of AFQT is 0.95, indicating that the measure is highly reliable. This figure is consistent with Bock and Moore's comment (1986, p. 196) that "various composites such as the AFQT composite . . . have reliabilities in excess of 0.90." Herrnstein and Murray also report that SES has a reliability of 0.76 (p. 574). This reliability is based on Cronbach's Alpha, however, which is an appropriate measure of reliability under the assumption that one has a set of measures of a single underlying variable. In the case of SES this assumption may not be defensible. Parents' education, the occupation of the head of the household, and parents' income are unlikely to measure a single underlying concept. Rather, we tend to think of these separate variables as combining to determine SES.

The true reliability of Herrnstein and Murray's SES measure is unknown. Ignorance about the reliability of SES does not mean, however, that we should ignore the potential bias induced by measurement error in the estimated effects of SES or AFQT. Because of high correlation between AFQT and SES, measurement error bias in the SES coefficient will be translated to the AFQT coefficient. At present we have discovered no way of obtaining an independent estimate of the reliability of Herrnstein and Murray's SES measure. Jencks et al. (1979) review a number of studies with different estimated reliabilities for the components of SES. From these estimates, a reliability of .85 for SES would seem to be conservative if we are concerned with measuring SES in a single year only. If measured SES changes from year to year during childhood, as it surely does, this reliability estimate is most likely too high if we are after a more permanent concept. In fact, even the .76 reliability reported by Herrnstein and Murray may be too high.

There is reason to suspect that the three components of Herrnstein and Murray's SES index are measured with considerable error. There is also evidence that errors in these variables can have important consequences for research results. Short-term measures of income, such as that used by Herrnstein and Murray, can lead to substantial understatements of the correlation between parents' income, on the one hand, and the income of adult children (Solon 1992; Zimmerman 1992), child health (Miller and Korenman 1994), and child development (Korenman, Miller, and Sjaastad 1995), on the other. The reporting and classification of occupations is another source of error (Jencks et al. 1979). And although years of schooling are reliably reported, measurement error in reported schooling can affect estimates of the returns to schooling (Ashenfelter and Krueger 1994).

Measurement error in independent variables leads to potentially severely biased and inconsistent estimates of regression parameters. Simple techniques are available to correct for measurement error in linear regression models when the measurement error is purely random. Some popular computer programs such as STATA (Stata Corporation 1993), which we have used for most of our analyses, contain routines for carrying out this correction.

Most of the models estimated by Herrnstein and Murray involve logit analyses. The correction of measurement error in logit analysis is an area of current research. Carroll, Ruppert, and Stefanski (1995) provide a detailed discussion. At present no software is available for the general situation for carrying out these corrections. Therefore, at this time we are able to examine the effects of measurement error only in the three cases where the dependent variable is continuous.

Table 7.3 reports estimates of the effects of AFQT and SES on family income, annual earnings, and education. We have assumed a reliability of .95 for AFQT and reliabilities of .85 or .76 for SES. (We postpone to a later section discussion of the effects of reliability corrections on estimates from models that include education controls.)

As one would expect, given the lower reliabilities for SES than AFQT, correcting for measurement error increases the size of the effect of SES relative to that of AFQT. In the case of income, when a reliability ratio of 0.76 is assumed for SES, SES has a slightly larger effect ($7,036) than AFQT ($6,047). When measurement error is corrected in the earnings equa-

TABLE 7.3
Effects of Reliability Corrections on Coefficient Estimates

	Coefficients (SEs)			Reliability Ratios[a]		
	zAFQT	zSES	zED	zAFQT	zSES	zED
1. Family income, 1989	6,977	4,578		1.00	1.00	
	(353)	(324)				
	6,825	5,675		0.95	0.85	
	(419)	(436)				
	6,047	7,036		0.95	0.76	
	(457)	(538)				
	4,135	3,623	4,613	1.00	1.00	1.00
	(421)	(330)	(379)			
	3,583	4,458	5,072	0.95	0.85	0.90
	(529)	(453)	(408)			
	3,189	5,634	4,713	0.95	0.76	0.90
	(541)	(571)	(514)			
2. Annual earnings, 1989,	4,866	1,531		1.00	1.00	
YR workers	(262)	(239)				
	5,072	1,762		0.95	0.85	
	(306)	(317)				
	4,855	2,162		0.95	0.76	
	(330)	(389)				
	3,040	910	3,092	1.00	1.00	1.00
	(306)	(243)	(279)			
	2,917	942	3,514	0.95	0.85	0.90
	(379)	(328)	(363)			
	2,842	1,175	3,445	0.95	0.76	0.90
	(386)	(409)	(371)			
3. Annual earnings, 1989,	4,433	2,059		1.00	1.00	
males, YR workers	(379)	(361)				
	4,515	2,469		0.95	0.85	
	(447)	(484)				
	4,199	3,052		0.95	0.76	
	(488)	(598)				
	2,798	1,450	2,790	1.00	1.00	1.00
	(451)	(370)	(426)			
	2,630	1,674	3,111	0.95	0.85	0.90
	(567)	(508)	(569)			
	2,499	2,114	2,966	0.95	0.76	0.90
	(578)	(642)	(584)			
4. Education, 1990 (z-score)	0.62	0.20		1.00	1.00	
	0.64	0.24		0.95	0.85	

(*table continues*)

TABLE 7.3 (*continued*)

| | Coefficients (SEs) | | | Reliability Ratios[a] | | |
	zAFQT	zSES	zED	zAFQT	zSES	zED
	(.01)	(.01)				
	0.61	0.29		0.95	0.76	

Notes: Models also include controls for race/ethnicity (3 dummy variables), age, and, where appropriate, gender. Sample sizes are, for outcomes (1) to (4): (1) 7,978 (2) 4,974 (3) 2,776 (4) 9,886.

[a]Reliability ratios are ratios of signal variance to total variance. The values for reliability of zAFQT are from Murray (personal communication) and Bock and Moore (1986). Reliability ratios for zSES are taken from Herrnstein and Murray (1994) and Jencks et al. (1979) (see text for discussion). The reliability ratio for education is the average of two values reported by Ashenfelter and Krueger (1994) based on their analyses of twins.

tions for all year-round workers (males and females, controlling for sex), the effect of SES increases (to $2,162, assuming a reliability ratio of 0.76) although it is still considerably smaller than the effect of AFQT ($4,855). When the analysis is restricted to men (part 3 of table 7.3) and we assume a reliability of 0.76 for SES, its effect ($3,052) begins to approach that of AFQT ($4,199).

When years of schooling is the dependent variable, correcting for measurement error increases the effect of SES (from .20 to .24 and .29), but it is still considerably smaller than that of AFQT (.62, .64, and .61).

Biases in the Effects of Parents' SES: Additional Family Background Characteristics

Herrnstein and Murray's SES index may not capture all relevant aspects of family socioeconomic background. Therefore, we examine the effects of controlling for several additional family characteristics: family arrangement when the respondent was fourteen years old (two-parent, parent and stepparent, single-parent, other); whether, at age fourteen: the respondent lived in an urban area; the respondent's family had a library card, received magazines regularly, and received newspapers regularly; whether an adult female in the household worked outside the home; the number of siblings of the respondent (dummy variables for none, two, three, and four or more); the age of the respondent's mother at the time of the respondent's birth (entered as a quadratic); whether the respondent is the eldest child in the family; and whether the respondent was born outside the United States. Surely, there are other important parental SES and family background components omitted.

Coefficients and standard errors for the full models are presented in appendix B. The results are summarized in table 7.4. In the first two columns

TABLE 7.4

Summary of Effects from Models of Socioeconomic Status and Child Development, with and without Detailed Family Background Controls

	OLS or Logit Coefficients (SEs)				Composite Effects (Absolute Values)	
	Herrnstein and Murray Controls[a]		Add Detailed FB Controls[b]			Race + FB + SES
					FB + SES	
	zAFQT	zSES	zAFQT	zSES		
Family income (1990 $) in 1989	6,975 (354)	4,580 (324)	6,516 (383)	3,615 (410)	6,157	6,108
In poverty in 1989	−0.95 (.05)	−0.33 (.04)	−0.93 (.05)	−0.24 (.05)	0.54	0.57
Annual earnings (1990 $), YR workers, in 1989	4,866 (270)	1,531 (246)	4,669 (271)	1,285 (279)	3,007	3,287
Yrs. schooling completed (z-score)	0.62 (.01)	0.20 (.01)	0.58 (.01)	0.18 (.01)	0.27	0.29
HS dropout	−1.82 (.06)	−0.48 (.04)	−1.76 (.06)	−0.40 (.05)	0.80	0.87
BA degree	1.76 (.06)	0.70 (.05)	1.72 (.06)	0.67 (.05)	0.90	0.89
High-IQ occ.	1.36 (.08)	0.39 (.07)	1.34 (.08)	0.30 (.08)	0.65	0.68
Out of LF 1+ mos. in 1989, men	−0.39 (.06)	0.02 (.05)	−0.40 (.06)	0.00 (.06)	0.43	0.45
Unemployed 1+ mos. in 1989, men	−0.44 (.07)	−0.09 (.07)	−0.42 (.07)	−0.04 (.08)	0.29	0.31
Married by age 30	−0.04 (.05)	−0.07 (.04)	0.01 (.05)	−0.09 (.05)	0.30	0.56
Divorced, first 5 years of marriage	−0.22 (.05)	0.18 (.05)	−0.27 (.05)	0.13 (.05)	0.25	0.34
Middle-class values index	0.75 (.04)	0.23 (.03)	0.73 (.04)	0.16 (.04)	0.47	0.51
Ever interviewed in jail, men	−0.91 (.08)	−0.06 (.07)	−0.88 (0.08)	−0.05 (0.09)	0.60	0.68
CHILD OUTCOMES, FIRSTBORN CHILDREN						
"Illegitimate" (out-of-wedlock) birth	−0.46 (.06)	−0.22 (.05)	−0.45 (.07)	−0.14 (.06)	0.58	1.14
Early AFDC use	−0.54 (.08)	−0.19 (.06)	−0.54 (.08)	−0.14 (.07)	0.55	0.67

(table continues)

TABLE 7.4 (continued)

	OLS or Logit Coefficients (SEs)					
	Herrnstein and Murray Controls[a]		Add Detailed FB Controls[b]		Composite Effects (Absolute Values)	
					FB + SES	Race + FB + SES
	zAFQT	zSES	zAFQT	zSES		
Poor, first 3 years of life	−1.32	−0.78	−1.35	−0.67	1.03	1.11
	(.16)	(.13)	(.16)	(.15)		
Mother smoked during	−0.52	−0.01	−0.49	−0.00	0.36	0.73
pregnancy	(.06)	(.05)	(.06)	(.06)		
Low birth weight	−0.35	−0.08	−0.41	−0.10	0.32	0.45
	(.10)	(.09)	(.11)	(.10)		
Ever in foster or relative	−0.42	−0.22	−0.41	−0.34	0.58	0.70
care?	(.10)	(.09)	(.13)	(.11)		
CHILD OUTCOMES, ALL CHILDREN[c]						
HOME score (percentiles)	6.9	4.4	6.1	3.0	6.4	9.0
	(0.5)	(0.5)	(0.5)	(0.5)		
Motor and social develop-	2.2	1.9	1.5	1.0	4.1	4.7
ment index (percentiles)	(0.6)	(0.5)	(0.7)	(0.6)		
PPV (standardized score)	6.8	3.7	6.2	3.3	5.0	8.2
	(0.5)	(0.4)	(0.5)	(0.5)		
PPVT, 6+ year olds	6.8	2.6	6.5	2.2	3.3	5.6
(standardized score)	(0.6)	(0.5)	(0.6)	(0.5)		
Behavior problems index	−1.6	−0.5	−1.5	−0.3	1.4	1.5
(standardized score;	(0.4)	(0.3)	(0.4)	(0.3)		
(higher = more problems)						

Notes: For complete models, see appendix B. For sample and variable descriptions, see table 7.1.

[a]Controls include AFQT score and SES score, age (z-score), and, where appropriate, dummy variables for gender, race/ethnicity (3 dummy variables), year, and child's age at the time of assessment. Standard errors are corrected for non-independence of observations among youths from the same baseline household.

[b]Detailed family background controls include family arrangement at age 14 (3 dummy variables); dummy variables for the following family characteristics at age 14: urban residence, adult female worked outside the home, family received magazines regularly, received newspapers regularly, had a library card; number of siblings (4 dummy variables); age of mother at birth of respondent (quadratic); whether the respondent was firstborn; and whether the respondent was born outside the United States.

[c]Models for "all children" are based on averages (across years) of outcomes and control variables for children who were assessed in more than one year. In fixed-effects models for children (i.e., first-cousin differences), standard errors are corrected for non-independence of observations among (child) siblings.

we repeat the results presented in table 7.2. In the third and fourth columns we present coefficients and standard errors for the AFQT and SES variables from models that include detailed controls for family socioeconomic background. Finally, in the last two columns of the table we present two "composite" estimates of the effects of family socioeconomic background (both in absolute values). The first is a standardized composite of the SES effect and the effects of the various family background characteristics described in the previous paragraph. The second composite adds to the first the effect of racial/ethnic identification. Since AFQT score is controlled, the effects of race/ethnicity may reflect, at least in part, additional effects of family socioeconomic background (also see Fischer et al. 1996).

The composite effects we have constructed may be unfamiliar to many readers. This procedure allows us to extend Herrnstein and Murray's methodology for comparing effects of AFQT and SES to compare the effects of AFQT to a single, yet more comprehensive, measure of family socioeconomic background. The composite effects are derived as follows. We first estimate a model for each outcome using the different controls for family socioeconomic background described above. For example, in a linear regression with dependent variable Y, family background components X, and AFQT we would have:

$$Y = b_0 + X b_1 + AFQT\, b_2 + e \qquad (1)$$

where b_1 is a vector of coefficients representing the effects of different family background measures.[7] Using our estimate of b_1 we then calculate the predicted (linear) component of Y, F, due to family background factors:

$$\hat{F} = X\, \hat{b}_1; \qquad (2)$$

Using the estimated form of the equation for Y (equation 1) we can rewrite (1) as:

$$Y = \hat{b}_0 + \hat{F} + AFQT\, \hat{b}_2 + \hat{e} \qquad (3)$$

We then standardize $\hat{F}$ to have standard deviation equal to one in the population, producing a new variable $\hat{F}^*$. We can then rewrite (3) as:

$$Y = \hat{b}_0 + \hat{F}^* \sigma_f + AFQT\, \hat{b}_2 + \hat{e} \qquad (4)$$

---

[7] The models also include terms for age and gender controls (not shown). The array X includes Herrnstein and Murray's parental SES index.

Since AFQT is scaled to have standard deviation one in the population, $\hat{\sigma}_f$ and $\hat{b}_2$ can be directly compared. The analogous procedure is used for logit models.[8]

The composite family background measures differ across dependent variables. Our procedure constructs the index for each model so as to maximize the effect of measured family background. This strategy is appropriate if one wishes to isolate the direct effects of measured IQ and measured family background. Our procedure differs from Herrnstein and Murray's because they use a fixed index of IQ (AFQT score) and a fixed index of parents' SES across all models. Given Herrnstein and Murray's position that AFQT measures a single underlying construct of intelligence, their treatment of the AFQT score is appropriate (although an area of future research is to investigate whether different components of AFQT differentially affect different measures of social and economic success).[9] However, we know of no theoretical or evidentiary basis for the use of a single index of parents' SES in all models.

Generally speaking, when family arrangement and the other family socioeconomic background variables are included in the models, the effect of AFQT is virtually unchanged and the effect of SES falls modestly (compare column 1 to column 3 and column 2 to column 4). However, in most cases the effects of many of the other FB (family socioeconomic background) variables are substantial (see appendix B), and the combined effects of the SES index and the FB variables typically far exceed those of SES alone (compare column 2 to column 5 or 6). For example, the effect of FB + SES reported in column 5 is at least 50 percent larger than the effect of SES alone (column 2) for the following outcomes: poverty, annual earnings, high school dropout, high-IQ occupation, out of the labor force, unemployment, married by age 30, middle class values index, and ever in jail, as well as nearly all the child outcomes. Strikingly, there are several outcomes—jail, marriage, out of labor force, and low birth weight—upon which the SES index has no discernible effect, and yet the composite FB effect is substantial.

Comparing the relative size of the AFQT and composite FB effects, it appears that the more closely related the outcome is to schooling attainment, the larger is the effect of AFQT relative to the FB composite. The strength

---

[8] This procedure is related to the more standard decomposition of the variance of the dependent variable. Specifically:

$$\text{Var}(Y) = \sigma_f^2 + b_2^2 + \sigma_f b_2 \, \text{corr}(F^*, \text{AFQT}) + \text{VAR}(e)$$

The coefficient of the family background effect, σ_f, is just the square root of the component of the variance of Y that is due solely to family background factors, σ_f^2.

[9] Currie and Thomas (1995) examine the effects of different components of mother's AFQT in analyses of child test scores.

of AFQT in predicting education and education-related outcomes further underscores the need to model carefully the joint determination of education, AFQT score, and the various adult outcomes. Other than schooling outcomes, the magnitude of the composite FB effect tends to be in the neighborhood of the AFQT effect, and the point estimate of the composite FB effect is larger than the AFQT effect for seven outcomes (out of the labor force, marriage, illegitimate birth, early AFDC use, foster care, HOME score, and motor and social development score) when race/ethnicity is excluded from the composite effect. The composite FB effect is larger than the AFQT effect for three other outcomes (divorce, low birth weight, and PPVT score for all children) when the effects of race/ethnicity are included in the composite.

Biases in the Effects of Parents' SES: Residual Family Background Effects

The results presented in table 7.4 suggest that the combined family socioeconomic background effect was considerably larger than the effect of the index of parents' SES alone. It is also possible to derive an omnibus estimate of the family background effect implied by the fixed-effect models. This effect captures the effects of all characteristics siblings have in common that are not included in the model (such as AFQT, age, and gender). Thus, for example, it includes not only the effect of having grown up in the same household, but also the effect of having grown up in the same neighborhood or state. This effect potentially includes similarities in such things as personality, motivation, and effort. With continuous dependent variables, we estimate directly the effect of the latent family background variable by conducting a one-way ANOVA (analysis of variance) analysis (by household) of the residual from the fixed-effect model. Here the residual is constructed to include all variance in the dependent variable not due to the observed independent variables. That is, it includes both the individual and family-specific components of the dependent variable, once we have removed the effects of AFQT and other observed variables that may differ among siblings. If we assume that the latent variable has variance one, then its coefficient is equal to the standard deviation of the household effect. These results are shown in table 7.5a.

With discrete outcomes, the same methodology is not available. Instead, we estimate a bivariate probit model. This model is is not as powerful since it is a random effects model, and so we must assume that any unobserved family component is uncorrelated with observed variables such as AFQT. However, we noted in our discussion of the fixed-effect models that SES appeared to be an adequate control for family background for the purpose of

TABLE 7.5A

Standardized Effects of Family Background and AFQT Score from Analyses of
Siblings, Continuous Outcomes

	Estimated Effect (SE)			
	OLS		Fixed Effects	
	zAFQT	zSES	zAFQT	zFB[a]
Family income, 1989 (N = 3,316)	7,296	4,487	5,558	12,482
	(622)	(577)	(890)	(543)
Annual earnings, 1989, YR	5,548	1,169	5,317	6,180
Workers (N = 1,579)	(604)	(459)	(765)	(526)
Yrs. schooling, 1990 (z-score)	0.59	0.18	0.45	0.50
(N = 4,758)	(.02)	(.02)	(.02)	(.01)

Notes: Other controls include: zAGE, black, Latino, other race, and, where appropriate,
gender.

FB: Family Background.

[a]See text for a discussion of the family background effects.

estimating the effects of AFQT. (The exceptions to this finding were outcomes for the children of NLSY respondents. However, we do not examine
child outcomes here.) As in the fixed-effect model, if we assume that the
latent variable has variance one, then its effect is the square root of the
intersibling correlation. The results of the bivariate probit analyses are reported in table 7.5b.

The first row of table 7.5a shows the imputed effect of family background
for family income. The implied effect of family background on income
($12,482) is considerably larger than that of SES ($4,487) or either AFQT
effect (OLS: $7,296, and FE: $5,558). The effect of family background on
annual earnings ($6,180) is far larger than that of SES alone ($1,169) and
is somewhat larger than the effect of AFQT score (OLS: $5,548, or FE:
$5,317). Finally the implied effect of family background on education (.50)
is far larger than the OLS estimate of SES's effect (.18), and is somewhat
larger than the AFQT fixed-effect estimate (.45).

Table 7.5b reports the results from the bivariate probit analyses. Results
are similar to those for income in table 7.5a in that in almost all cases the
effect of the latent variable and the combined effect of SES and the latent
variable are larger than the effect of AFQT, often considerably so. The sole
exception is the probability of receiving a BA degree, where the effects are
of nearly equal size. The results in table 7.5b suggest there is a very large
latent family background component that is orthogonal to the parental SES
index, but has substantial effects on many outcomes.

Caution should be used in interpreting the estimates in tables 7.5a and

TABLE 7.5B

Standardized Effects of Family Background and AFQT from Bivariate Probit Analyses of Siblings

	Estimated Effects (SEs)			
			Absolute Value of Effect	
	zAFQT	zSES	Latent FB[a]	Total FB[b]
In poverty in 1989	−0.37	−0.18	0.65	0.68
	(.04)	(.04)	(.04)	(.01)
HS dropout	−0.64	−0.29	0.78	0.83
	(.04)	(.04)	(.03)	(.01)
BA degree	0.68	0.24	0.75	0.79
	(.04)	(.03)	(.03)	(.01)
Out of labor force 1+ mos. in 1989	−0.21	−0.08	0.54	0.55
(men)	(.03)	(.03)	(.04)	(.004)
Unemployed 1+ mos. in 1989 (men)	−0.20	−0.11	0.74	0.75
	(.03)	(.03)	(.03)	(.004)
Married by age 30	0.10	−0.03	0.37	0.37
	(.06)	(.07)	(.13)	(.01)
Divorced, first 5 years of marriage	−0.19	0.17	0.21	0.27
	(.07)	(.06)	(.26)	(.004)
Ever interviewed in jail, men	−0.19	−0.13	0.96	0.96
	(.03)	(.04)	(.01)	(.004)
Middle class values index	0.47	0.12	0.55	0.56
	(.04)	(.03)	(.05)	(.01)
High-IQ occupation	0.25	0.06	0.73	0.73
	(.04)	(.04)	(.04)	(.004)

Notes: Other controls include: zAGE, black, Latino, other race, and, where appropriate, gender. See table 7.1 for variable and sample definitions.

FB: family background

[a]The latent effect is the square root of the cross-equation correlation for siblings.

[b]The total effect is the square root of the sum of the SES effect squared plus the latent effect squared.

7.5b. These estimates attribute to family background all common variance among siblings in the outcome variables that is independent of the effect of AFQT score, gender, and age. For example, the total family background effects include genetic traits that are common to siblings and orthogonal to AFQT score. Similarly, if siblings have grown up in the same places, any effects of location on outcomes will be included in our estimates of the effect of family background. Nonetheless, our estimates do not simply reaffirm Herrnstein and Murray's acknowledgment that the explanatory power of their models is low. *Rather, our sibling models demonstrate that the family one is born into has a very large effect on chances of success in adulthood, independent of measured intelligence.*

The Role of Education

Herrnstein and Murray do not present estimates of the effects of schooling on most of the outcomes they examine. As noted, given the potential for policies to change individual educational attainment, this omission is likely to be important. Also, they examine in only a limited way the effect that controlling for education has on their estimates of the effects of AFQT. In appendixes 6 and 8 as well as in several diagrams in the main body of *The Bell Curve*, Herrnstein and Murray present results from models for two education groups (high school graduates and college graduates). In general, however, it is not obvious from these analyses how sensitive the AFQT effects are to inclusion of controls for education. Furthermore, it is not possible to determine from these analyses the partial effect of education (net of AFQT score). Education may be an important source of omitted variable bias since AFQT and schooling are correlated 0.64.

Herrnstein and Murray argue against including education controls in their models since education may be determined in part by an individual's intelligence (p. 124).[10] Their argument is that if one includes education in the models, the effect of AFQT score would be understated because part of the effect of intelligence is indirect, through education. This objection points to an area of confusion in *The Bell Curve*. Throughout section II, Herrnstein and Murray are unclear about whether, in comparing the effects of AFQT and SES, they intend to contrast the partial (i.e., direct) effects of the variables on an outcome—that is, the effects of AFQT and SES net of the effect of other variables—or the "total" effects of these two variables (their direct effects plus their indirect effects through other variables such as education).

[10] Herrnstein and Murray list three additional objections to including schooling controls: (1) the effects of education may be nonlinear; (2) schooling and AFQT score are likely to be collinear; AFQT score are likely to be collinear; and (3) the relationship between schooling and intelligence is complex: "The effects of education, whatever they may be, depend on the coexistence of suitable cognitive abilities in ways that often require complex and extensive modeling of interaction effects—once again, problems that we hope others will take up but would push us far beyond the purposes of this book" (p. 125).

The first objection is easily addressed by allowing schooling to have nonlinear effects. As for the second objection, the problem of multicollinearity amounts to whether there are enough data to estimate coterminously precise effects of education and AFQT score. In effect, by excluding schooling controls, Herrnstein and Murray overstate the magnitude and precision of their AFQT estimates (e.g., Goldberger 1991, pp. 248–250). As for the final objection, we agree that further work is needed on the complex and possibly interacting relationship between intelligence and schooling. Nonetheless, there is no reason to believe that a model that includes schooling controls in a crude way is inferior to one that omits them altogether.

Furthermore, if one wants to contrast total effects and thus account for the indirect effects of AFQT through education, one should also account for the possible indirect effects of SES through AFQT (and education) on different outcomes.

A critical question is, therefore, whether effects of AFQT are direct or primarily indirect through education. In the latter situation, it is because individuals who have higher AFQT scores tend to get more education, and education directly affects an outcome, that outcomes differ by AFQT score. In this case, the relation between AFQT and an outcome might be changed by policies that alter the relationship between AFQT and schooling. In fact, in *The Bell Curve* Herrnstein and Murray recognize that the relationship between schooling and IQ is malleable when they argue that higher education has become increasingly selective with respect to IQ, and again in chapter 18 when they discuss the "dumbing down" of American education.

Schooling attainment can potentially be manipulated by public policy. If education has a substantial effect on various outcomes, then Herrnstein and Murray's pessimism about society's ability to change individual outcomes may be unwarranted. That is, even if additional education has no effect on IQ, an increase in an individual's education level may enhance his or her chances of success (Hauser and Carter 1995; Jencks et al. 1979).

Table 7.2 reports estimates when education is included as an independent variable. In eleven of twenty-three cases the inclusion of education reduces the effect of AFQT by more than 25 percent. In many cases the standardized effect of education is larger than that of AFQT. In the OLS and standard logit analyses, education has a larger effect than AFQT for family income, annual earnings, high-IQ occupations, the middle-class values index, whether the mother smoked during pregnancy, HOME index, and child's motor and social development index. Parallel changes are found in the fixed-effect models.[11]

The inclusion of education controls also substantially changes the effect of parental SES. This result is hardly surprising, since previous research has repeatedly shown that much of the effect of parental SES on status attainment works indirectly through education. In six of twenty-three cases the effect of SES is reduced by more than 25 percent. It is notable that including education has little impact on the estimates of the effects of SES on the outcomes associated with the children of NLSY respondents.

One might argue that it is appropriate to exclude education controls because Herrnstein and Murray intend to compare the total effects of AFQT

---

[11] Appendix C presents analyses of family income and annual earnings where we have adjusted fixed-effects estimates for measurement error in AFQT scores and education. In models of family income, the effect of AFQT score falls slightly and the effect of education rises markedly (from 4,305 to 5,627) when we correct for measurement error. Both effects rise slightly in models of annual earnings.

score and parental SES. Even in this case, however, the omission of education is problematic since education may affect AFQT scores. If so, then these
analyses understate the effect of parental SES (because parental SES affects
education) and overstates the effect of AFQT.[12]

Indeed, Herrnstein and Murray argue that education has a minimal effect
on AFQT scores. In appendix 3 of *The Bell Curve* Herrnstein and Murray
carry out an analysis of the possible effects of education on AFQT using
earlier measures of IQ as a control variable. They find that an increase in
education of one year increases a youth's percentile ranking in the
AFQT distribution by only 2.2 points, or when they use the standardized
AFQT score, by .074 of a standard deviation, about one IQ point per year of
education.

In recent work with the NLSY, however, Neal and Johnson (1995) have
found, using quarter of birth as an instrument for educational attainment, that
each additional year of education increases AFQT score by more than three
points (a large effect). Furthermore, our reanalysis of Herrnstein and Murray's data (Winship and Korenman 1997) revealed that seven observations
included in Herrnstein and Murray's analyses had years of schooling equal
to − 5, a missing value code in the NLSY. Furthermore, the results presented
on page 591 are from analyses that do not include age at first test, although
they state on page 590 that age at first test was included. When missing data
are treated appropriately and age at first test included as a control, and with
conservative reliability corrections, the effect of education on AFQT more
than doubles to about 2.7 IQ points for every year of education (Winship and
Korenman 1997).

A considerable modeling effort is needed to sort out the possible mutual
effects of education and AFQT score on each other, and to account for the
indirect effects of SES on various outcomes through its effect on AFQT. We
have begun to develop such models in two related papers (Winship and
Korenman 1997, and Winship and Korenman forthcoming). Nonetheless,
from the analyses reported here we learn that estimates of the direct effects
of AFQT, where we control for education, are often substantially smaller
than the effects of AFQT reported in *The Bell Curve*. Furthermore, education
has large effects on many outcomes, controlling for AFQT score.

Conclusion

The purpose of section II of *The Bell Curve* and chapter 14 is to demonstrate
the importance of AFQT score in determining a variety of outcomes. Herrnstein and Murray summarize their results in the following way: "If a white

---

[12] We also do not control for quality of education. Presumably doing so would further increase the effects of education and reduce the effects of AFQT score.

child of the next generation could be given a choice between being disadvantaged in socioeconomic status or disadvantaged in intelligence, there is no question about the right choice" (p. 135). Herrnstein and Murray are confident that innate intelligence is the principal determinant of economic and social success.

In their 1979 book, *Who Gets Ahead?* Christopher Jencks et al., using a large number of data sets, analyze the importance of intelligence, education, family background, and noncognitive abilities in determining various economic outcomes. Jencks et al. conclude that all four sets of factors are important, that no single factor dominates the others, and that their relative importance differs across samples and outcomes.

Which conclusion is right? Are Herrnstein and Murray correct in asserting that intelligence is the dominant factor in determining social and economic success? Or, as Jencks et al. assert, is intelligence just one of several important factors including education and family background? Although we mostly confirm with sibling analyses Herrnstein and Murray's finding that the effects of AFQT are substantial and robust,[13] on balance our results are closer to Jencks et al.'s. Although we have not replicated the Jencks et al. analyses, we do find evidence that the partial effects of family background and schooling are as large as, and in many cases larger than, those of AFQT in predicting a variety of outcomes. The large partial effects we find for education (net of AFQT score and family background) are particularly important given Herrnstein and Murray's pessimism about the potential of social policies to change outcomes. In addition, in models that exclude schooling controls, the effects of family background are as large as or larger than the effects of AFQT score.

In reaching these conclusions we have ignored the potentially serious problem of the endogenous determination of AFQT score. For example, if family socioeconomic background and schooling quality are important determinants of AFQT score at ages fifteen to twenty-three, then the estimates of AFQT score and parental SES that we have presented may exaggerate the importance of AFQT score relative to family background in influencing socioeconomic outcomes. The endogeneity of AFQT scores is a subject of ongoing investigation (see, e.g., Neal and Johnson 1995; Rogers and Spriggs 1995).

---

[13] An exception to our finding of robust effects of AFQT are analyses of the developmental outcomes of young children of NLSY female sample members. Effects of mother's AFQT score are small and not significant when the comparison is made between the children of mothers who are sisters (i.e., first cousins). This finding also stands in contrast to the findings of Currie and Thomas (1995), who report substantial effects of mother's AFQT score after adding controls for mother's education and permanent income. (They do not conduct analyses of sibling differences, however.)

APPENDIX A

Estimated Effects from Models of Socioeconomic Status, by Race

	OLS Coefficients (SEs)							
	Full Sample[a]			Siblings XSEC[a]			Siblings FE[b]	
	zAFQT	zSES	zED	zAFQT	zSES	zED	zAFQT	zED
FAMILY INCOME (1990$), 1989								
Whites	6,627	4,146		7,003	5,208		6,166	
	(500)	(481)		(855)	(877)		(1562)	
	3,765	3,840	4,713	4,084	3,849	5,043	3,910	5,335
	(595)	(500)	(542)	(954)	(916)	(942)	(1578)	(1442)
Number of obs.		4468			1811		1811	
Blacks	6,923	5,352		7,108	3,586		3,685	
	(651)	(574)		(1112)	(1023)		(1384)	
	4,582	4,647	4,201	5,393	3,263	2,849	1,932	3,408
	(756)	(581)	(706)	(1532)	(982)	(1577)	(1807)	(1594)
Number of obs.		1931			861		861	
Latinos	8,425	2,272		8,629	3,038		6,444	
	(863)	(698)		(1365)	(932)		(2000)	
	5,912	1,934	3,839	6,740	2,859	3,354	5,900	1,325
	(1031)	(697)	(876)	(1466)	(916)	(1172)	(2083)	(2232)
Number of obs.		1225			501		501	
ANNUAL EARNINGS, 1989 YEAR-ROUND WORKERS								
Whites	5,056	1,923		6,007	1,410		6,412	
	(389)	(375)		(913)	(804)		(1433)	
	2,906	885	3,663	4,084	591	3,163	4,738	3,061
	(455)	(388)	(415)	(922)	(819)	(903)	(1299)	(1457)
Number of obs.		2823			878		878	
Blacks	5,145	1,362		4,539	1,181		3,046	
	(439)	(393)		(933)	(631)		(881)	
	3,613	859	2,949	3,313	1,047	2,097	2,213	1,458
	(502)	(396)	(490)	(1029)	(622)	(757)	(1017)	(964)
Number of obs.		1161			401		401	
Latinos	3,741	1,283		5,138	926		5,469	
	(583)	(470)		(1154)	(870)		(1570)	
	2,984	1,228	1,158	4,555	963	877	4,838	1,158
	(698)	(470)	(591)	(1212)	(851)	(883)	(1761)	(1002)
Number of obs.		796			248		248	
YEARS OF SCHOOLING COMPLETED, 1990 (Z-SCORE)								
Whites	0.60	0.28		0.55	0.30		0.40	
	(.01)	(.01)		(.02)	(.02)		(.03)	
Number of obs.		5261			2385		2385	

(*table continues*)

APPENDIX A (*continued*)

	OLS Coefficients (SEs)							
	Full Sample[a]			*Siblings XSEC*[a]			*Siblings FE*[b]	
	zAFQT	zSES	zED	zAFQT	zSES	zED	zAFQT	zED
Blacks	0.55	0.17		0.57	0.13		0.50	
	(.02)	(.02)		(.03)	(.03)		(.04)	
Number of obs.		2603			1415			1415
Latinos	0.71	0.07		0.63	0.02		0.48	
	(.03)	(.02)		(.05)	(.03)		(.05)	
Number of obs.		1603			778			778

Notes: See table 7.1 for description of dependent variables and samples.

XSEC: cross-section; FE: fixed-effects; YR: year-round

[a]Models contain controls for age (z-score) and gender. Standard errors are corrected for non-independence of observations among youths from the same baseline household.

[b]Sibling fixed-effects models are sibling differences estimated by including in the regression models a dummy variable for each family of origin.

APPENDIX B
Estimated Effects from Models of Socioeconomic Status and Child Development with Detailed Family Background Controls

	OLS or Logit Coefficients (SEs)								
	Ann. Income	Poor	Ann. Earns.	Years Schl.	HS Drop	BA	High-IQ Occ	Out of LF	Unemp
SES + FB (abs. value)	6,157	0.54	2,767	0.27	0.80	0.90	0.65	0.43	0.29
SES + FB + Race (abs. value)	6,108	0.57	2,251	0.29	0.87	0.89	0.68	0.45	0.31
zAFQT	6,515	−0.93	4,669	0.58	−1.76	1.71	1.34	−0.40	−0.42
	(383)	(.05)	(271)	(.01)	(.06)	(.06)	(.08)	(.06)	(.07)
zSES	3,614	−0.24	1,285	0.18	−0.40	0.67	0.30	0.00	−0.04
	(409)	(.05)	(279)	(.01)	(.05)	(.05)	(.08)	(.06)	(.08)
zAGE	1,806	−0.03	1,580	−0.03	0.11	−0.10	−0.17	−0.08	−0.05
	(296)	(0.04)	(220)	(.01)	(.04)	(.04)	(.07)	(.05)	(.07)
Black	115	0.17	892	0.57	−1.72	1.24	1.00	0.16	0.05
	(749)	(.09)	(548)	(.02)	(0.11)	(.11)	(.18)	(.12)	(.15)
Latino	2,418	−0.07	917	0.25	−0.64	0.28	0.87	0.08	−0.23
	(910)	(.12)	(673)	(.03)	(0.12)	(.14)	(.21)	(.14)	(.21)
Other race	−1,865	0.37	−1,931	−0.03	0.61	0.01	0.17	0.32	0.03
	(1,422)	(.16)	(719)	(.04)	(.17)	(.20)	(.32)	(.22)	(.31)
Female	−1,410	0.79	−7,635	0.09	−0.35	0.28	−0.22	—	—
	(562)	(.07)	(405)	(.01)	(.07)	(.07)	(.13)		
FAMILY ARRANGEMENT, AGE 14									
Mother only	−3,721	0.42	160	−0.01	0.44	−0.05	0.00	0.37	0.35
	(779)	(.09)	(581)	(.02)	(.10)	(.13)	(.21)	(.12)	(.16)
Step	−3,776	0.28	−369	−0.17	0.83	−0.69	0.12	0.40	0.05
	(859)	(.11)	(693)	(.02)	(.11)	(.14)	(.22)	(.14)	(.19)

Other	-5,160 (1,191)	0.40 (.05)	-236 (373)	-0.06 (.04)	0.66 (.16)	-0.20 (.25)	-0.71 (.61)	0.73 (.20)	0.50 (.27)
AGE 14									
Urban residence	727 (651)	0.35 (.10)	787 (434)	-0.00 (.02)	0.27 (.09)	-0.06 (.10)	0.20 (.17)	0.39 (.13)	0.06 (.15)
Adult female worked	-384 (588)	-0.10 (.08)	-399 (433)	-0.04 (.02)	0.15 (.08)	-0.15 (.08)	0.24 (.13)	0.01 (.09)	-0.04 (.13)
Magazines	920 (652)	-0.10 (.08)	993 (467)	0.09 (.02)	-0.29 (.08)	0.21 (.09)	0.39 (.17)	0.02 (.10)	-0.10 (.14)
Newspapers	474 (653)	-0.13 (.08)	-69 (442)	-0.02 (.05)	-0.09 (.09)	-0.18 (.12)	0.05 (.20)	-0.07 (.11)	0.00 (.15)
Library card	1,676 (595)	0.03 (.08)	1,218 (421)	-0.03 (.03)	-0.17 (.08)	0.15 (.10)	0.21 (.19)	0.19 (.10)	0.12 (.14)
NUMBER OF SIBS									
None	-1,576 (1,860)	0.02 (.28)	-1,279 (1,050)	-0.02 (.05)	-0.44 (0.32)	-0.22 (.21)	0.24 (.33)	-0.18 (.33)	0.05 (.41)
Two	-1,046 (1179)	-0.03 (.16)	489 (789)	-0.03 (.03)	0.06 (.16)	-0.16 (.11)	0.01 (.19)	0.09 (.18)	-0.12 (.24)
Three	-2,725 (1,149)	0.09 (.15)	-67 (772)	-0.09 (.03)	0.06 (.16)	-0.35 (.12)	0.30 (.20)	-0.04 (.18)	0.14 (.24)
Four or more	-3,297 (1,073)	0.31 (.14)	-336 (728)	-0.14 (.03)	0.37 (.15)	-0.51 (.12)	-0.03 (.20)	0.20 (.16)	0.26 (.22)
Age mother at birth	1,157 (289)	-0.10 (.04)	47 (269)	0.02 (.01)	-0.02 (.04)	0.05 (.05)	0.09 (.09)	0.01 (.05)	-0.04 (.08)

(table continues)

APPENDIX B (*continued*)

	OLS or Logit Coefficients (SEs)								
	Ann. Income	Poor	Ann. Earns.	Years Schl.	HS Drop	BA	High-IQ Occ	Out of LF	Unemp
(Age mother squared)/100	−1,926	0.16	−74	−0.02	0.01	−0.03	−0.12	−0.02	0.03
	(504)	(.07)	(481)	(.02)	(.07)	(.09)	(.15)	(.09)	(.14)
Firstborn	253	−0.12	−366	0.01	−0.08	−0.10	0.05	−0.08	−0.05
	(801)	(.11)	(631)	(.02)	(.11)	(.10)	(.17)	(.14)	(.18)
Foreign-born	7,215	−0.55	−4,091	0.06	−0.29	0.77	0.69	−0.25	−0.44
	(1,438)	(.18)	(796)	(.04)	(.15)	(.19)	(.27)	(.21)	(.30)
Number of obs	7,977	7,977	5,009	9,885	8,739	9,588	7,944	4,144	3,225

	OLS or Logit Coefficients (SEs)									
	Mar.	Div.	MC Values	Ever Jail	Illeg. Birth	Early AFDC	Early Pov.	Smoke	LBW	Foster Care
Combined FB (abs. value)	0.30	0.25	0.47	0.60	0.58	0.55	1.04	0.36	0.32	0.58
	(.05)	(.05)	(.04)	(.08)	(.07)	(.08)	(.16)	(.06)	(.11)	(.13)
Combined FB & Race (abs. value)	0.56	0.34	0.50	0.68	1.14	0.67	1.11	0.73	0.45	0.70
	(.05)	(.05)	(.04)	(.09)	(.06)	(.07)	(.15)	(.06)	(.10)	(.11)
zAFQT	0.01	−0.27	0.73	−0.88	−0.45	−0.54	−1.35	−0.49	−0.41	−0.41
	(.05)	(.05)	(.04)	(.08)	(.07)	(.08)	(.16)	(.06)	(.11)	(.13)
zSES	−0.09	0.13	0.16	−0.05	−0.14	−0.14	−0.67	−0.00	−0.10	−0.34
	(.05)	(.05)	(.04)	(.09)	(.06)	(.07)	(.15)	(.06)	(.10)	(.11)
zAGE	0.07	−0.03	−0.02	0.02	−0.21	−0.16	−0.34	0.08	0.13	0.20
	(.08)	(.04)	(.03)	(.06)	(.05)	(.06)	(.10)	(.04)	(.08)	(.08)
Black	−1.26	−0.35	−0.22	0.40	1.91	0.55	0.51	−1.15	0.73	0.69
	(.10)	(.12)	(.08)	(.17)	(.11)	(.13)	(.22)	(.12)	(.21)	(.21)

Latino	−0.34	−0.36	0.15	−0.10	0.20	−0.18	−0.41	−1.50	0.43	0.20
	(.12)	(.13)	(.09)	(.22)	(.14)	(.17)	(.31)	(.16)	(.25)	(.27)
Other race	−0.15	0.41	−0.32	0.78	0.03	0.07	0.24	−0.13	0.50	0.07
	(.20)	(.15)	(.14)	(.29)	(.21)	(.25)	(.43)	(.19)	(.36)	(.44)
Female	0.42	0.12	0.34	—	—	—	—	—	—	—
	(.07)	(.08)	(.05)							
FAMILY ARRANGEMENT, AGE 14										
Mother only	−0.19	0.10	−0.51	0.52	0.65	0.38	0.64	0.17	−0.13	−0.11
	(.11)	(.12)	(.08)	(.17)	(.12)	(.13)	(.22)	(.11)	(.19)	(.20)
Step	0.08	0.22	−0.67	0.78	0.44	0.56	0.91	0.41	−0.30	0.41
	(.12)	(.11)	(.09)	(.17)	(.12)	(.14)	(.26)	(.12)	(.24)	(.21)
Other	−0.28	0.19	−0.66	0.74	0.43	0.42	0.72	0.31	−0.08	−0.04
	(.18)	(.19)	(.16)	(.25)	(.19)	(.21)	(.33)	(.19)	(.30)	(.33)
AGE 14										
Urban residence	−0.16	−0.02	−0.18	0.32	0.39	0.32	0.05	0.14	0.01	0.22
	(.10)	(.09)	(.07)	(.18)	(.12)	(.13)	(.22)	(.10)	(.19)	(.20)
Adult female worked	0.21	0.14	−0.05	0.27	−0.11	−0.02	−0.33	0.06	−0.04	−0.09
	(.08)	(.08)	(.06)	(.14)	(.09)	(.10)	(.19)	(.08)	(.15)	(.17)
Magazines	0.06	−0.08	0.23	−0.22	−0.11	−0.28	−0.15	−0.26	0.08	0.11
	(.09)	(.09)	(.06)	(.14)	(.10)	(.11)	(.20)	(.10)	(.17)	(.18)
Newspapers	0.05	−0.14	0.06	0.06	−0.04	0.03	0.07	0.23	0.01	−0.10
	(.10)	(.10)	(.07)	(.15)	(.11)	(.12)	(.20)	(.10)	(.18)	(.18)
Library card	−0.17	0.26	−0.06	0.02	0.13	0.23	0.03	0.02	0.08	−0.17
	(.09)	(.09)	(.07)	(.14)	(.10)	(.12)	(.19)	(.09)	(.18)	(.18)

(*table continues*)

APPENDIX B (continued)

					OLS or Logit Coefficients (SEs)					
	Mar.	Div.	MC Values	Ever Jail	Illeg. Birth	Early AFDC	Early Pov.	Smoke	LBW	Foster Care
NUMBER OF SIBS										
None	0.07	0.22	0.07	−1.10	−0.10	0.63	−0.05	−0.40	−0.11	−0.03
	(.23)	(.25)	(.18)	(.77)	(.32)	(.35)	(.60)	(.32)	(.66)	(.74)
Two	0.26	−0.05	0.07	0.35	−0.09	−0.01	−0.45	0.00	−0.11	0.47
	(.13)	(.14)	(.10)	(.29)	(.18)	(.22)	(.41)	(.16)	(.34)	(.38)
Three	0.19	−0.19	0.12	0.11	0.10	0.01	0.01	−0.02	0.38	0.52
	(.13)	(.14)	(.10)	(.30)	(.18)	(.21)	(.38)	(.15)	(.32)	(.37)
Four or more	0.38	−0.07	−0.01	0.46	0.24	0.34	0.35	−0.04	0.14	0.28
	(.12)	(.13)	(.09)	(.27)	(.16)	(.19)	(.34)	(.15)	(.30)	(.35)
Age mother at birth	−0.03	−0.09	0.04	0.03	−0.11	−0.07	−0.05	−0.12	0.06	−0.17
	(.05)	(.04)	(.03)	(.08)	(.05)	(.06)	(.10)	(.05)	(.09)	(.08)
(Age mother squared)/100	0.01	0.15	−0.07	−0.09	0.20	0.00	0.07	0.19	−0.09	0.00
	(.08)	(.08)	(.06)	(.15)	(.09)	(.00)	(.18)	(.09)	(.15)	(.00)
Firstborn	0.03	0.08	−0.06	−0.08	−0.07	−0.10	0.00	−0.41	0.08	−0.04
	(.10)	(.11)	(.08)	(.19)	(.13)	(.15)	(.28)	(.12)	(.23)	(.23)
Foreign-born	0.17	−0.18	0.15	−0.35	−0.80	−0.91	−1.20	−0.74	−1.02	−1.42
	(.16)	(.18)	(.12)	(.29)	(.21)	(.26)	(.47)	(.23)	(.45)	(0.54)
Number of obs	4,221	4,684	7,692	4,809	3,448	2,683	1,369	3,333	3,325	3,475

OLS or Logit Coefficients (SEs)

	HOME	MOSO	PPVT	PPVT6	BPI
SES + FB (abs. value)	6.4	4.1	5.0	3.3	1.4
SES + FB + Race (abs. value)	9.0	4.7	8.2	5.6	1.5
zAFQT	6.1	1.5	6.2	6.5	−1.5
	(0.5)	(0.7)	(0.5)	(0.6)	(0.4)
zSES	3.0	1.0	3.3	2.2	−0.3
	(0.5)	(0.6)	(0.4)	(0.5)	(0.3)
zAGE	1.7	−0.6	−0.4	−0.6	0.0
	(0.4)	(0.5)	(0.4)	(0.5)	(0.3)
Year 1	−1.9	0.4	2.4	1.7	5.5
	(2.0)	(1.3)	(0.9)	(1.3)	(1.0)
Year 2	−0.0	3.9	−0.2	−0.9	3.8
	(1.5)	(1.4)	(0.9)	(1.3)	(0.8)
Child's age (months) or age group = #1[a]	−5.1	−0.19	0.07	0.00	0.02
	(1.1)	(0.05)	(.01)	(.02)	(.01)
Child's age group = #2	−3.2	—	—	—	—
	(1.1)				
Black	−11.2	1.8	−11.3	−8.7	−1.4
	(1.0)	(1.3)	(0.8)	(1.0)	(0.6)
Latino	−1.6	−3.9	−6.1	−3.7	−2.3
	(1.2)	(1.4)	(1.1)	(1.3)	(0.8)
Other race	−3.8	3.3	−1.4	−1.0	−0.5
	(1.8)	(2.3)	(1.1)	(1.5)	(1.1)

(table continues)

APPENDIX B (continued)

	OLS or Logit Coefficients (SEs)				
	HOME	MOSO	PPVT	PPVT6	BPI
FAMILY ARRANGEMENT AGE 14					
Mother only	-0.7	-0.6	1.2	0.0	1.4
	(1.1)	(1.3)	(0.9)	(1.0)	(0.7)
Step	-2.3	-3.2	0.8	0.8	2.3
	(1.2)	(1.4)	(0.8)	(1.1)	(0.7)
Other	-2.3	-2.3	0.5	0.1	2.0
	(1.7)	(2.3)	(1.4)	(1.8)	(1.0)
AGE 14					
Urban residence	1.5	-0.9	-1.1	-0.6	-0.2
	(0.9)	(1.2)	(0.7)	(1.0)	(0.6)
Adult female worked	-0.3	-0.4	-1.0	-0.0	0.9
	(0.8)	(0.9)	(0.6)	(0.8)	(0.5)
Magazines	2.0	2.2	0.7	0.3	-0.8
	(0.9)	(1.1)	(0.7)	(0.9)	(0.5)
Newspapers	2.2	0.8	0.8	0.7	0.1
	(0.9)	(1.2)	(0.7)	(1.0)	(0.6)
Library card	5.1	4.9	2.3	0.8	-0.2
	(0.9)	(1.1)	(0.7)	(0.9)	(0.6)
NUMBER OF SIBS					
None	3.3	-3.1	0.9	3.2	1.0
	(2.3)	(3.7)	(2.0)	(2.4)	(1.6)
Two	0.5	-3.0	0.7	-0.6	0.9
	(1.5)	(1.7)	(1.1)	(1.7)	(0.9)

Three	0.4	−0.6	−0.4	−2.7	1.2
	(1.4)	(1.8)	(1.1)	(1.6)	(0.9)
Four or more	−1.4	−2.7	−2.5	−1.5	0.9
	(1.3)	(1.7)	(1.0)	(1.5)	(0.8)
Age mother at birth	0.5	−0.1	0.3	0.5	−0.5
	(0.4)	(0.6)	(0.4)	(0.4)	(0.3)
(Age mother squared)/100	−0.8	0.4	−0.3	−0.0	1.0
	(0.8)	(1.1)	(0.6)	(0.1)	(0.5)
First born	−1.4	−2.5	−1.1	−1.1	0.1
	(1.1)	(1.4)	(0.9)	(1.1)	(0.7)
Foreign born	1.8	0.7	−6.1	−4.1	−0.0
	(1.7)	(1.9)	(1.7)	(1.8)	(1.0)
Number of obs	6,711	4,101	4,707	1,784	4,645

Note: See table 7.1 for a description of dependent variables and samples.

[a] Child's age group for HOME score; age at assessment in months for other outcomes.

APPENDIX C
Effects of Reliability Corrections on Fixed-Effect Coefficient Estimates

	Fixed-Effects Coefficients (SEs)		Reliability Ratios[a]	
	zAFQT	zED	zAFQT	zED
1. Family income, 1989	5,558 (975)		1.00	
	3,610 (1,044)	4,305 (963)	1.00	1.00
	6,558 (1,049)		0.85	
	3,554 (1,297)	5,627 (1,298)	0.85	0.77
2. Earnings, 1989 (year-round workers)	5,317 (852)		1.00	
	4,023 (821)	2,341 (856)	1.00	1.00
	6,228 (659)		0.86	
	4,493 (873)	2,677 (800)	0.86	0.80

Note: Models also include controls for age and sex.

[a]Reliability ratios are ratios of signal variance to total variance. The values for reliability of AFQT score are based on Murray (personal communication) and Bock and Moore (1986); the reliability ratio of education is based on Ashenfelter and Krueger (1994). These values are adjusted for use in fixed-effect estimation using the intrafamily correlation of test scores and education. See also chapter footnotes.

References

Ashenfelter, Orley, and Alan B. Krueger. 1994. "Estimates of the Economic Return to Schooling from a New Sample of Twins." *American Economic Review* 84, no. 5: 1157–1173.

Baker, Paula C., and Frank Mott. 1989. *NLSY Child Handbook 1989*. Columbus, OH: Center for Human Resource Research–The Ohio State University.

Bock, R. Darrell, and Elise G. J. Moore. 1986. *Advantage and Disadvantage: A Profile of American Youth*. Hillsdale, NJ: Lawrence Erlbaum Associates.

Carroll, R. J., D. Ruppert, and L. A. Stefanski. 1995. *Measurement Errors in Nonlinear Models*. London: Chapman Hall.

Center for Human Resources Research. 1994. *NLS Handbook 1994*. Columbus: Ohio State University.

Chamberlain, Gary. 1980. "Analysis of Covariance with Qualitative Data." *Review of Economic Studies* 47: 225–238.

Currie, Janet, and Duncan Thomas. 1995. "Race, Children's Cognitive Achievement and *The Bell Curve.*" NBER Working Paper no. 5240, August.

Fischer, Claude S., Michael Hout, Martin Sanchez Jankowski, Samuel R. Lucas, Ann Swidler, and Kim Voss. 1996. *Inequality by Design: Cracking the Bell Curve Myth.* Princeton, NJ: Princeton University Press.

Garfinkel, Irwin, and Sara S. McLanahan. 1986. *Single Mothers and Their Children: A New American Dilemma.* Washington DC: Urban Institute Press.

Goldberger, Arthur S. 1991. *A Course in Econometrics.* Cambridge, MA: Harvard University Press.

Goldberger, Arthur S., and Charles Manski. 1995. Review Article: *The Bell Curve* by Herrnstein and Murray. *Journal of Economic Literature* 33 (June): 762–776.

Griliches, Zvi. 1979. "Sibling Estimates: The Beginnings of a Survey." *Journal of Political Economy* 87 (part 1): S37–S64.

Hauser, Robert M., and Wendy Y. Carter. 1995. "*The Bell Curve* as a Study of Social Stratification." Unpublished paper, Sociology Department, University of Wisconsin, Madison.

Heckman, James J. 1995. "A review of *The Bell Curve: Intelligence and Class Structure in American Life* by Richard Herrnstein and Charles Murray." *REASON* (March). Reprinted in the *Harris School Report, University of Chicago* (Summer 1995): 49–56.

Herrnstein, Richard J., and Charles Murray. 1994. *The Bell Curve: Intelligence and Class Structure in American Life.* New York: Free Press.

Hunt, Earl. 1995. "The Role of Intelligence in Modern Society." *American Scientist* (July/August): 355–368.

Jencks, Christopher, et al. 1979. *Who Gets Ahead? The Determinants of Economic Success in America.* New York: Basic Books.

Korenman, Sanders D., Jane E. Miller, and John E. Sjaastad. 1995. "Long-Term Poverty and Child Development in the United States: Evidence from the NLSY." *Children and Youth Services Review* 17, no. 1/2: 127–155.

Miller, Jane E., and Sanders D. Korenman. 1994. "Poverty and Children's Nutritional Status in the United States." *American Journal of Epidemiology* 140, no. 3: 233–243.

Murray, Charles. 1984. *Losing Ground: American Social Policy 1950–1980.* New York: Basic Books.

Neal, Derek A., and William R. Johnson. 1995. "The Role of Pre-Market Factors in Black-White Wage Differences." NBER Working Paper no. 5124, May.

Rodgers, William M., and William E. Spriggs. 1995. "What Does AFQT Really Measure: Race, Wages, Schooling and the AFQT Score." Mimeo, College of William and Mary, March.

Solon, Gary S. 1992. "Intergenerational Income Mobility in the United States." *American Economic Review* 82, no. 3: 393–408.

STATA Corporation. 1993. *STATA Reference Manual: Release 3.1.* 6th ed. College Station, TX.

Winship, Christopher, and Sanders D. Korenman. 1997. "Does Staying in School Make You Smarter? The Effect of Education on IQ in *The Bell Curve.*" In *Intelligence, Genes and Success: Scientists Respond to "The Bell Curve,"* ed. Bernie

Devlin, Stephen Fienberg, Daniel Resnick, and Kathryn Roeder. New York: Springer-Verlag, pp. 215–234.

Winship, Christopher, and Sanders D. Korenman. Forthcoming. "Economic Success and the Evolution of Schooling and Mental Ability." In *When Schools Make a Difference*, ed. Susan E. Mayer and Paul E. Peterson.Washington, DC: Brookings Institution.

Zimmerman, David. 1992. "Regression Toward Mediocrity in Economic Stature." *American Economic Review* 82, no. 3: 409–429.

Eight

Occupational Status, Education, and Social Mobility in the Meritocracy*

ROBERT M. HAUSER, JOHN ROBERT WARREN,
MIN-HSIUNG HUANG, AND WENDY Y. CARTER

IN THIS CHAPTER we use indexes of the socioeconomic standing of occupations to measure trends and differentials in intergenerational social mobility and in the effects of social background, educational attainment, and measured mental ability on occupational standing. We begin with an overview of the measurement of occupational status. This concept may be unfamiliar to some readers, and comparability among later findings depends on some of the details of index construction. We turn next to an examination of trends in aggregate intergenerational mobility, trends in occupational social standing, and trends in the effects of social background and educational attainment on occupational standing. In these analyses we use several sets of national survey data that contain appropriate measurements: the 1962 and 1973 Occupational Changes in a Generation Surveys (OCG), the 1986–1988 Surveys of Income and Program Participation (SIPP), and the 1972–1990 General Social Surveys of the National Opinion Research Center (GSS). These surveys are each sufficiently large to permit some level of disaggregation by race, age, and sex, but only one of them, the GSS, contains even a crude direct measure of mental ability. Thus, there is a tradeoff between national and temporal scope, on the one hand, and examination of the role of mental ability in the stratification process, on the other. Finally, using data from the National Longitudinal Survey of Youth (NLSY) and from the Wisconsin Longitudinal Survey (WLS), we focus on the role of measured mental ability in occupational standing. The NLSY is a high-quality national survey, but its population coverage is limited to cohorts aged fourteen to twenty-one in

* Support for this research was provided by the National Science Foundation (SBR-9320660), the National Institute on Aging (AG-9775), the Office of the Assistant Secretary for Planning and Evaluation, U.S. Department of Health and Human Services, the Vilas Estate Trust, and the Center for Demography and Ecology at the University of Wisconsin–Madison. The opinions expressed herein are those of the authors. We thank Linda Jordan for programming assistance. Address correspondence to Robert M. Hauser, Department of Sociology, The University of Wisconsin–Madison, 1180 Observatory Drive, Madison, Wisconsin 53706, or e-mail to HAUSER@SSC.WISC.EDU.

1979, which have been followed through 1993. The WLS is a regional sample of men and women who have been followed from their high school graduation in 1957 to ages fifty-three and fifty-four in 1992–1993.

Socioeconomic Status

Socioeconomic status is typically used as a shorthand expression for variables that characterize the placement of persons, families, households, census tracts, or other aggregates with respect to the capacity to create or consume goods that are valued in our society. Thus, socioeconomic status may be indicated by educational attainment, by occupational standing, by social class, by income (or poverty), by wealth, by tangible possessions such as home appliances or libraries, houses, cars, and boats, or by degrees from elite colleges and universities. At some times, it has also been taken to include measures of participation in social, cultural, or political life.

Job-holding is the most important social and economic role played by most adults outside their immediate family or household. When we meet someone new, our first question is often "What do you do?" and that is a very good question. Job-holding defines how we spend much of our time, and it provides strong clues about the activities and circumstances in which that time is spent. Job-holding tells us about the technical and social skills that we bring to the labor market, and for most people job-holding delimits current and future economic prospects. Thus, even for persons who are not attached to the labor market, past jobs or the jobs held by other members of the same family or household provide information about economic and social standing. As market labor has become nearly universal among adult women as well as men, it is increasingly possible to characterize individuals in terms of their own current or past jobs.

There is a long-standing and well-developed methodology for measuring one aspect of socioeconomic status using characteristics of job-holders.[1] The procedure is to link census occupation lines to a weighted average of occupational educational attainment and occupational income or earnings, thus providing a scalar measure of occupational status. Beginning with Duncan (1961), the weights of occupational education and income have usually been chosen by regressing popular ratings of occupational prestige on these occupational characteristics.

Occupational status appears to indicate a reliable and powerful characteristic of persons or households by dint of its temporal stability and substantial correlation with other social and economic variables. Some economists have suggested that occupational status may be a better indicator of long-

---

[1] Hauser and Warren (1997) have comprehensively reviewed the history and methodology of occupational status measurement in the United States.

term or permanent income than is income at a single point in time (Gold-berger 1989; Zimmerman 1992). However, unlike permanent income, occu-pational status can be measured well at a single point in time, and occupa-tional education, rather than income, appears to account for the persistence of occupational standing (Hauser and Warren 1997).[2] Because past as well as current occupations can be ascertained reliably, even by proxy or retrospec-tively, status indexes can be used to measure persistence and change in occu-pational standing across generations and within the career.

Occupational status indexes have disadvantages as well as advantages. A scalar measure of occupational standing obviously cannot reflect everything about a job that might be relevant to other social, economic, or psychologi-cal variables (Jencks et al. 1988; Rytina 1992; Hauser and Logan 1992), nor is there a strong theoretical basis for the concept of occupational socio-economic status (Hodge 1981). Moreover, some common occupations do not fit typical relationships among socioeconomic characteristics and occupa-tional prestige (Hauser and Warren 1997); in particular, farm occupations are often given special treatment. Because the occupational education of women typically exceeds that of men, while the occupation earnings or income of men typically exceeds that of women, composite indexes of occupational status do not provide an accurate account of gender differences in occupa-tional standing (Boyd 1986; Warren et al. 1998). Measures of occupational status do not tell us everything about social standing, and they should be used in combination with other socioeconomic variables, such as educational attainment, income, earnings, and wealth.

In our analyses of occupational standing, we use survey data that have been classified into census occupational systems from the 1960s to the 1980s. This creates a problem of comparability. The Duncan SEI was con-structed by regressing occupational prestige for forty-five occupations in a 1947 NORC survey on the characteristics of male workers in 1950 (Duncan 1961). It was subsequently updated for use with the 1960- and 1970-basis census occupational classifications (Hauser and Featherman 1977). Prestige ratings of all occupations were obtained in the 1960s (Siegel 1971), and Stevens and Featherman (1981) constructed a new socioeconomic index for men (MSEI2), based upon characteristics of male workers in 1970. This was subsequently updated for use with the 1980 census classification (Stevens and Cho 1985).

We use the Duncan SEI in analyses of the 1962 and 1973 OCG data when the occupations in each survey have been coded into the 1960 census occu-pational classification, and also in analyses of the WLS data. The 1973 OCG

---

[2] That is, correlations of occupational income across generations or within the career are much smaller than correlations of occupational education (Hauser and Warren 1997; Warren et al. 1998).

data were doubly coded, into both the 1960 and the 1970 census classifications. We use MSEI2 in analyses of the 1973 OCG data when they have been coded into the 1970 census occupational classification, thus providing a bridge between analyses using the Duncan SEI and those using MSEI2. We also use MSEI2 in analyses of the 1972–1990 GSS, the NLSY, and the 1986–1988 SIPP.[3]

Trends in Aggregate Status Mobility

For much of this century, interest in social mobility focused on the question of whether "America was still the land of opportunity," that is, whether children were able to move up in the social structure relative to their parents. Reliable national data on mobility became available only in the 1960s, with the first Occupational Changes in a Generation Survey, which was carried out as a supplement to the March 1962 Current Population Survey (CPS).[4] Contrary to many suppositions, the 1962 OCG data showed a predominant flow of upward mobility from one generation of men to the next, which had been fed in large part by the movement from farm to city (Duncan 1965; Blau and Duncan 1967). The second OCG survey, which Featherman and Hauser directed as a supplement to the March 1973 CPS, continued to show a predominant flow of upward mobility among U.S. men (Featherman and Hauser 1978).[5]

It is now much less clear whether the predominance of upward mobility will continue, even though one might well argue that future upward mobility will be spurred by the large flow of foreign migrants to the United States. For example, figure 8.1 shows a time series of trends in mean father-to-son status mobility for cohorts of white, U.S. men born between the beginning of World War I and the late 1950s. The data are from the annual series of General Social Surveys carried out between 1972 and 1990, along with the 1973 OCG survey and the 1986–1988 SIPP supplements. For obvious reasons, each age grouping or survey covers a different, but overlapping set of cohorts. Although the data are somewhat irregular, at least in part because the average cell size is well under 200, the GSS series suggests that a plateau of aggregate upward mobility was reached in birth cohorts of the late 1920s to the early 1940s. Fortunately, the data points from the much larger ten-year age groups in the 1973 OCG and 1986–1988 SIPP fall neatly into the pat-

[3] The GSS and NLSY data were coded into the 1970 system, and SIPP data were coded into the 1980 system.

[4] The 1962 OCG survey included 20,700 U.S. men in the civilian noninstitutional population, plus those living in family quarters in military installations (Featherman and Hauser 1978, appendix B).

[5] The 1973 OCG survey covered 33,613 U.S. men in the civilian, noninstitutional population, including oversamples of black and Hispanic men drawn from previously retired CPS rotation groups.

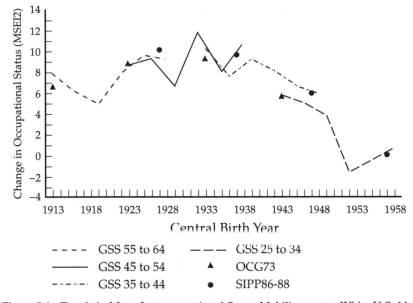

Figure 8.1. Trends in Mean Intergenerational Status Mobility among White U.S. Men by Age: General Social Survey, 1972 to 1990

tern of the GSS series. The largest intergenerational shift, just under ten points on MSEI2, corresponds to a bit less than half a standard deviation in the status of sons and a bit more than half a standard deviation in the status of fathers.[6]

There has been a steady decline in the aggregate intergenerational status mobility of cohorts born after the end of World War II. At least at young ages, there appears to have been no net upward mobility among white men born after 1950. Even in the absence of expanding opportunities in high-status occupations, a finding of declining intergenerational mobility is by no means a necessity, for continuing upward mobility could also be fed by status differentials in fertility. Our finding echoes recent claims, offered by scholars as well as politicians, that "today's high school graduates make less than their fathers did" (Murnane and Levy 1993). However, it locates declining intergenerational mobility chances in earlier cohorts, and it has a stronger conceptual basis. Murnane and Levy's pronouncement was based on intercohort comparisons, not on an intergenerational comparison. It also fails to acknowledge intergenerational educational mobility. That is, many of today's high school graduates are not the sons of high school graduates, and many of the sons of high school graduates are not high school graduates.

---

[6] In all of the surveys except the GSS, the term *father's occupation* actually refers to the head of the household in the respondent's family of orientation. Thus, the referent is a stepfather or a mother in an increasing share of cases among younger cohorts, especially among blacks.

One should not jump from the data of figure 8.1 to the conclusion that net immobility will last throughout the lives of recent cohorts of U.S. men, for the status of men's jobs typically grows from career entry to midlife. Table 8.1 shows the means and standard deviations of the SEI and MSEI2 for nonblack men in the two OCG surveys and the 1986–1988 SIPP.[7] Both the 1962 and 1973 surveys asked men about their first full-time civilian job held after leaving school for the last time, and the 1973 survey also asked about men's jobs in 1962.[8] Thus, both of the OCG surveys provide intragenera-

TABLE 8.1

Means and Standard Deviations of Occupational Status: Nonblack men, 1962 and 1973 Occupational Changes in a Generation Surveys (OCG) and 1986–1988 Surveys of Income and Program Participation (SIPP)

	Age 25 to 34		Age 35 to 44		Age 45 to 54		Age 55 to 64	
Variable	Mean	Std Dev	Mean	Std Dev	Mean	Std Dev	Mean	Std Dev
1962 OCG (1960-BASIS DUNCAN SEI)								
Current job	40.4	25.0	40.7	24.7	38.1	23.6	36.9	24.2
First job	30.0	22.8	27.2	21.1	25.3	20.1	25.9	20.4
Father's job	30.4	21.7	28.7	21.8	26.6	20.5	25.9	20.4
1973 OCG (1960-BASIS DUNCAN SEI)								
Current job	42.6	25.0	44.4	25.5	43.0	25.3	38.5	24.9
First job	36.7	25.4	36.4	25.9	33.2	24.6	28.9	22.7
Father's job	33.8	23.9	30.0	22.4	28.0	21.4	26.5	20.9
1973 OCG (1970-BASIS MSEI2)								
Current job	37.6	20.8	38.9	20.9	37.2	20.0	34.5	19.3
Job in 1962	—	—	36.1	20.2	36.0	19.6	34.3	19.0
First job	33.6	21.1	33.4	21.5	30.9	20.0	28.0	18.3
Father's job	31.8	17.7	29.6	16.5	28.4	15.5	27.8	15.1
1986–1988 SIPP (1980-BASIS MSEI2)								
Current job	37.8	20.6	40.9	21.0	41.9	21.1	41.1	21.3
Father's job	37.9	19.6	35.0	18.0	32.2	16.7	31.0	15.8

[7] The appendix gives approximate sample sizes for the 1962 OCG survey, the 1973 OCG survey, and the 1986–1988 SIPP. In the case of the two OCG surveys, the reported counts have been adjusted downward, by factors of 0.62 and 0.75, respectively, in light of the Census Bureau's reports of sampling variability (Featherman and Hauser 1978, pp. 507–514).

[8] The first job questions were not comparable between the 1962 and 1973 OCG surveys. The 1962 instrument failed to anchor school-leaving in time, and it often elicited responses that must have pertained to jobs held well before respondents had completed their schooling (Duncan et al. 1972, pp. 210–224). In 1973 Featherman and Hauser anchored the first job item with questions about the highest grade of school completed and the date of school-leaving.

tional as well as intergenerational measures of net status mobility. Across all age groups, there is little net mobility from fathers' occupations to sons' first jobs, and most of the net upward mobility occurs between sons' first jobs and those held at ages thirty-five to forty-four.

Table 8.2 gives means and standard deviations of occupational status among black men in the OCG and SIPP surveys. The 1962 OCG data provide striking evidence of the low occupational status of black men and of their low net intergenerational mobility in the pre–civil rights era. There was substantial growth in occupational standing, even among relatively old black men, between 1962 and 1973, and the miserable stasis of the pre–civil rights era was replaced by a predominant pattern of net upward mobility. There was continued improvement in the status of current jobs between 1973 and 1986–1988 among black men at ages thirty-five and above, but strikingly little change in the youngest age group.[9]

TABLE 8.2

Means and Standard Deviations of Occupational Status: Black men, 1962 and 1973 Occupational Changes in a Generation Surveys (OCG) and 1986–1988 Surveys of Income and Program Participation (SIPP)

Variable	Age 25 to 34		Age 35 to 44		Age 45 to 54		Age 55 to 64	
	Mean	Std Dev	Mean	Std Dev	Mean	Std Dev	Mean	Std Dev
1962 OCG (1960-BASIS DUNCAN SEI)								
Current job	18.3	16.3	19.2	16.1	17.2	13.9	14.9	12.7
First job	16.6	14.2	15.8	13.3	13.0	10.1	13.8	12.7
Father's job	17.4	15.3	14.8	11.3	16.2	11.6	16.2	12.5
1973 OCG (1960-BASIS DUNCAN SEI)								
Current job	29.1	21.7	27.8	21.2	23.4	18.8	18.9	16.2
First job	24.2	20.0	20.7	19.1	18.4	16.3	15.4	15.1
Father's job	17.5	15.5	16.3	14.3	14.3	11.8	14.0	10.4
1973 OCG (1970-BASIS MSEI2)								
Current job	27.3	16.6	27.1	17.0	24.0	14.0	21.0	10.7
Job in 1962	—	—	24.3	15.0	23.0	13.1	21.1	10.7
First job	23.9	14.6	22.9	15.2	21.0	12.1	19.7	10.6
Father's job	21.5	11.2	21.0	10.4	20.4	9.1	20.3	7.4
1986–1988 SIPP (1980-BASIS MSEI2)								
Current job	29.6	17.7	35.9	17.0	30.2	18.4	27.6	16.1
Father's job	28.4	13.5	27.3	13.0	24.6	10.2	26.7	12.5

[9] We are somewhat mistrustful of comparisons of net intergenerational mobility between the 1973 OCG and SIPP among blacks. Levels of parental status in SIPP appear unreasonably high relative to those in the 1973 OCG, and we suspect some lack of comparability in the identification of nonpaternal household heads.

Trends in Intergenerational Status Persistence

Throughout the period for which data are available, intergenerational correlations of occupational status have declined among white men, and they have increased irregularly among black men. There is a great deal of evidence to support the first of these assertions. It is supported by the evidence of linear and canonical correlations and loglinear models of early, small mobility surveys and of the 1962 and 1973 OCG data (Hauser et al. 1975b; Hauser et al. 1975a; Featherman and Hauser 1978, chaps. 2–3), and by canonical and loglinear models of the 1972 to 1990 GSS data (Hout 1988; Hauser and Logan 1992). As Featherman and Hauser (1978, p. 135) concluded, "If there is a trend in the volume of occupational mobility, it is toward greater movement."[10]

Table 8.3 assembles regressions of men's or women's occupational status on fathers' occupational status from the two OCG surveys and from the 1986–1988 SIPP, thus extending the existing trend data. Because of the change in scales, it is possible to compare lines pertaining to the 1962 and 1973 OCG surveys in the SEI metric and lines pertaining to the 1973 and the 1986–1988 SIPP in the MSEI2 metric, but not to make direct comparisons between the 1962 OCG and the 1986–1988 SIPP. Among nonblack men, each of the paired, age-specific comparisons shows a decline in the regression of a man's current occupational status on that of his father by about 8 percent between 1962 and 1973 and by about 13 percent between 1973 and 1986. For example, at age twenty-five to thirty-four, the slope declined from 0.45 to 0.37 between 1962 and 1973 (in the SEI metric), and it declined from 0.42 to 0.35 between 1973 and 1986 (in the MSEI2 metric). At the same time, there has been no monotonic change across age groups in the regression of the status of a man's first occupation on that of his father. For example, within the 1973 OCG survey, the regressions were slightly larger at ages thirty-five to fifty-four than at younger or older ages. This suggests that the reduction in intergenerational stratification has occurred by way of increasing mobility after career entry.

The story is quite different in the black population, where the 1962 OCG survey provided meager evidence of intergenerational stratification. O. D. Duncan (1969) characterized this as a perverse form of equality of opportunity, in which black families could not pass advantage—or disadvan-

---

[10] The senior author raised this observation in a conversation with Charles Murray shortly before publication of *The Bell Curve*, suggesting that it was inconsistent with the book's thesis that social stratification was increasing as a consequence of cognitive stratification. Murray responded that he did not expect such rigidification to occur until after the beginning of the twenty-first century. *The Bell Curve* does not refer to any evidence about trends in social mobility in the United States.

TABLE 8.3

Intergenerational Regressions of Occupational Status: 1962 and 1973 Occupational Changes in a Generation Surveys (OCG) and 1986–1888 Surveys of Income and Program Participation (SIPP)

Group and Variables	Age 25 to 34	Age 35 to 44	Age 45 to 54	Age 55 to 64
NONBLACK MEN				
Father's Occupation and Current Occupation				
1962 OCG (1960-basis Duncan SEI)	0.45	0.47	0.47	0.44
1973 OCG (1960-basis Duncan SEI)	0.37	0.42	0.44	0.46
1973 OCG (1970-basis MSEI2)	0.42	0.46	0.47	0.47
1986–1988 SIPP (1980-basis MSEI2)	0.35	0.37	0.42	0.44
Father's Occupation and First Occupation				
1962 OCG (1960-basis Duncan SEI)	0.42	0.39	0.42	0.42
1973 OCG (1960-basis Duncan SEI)	0.43	0.48	0.48	0.44
1973 OCG (1970-basis MSEI2)	0.45	0.51	0.50	0.47
BLACK MEN				
Father's Occupation and Current Occupation				
1962 OCG (1960-basis Duncan SEI)	0.18	0.25	0.10	0.17
1973 OCG (1960-basis Duncan SEI)	0.44	0.32	0.32	0.24
1973 OCG (1970-basis MSEI2)	0.41	0.33	0.29	0.20
1986–1988 SIPP (1980-basis MSEI2)	0.51	0.28	0.30	−0.04
Father's Occupation and First Occupation				
1962 OCG (1960-basis Duncan SEI)	0.24	0.13	0.03	0.15
1973 OCG (1960-basis Duncan SEI)	0.50	0.30	0.32	0.40
1973 OCG (1970-basis MSEI2)	0.47	0.30	0.30	0.24
NONBLACK WOMEN: FATHER'S OCCUPATION AND CURRENT OCCUPATION				
1986–1988 SIPP (1980-basis MSEI2)	0.25	0.23	0.26	0.29

(*table continues*)

TABLE 8.3 (*continued*)

Group and Variables	Age 25 to 34	Age 35 to 44	Age 45 to 54	Age 55 to 64
BLACK WOMEN: FATHER'S OCCUPATION AND CURRENT OCCUPATION				
1986–1988 SIPP (1980-basis MSEI2)	0.23	0.39	0.17	0.20

tage—from one generation to the next. Instead, regardless of stratum of origin, low-status jobs were the rule. As occupational opportunities expanded in the black population, social stratification increased. The intergenerational status regression increased at every age between the 1962 and 1973 OCG surveys, and it increased at ages twenty-five to thirty-four between the 1973 OCG survey and the 1986–1988 SIPP.[11] Among black men, the regressions of the status of first jobs on fathers' occupations in the two OCG surveys also suggest increasing stratification in more recent cohorts. One might suspect that the mixed findings of trend among black men reflect the combination of the entry of blacks into the economic mainstream and the secular decline in occupational stratification that is more easily observed among whites.

The last two panels of table 8.3 show the observed intergenerational regressions for women in the 1986–1988 SIPP. These, of course, provide no evidence about trend. The estimates suggest that intergenerational stratification among white women is slightly less than among white men (relative to the status of mostly male family heads). There is no clear pattern to the gender differences in stratification among blacks, nor are there consistent differences in the regressions between black and white women.

Intergenerational Regressions and the Effects of Family Origins

In focusing on intergenerational status regressions, we do not claim that they are the best indicators of the social stratification of opportunity. On the contrary, we think that they are not and that it would be far preferable to create time-series in resemblance among siblings. Such indicators would reflect the global correlation between the family of orientation and socioeconomic outcomes, and they would not depend either on a specific choice of variables pertaining to the family of orientation or to the problems of measuring such variables retrospectively or by proxy, along with adult outcomes (Jencks

---

[11] We have no explanation other than sampling variability for the negative regression among black men aged fifty-five to sixty-four in the 1986–1988 SIPP.

et al. 1972; Hauser and Featherman 1976; Olneck 1977; Griliches 1979; Hauser and Mossel 1985; Hauser and Sewell 1986; Kuo and Hauser 1995). For example, using the 1973 OCG data Hauser and Featherman (1976, p. 117) estimated correlations between the educational attainments of American brothers in nine cohorts. These estimates range from 0.62 to 0.70 after correction for response error, thus suggesting a very powerful role for the family in educational stratification. That is, between 62 and 70 percent of the variance in educational attainment lies between families. Analyses of WLS data suggest that family resemblance in occupational status is substantially less than that in educational attainment (Hauser and Sewell 1986, p. s109). After correcting for response error, Hauser and Sewell estimated between-family variance components of 49 percent of the variance in mental ability, 46 percent of the variance in educational attainment, 41 percent of the variance in the status of first jobs, and 38 percent of the variance in current occupations.

Sibling pair data can be drawn from national samples in the original National Longitudinal Surveys of Labor Market Experience (Altonji and Dunn 1991), the Panel Study of Income Dynamics (Solon et al. 1991), and—most important—the 1979 National Longitudinal Study of Youth (NLSY) (Korenman and Winship 1996). There are also good data on siblings in the Wisconsin Longitudinal Study, a large regional sample. Thus, it is no longer necessary to say that sibling studies are small, local, and nonrepresentative. However, with one exception (the 1994 GSS), there are no large surveys of socioeconomic resemblance among siblings that cover the full adult population across all ages, nor do repeated cross-section surveys of siblings provide a base for trend comparisons.

Hauser and Featherman's analyses of the 1973 OCG data on the education of brothers in different age cohorts were recently elaborated by Kuo and Hauser (1995, pp. 155–156), who estimated trends in family stratification of education among black men and among white men. The main trend in both populations was declining inequality of educational attainment. There were reductions in all sources of variance in schooling: measured between-family effects, unmeasured between-family effects, and within-family effects. As educational inequality declined, the share of within-family variance increased over time among white men, while it decreased over time among black men (after correction for response variability). Unfortunately, there is no comparable time-series for occupational status (or earnings), but the 1997 NLSY should eventually make it possible to compare the early 1990s with the early twenty-first century in two cohorts of American youth.[12]

---

[12] Efforts by the senior author, among others, to include questions about the educational attainment and occupational status of siblings in the 1986–1988 SIPP family background mod-

In the 1994 GSS, Robert D. Mare and Robert M. Hauser designed a supplementary module on families and social stratification. It had two major components. First, the GSS module asked some 3,000 respondents about the education and occupational standing of several relatives, including siblings, children, parents, spouses, and in-laws. Second, a supplementary Survey of American Families (SAF) interviewed a randomly selected brother or sister of 1,155 of the GSS respondents.[13] Both the GSS and the SAF ask about early career jobs as well as about current occupations (and earnings), so it may be possible to measure trends in the status resemblance of siblings within the GSS-SAF. Several questions were asked both directly and by proxy in the GSS and SAF, and it thus will eventually be possible to correct for random and some forms of nonrandom response error.

Table 8.4 gives preliminary estimates of sibling correlations, based on data reported by the 1994 GSS respondents.[14] To our knowledge, these are the first such correlations observed for even a moderately large random sample of the adult population of the United States. The correlations between educational attainments and occupational statuses of siblings are shown in boldface. Among the four combinations of brothers and sisters, the correlations range from 0.40 to 0.49 in the case of educational attainment and from 0.24 to 0.29 in the case of occupational status. Even though the estimated correlations will increase when they have been corrected for response error, we think the estimates suggest surprisingly low levels of correlation. For example, among the OCG brothers surveyed in 1973, Hauser and Featherman (1976, p. 117) observed education correlations ranging from 0.515 to 0.590. Moreover, in the WLS sample, which has sometimes been dismissed as "too homogeneous," the uncorrected correlation between brothers' occupational statuses in the mid 1970s was 0.29 (Hauser and Sewell 1986). Our preliminary finding is that the 1994 GSS sibling data provide no stronger evidence of family stratification in occupational status than we see in recent intergenerational status correlations and regressions. Indeed, in the GSS the intergenerational occupational correlations—of father's status with respondent's or sibling's status—are as large or larger than the corresponding sibling correlations.

---

ule were rejected by the U.S. Bureau of the Census and the Office of Management and Budget on the grounds that they had no immediate policy relevance. For the same reason, the family background module was dropped from SIPP after 1988, and it was not included in the redesign of SIPP for 1996 and beyond. In our opinion this is a tragic loss of an important social indicator series.

[13] The Survey of American Families completed its field operations late in 1995, and documentation and data from the survey are in the public domain at http://dpls.dacc.wisc.edu/Saf/.

[14] These correlations are based upon our recodes of the 1994 GSS occupation and industry reports, so they cannot be reproduced from the public-use version of the GSS data.

TABLE 8.4

Correlations among Selected Socioeconomic Variables: 1994 General Social Survey

	(1)	(2)	(3)	(4)	(5)	(6)	(7)
MALE RESPONDENT, MALE SIBLING (N = 351)							
(1) Father's occupational status	1.00						
(2) Father's educational attainment	0.66	1.00					
(3) Mother's educational attainment	0.50	0.69	1.00				
(4) Respondent's educational attainment	0.41	0.42	0.35	1.00			
(5) Respondent's occupational status	0.34	0.27	0.19	0.60	1.00		
(6) Sibling's educational attainment	0.41	0.48	0.49	**0.47**	0.27	1.00	
(7) Sibling's occupational status	0.28	0.28	0.25	0.34	**0.29**	0.62	1.00
Mean	36.7	11.3	11.4	14.1	37.6	13.6	38.6
Standard deviation	14.5	4.2	3.4	2.7	14.4	3.0	15.9
MALE RESPONDENT, FEMALE SIBLING (N = 338)							
(1) Father's occupational status	1.00						
(2) Father's educational attainment	0.62	1.00					
(3) Mother's educational attainment	0.39	0.57	1.00				
(4) Respondent's educational attainment	0.40	0.47	0.32	1.00			
(5) Respondent's occupational status	0.34	0.33	0.13	0.60	1.00		
(6) Sibling's educational attainment	0.32	0.42	0.42	**0.44**	0.28	1.00	
(7) Sibling's occupational status	0.28	0.25	0.17	0.32	**0.27**	0.58	1.00
Mean	37.4	11.3	11.4	13.9	39.3	13.6	37.7
Standard deviation	14.3	4.0	3.1	2.9	14.4	2.7	15.3
FEMALE RESPONDENT, MALE SIBLING (N = 414)							
(1) Father's occupational status	1.00						
(2) Father's educational attainment	0.65	1.00					
(3) Mother's educational attainment	0.37	0.62	1.00				
(4) Respondent's educational attainment	0.39	0.41	0.38	1.00			

(table continues)

TABLE 8.4 (*continued*)

	(1)	(2)	(3)	(4)	(5)	(6)	(7)
(5) Respondent's occupational status	0.32	0.26	0.22	0.58	1.00		
(6) Sibling's educational attainment	0.34	0.44	0.39	**0.40**	0.29	1.00	
(7) Sibling's occupational status	0.27	0.31	0.21	0.31	**0.25**	0.65	1.00
Mean	35.4	11.1	11.2	13.7	37.1	13.5	39.0
Standard deviation	13.3	4.0	3.2	2.5	14.3	2.8	15.0
FEMALE RESPONDENT, FEMALE SIBLING (N = 429)							
(1) Father's occupational status	1.00						
(2) Father's educational attainment	0.65	1.00					
(3) Mother's educational attainment	0.44	0.68	1.00				
(4) Respondent's educational attainment	0.40	0.47	0.40	1.00			
(5) Respondent's occupational status	0.29	0.26	0.25	0.62	1.00		
(6) Sibling's educational attainment	0.42	0.46	0.42	**0.49**	0.27	1.00	
(7) Sibling's occupational status	0.30	0.27	0.22	0.30	**0.24**	0.64	1.00
Mean	36.8	11.2	11.1	13.8	37.7	13.5	37.3
Standard deviation	14.3	4.2	3.4	2.7	14.8	2.5	14.9

Note: All occupations have been coded using the 1980 Census occupational classification and mapped into the Stevens-Cho MSEI2. Correlations between educational attainments and occupational statuses of siblings are shown in boldface.

Measured Social Background and Occupational Status

Father's or head of family's occupational status is a convenient proxy measure of social background, and by looking at its relationship with men's or women's occupational status, we maintain the metaphor of social mobility. However, social background consists of a much larger array of conditions of upbringing, each of which may affect adult outcomes directly or indirectly and whose effects are usually considered antithetical to notions of meritocratic achievement or selection. We have already considered some effects of race and sex, but a reasonable array of social background variables would also include maternal and paternal education and income, family structure and size, and regional and urban origin. Unfortunately, the OCG and SIPP surveys do not include a good measure of income in the family of orientation,[15] but we think that its exclusion from our analyses is not critically important in light of the available evidence of its overlap with other socioeconomic measures (Sewell and Hauser 1975; Hauser and Sweeney 1997).

Using the 1962 and 1973 OCG surveys, we have regressed occupational status (SEI) on father's educational attainment, father's occupational status, number of siblings, intact family, farm origin, and southern origin. Using the 1973 OCG survey and the 1986–1988 SIPP, we have regressed occupational status (MSEI2) on those variables, plus mother's educational attainment and—among nonblack men or women—Hispanic origin. None of the findings of these analyses is new or surprising, and the details have been presented elsewhere (Featherman and Hauser 1978). With minor exceptions, men and women are advantaged in the occupational structure if they have highly educated, high-status parents, if their families are small and intact, and if they were born outside the South, not raised on a farm, and are not of Spanish origin or descent.

In the present context, we think the most important questions are whether there has been any change in the degree to which family background influences occupational success through schooling and how the effects of schooling have changed across time. There is a long tradition of studies of omitted variable bias in estimates of the economic returns to schooling, and in this respect sociological studies of occupational attainment parallel economic studies of earnings. The prevailing wisdom is that socioeconomic origins affect adult attainments primarily through schooling. This implies that the direct effects of origins—say, the effect of parent's income on child's income—are interesting but relatively minor (Sewell and Hauser 1975). Absent lagged effects of social background, there is also less concern about omitted variable bias in the returns to schooling, though the effect of ability, motivation, or other intermediate variables, as well as those of social background, could lead to bias in estimated returns to schooling.[16] There have been occasional proposals that errors in the measurement of social background lead to underestimates of its influence and overestimates of the effects of schooling (Bowles 1972; Bowles and Gintis 1976; Rytina 1992), but in our judgment these proposals have not been supported by the evidence (Bielby and Hauser 1977; Bielby et al. 1977; Hauser and Logan 1992). For example, when Bielby, Hauser, and Featherman (1977) adjusted the 1973 OCG data for response errors in socioeconomic variables, they found even

---

[15] The 1973 OCG survey did include a retrospective item about income in the family of orientation, which was highly reliable ($r = 0.91$). However, in a validation search of Wisconsin census records, Featherman (1980) found a correlation of only 0.28 between that item and the income of the respondent's family at the census nearest his sixteenth birthday.

[16] Hauser and Sewell (1986) find little evidence that effects of measured or unmeasured family effects or academic ability reduce naive estimates of the return to postsecondary schooling among men in the WLS sample.

stronger evidence for a mediating role of schooling in the stratification process. Thus, we have no reluctance to look for evidence of change in a series
of ordinary regression analyses.

Table 8.5 gives summary measures of fit (adjusted R^2) and dispersion
(standard error of estimate) in regressions of current occupational status on
social background, on schooling, and on the combination of social background and schooling. (In the next section we will look closely at the effects
of schooling on occupational status.) With minor exceptions, regardless of the survey and year or population group, the findings in table 8.5 are
consistent.

> While social background accounts for about 15 to 20 percent of the
> variance in occupational status—equivalent to an intergenerational
> correlation between 0.39 and 0.45—schooling alone accounts for a
> far larger but more variable share of the variance in occupational
> standing. Among white men, these shares range from 0.31 to 0.53;
> among white women, from 0.29 to 0.36; among black men, from
> 0.19 to 0.60; among black women, from 0.36 to 0.53.

> Whatever the explanatory power of schooling, social background adds
> little to it. With few exceptions, the vectors of social background
> variables add no more than one or two percentage points to the ex-
> plained variance in occupational status. Indeed, in some cases the
> adjusted R^2 declines when the vector of social background variables
> is added to the equation; their contribution is worth less than the cost
> in degrees of freedom.

> Finally, both among nonblack men and black men, dispersion in occu-
> pational outcomes has increased, net of the effects of social back-
> ground and schooling. That is, in comparisons between the 1962 and
> 1973 OCG surveys (in the SEI metric), and between the 1973 OCG
> and the 1986–1988 SIPP (in the MSEI2 metric), standard errors of
> estimate increase over time for men of the same age in successive
> surveys. If occupational inequality has increased from the 1960s to
> the 1980s, some components of the increase are independent of
> changes in the distribution and effects of social background and
> schooling.

Effects of Schooling on Occupational Status

The analyses in table 8.5 are based on a simple, piecewise linear specification of the regression of occupational status on schooling:

$$Y = \alpha + \beta X_1 + \beta_2 X_2 + \beta_3 X_3 \ldots \tag{1}$$

TABLE 8.5

Measures of Dispersion and Fit in Selection Regression Analyses of Occupational Status on Social Background and Schooling: 1962 and 1973 Occupational Changes in a Generation Surveys (OCG) and 1986–1988 Surveys of Income and Program Participation (SIPP)

Population and Model	Age 25 to 34		Age 35 to 44		Age 45 to 54		Age 55 to 64	
	Err. of Est.	Adj. R-Sq.	Err. of Est.	Adj. R-Sq.	Err. of Est.	Adj. R-Sq.	Err. of Est.	Adj. R-Sq.
NONBLACK MEN								
1962 OCG (1960-basis Duncan SEI)								
Background	22.2	0.21	21.8	0.22	21.2	0.19	22.0	0.18
Education	18.2	0.47	18.5	0.44	18.8	0.37	20.2	0.31
Background and education	17.9	0.49	18.2	0.46	18.4	0.39	19.6	0.34
1973 OCG (1960-basis Duncan SEI)								
Background	22.7	0.18	22.9	0.19	22.9	0.18	22.4	0.19
Education	19.2	0.41	19.1	0.44	19.7	0.39	19.8	0.37
Background and education	19.0	0.42	18.9	0.45	19.4	0.41	19.4	0.39
1973 OCG (1970-basis MSEI2)								
Background	18.6	0.20	18.5	0.21	17.9	0.20	17.4	0.19
Education	14.6	0.51	14.3	0.53	14.5	0.47	14.7	0.42
Background and education	14.5	0.51	14.2	0.54	14.4	0.48	14.5	0.44
1986–1988 SIPP (1980-basis MSEI2)								
Background	18.8	0.16	19.3	0.15	19.3	0.16	19.4	0.17
Education	15.7	0.42	15.9	0.42	15.7	0.44	15.5	0.47
Background and education	15.5	0.43	15.8	0.43	15.7	0.45	15.3	0.48
NONBLACK WOMEN								
1986–1988 SIPP (1980-basis MSEI2)								
Background	16.6	0.13	16.8	0.12	16.6	0.14	15.8	0.13
Education	14.9	0.29	14.6	0.33	14.2	0.36	14.2	0.29
Background and education	14.8	0.31	14.6	0.34	14.1	0.38	14.1	0.31

(table continues)

TABLE 8.5 (*continued*)

Population and Model	Age 25 to 34		Age 35 to 44		Age 45 to 54		Age 55 to 64	
	Err. of Est.	Adj. R-Sq.	Err. of Est.	Adj. R-Sq.	Err. of Est.	Adj. R-Sq.	Err. of Est.	Adj. R-Sq.
BLACK MEN								
1962 OCG (1960-basis Duncan SEI)								
Background	15.2	0.14	15.2	0.11	14.0	−0.02	12.6	0.01
Education	12.9	0.38	14.1	0.22	12.5	0.19	11.1	0.24
Background and education	12.8	0.39	13.9	0.25	12.6	0.17	11.4	0.19
1973 OCG (1960-basis Duncan SEI)								
Background	19.8	0.17	20.1	0.10	17.9	0.09	15.3	0.10
Education	16.9	0.39	15.7	0.45	15.4	0.33	13.1	0.35
Background and education	16.6	0.41	15.5	0.47	15.3	0.34	12.9	0.36
1973 OCG (1970-basis MSEI2)								
Background	15.3	0.15	16.3	0.08	13.1	0.12	10.3	0.08
Education	12.4	0.45	10.8	0.60	10.6	0.43	7.7	0.48
Background and education	12.3	0.46	10.7	0.60	10.4	0.45	7.7	0.48
1986–1988 SIPP (1980-basis MSEI2)								
Background	16.2	0.16	17.3	0.12	17.2	0.13	13.9	0.25
Education	14.1	0.37	14.6	0.38	12.8	0.52	13.1	0.34
Background and education	13.9	0.39	14.3	0.40	12.9	0.51	12.7	0.38
BLACK WOMEN								
1986–1988 SIPP (1980-basis MSEI2)								
Background	15.9	0.12	18.8	0.13	16.3	0.19	17.6	0.07
Education	13.6	0.36	15.2	0.43	12.5	0.53	13.5	0.45
Background and education	13.3	0.39	15.0	0.44	12.3	0.54	13.2	0.47

where Y = occupational status, X_1 = years of graded schooling (with a maximum of 12), X_2 = years of postsecondary schooling (with a minimum of 0 for completion of twelve or fewer grades), and X_3 = 0 for eleven or fewer years of schooling and X_3 = 1 for twelve or more years of schooling. This specification provides a convenient summary of the relationship between schooling and occupational status. For example, figures 8.2 and 8.3 show the relationship between fitted and observed mean levels of occupational status (MSEI2), net of measured social background, among nonblack and black men at ages thirty-five to forty-four in the 1973 OCG survey. The approximation is close except for a tendency to overestimate the occupational status of persons who completed some college. We think that the specification is both close enough and simple enough to facilitate comparisons among groups in the effects of schooling on occupational status.

The most salient feature of the fit in figures 8.2 and 8.3 is that the effect of postsecondary schooling on occupational status is far larger than that of graded schooling. Indeed, the effect of graded schooling is slight, both among black men and among nonblack men. It is our strong suspicion that some estimates of lower returns to schooling among blacks than among whites rest on comparisons of (mis-specified) simple linear regressions. Lower slopes will be estimated among blacks merely because they complete fewer years of schooling. That is, observations for blacks are concentrated in the region of graded schooling, where returns are low.

Table 8.6 gives estimates of the effects of schooling on occupational status by race, sex, and year in the OCG surveys and SIPP. All of the reported estimates are net of measured social background. In general, the findings are similar to those in figures 8.2 and 8.3; that is, the effects of high school graduation and postsecondary schooling are large, whereas those of graded schooling are small. There are also important changes and differentials.

The effects of graded schooling on occupational status have been negligible among blacks from the 1960s through the 1980s. Among nonblacks, those effects were small in the 1960s, and by the 1980s there was no longer any effect of graded schooling on occupational status. Of course, given the growth of schooling, those noneffects are now of little importance in the population at large.

Nonblack men have enjoyed substantial effects of high school graduation and of postsecondary schooling. In the one series we can observe for nonblack women, the effect of high school graduation is larger at every age than that of postsecondary schooling. White women appear to have a higher payoff than white men for high school completion, but a lower payoff for postsecondary schooling. There is a similar differential in the effects of schooling between black women and men in the late 1980s.

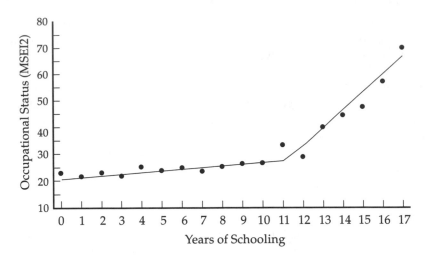

Figure 8.2. Occupational Socioeconomic Status (MSEI2) by Education: Nonblack Men Aged 35 to 44 in 1973. *Note:* Effects of years of schooling are net of social background: mother's education, father's education, head of family's occupational status, number of siblings, intact family, farm origin, Hispanic origin, and region of birth.

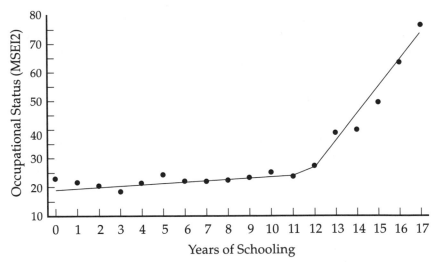

Figure 8.3. Occupational Socioeconomic Status (MSEI2) by Education: Black Men Aged 35 to 44 in 1973. *Note:* Effects of years of schooling are net of social background: mother's education, father's education, head of family's occupational status, number of siblings, intact family, farm origin, Hispanic origin, and region of birth.

TABLE 8.6

Effects of Educational Attainment on Occupational Status Net of Social Background: 1962 and 1973 Occupational Changes in a Generation Surveys (OCG) and 1986–1988 Surveys of Income and Program Participation (SIPP)

Population and Variables	Age 25 to 34		Age 35 to 44		Age 45 to 54		Age 55 to 64	
	Estimate	Std. Error	Estimate	Std. Error	Estimate	Std. Error	Estimate	Std. Error
NONBLACK MEN								
1962 OCG (1960-basis Duncan SEI)								
Graded school	1.30	0.31	1.35	0.24	2.14	0.24	2.17	0.26
Postsecondary school	7.16	0.24	6.16	0.25	5.24	0.31	3.96	0.42
High school graduation	5.79	1.37	8.50	1.18	4.37	1.26	4.17	1.67
1973 OCG (1960-basis Duncan SEI)]								
Graded school	0.88	0.29	1.49	0.25	1.53	0.23	1.52	0.25
Postsecondary school	6.74	0.16	6.52	0.18	6.17	0.20	5.93	0.28
High school graduation	7.06	1.17	6.46	1.15	7.16	1.09	6.39	1.24
1973 OCG (1970-basis MSEI2)								
Graded school	0.29	0.2	0.60	0.18	0.67	0.17	0.68	0.19
Postsecondary school	6.93	0.13	6.75	0.14	6.27	0.15	5.85	0.21
High school graduation	4.13	0.87	4.64	0.84	4.82	0.80	5.50	0.93
1986–1988 SIPP (1980-basis MSEI2)								
Graded school	−0.14	0.25	−0.35	0.24	0.71	0.28	0.54	0.26
Postsecondary school	5.73	0.11	5.46	0.12	5.27	0.14	5.70	0.18
High school graduation	4.15	1.00	5.15	1.15	4.19	1.23	3.16	1.25
NONBLACK WOMEN								
1986–1988 SIPP (1980-basis MSEI2)								
Graded school	−0.70	0.30	0.16	0.29	0.72	0.31	0.42	0.32
Postsecondary school	3.95	0.12	4.17	0.12	4.38	0.17	3.73	0.22
High school graduation	8.45	1.19	7.91	1.25	3.12	1.25	6.78	1.34

(table continues)

TABLE 8.6 (continued)

Population and Variables	Age 25 to 34		Age 35 to 44		Age 45 to 54		Age 55 to 64	
	Estimate	Std. Error	Estimate	Std. Error	Estimate	Std. Error	Estimate	Std. Error
BLACK MEN								
1962 OCG (1960-basis Duncan SEI)								
Graded school	0.23	0.41	0.48	0.33	0.80	0.34	0.84	0.34
Postsecondary school	8.95	0.98	6.08	1.05	8.02	1.38	7.09	1.94
High school graduation	0.67	2.53	1.15	2.83	-2.62	3.14	-0.91	5.98
1973 OCG (1960-basis Duncan SEI)								
Graded school	0.64	0.53	0.67	0.41	1.20	0.32	0.54	0.32
Postsecondary school	7.72	0.57	9.04	0.60	7.34	0.76	9.59	1.09
High school graduation	6.17	2.14	4.65	2.14	1.20	2.32	0.52	2.82
1973 OCG (1970-basis MSEI2)								
Graded school	0.28	0.35	0.41	0.26	0.49	0.20	0.28	0.17
Postsecondary school	7.31	0.39	9.31	0.37	7.14	0.47	8.56	0.59
High school graduation	2.96	1.44	2.57	1.34	1.30	1.41	-0.94	1.51
1986–1988 SIPP (1980-basis MSEI2)								
Graded school	0.50	1.16	-0.14	0.72	0.51	0.54	0.47	0.49
Postsecondary school	5.35	0.40	5.57	0.44	6.56	0.52	3.49	0.79
High school graduation	3.58	2.76	6.00	2.62	1.29	2.60	3.30	3.14
BLACK WOMEN								
1986–1988 SIPP (1980-basis MSEI2)								
Graded school	0.39	1.10	-0.79	0.82	0.85	0.62	0.30	0.59
Postsecondary school	4.55	0.32	6.03	0.39	6.98	0.58	6.01	0.69
High school graduation	7.56	3.16	9.10	2.97	5.05	2.39	8.17	3.27

Black and nonblack women have similar returns to high school graduation in the 1980s, but the effect of postsecondary schooling is consistently larger among black than among nonblack women. This may be
due to the more continuous employment histories of black women.

At younger ages, black men have experienced increasing returns to high
school graduation, both between the 1960s and 1970s and between
the 1970s and the 1980s. By the 1980s those effects were similar to
the effects of high school graduation among nonblack men. Effects of
high school graduation have remained low among black workers at
older ages.

In the 1960s and 1970s, effects of postsecondary schooling on the occupational status of black men were consistently larger than among
nonblack men; this differential is no longer clear in the 1980s.

In our opinion, the main story here is that there has been relatively little
change in the effects of schooling on occupational status. Occupational effects of graded schooling have been low, and they have remained low or
disappeared. Returns to postsecondary schooling have been high, and they
have remained high. The most conspicuous change is the increasing value of
high school graduation among young black men. Public perception of the
growing importance of schooling in social and economic success has played
an important part in discussions of "the meritocracy." What accounts for that
perception if the effects of schooling on occupational standing have not
changed very much?

First, since the early 1970s there have been major changes in the effects of
schooling on earnings, and these have increased the relative value of high
school graduation and college attendance (Murphy and Welch 1989). Second, and—we think—equally important, schooling has become more important because levels of educational attainment have increased. More of the
population has completed levels of schooling where the expected returns to
schooling are high. For example, figures 8.4 and 8.5 show the distribution by
age in 1992 of educational credentials among blacks and among non-
Hispanic whites.[17] The age differences in education reflect intercohort
changes in educational attainment. Although the trends are damped by the
tendency of adults to complete higher degrees at older ages, the cross-
sectional age comparisons amply demonstrate the expansion of postsecondary schooling among blacks and whites and the rapid decline of the share of
the black population with no high school credential. Similar observations
might be offered with respect to growth in postsecondary schooling among
women relative to men. Moreover, the general population has moved into
levels of the educational distribution where returns are high at the same time

[17] These data are based on the Census Bureau's post-1990 classification of educational
credentials.

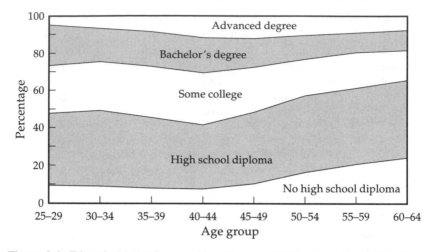

Figure 8.4. Educational Attainment: Non-Hispanic Whites Aged 25 to 64, March 1992 Current Population Survey

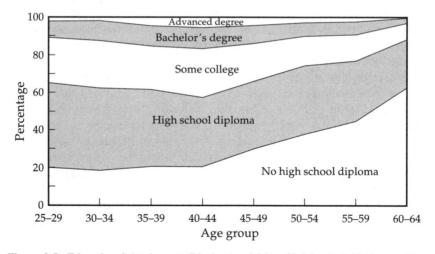

Figure 8.5. Educational Attainment: Blacks Aged 25 to 64, March 1992 Current Population Survey

that previously noncompeting groups—women and blacks—have moved into the same segments of the labor market.

Mental Ability, Merit, and Occupational Status

In this section we first offer a few observations about relationships among measured mental ability, schooling, and occupational status, and we then turn to a more intensive analysis of the effects of ability and of other social and psychological variables on occupational status in a large, long-term study of the life course. It is not clear to us why the term *merit* should be identified so closely with mental ability as distinct from many other conditions and traits that improve the chances of social and economic success. Among these, for example, one might list ambition or drive, perseverance, responsibility, personal attractiveness, and physical or artistic skills or talents, along with access to favorable social and economic networks and resources.[18] To be sure, cognitive functioning plays an important role in the occupational structure of complex societies, but it is surely not the only identifiable factor in achievement beyond the initial conditions of race, sex, and socioeconomic origin. One factor contributing to the conflation of merit with mental ability is surely the preoccupation with intelligence and its consequences in a long tradition of psychology, whose latest unfortunate manifestation is the Herrnstein and Murray (1994) book, *The Bell Curve*. In our opinion, some economic thought has catered to this unidimensional notion of merit by treating ability as an unmeasured residual. To be sure, the theoretical content of the economic concept of ability is potentially broader, but gradually it has become identified with the psychologist's measurements of the same name, rather than with an array of variables beyond those that are easily quantifiable in economic research.

Early in *The Bell Curve* there is a wonderfully written but purely speculative passage that argues that occupations have become more and more segregated by intelligence throughout the course of the twentieth century (Herrnstein and Murray 1994, pp. 51–61). Over the course of this century, Herrnstein and Murray argue, ability has increased in importance with respect to occupational and economic success. That, in turn, has tended to segregate people in the higher reaches of the occupational distribution, and this leads through social isolation to mutual sociation, to elitism, and, finally, by dint of genetic inheritance, to persistence of membership across generations in the cognitive elite. They also suggest that the isolation of the elite from the everyday lives of the nonelite could eventually lead to social disaster. We suspect that to the extent cognitive elitism and isolation has grown, it has far

[18] See, for example, the work of Clausen (1993), *American Lives*, which follows the careers of a small California sample from youth to old age.

more to do with growth in education, growth of complex, high-status occupations, and growth in complex organizations than with selection on ability per se. Herrnstein and Murray conclude, "Even as recently as midcentury, America was still a society in which most bright people were scattered throughout a wide range of jobs. As the century draws to a close, a very high proportion of that same group is now concentrated within a few occupations that are highly screened for IQ."

Herrnstein and Murray's text offers no data about trends in the joint distribution of IQ and occupation: It rests entirely on the growth of occupations whose incumbents have high levels of schooling. See, especially, their graph at p. 56, "The top IQ decile becomes rapidly more concentrated in high-IQ professions from 1940 onward," which displays time-series in three different scalar transformations of the number of workers in selected professional and technical occupations. The evidence that Herrnstein and Murray present about occupations and the cognitive elite combines real data about the growth of key knowledge-based occupations with unfettered speculation about constancy in the measured ability of the incumbents of those elite occupations (and in the population at large). "Increasing cognitive isolation" is no more than a speculative extrapolation from the growth of knowledge-based occupations.

To test the original proposition, we looked at data for 13,000 persons in the GSS in the eleven years from 1974 to 1993 in which a ten-item verbal ability test had been administered. We looked at the share of employed persons, aged twenty-five to sixty-four, who answered all ten questions correctly, relative to the share of such persons who gave fewer correct answers; about 6 percent of the population met this standard of cognitive ability. Then we classified occupations into those that represented the cognitive elite, as defined by Herrnstein and Murray, versus all other occupations.[19] Figure 8.6 shows trends in the chances that persons in elite and in nonelite occupations answered ten questions correctly and trends in the chances that persons in elite occupations answered ten questions correctly relative to the chances that persons in nonelite occupations answered ten questions correctly. (Each series has two components because the GSS used 1970-basis occupation codes from 1974 to 1990, and it used 1980-basis occupation codes from 1988 to 1993.) The first two measures are expressed in the natural log of the odds of answering the questions correctly, and the third measure is the difference between the first two. Over the twenty years covered by the GSS, the story is very simple. Cognitive performance has been essentially stable in nonelite occupations. It is higher in elite than in nonelite occupations, but

[19] The elite occupations are accountant, architect, chemist, college teacher, computer scientist, dentist, engineer, lawyer, mathematician, natural scientist, physician, and social scientist (Herrnstein and Murray 1994, p. 56).

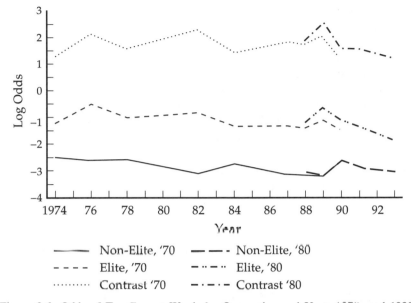

Figure 8.6. Odds of Ten Correct Words by Occupation and Year: 1970- and 1980-Basis Occupational Classification Systems, General Social Survey, 1974 to 1993. *Note:* Data are shown for years in which GSS data are available and interpolated for intermediate years.

appears to have declined slightly in elite occupations. Consequently, there has been a slight decline in the difference in verbal ability between persons in elite and in nonelite occupations. The finding is unchanged if we restrict the sample to nonminorities, and it is unchanged if we choose a less stringent criterion of cognitive performance—getting nine of the ten answers right. The time-series based on the GSS data not only fails to support Herrnstein and Murray, but tends to contradict their thesis.[20]

The Bell Curve offers other strong statements and speculations about the relationship between mental ability and occupational status, but it offers little evidence to back them up. To be sure, there are only a few sets of national data that include measures of mental ability as well as socioeconomic variables, and most of those are limited to samples of youth, either in the general population or in school-based samples. Few studies provide the extended window of observation that one would like in order to measure long-term

[20] Weakliem, McQuillan, and Schauer (1995) have carried out additional analyses of the GSS data and reached parallel conclusions about the lack of trends in relationships between verbal ability and social class. For a thorough critique of Herrnstein and Murray's trend hypothesis and additional data on trends in relationships between verbal ability and social background, educational attainment, occupational status, and earnings, see Hauser and Huang (1997).

effects of mental ability on occupational outcomes. One of the best available resources of this kind is probably the National Longitudinal Survey of Youth (NLSY), from which a variety of data through 1990 were used in *The Bell Curve*. However, there is very little analysis of occupational attainment in the book, based either on the NLSY or on other readily available data resources.

For example, in a summary passage Herrnstein and Murray write, "Whatever the reason for the link between IQ and occupation, it goes deep. If you want to guess an adult male's job status, the results of his childhood IQ test help you as much as knowing how many years he went to school" (p. 51). Surprisingly, the supporting text (p. 53) makes no reference to the NLSY. This is curious, since the only research discussed in the text is McCall's study of forty-six to ninety children of each sex in the Fels Longitudinal Study, for whom educational attainment and occupation had been ascertained at ages twenty-six or later. Herrnstein and Murray report, "The IQ scores they got when they were 7 or 8 years old were about as correlated with the status level of their adult jobs as their adult IQ would have been. Inasmuch as childhood IQ is more correlated with status than completed education, as it is in some studies, the thesis that IQ scores really just measure educational level is weakened." The Fels sample, born between 1930 and 1943, is reported to contain "families from the top 85 percent of the socioeconomic scale and is somewhat skewed to the right in educational attainment" (McCall 1977, p. 482). That is surely the case, for McCall reports that 34 percent of the women and 56 percent of the men in the sample had graduated from college. These percentages are exceptionally high for the relevant cohorts, and they lead us to doubt whether the samples could possibly yield estimates of correlations that would be valid for the general population.[21] None of these qualifications is mentioned by Herrnstein and Murray.

Among youth in the contemporary United States, there are substantial correlations between mental ability, measured in adolescence, with both educational attainment and occupational status, but the correlation between ability and occupation is not larger than that between educational attainment and occupation. Table 8.7 shows correlations among years of schooling, Armed Forces Qualification Test scores (1989 revision), and occupational status in four subgroups of the NLSY sample. The data pertain to youth in the cross-section sample in the four youngest birth cohorts, born in 1961 to 1964, who were very likely to have taken the Armed Services Vocational Aptitude Battery (ASVAB) before school-leaving.[22] Thus, the observation of completed

[21] It is a bit off the subject but worth noting that McCall's report—ignored by Herrnstein and Murray—comments that "to predict child's attained education . . . for sheer predictive purposes father's education level was more accurate than the child's own IQ, which contributed no substantial additional predictive power" (McCall 1977, p. 483).

[22] Because of the narrow age-range of this sample, we have not adjusted AFQT scores for age or grade in school at administration of the test.

TABLE 8.7
Correlations between AFQT (1989 Revision), Educational Attainment (1988), and Occupational Status (MSEI2) in the National Longitudinal Study of Youth: Cohorts Born between 1961 and 1964

Subgroup	Schooling	1989 Job	1990 Job	1991 Job	1992 Job	1993 Job
NONBLACK MEN (N = 1,202)						
Schooling	1.00	0.61	0.64	0.62	0.59	0.61
AFQT	0.66	0.51	0.54	0.51	0.51	0.55
NONBLACK WOMEN (N = 1,159)						
Schooling	1.00	0.52	0.56	0.51	0.48	0.50
AFQT	0.62	0.43	0.46	0.42	0.38	0.43
BLACK MEN (N = 169)						
Schooling	1.00	0.64	0.56	0.53	0.57	0.54
AFQT	0.54	0.54	0.59	0.49	0.54	0.50
BLACK WOMEN (N = 189)						
Schooling	1.00	0.55	0.55	0.53	0.43	0.47
AFQT	0.48	0.49	0.46	0.41	0.49	0.40

schooling, from the 1988 NLSY survey, pertains to the sample at ages twenty-four to twenty-eight, and the observations of occupational status cover ages from twenty-five to thirty-two. The data permit twenty comparisons of the correlation between AFQT and occupational status with that between educational attainment and occupational status. In just two of those, both in the rather small black samples, the correlation of status with the AFQT is larger than with educational attainment. In the remaining cases, and especially among nonblack youth, the correlations between schooling and occupational status are often much larger than those between the AFQT and occupational status.

Ability and Occupational Status in the Life Course

The senior author of this paper, among others, has followed a cohort of ten thousand Wisconsin high school students since their graduation in 1957 (Sewell and Hauser 1992b). The most recent follow-up of the Wisconsin Longitudinal Study (WLS) was in 1992–1993, when the sample was fifty-three to fifty-four years old (Hauser et al. 1992). It thus provides a valuable opportunity for us to look at the evolution of socioeconomic achievements over much of the life course.

A survey of background, school experiences, and aspirations among all high school seniors in Wisconsin public, private, and parochial schools was conducted in the spring of 1957. From this survey, a one-third random sample of 4,994 men and 5,323 women was drawn. Information on parental income, student's measured intelligence, and high school rank were taken from school and public records with proper precautions to protect the confidentiality of individual information. In 1975 a follow-up study was conducted in which almost 90 percent of the original sample members were located and interviewed by telephone (Clarridge et al. 1978). These data provide a full record of social background, youthful aspirations, schooling, military service, family formation, labor-market experiences, and social participation of the original respondents. During 1992 and 1993, we followed up the sample for the first time since 1975, and we interviewed 91 percent of surviving 1975 respondents.

The WLS sample is broadly representative of middle-aged white American men and women who have completed at least a high school education. Among American women and men aged fifty to fifty-four in 1990 and 1991, approximately 66 percent are whites of non-Hispanic background who completed at least twelve years of schooling (Kominski and Adams 1992). In light of the essential stability of occupational returns to postsecondary schooling over the past thirty years, we think that the experience of the Wisconsin cohort is highly relevant to the contemporary discussion of meritocracy and inequality. Some strata of American society are not represented in the WLS. Everyone in the original sample graduated from high school. Sewell and Hauser (1975) estimated that about 75 percent of Wisconsin youth graduated from high school in the late 1950s. Minorities are not well represented; there are only a handful of African-American, Hispanic, or Asian persons in the sample. About 19 percent of the WLS sample is of farm origin, and that is consistent with national estimates of persons of farm origin in cohorts born in the late 1930s. At each reinterview, roughly 70 percent of the sample lived in Wisconsin, and 30 percent lived elsewhere in the United States or abroad.

Despite its limitations, the WLS provides a long-term look at the development of the life course from adolescence to midlife in a cohort of men and women who resemble a large segment of the U.S. population. The sample is large, and sample retention is very high; compare Jencks et al. (1979, pp. 6–7) and Center for Human Resource Research (1992, p. 1). Measurements are of high (and often of known) quality. Moreover, the WLS has fared well in comparisons of findings with national studies of comparable populations (Sewell and Hauser 1975; Jencks et al. 1983; Corcoran et al. 1992).

Our analysis of the WLS data is based upon the well-known social psychological model of attainment that was originally developed using data for the same cohort from the senior year of high school, 1957, through the seven years that usually encompass college attendance and entry into careers and marriage (Sewell et al. 1969; Sewell et al. 1970; Sewell 1971; Sewell and

Hauser 1975). In the present analysis we seek to learn whether, and in what ways, the conditions of early career success continue to influence socio-economic outcomes later in life.

To anticipate some findings, we note that adolescent IQ and educational attainment are both moderately correlated with occupational status from youth to maturity, but the educational correlations are much larger, at least early in the career. Among WLS men, the correlation between years of schooling and the status of first full-time civilian jobs is 0.77, and among WLS women, the correlation is 0.50. By age fifty-three to fifty-four, these correlations fall to 0.54 and 0.37, respectively. The correlation between Henmon-Nelson IQ score and status of the first job is 0.44 among men and 0.33 among women. At ages fifty-three to fifty-four, the correlations are 0.39 and 0.37. Thus, the correlations of occupation with educational attainment decline across the life course, whereas those with IQ are relatively stable. This suggests that there is something more to ability than its validation through schooling, but the correlation of IQ with occupational status is also not impressively large.

A Social Psychological Model of Attainment

In this section we first briefly review our social psychological model of achievement. Second, we report a regression analysis of the occupational status of WLS men and women, which follows the influence of social background, ability, and aspiration from adolescence through maturity. Last, we report a parallel, canonical analysis of occupational status across the life course; this identifies patterns of constancy and change in the influence of earlier life conditions and experiences.

Our analysis is based upon a social psychological model of attainment, which is shown schematically in figure 8.7. Briefly, it elaborates the well-known Blau-Duncan model of occupational achievement by introducing social psychological variables related to school experience and aspiration, as well as a more extensive set of social background characteristics.[23] The model is block-recursive, and all save two of the blocks shown in figure 8.7 represent more than one variable. The idea of the model is that social background affects school performance, while background and performance affect social support for post–high school education. All three prior constructs affect levels of aspiration, which in turn affect the ultimate level of post–high school educational attainment. Finally, educational attainment, along

[23] Our work with the model is reviewed by Sewell and Hauser (1992a and 1992b). It has been used previously in three comparative analyses of the attainment of women and men in young adulthood (Sewell 1971; Hauser et al. 1976; Sewell et al. 1980). We have modified the content of some of the blocks of variables in the model relative to earlier versions of it.

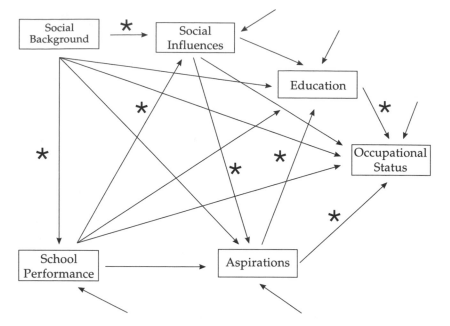

Figure 8.7. A Social Psychological Model of Socioeconomic Attainment

with all of the previous variables, affects occupational status. Although the diagram and our description of it suggest that each variable in turn can directly affect all of the variables in the blocks that follow it, we expect to find that the major effects approximate a modified causal chain (Sewell et al. 1969; Sewell et al. 1970; Hauser et al. 1983). The most important paths in the model, noted with asterisks in the diagram, are those from social background to school performance, from social background and school performance to the social influences, from the social influences to aspiration, from aspiration to schooling and socioeconomic attainment, and from schooling to attainment. Thus, the model purports to account for the influence of social background and school performance on attainment by way of social support and aspiration.

Variables

Table 8.8 shows the means and standard deviations of the variables used in the present analysis for men and women and for two sample definitions. Throughout, we limit the analysis to men and women who responded both in 1975 and 1992–1993 and for whom all of the variables in the model up through educational attainment had been ascertained. In the first column of

TABLE 8.8

Means and Standard Deviations of Social, Psychological, and Occupational Variables by Sex: Wisconsin Longitudinal Study

Variable	All Men in Sample			Men Reporting Jobs at Each Observation (N = 3080)		All Women in Sample			Women Reporting Jobs at Each Observation (N = 1489)	
	Mean	SD	N	Mean	SD	Mean	SD	N	Mean	SD
Parents' Income	8.65	0.58	3,360	8.65	0.58	8.64	0.58	3,747	8.61	0.54
Father's Occupation (SEI)	34.5	23.2	3,360	34.3	23.2	34.7	23.2	3,747	33.1	22.6
Father's Education	9.8	3.4	3,360	9.7	3.4	9.6	3.3	3,747	9.5	3.2
Mother's Education	10.6	2.8	3,360	10.6	2.8	10.3	2.8	3,747	10.3	2.7
Farm Background	0.20	0.40	3,360	0.21	0.40	0.20	0.40	3,747	0.22	0.42
Intact Family	0.92	0.28	3,360	0.92	0.28	0.92	0.28	3,747	0.92	0.27
Sibship Size	3.2	2.5	3,360	3.2	2.5	3.3	2.5	3,747	3.3	2.6
IQ (Henmon-Nelson)	101.9	15.1	3,360	101.5	15.0	101.4	14.3	3,747	101.8	14.7
Academic Program	0.66	0.48	3,360	0.64	0.48	0.55	0.50	3,747	0.55	0.50
High School Rank	98.1	14.5	3,360	97.8	14.5	105.0	14.1	3,747	105.1	14.7
Teacher's Encouragement	0.46	0.50	3,360	0.45	0.50	0.43	0.50	3,747	0.44	0.50
Parents' Encouragement	0.60	0.49	3,360	0.59	0.49	0.48	0.50	3,747	0.49	0.50
Friends' College Plans	0.37	0.48	3,360	0.36	0.48	0.39	0.49	3,747	0.39	0.49
College Plans	0.48	0.50	3,360	0.47	0.50	0.50	0.50	3,747	0.50	0.50
Occupational Aspiration (SEI)	54.3	23.5	3,360	53.9	23.5	49.1	13.1	3,747	48.7	13.1
Educational Attainment	13.9	2.5	3,360	13.8	2.4	13.1	1.8	3,747	13.1	1.9
First Occupation (SEI)	40.7	27.1	3,192	40.4	27.0	46.8	18.5	3,482	47.2	18.8
1970 Occupation (SEI)	50.2	24.7	3,212	49.8	24.8	47.3	20.2	1,660	46.9	20.1
1975 Occ. (SEI from 1975)	51.5	24.5	3,334	50.8	24.7	45.1	20.4	2,709	47.1	20.1
1975 Occ. (SEI from 1992)	51.0	24.7	3,338	50.3	24.7	45.6	20.5	3,464	47.6	20.2
1992 Occupation (SEI)	51.6	24.7	3,339	50.8	24.7	48.6	20.9	3,466	50.1	20.6

Table 8.8, conditional on that selection of cases, we show means and standard deviations for all individuals who reported the variable in question. In the second column, the descriptive statistics are limited to the individuals who reported each of five jobs covered in the analysis.

Social background variables include parents' income, father's occupation, mother's and father's educational attainments, farm origin, family structure (intact or non-intact), and number of siblings. Parents' income was obtained from Wisconsin state tax records for 1957 to 1960, the years during which respondents were most likely to have attended college. It is expressed here as the natural log of the four-year average. Father's occupation and the educational attainment of each parent were reported in the 1975 survey; in a small number of cases missing data were filled in with information from tax records or from the 1957 survey. Father's occupation was coded into categories of the classification of occupations and industries for the U.S. census of 1970, and for the regression analysis this was mapped into the Duncan SEI.

School performance includes mental ability, high school program, and rank in high school class. Mental ability is based on the Henmon-Nelson test, normed on the population of Wisconsin high school juniors to which it was routinely administered during the 1950s. The scores were obtained from records of the Wisconsin State Testing Service at the University of Wisconsin–Madison. High school program is a dummy variable, obtained by comparing student's 1957 report of the number of courses taken in several subject matter areas to the contemporary requirements for entrance to the University of Wisconsin. Students were coded as in a college preparatory program if they reported completing the University of Wisconsin entrance requirements. Rank in high school class was reported by the schools, transformed to percentile rank, and then transformed to a normal deviate with a mean of 100 and a standard deviation of 15. It is thus expressed in the same metric and has nominally the same distribution as the Henmon-Nelson IQ scores.

Social influences are represented by the respondent's perception of encouragement from parents and from teachers to attend college and by perception of whether most friends planned to attend college. Aspirations include educational plans in the year after high school graduation and the occupation that the respondent eventually hoped to enter. For this analysis, we used the student's reports from the 1957 survey. The 1957 reports of occupational aspiration were recently recoded to 1970 census standards and mapped into the Duncan scale.

Educational attainment is the number of years of regular (academic) schooling completed by the respondent, as reported in the 1975 survey. Occupational status is based on reports of occupation, industry, and class of worker from the 1975 and 1992 surveys: first full-time job after leaving school for the last time, job in 1970, current or last job in 1975 (as reported in 1975), job in 1975 (as reported in 1992–1993), and current or last job in 1992–1993.[24]

We have used both the 1975 and 1992–1993 reports of 1975 occupations in order to assess the comparability of the data collected in the two widely separated follow-up surveys. In the 1992–1993 survey, we asked about jobs in 1975 for two reasons. First, we wanted to establish an anchor in the telephone interview for the respondent to use in giving us an occupational history since 1975. Thus, early in the occupation section we said, "When we last talked to you in [month] 1975, you told us that you were working at [name of firm]. What kind of work were you doing?" Second, we wanted to ascertain the reliability of occupational reports across the eighteen-year period between the two surveys. Although the two measurements were in some sense dependent, by virtue of the deliberate linkage in time and place, the occupation and industry reports were otherwise ascertained and coded independently. In both surveys, the several possible occupation reports were also coded independently within interviews, and no information from the 1975 surveys was used in coding the 1992–1993 data. Note that many fewer women had complete occupational histories than men. Of course, women were less likely than men to have had continuous employment histories. However, this loss of data occurred in part because of the seemingly large discrepancy between the number of women for whom there were contemporaneous occupation reports in 1975 (2,523) and for whom there were retrospective reports (1,987); there was only a small difference in the corresponding counts among men. This occurred because the contemporaneous 1975 reports referred to a current or last job held within the past five years, whereas the retrospective reports covered only current employment in the month of the 1975 interview. All of the occupations held by respondents were mapped into the Duncan SEI.

There were essentially no differences in the characteristics of the samples generated by our two population definitions. However, regardless of the method used to define the sample, there were significant differences between women and men in late adolescence (compare the entries for men and women in table 8.8). There were no sex differences in social background or mental ability, but 66 percent of men and only 55 percent of women completed a college preparatory program in high school. At the same time, women's high school ranks were substantially higher than those of men (by

[24] We collected an occupational history from 1975 to 1992–1993 of up to four employers or businesses and the first and last jobs with each employer/business, and we plan to include other occupations held from 1975 to 1992–1993 in future analyses. This data collection scheme does not in principle give us a continuous or complete job history. It leaves out the middle employment spells for persons who were employed in more than four establishments. However, for this cohort, employment patterns were sufficiently stable by 1975 to give us complete and continuous histories for more than 90 percent of respondents.

seven points, or nearly half a standard deviation). Despite the higher grades of women, men were slightly more likely than women to report that their teachers had encouraged them to attend college (46 percent versus 43 percent), but men were much more likely than women to report that their parents had encouraged college attendance (60 percent versus 48 percent). Consequently, it was somewhat surprising to find that women were more likely than men to report that their friends were planning to attend college, and that women were more likely than men to plan to attend college in the year following high school graduation.[25] However, women aspired to lower-status occupations than men.

Ultimately, men of the WLS obtained almost a year more schooling than women. Men gained about ten points in status from their first to 1970 occupations, but little growth occurred after that. Among all women, there was virtually no change in occupational status from first jobs to 1970 jobs. Status decreased from 1970 to 1975, but it increased by 1992–1993 to a higher level than in the early career. However, among fully employed women there was slow growth in occupational status after 1970. At every stage of the career after the first job, and regardless of continuity of employment, women's jobs were lower in status than men's jobs.

In tables 8.9 and 8.10 we have arrayed selected coefficients of successive reduced-form regressions of occupational status on prior variables in the social psychological model of figure 8.7. By entering variables in succession, from least to most proximate to the outcome variables, we estimate the total effects of each block of variables in turn, as well as a decomposition of the influence of each variable through subsequent intervening variables (Alwin and Hauser 1975). Although this analysis tells us about the effects of the variables in the model, it provides no information about the relationships among the occupational status measures. That is, in the present analysis we have not attempted to model the occupational career. We think that the successive reduced-form regressions are of interest in their own right.

After examining the regressions for occupational status in 1992–1993, we focus our attention on comparisons among the several reduced-form regressions of the occupational outcomes. In the former analysis we use all of the observations from the 1992–1993 survey; in the latter we restrict our attention to men and women with complete occupation histories. In the second stage of the analysis we ask how different are the reduced-form regressions across the several measures of occupational status. We specify MIMIC (multiple-indicator, multiple-cause) models of occupational status, and these permit us to test for differences among the five possible occupational status regressions (Hauser and Goldberger 1971; Joreskog and Goldberger 1975).

---

[25] A substantial minority of men, but not of women, planned to enter military service soon after completing high school.

TABLE 8.9

Regression of Occupational Status (SEI) of 1992 Job on Social Psychological Variables and Schooling: Men and Women in the Wisconsin Longitudinal Study

Variables Added to Model	Men (N = 3,339)					Women (N = 3,466)				
	Social Origins	School Perform.	Others' Influence	Aspirations	Schooling	Social Origins	School Perform.	Others' Influence	Aspirations	Schooling
Parents' income	4.14	3.13	2.25	2.15	1.63	3.57	3.02	2.92	2.74	2.08
	(0.81)	(0.75)	(0.74)	(0.73)	(0.70)	(0.72)	(0.68)	(0.68)	(0.68)	(0.67)
Father's occ. (SEI)	0.15	0.09	0.06	0.05	0.04	0.08	0.05	0.04	0.04	0.02
	(0.02)	(0.02)	(0.02)	(0.02)	(0.02)	(0.02)	(0.02)	(0.02)	(0.02)	(0.02)
Father's education	0.53	0.25	0.18	0.12	-0.10	0.25	0.00	-0.07	-0.09	-0.13
	(0.15)	(0.14)	(0.14)	(0.14)	(0.13)	(0.13)	(0.13)	(0.13)	(0.13)	(0.12)
Mother's education	0.53	0.29	0.19	0.14	0.08	0.83	0.41	0.33	0.28	0.19
	(0.17)	(0.16)	(0.15)	(0.15)	(0.14)	(0.15)	(0.14)	(0.14)	(0.14)	(0.14)
Farm background	-5.30	-5.57	-5.27	-4.29	-4.24	1.71	0.91	0.75	0.49	-0.39
	(1.15)	(1.07)	(1.06)	(1.06)	(1.01)	(1.01)	(0.96)	(0.96)	(0.95)	(0.94)
Intact family	-1.56	-2.12	-2.14	-2.22	-2.08	-0.85	-1.27	-1.41	-1.42	-1.02
	(1.50)	(1.39)	(1.37)	(1.35)	(1.29)	(1.28)	(1.22)	(1.21)	(1.21)	(1.19)
Number of siblings	-0.43	-0.07	0.10	0.15	0.18	-0.41	-0.14	-0.06	-0.04	-0.01
	(0.17)	(0.16)	(0.16)	(0.15)	(0.15)	(0.14)	(0.14)	(0.14)	(0.14)	(0.13)
IQ (Henmon-Nelson)		0.29	0.26	0.24	0.18		0.24	0.23	0.23	0.21
		(0.03)	(0.03)	(0.03)	(0.03)		(0.03)	(0.03)	(0.03)	(0.03)
Academic program		6.17	3.42	2.37	1.67		3.35	2.04	1.75	1.51
		(0.90)	(0.92)	(0.91)	(0.87)		(0.76)	(0.79)	(0.80)	(0.78)

(table continues)

TABLE 8.9 (continued)

Variables Added to Model	Men (N = 3,339)					Women (N = 3,466)				
	Social Origins	School Perform.	Others' Influence	Aspirations	Schooling	Social Origins	School Perform.	Others' Influence	Aspirations	Schooling
High school rank		0.28	0.17	0.12	-0.01		0.22	0.19	0.17	0.13
		(0.03)	(0.03)	(0.03)	(0.03)		(0.03)	(0.03)	(0.03)	(0.03)
Teacher's encouragement			3.95	3.00	2.08			2.02	1.51	1.31
			(0.87)	(0.87)	(0.83)			(0.78)	(0.78)	(0.77)
Parents' encouragement			5.08	2.69	1.81			2.16	1.04	0.31
			(0.93)	(0.95)	(0.91)			(0.81)	(0.88)	(0.87)
Friends' college plans			5.59	3.90	1.22			1.94	1.33	0.45
			(0.89)	(0.90)	(0.87)			(0.80)	(0.82)	(0.81)
College plans				4.50	0.91				1.30	-0.67
				(0.97)	(0.95)				(0.87)	(0.88)
Occ. aspirations (SEI)				0.14	0.10				0.16	0.08
				(0.02)	(0.02)				(0.03)	(0.03)
Education					3.52					2.53
					(0.20)					(0.24)
Constant	3.64	-42.33	-23.59	-20.52	-37.14	5.83	-32.39	-26.63	-29.12	-42.94
	(6.81)	(6.76)	(6.83)	(6.77)	(6.54)	(5.95)	(6.26)	(6.32)	(6.32)	(6.36)
R-Squared	0.116	0.241	0.270	0.292	0.353	0.065	0.159	0.167	0.176	0.202
SE of estimate	23.26	21.56	21.14	20.84	19.92	20.27	19.23	19.15	19.06	18.75

For example, at one extreme, the regression of occupational status in 1992–1993 on the several variables in our model might be indistinguishable from the regressions of the other four status measures on the same variables. At the other extreme, the relative weights of the explanatory variables in the five regressions might vary so widely across the life course that each equation requires separate examination. Between the extremes, we might find regular, scalar gradations in the effects of the explanatory variables on occupational status, for example, that effects on occupational status decline regularly across the life course, as suggested by Sewell et al. (1980). Or we might find such regular gradations combined with a few significant departures from them. In the case of occupational status, the MIMIC models also permit us to test some ideas about the structure of the career. For example, if a single latent factor could account for the correlations among occupational status variables across the life course, one might ask whether there was a career at all, or whether the jobs held over time were merely sampled at random from those initially accessible to a person.

Table 8.9 shows the reduced-form regressions of occupational status in 1992–1993 on the variables in our social psychological model. Reading the columns from left to right, the total effect of each variable is given by its coefficient in the first equation in which it appears.[26] The mediation of effects through intervening blocks of variables in the model can be observed by seeing how the coefficient of a variable changes from column to column. For example, looking at the total effect of father's education among men (0.53), about half is explained by the influence of father's education on the school performance of young men, for the coefficient falls to 0.25 when the three school performance variables are added to the equation.

Occupational Status In 1992–1993

As expected, the four socioeconomic background variables (parents' income, father's occupational status, and mother's and father's educational attainments) have significant total effects of the expected sign on occupational status in 1992–1993. In one case, the coefficients differ significantly between men and women. The effect of father's occupational status on son's occupational status exceeds that of father's occupational status on daughter's status.[27] Among all four socioeconomic variables, a substantial share of the

---

[26] Throughout this discussion, our rule of thumb for statistical significance is that a coefficient, or a gender difference in coefficients, should exceed twice its standard error. Standard errors are shown below the regression coefficients in each table. In samples this large, one might reasonably demand a higher standard (Raftery 1995).

[27] There is an interesting asymmetry in the effects of maternal and paternal educational attainment on occupational status. The effect of mother's education on daughter's status appears larger than that of father's education.

effect is mediated by differences in school performance. Only two of the socioeconomic variables have significant effects on occupational status after schooling enters the equation: parents' income and father's occupational status. The latter effect occurs only among men. In the final equation, none of the effects of the socioeconomic background variables differ between men and women.

The total effect of having a father who farmed is large and negative among men.[28] It leads to more than a five-point loss in status. There is no corresponding effect among women. Indeed, the total effect of farm background on daughters' status is positive, and the gender difference in the effect of farming is significant in every reduced-form equation. Perhaps the effect of farm origin is explained by the small number of WLS men who entered farming themselves, for less than half of the effect is mediated by later variables in the model.

There is no effect of growing up in a nonintact family in the Wisconsin sample. Recall that only about 8 percent of WLS respondents lived in nonintact families in 1957 (table 8.8), and in about half of those cases, widowhood was the source of that family structure. Thus, nonintact families have neither the prevalence nor the same sources as in younger cohorts.

The other family structure variable, number of siblings, plays a less ambiguous role in occupational attainment in 1992–1993. Its total effects on occupational status in 1992–1993 are large, statistically significant, and negligibly different between men and women. An additional child in the family of orientation leads to a loss of about 0.4 points in occupational status at ages fifty-three to fifty-four. However, the model accounts fully for the effect of size of sibship. Most of the effect is explained by differences in school performance in larger and smaller sibships, and the remainder is explained by differences in social influences on postsecondary schooling. There are no significant effects of size of sibship in the last three reduced-form equations.

Each of the three school performance variables has a large and statistically significant effect on occupational status at ages fifty-three to fifty-four. Roughly speaking, an increase of four points of mental ability or (on the same scale) high school rank leads to a one-point increment in status on the Duncan scale. Among men and women, the effect of mental ability persists; it remains significant in the final reduced-form equation. The effect of high school rank among men is fully explained by the model; it has no effect once educational attainment is controlled. Although high school rank remains significant in the final equation for women, its coefficient is about 40

---

[28] The effects of farm origin differ from those reported in previous analyses of the WLS data. Farm origin is based strictly on whether the respondent's father was a farmer in 1957; it does not confound farm occupation with rural residence. It should be kept in mind that the effect of farm origin in these equations depends on the placement of farm occupations in the Duncan scale.

percent lower than the total effect. The differential persistence of the effects of IQ and of high school rank suggests that there is more to school performance than the sanctioned approval of teachers.

Completion of an academic high school program increases men's occupational status by about six points, and it increases women's occupational status by more than three points. The total effect is significantly larger among men than women, but there are no significant gender differences in the effects of an academic program once social influences have entered the model. The intermediate variables account for almost three-quarters of the effect of an academic program among men and for about half the effect among women. In the final model, completion of a college preparatory program is worth about 1.5 points in occupation status among men and women, but this remaining effect is of borderline statistical significance. Thus, among men and among women, there appears to be greater persistence across the career in the influence of IQ than in that of high school rank or academic program.

Despite their specific reference to postsecondary schooling rather than to careers, the social influence variables (teachers' and parents' encouragement to attend college and friends' college plans) have substantial positive effects on occupational status at age fifty-three to fifty-four. The total effects are substantially larger among men than among women, and even among women, each positive social influence is worth about two points in occupational status. Among men, each of the three positive effects is about as large as the negative effect of farm background. Among women and men, the effects of the social influence variables are largely explained by aspirations and postsecondary schooling. In the final model, there remains a significant effect of teachers' encouragement among men, but there are no significant gender differences in the effects of any of the social influence variables.

Among women, having planned to attend college is worth about 1.3 points in occupational status, but this effect is not statistically significant. For men the effect is significantly larger, 4.5 points. However, among both men and women, the effect of planning to attend college is completely explained by post–high school education. That is, educational plans affect occupational status at midlife only if they have been realized in completed schooling.

The effect of occupational aspiration is similar and highly significant for both men and women. A ten-point increase in occupational aspiration in high school is worth 1.5 points in occupational status at ages fifty-three to fifty-four. Only part of these effects is mediated by educational attainment. When all other variables in the model have been controlled, a ten-point increase in occupational aspiration is still worth about one point in occupational status at midlife.

Finally, after all earlier variables have entered the model, there is a large effect of educational attainment on occupational status in 1992–1993 among men and women. Each year of post–high school educational attainment leads to a 2.5-point increase in status on the Duncan scale among women and to a 3.5-point increase in status among men. This gender difference in the effect of educational attainment is statistically significant.

Overall, the model is moderately powerful in predicting occupational status. It accounts for 35 percent of the variance among men and 20 percent of the variance among women. However, the model actually leaves less to be explained among women than among men; note that the standard errors of estimate in each equation are smaller among women than among men. We believe that the models are more powerful than they appear thus far in the analyses. First, we have not corrected for measurement error in occupational status or other variables. Second, because occupations in 1992–1993 are so far removed from high school, we thought it likely that intervening career experiences could attenuate the influence of social and psychological conditions in young adulthood. For these reasons, we have elaborated the reduced-form equations of table 8.9 by incorporating five reports of occupational standing across the career: first full-time job after leaving school; 1970 job; 1975 job (both contemporaneous and retrospective reports); and 1992–1993 job.

A MIMIC Model of Occupational Status

In order to discipline our interpretations of the changing effects of the variables in our model on occupational status across the life course, we specified and estimated a series of MIMIC models of occupational status (Hauser and Goldberger 1971; Joreskog and Goldberger 1975). The structure of the social psychological model remains unchanged, but we impose a series of restrictions on the effects of the variables in the model. All of these models have in common the specification that prior variables affect occupational status through a single common factor, so the effects of those variables on each status outcome must be proportional, if not identical to one another.

For example, the final reduced-form equation of the model may be written as follows:

$$\eta_1 = \Sigma_{16}^1 \gamma_{1j} x_j$$
$$\eta_i = \beta_{i1} \eta_1 + \zeta_i \qquad (2)$$
$$y_i = \eta_i, \; i = 2 \ldots 6$$

where η_1 is a linear composite of the sixteen explanatory variables (x_j); the γ_{1j} are regression coefficients; the η_i are nominally true values of successive occupational status scores, from $\eta_2 =$ status of first job to $\eta_6 =$ status of current or last job in 1992–1993; the β_{i1} are slopes of the occupational status scores on the linear composite; the ζ_i are disturbances in occupational status scores; and the y_i are observed occupational status variables. The distinction between the y_i and the η_i is empirically empty here, but will become useful below. In this model, sixty overidentifying restrictions are generated by the specification that the x_j affect the y_i only by way of the linear composite, η_i. However, the model places no restrictions on the variances or covariances of the disturbances in the η_i, var$[\zeta_i, \zeta_i] = \psi_{ii'}$.[29]

First, we consider a model in which the effects of all variables on each of the five occupational status outcomes is exactly the same, while the relationships among those outcomes are completely unconstrained. Thus, we add the restriction $\beta_i = 1$ for all i to the model in equations 2. This model would be rejected at conventional significance levels for men ($L^2 = 454.4$ with 64 df) and for women ($L^2 = 119.0$ with 64 df). Second, we specify a model in which the effects of prior variables on occupational status are not necessarily equal, but must be proportional to one another. That is, we release the previous constraint on the β_i. Again, there is no constraint on the relationships among the status outcomes. The fit improves among men ($L^2 = 168.6$ with 60 df) and among women ($L^2 = 104.5$ with 60 df).[30] Third, we accept the second model, but add the constraint that a single common factor explains the covariance structure of the occupational status outcomes. In this model, $\psi_{ii'} = 0$ for $i \neq i'$. This model also fits badly ($L^2 = 317.2$ with 65 df among men and $L^2 = 199.4$ with 65 df among women), which is to say that a full model of status outcomes would need to specify a structure for the occupational career.

Given our findings from the second model, we specified a modified version of it, which fits about as well ($L^2 = 180.8$ with 62 df among men and $L^2 = 110.3$ with 62 df among women). Since two of the five occupational status reports pertain to the same (1975) job, we have treated those two reports as indicators of a single latent variable. The reliability of the two reports across the eighteen-year span, incidentally, is 0.83 for men and 0.75 for women. Also, we have "borrowed" the error variance estimates for the contemporaneous and retrospective reports of occupation in 1975 and imposed them, correspondingly, on the other reports, depending on whether they were obtained contemporaneously or retrospectively. Formally, the equation for the linear composite in explanatory variables is unchanged:

$$\eta_1 = \Sigma_{16}^1 \, \gamma_j \, x_j. \tag{3}$$

---

[29] Note that a somewhat different setup is required to estimate the other reduced-form equations, subject to the same constraints.

[30] These and all other fit statistics reported herein would nominally lead to model rejection at conventional levels of statistical significance because of the relatively large sample sizes. However, the values of Raftery's (1995) Bayesian Information Criterion (BIC) fall into an acceptable range for all models.

The linear composite, η_1, affects four occupational status outcomes, $\eta_2 \ldots \eta_6$, one for each of first job, 1970 job, 1975 job, and 1992–1993 job, in that order:

$$\eta_2 = \eta_1 + \zeta_2$$
$$\eta_3 = \beta_{31} \eta_1 + \zeta_3$$
$$\eta_4 = \beta_{41} \eta_1 + \zeta_4 \qquad (4)$$
$$\eta_5 = \beta_{51} \eta_1 + \zeta_5.$$

Again, we place no restrictions on the variances or covariances of the disturbances, $\text{var}[\zeta_i, \zeta_{i'}] = \psi_{ii'}$. Finally, unlike the models of equations 2, there is a nontrivial measurement model:

$$y_1 = \eta_2 + \epsilon_1$$
$$y_2 = \eta_3 + \epsilon_2$$
$$y_3 = \eta_4 + \epsilon_3 \qquad (5)$$
$$y_4 = \eta_4 + \epsilon_4$$
$$y_5 = \eta_5 + \epsilon_5,$$

where y_3, contemporaneous report of 1975 job, and y_4, retrospective report of 1975 job, each depend on the same latent factor, η_4. Also, we specify that, for $\text{var}[\epsilon_i] = \theta_i$, $\theta_1 = \theta_2 = \theta_4$, and $\theta_3 = \theta_5$, and we specify two free covariances between errors in report of occupational status, $\text{cov}[\epsilon_i \epsilon_{i'}] = \theta_{ii'}$, θ_{23}, and θ_{45}. That is, we allow correlation between errors in reports about jobs that were ascertained in the same section of an interview on the same occasion.

After examining residuals from the fit of this model, we added one more parameter each to the models for men and for women. In the case of men, we added a direct effect of educational attainment on the status of the first job ($\gamma_{2,13}$), and this improved the fit markedly ($L^2 = 80.2$ with 61 df). For women, we added a direct effect of IQ on the status of the job in 1992–1993 (γ_{58}), and we also equated the metrics of status of first and 1970 job, yielding $L^2 = 76.5$ with 62 df. Neither of these models would be rejected at even the $p = 0.05$ probability level.

Except for the two parameters just mentioned, the model imposes proportionality constraints on effects of earlier variables on the status of first job, job in 1970, job in 1975, and job in 1992–1993. If we take the occupational status of the first job as the standard, the constants of proportionality are 1.00, 1.44, 1.39, and 1.29 among men, and they are 1.00, 1.00, 0.94, and 0.69 among women. Thus, among women, the main change that occurs across the life course in the effects of the variables in our model on occupational status is that they decline. Among men, most effects (except that of education) increase from the first to later occupations, and there is some indication that the effects decline by midlife. Again, the only exceptions to this general pattern are that the effect of education on the status of men's first jobs is unusually large, and the effect of IQ on the status of women's 1992–1993 jobs is unusually large.

The final equations account for 71, 52, 49, and 42 percent of the variance in status of men's jobs, and among women, they account for 48, 40, 34, and 27 percent of the variance. Change in the predicted variance of successive occupational status scores accounts in part for the declining power of the model to account for the variance in occupational standing across the career. In addition, the disturbance variances in occupational status increase across the career. For example, among men, the standard error of estimate for first jobs is 13.4, whereas it is 17.2 for jobs in 1992–1993, and among women, the standard error of estimate for first jobs is 11.3, whereas it is 15.5 for jobs in 1992–1993. As in our regression analysis of jobs in 1992–1993, the so-cial psychological model explains a smaller share of the variance for women than for men, but it also leaves a smaller component of variance unexplained for women than for men.

Table 8.10 gives estimates from the MIMIC model of the regressions of each occupational status on all prior variables in the model for men and women. For example, the fourth column of estimates in each panel of table 8.10 is a constrained version of the fifth column of estimates in each panel of table 8.9. By reading from left to right within each panel, we can see the evolution of effects across the life course. Thus, among men, all effects except that of schooling increase slightly between the first job and the job in 1970, and the effects on later jobs decrease slightly. The effect of schooling is uniquely high at men's entry into the labor force, and it drops to about half the entry value at any later point in the career. Men's occupational status at career entry is modestly affected by IQ, net of other variables, and this effect increases by about a third for occupations later in the career. Among women, the model specifies no differences between effects on the status of first and 1970 jobs, but the effects of all variables except IQ decline later in the career. The direct effect of IQ on women's occupational status is unique in almost tripling between career entry and midlife.

Thus, there are persistent and, indeed, growing effects of IQ on occupa-tional status throughout the careers of the Wisconsin high school graduates. However, relative growth does not indicate absolute importance; there may be less here than meets the eye. In the reduced-form equation for occupa-tional status in 1992–1993, subject to the MIMIC constraints, the total ef-fects of ability are 0.236 among men and 0.303 among women. That is, a ten-point shift in IQ yields two to three points in occupational status. The standardized coefficient of ability is 0.157 among men and 0.245 among women. In the final equations, the effects of ability are 0.116 among men and 0.279 among women. The corresponding standardized coefficients are 0.077 and 0.226. Such effects would seem unlikely to dominate the process of social stratification in the United States.

TABLE 8.10

Canonical Regression of Occupational Status (SEI) on Social Psychological Variables and Schooling: Men and Women in the Wisconsin Longitudinal Study

Variables Added to Model	Men (N = 3,080)				Women (N = 1,489)			
	First Job	1970 Job	1975 Job	1992–1993 Job	First Job	1970 Job	1975 Job	1992–1993 Job
Parents' income	1.13	1.62	1.57	1.45	0.93	0.93	0.88	0.65
	(0.41)	(0.58)	(0.56)	(0.52)	(0.74)	(0.74)	(0.70)	(0.51)
Father's occ.	0.04	0.05	0.05	0.05	0.02	0.02	0.02	0.01
(SEI)	(0.01)	(0.02)	(0.02)	(0.02)	(0.02)	(0.02)	(0.02)	(0.01)
Father's	0.01	0.02	0.02	0.02	0.20	0.20	0.18	0.14
education	(0.08)	(0.11)	(0.10)	(0.10)	(0.13)	(0.13)	(0.12)	(0.09)
Mother's	−0.01	−0.02	−0.02	−0.02	0.02	0.02	0.02	0.01
education	(0.08)	(0.12)	(0.12)	(0.11)	(0.14)	(0.14)	(0.14)	(0.10)
Farm back-	−3.72	−5.36	−5.17	−4.79	−0.05	−0.05	−0.05	−0.04
ground	(0.61)	(0.84)	(0.81)	(0.75)	(0.94)	(0.94)	(0.88)	(0.65)
Intact family	−0.99	−1.42	−1.37	−1.27	1.09	1.09	1.03	0.75
	(0.72)	(1.04)	(1.00)	(0.93)	(1.26)	(1.26)	(1.19)	(0.87)
Number of	−0.02	−0.03	−0.03	−0.02	−0.17	−0.17	−0.16	−0.12
siblings	(0.08)	(0.12)	(0.12)	(0.11)	(0.14)	(0.14)	(0.13)	(0.09)
IQ (Henmon-	0.09	0.13	0.13	0.12	0.11	0.11	0.11	**0.28**
Nelson)	(0.02)	(0.03)	(0.03)	(0.02)	(0.03)	(0.03)	(0.03)	(0.04)
Academic	1.34	1.93	1.86	1.73	−0.51	−0.51	−0.48	−0.35
program	(0.50)	(0.71)	(0.68)	(0.64)	(0.80)	(0.80)	(0.75)	(0.55)
High school	0.03	0.04	0.03	0.03	0.21	0.21	0.20	0.15
rank	(0.02)	(0.03)	(0.03)	(0.02)	(0.03)	(0.03)	(0.03)	(0.02)
Teacher's	1.30	1.88	1.81	1.68	−1.23	−1.23	−1.15	−0.85
encouragement	(0.48)	(0.69)	(0.66)	(0.61)	(0.80)	(0.80)	(0.75)	(0.56)
Parents'	1.41	2.04	1.96	1.82	0.26	0.26	0.25	0.18
encouragement	(0.53)	(0.76)	(0.73)	(0.68)	(0.89)	(0.89)	(0.84)	(0.62
Friends' college	1.22	1.76	1.70	1.58	0.52	0.52	0.49	0.36
plans	(0.50)	(0.72)	(0.70)	(0.65)	(0.81)	(0.81)	(0.76)	(0.56)
College plans	−0.42	−0.60	−0.58	−0.54	−2.90	−2.90	−2.73	−2.00
	(0.54)	(0.78)	(0.76)	(0.70)	(0.89)	(0.89)	(0.84)	(0.63)
Occ. aspirations	0.09	0.13	0.13	0.12	0.18	0.18	0.17	0.12
(SEI)	(0.01)	(0.02)	(0.02)	(0.01)	(0.03)	(0.03)	(0.03)	(0.02)
Education	**7.11**	4.07	3.93	3.64	3.75	3.75	3.54	2.60
	(0.17)	(0.18)	(0.17)	(0.17)	(0.23)	(0.23)	(0.23)	(0.24)
R-Squared	0.714	0.520	0.487	0.418	0.475	0.397	0.336	0.272
SE of estimate	13.40	15.66	16.13	17.21	11.28	13.21	14.18	15.51

Note: Analysis is based on Duncan SEI of first full-time civilian occupation, 1970 occupation, 1975 occupation (as reported in 1975 and 1992–1993), and 1992–1993 occupation. Boldface entries violate canonical restrictions.

As we might have expected from our national findings, if there is a key variable in the occupational attainment of men and women, it is educational attainment. Even after social background, ability, and other social psychological variables are controlled, there is a large and persistent effect of post–high school education on occupational success across the life course. Furthermore, adolescent occupational aspirations have strong and persistent effects on the occupational success of men and of women. In addition, there are gender-specific influences on occupational success. Farm background is a persistent handicap to men, whereas good high school grades continue to improve women's occupational chances. Finally, relative to ability, there are weaker but still substantial and persistent effects of parents' income, father's occupational status, academic program, teachers' encouragement, parents' encouragement, and friends' college plans on men's occupational standing. In short, although mental ability plays a significant role in the process of occupational stratification, the Wisconsin findings also strongly support the conclusion that education and other social psychological variables are even more important. There are elements of "merit" in the schooling and psychological variables, so the Wisconsin findings lend weight to our earlier observation that it is inappropriate to identify merit too strongly with mental ability.

APPENDIX

Effective Sample Counts: 1962 and 1973 Occupational Changes in a Generation Surveys (OCG) and 1986–1988 Surveys of Income and Program Participation (SIPP)

Group and Survey	Age 25 to 34	Age 35 to 44	Age 45 to 54	Age 55 to 64
NONBLACK MEN				
1962 OCG (1960-basis Duncan SEI)	2,552	2,898	2,521	1,742
1973 OCG (1960-basis Duncan SEI)	5,285	4,315	4,404	2,997
1973 OCG (1970-basis MSEI2)	5,366	4,383	4,441	3,018
1986–1988 SIPP (1980-basis MSEI2)	6,109	4,963	3,275	2,269
BLACK MEN				
1962 OCG (1960-basis Duncan SEI)	263	280	231	147
1973 OCG (1960-basis Duncan SEI)	659	520	482	286
1973 OCG (1970-basis MSEI2)	796	641	597	354
1986–1988 SIPP (1980-basis MSEI2)	616	470	281	184
NONBLACK WOMEN				
1986–1988 SIPP (1980-basis MSEI2)	4,856	4,141	2,628	1,708
BLACK WOMEN				
1986–1988 SIPP (1980-basis MSEI2)	639	526	308	195

References

Altonji, Joseph G., and Thomas A. Dunn. 1991. "Relationships among the Family Incomes and Labor Market Outcomes of Relatives." *Research in Labor Economics* 12: 269–310.

Alwin, Duane F., and Robert M. Hauser. 1975. "The Decomposition of Effects in Path Analysis." *American Sociological Review* 40: 37–47.

Bielby, William T., and Robert M. Hauser. 1977. "Response Error in Earnings Functions for Nonblack Males." *Sociological Methods and Research* 6: 241–280.

Bielby, William T., Robert M. Hauser, and David L. Featherman. 1977. "Response Errors of Black and Nonblack Males in Models of the Intergenerational Transmission of Socioeconomic Status." *American Journal of Sociology* 82: 1242–1288.

Blau, Peter M., and Otis Dudley Duncan. 1967. *The American Occupational Structure*. New York: John Wiley and Sons.

Bowles, Samuel. 1972. "Schooling and Inequality from Generation to Generation." *Journal of Political Economy* 80: S219–S251.

Bowles, Samuel, and Herbert Gintis. 1976. *Schooling in Capitalist America*. New York: Basic Books.

Boyd, Monica. 1986. "Socioeconomic Indices and Sexual Inequality: A Tale of Scales." *Canadian Review of Sociology and Anthropology* 23, no. 4: 457–480.

Center for Human Resource Research, Ohio State University. 1992. *NLS Update: The National Longitudinal Studies of Labor Market Experience* 73.

Clarridge, Brian R., Linda L. Sheehy, and Taissa S. Hauser. 1978. "Tracing Members of a Panel: A 17-Year Follow-up." In *Sociological Methodology 1978*, ed. Karl F. Schuessler, pp. 185–203. San Francisco: Jossey-Bass.

Clausen, John A. 1993. *American Lives: Looking Back at the Children of the Great Depression*. New York: Free Press.

Corcoran, Mary, Roger Gordon, Deborah Laren, and Gary Solon. 1992. "The Association between Men's Economic Status and Their Family and Community Origins." *Journal of Human Resources* 27, no. 4: 575–601.

Duncan, Otis Dudley. 1961. "A Socioeconomic Index for All Occupations." In *Occupations and Social Status*, ed. Albert J. Reiss Jr., pp. 109–138. New York: Free Press.

———. 1965. "Social Origins of Salaried and Self-Employed Professional Workers." *Social Forces* 44: 186–189.

———. 1969. "Inequality and Opportunity." *Population Index* 35: 361–366.

Duncan, Otis Dudley, David L. Featherman, and Beverly Duncan. 1972. *Socioeconomic Background and Achievement*. New York: Seminar Press.

Featherman, David L. 1980. "Retrospective Longitudinal Research: Methodological Considerations." *Journal of Economics and Business* 32, no. 2: 152–169.

Featherman, David L., and Robert M. Hauser. 1978. *Opportunity and Change*. New York: Academic Press.

Goldberger, Arthur S. 1989. "Economic and Mechanical Models of Intergenerational Transmission." *American Economic Review* 79, no. 3: 504–513.

Griliches, Zvi. 1979. "Sibling Models and Data in Economics: Beginnings of a Survey." *Journal of Political Economy* 87: S37–S64.

Hauser, Robert M., Peter J. Dickinson, Harry P. Travis, and John N. Koffel. 1975a. "Structural Changes in Occupational Mobility among Men in the United States." *American Sociological Review* 40: 585–598.

Hauser, Robert M., and David L. Featherman. 1976. "Equality of Schooling: Trends and Prospects." *Sociology of Education* 49: 99–120.

———. 1977. *The Process of Stratification: Trends and Analyses*. New York: Academic Press.

Hauser, Robert M., and Arthur S. Goldberger. 1971. "The Treatment of Unobservable Variables in Path Analysis." In *Sociological Methodology*, ed. Herbert L. Costner, pp. 81–117. San Francisco: Jossey-Bass.

Hauser, Robert M., and Min-Hsiung Huang. 1997. "Verbal Ability and Socioeconomic Success: A Trend Analysis." *Social Science Research* 26 (September): 331–376.

Hauser, Robert M., John N. Koffel, Harry P. Travis, and Peter J. Dickinson. 1975b. "Temporal Change in Occupational Mobility: Evidence for Men in the United States." *American Sociological Review* 40: 279–297.

Hauser, Robert M., and John A. Logan. 1992. "How Not to Measure Intergenerational Occupational Persistence." *American Journal of Sociology* 97, no. 6: 1689–1711.

Hauser, Robert M., and Peter A. Mossel. 1985. "Fraternal Resemblance in Educational Attainment and Occupational Status." *American Journal of Sociology* 91: 650–673.

Hauser, Robert M., and William H. Sewell. 1986. "Family Effects in Simple Models of Education, Occupational Status, and Earnings: Findings from the Wisconsin and Kalamazoo Studies." *Journal of Labor Economics* 4: S83–S115.

Hauser, Robert M., William H. Sewell, and Duane F. Alwin. 1976. "High School Effects on Achievement." In *Schooling and Achievement in American Society*, ed. William H. Sewell, Robert M. Hauser, and David L. Featherman, pp. 309–341. New York: Academic Press.

Hauser, Robert M., William H. Sewell, John A. Logan, Taissa S. Hauser, Carol Ryff, Avshalom Caspi, and Maurice M. MacDonald. 1992. "The Wisconsin Longitudinal Study: Adults as Parents and Children at Age 50." *IASSIST Quarterly* 16, no. 2: 23–38.

Hauser, Robert M., and Megan M. Sweeney. 1997. "Does Poverty in Adolescence Affect the Life Chances of High School Graduates?" In *Growing Up Poor*, ed. Greg Duncan and Jeanne Brooks-Gunn, pp. 541–595. New York: Russell Sage Foundation.

Hauser, Robert M., Shu-Ling Tsai, and William H. Sewell. 1983. "A Model of Stratification with Response Error in Social and Psychological Variables." *Sociology of Education* 56: 20–46.

Hauser, Robert M., and John Robert Warren. 1997. "Socioeconomic Indexes for Occupations: A Review, Update, and Critique." In *Sociological Methodology 1997*, ed. Adrian Raftery, pp. 177–298. Boston: Blackwell.

Herrnstein, Richard J., and Charles Murray. 1994. *The Bell Curve: Intelligence and Class Structure in American Life*. New York: Free Press.

Hodge, Robert W. 1981. "The Measurement of Occupational Status." *Social Science Research* 10: 396–415.

Hout, Michael. 1988. "More Universalism, Less Structural Mobility: The American Occupational Structure in the 1980s." *American Journal of Sociology* 93, no. 6: 1358–1400.

Jencks, Christopher S., Lauri Perman, and Lee Rainwater. 1988. "What Is a Good Job? A New Measure of Labor Market Success." *American Journal of Sociology* 93, no. 6: 1322–1357.

Jencks, Christopher, Susan Bartlett, Mary Corcoran, James Crouse, David Eaglesfield, Gregory Jackson, Kent McClelland, Peter Mueser, Michael Olneck, Joseph Schwartz, Sherry Ward, and Jill Williams. 1979. *Who Gets Ahead? The Determinants of Economic Success in America*. New York: Basic Books.

Jencks, Christopher, James Crouse, and Peter Mueser. 1983. "The Wisconsin Model of Status Attainment: A National Replication with Improved Measures of Ability and Aspiration." *Sociology of Education* 56: 3–19.

Jencks, Christopher, Marshall Smith, Henry Acland, Mary Jo Bane, David Cohen, Herbert Gintis, Barbara Heyns, and Stephan Michelson. 1972. *Inequality: A Reassessment of the Effect of Family and Schooling in America*. New York: Basic Books.

Joreskog, Karl G., and Arthur S. Goldberger. 1975. "Estimation of a Model with Multiple Indicators and Multiple Causes of a Single Latent Variable." *Journal of the American Statistical Association* 70: 631–639.

Kominski, Robert, and Andrea Adams. 1992. "Educational Attainment in the United States: March 1991 and 1990." In *Current Population Reports*, p. 462. Washington, DC: U.S. Government Printing Office.

Korenman, Sanders, and Christopher Winship. 1996. "A Reanalysis of *The Bell Curve*." Unpublished paper. February.

Kuo, Hsiang-Hui Daphne, and Robert M. Hauser. 1995. "Trends in Family Effects on the Education of Black and White Brothers." *Sociology of Education* 68, no. 2: 136–160.

McCall, Robert B. 1977. "Childhood IQ's as Predictors of Adult Educational and Occupational Status." *Science* 197: 482–483.

Murphy, Kevin, and Finis Welch. 1989. "Wage Premiums for College Graduates: Recent Growth and Possible Explanations." *Educational Researcher* 18, no. 4: 17–26.

Murnane, Richard J., and Frank Levy. 1993. "Why Today's High-School Educated Males Earn Less Than Their Fathers Did: The Problem and an Assessment of Responses." *Harvard Educational Review* 63, no. 1: 1–20.

Olneck, Michael R. 1977. "On the Use of Sibling Data to Estimate the Effects of Family Background, Cognitive Skills, and Schooling: Results from the Kalamazoo Brothers Study." In *Kinometrics: Determinants of Socioeconomic Success within and between Families*, ed. Paul Taubman, pp. 125–162. Amsterdam: North-Holland.

Raftery, Adrian E. 1995. "Bayesian Model Selection in Social Research." In *Sociological Methodology 1995*, vol. 25, ed. Peter V. Marsden, pp. 111–163. Cambridge: Basil Blackwell.

Rytina, Steve. 1992. "Scaling the Intergenerational Continuity of Occupation: Is Occupational Inheritance Ascriptive After All?" *American Journal of Sociology* 97, no. 6: 1658–1688.

Sewell, William H. 1971. "Inequality of Opportunity for Higher Education." *American Sociological Review* 36: 793–809.

Sewell, William H., Archibald O. Haller, and George W. Ohlendorf. 1970. "The Educational and Early Occupational Status Attainment Process: Replication and Revision." *American Sociological Review* 35: 1014–1027.

Sewell, William H., Archibald O. Haller, and Alejandro Portes. 1969. "The Educational and Early Occupational Attainment Process." *American Sociological Review* 34: 82–92.

Sewell, William H., and Robert M. Hauser. 1975. *Education, Occupation, and Earnings: Achievement in the Early Career*. New York: Academic Press.

———. 1992a. "The Influence of The American Occupational Structure on the Wisconsin Model." *Contemporary Sociology* 21, no. 5: 598–603.

———. 1992b. "A Review of the Wisconsin Longitudinal Study of Social and Psychological Factors in Aspirations and Achievements, 1963–1993." CDE Working Papers, no. 92-1. Center for Demography and Ecology, University of Wisconsin–Madison.

Sewell, William H., Robert M. Hauser, and Wendy C. Wolf. 1980. "Sex, Schooling and Occupational Status." *American Journal of Sociology* 86: 551–583.

Siegel, Paul M. 1971. "Prestige in the American Occupational Structure," Ph.D. diss., University of Chicago.

Solon, Gary, Mary Corcoran, Roger Gordon, and Deborah Laren. 1991. "A Longitudinal Analysis of Sibling Correlations in Economic Status." *Journal of Human Resources* 26, no. 3: 509–534.

Stevens, Gillian, and Joo Hyun Cho. 1985. "Socioeconomic Indexes and the New 1980 Census Occupational Classification Scheme." *Social Science Research* 14: 74–168.

Stevens, Gillian, and David L. Featherman. 1981. "A Revised Socioeconomic Index of Occupational Status." *Social Science Research* 10, no. 4: 364–395.

Warren, John Robert, Jennifer T. Sheridan, and Robert M. Hauser. 1998. "Choosing a Measure of Occupational Standing: How Useful Are Composite Measures in Analyses of Gender Inequality in Occupational Attainment?" *Sociological Methods and Research* 27 (August): 3–76.

Weakliem, David, Julia McQuillan, and Tracy Schauer. 1995. "Toward Meritocracy? Changing Social-Class Differences in Intellectual Ability." *Sociology of Education* 68: 271–286.

Zimmerman, David J. 1992. "Regression toward Mediocrity in Economic Stature." *American Economic Review* 82: 409–429.

Nine

Understanding the Role of Cognitive Ability in Accounting for the Recent Rise in the Economic Return to Education*

JOHN CAWLEY, JAMES HECKMAN, LANCE LOCHNER, AND EDWARD VYTLACIL

IN THE LAST TWENTY YEARS there has been an increasing wage gap between those with high and those with low levels of education. There is some debate about whether this represents a rising wage return to cognitive ability or a rising return to formal education. The answer has important consequences for policy. If the rising wage gap is due to a rise in the return to education, then there is reason for optimism that those with low wages can be educated or trained for higher-wage jobs. However, if the increasing wage gap is due to a rise in the return to cognitive ability, there may be less optimism that education or training can increase the wages of the less able, because cognitive ability is much harder to change, even for adolescents.

This chapter examines the role of ability in the recent rise in the wage return to education. The consensus view is that much of the increase in the return to education is attributable to an increase in the return to ability. For example, Blackburn and Neumark (1993) report that the rise in the return to education is concentrated among those with both high education and high ability. Murnane, Willett, and Levy (1995) conclude that 38 percent of the rise in the return to education for twenty-four-year-old males from 1978 to 1986 can be attributed to a rise in the return to ability.

In the standard view, employers are assumed to value cognitive skills, and their valuation of these skills as reflected in wages rose in the 1980s. Those with high ability tend to acquire a high level of education, so failure to control for ability in regressions of wages on education will cause an upward bias in the estimated economic return to education. This is the classic ability bias model discussed in Griliches and Mason (1972) applied to changes over time in the coefficient on education in a wage equation.

* For their helpful comments, we thank the participants in the Conference on Meritocracy and Inequality held at the University of Wisconsin, December 1995. We especially thank our discussant, Robert Moffitt. This research is supported by NIH R01-HD-34958-01, NIH R01-HD32058-03, and NSF 97-09-873.

In this interpretation, earnings of person i at time t are payments for a vector of person-specific characteristics c_i:

$$Y_{it} = P_{1t}c_{1i} + P_{2t}c_{2i} + \ldots P_{Nt}c_{Ni} \tag{1}$$

where Y_{it} is the earnings (or log earnings) of individual i at time t; $c_{1i}, \ldots, c_{Ni}$ are the characteristics possessed by person i and $P_{1t}, \ldots, P_{Nt}$ are their prices. The characteristics include ability and education. The coefficients on the characteristics are their prices or "returns." Prices may change, but after the schooling years characteristics do not change, except possibly work experience, which is interpreted as a characteristic. Failure to control for ability (assumed to be a characteristic) biases the coefficient on schooling. The rise in the return to schooling may simply proxy the rise in the return to ability because schooling and ability are positively correlated.

This interpretation of the earnings equation implicitly governs the recent literature in economics and sociology. It takes a fundamentally static view of skills and ignores the dynamics of skill formation over the life cycle and how these dynamics are affected by changes in skill prices to which rational agents respond. Post-school investment in human capital is an important empirical phenomenon. About 25 percent of all human capital investment is made on the job (Heckman, Lochner, and Taber 1998).

Post-school investment is greatest for young workers; the more able forgo earnings and invest more than the less able. Within ability classes, the more educated invest more than the less educated. Abstracting from time series changes in skill prices, post-school investment obscures the role of ability on earnings for samples of young workers. Because the younger and the more able invest more, the potential earnings are understated and ability-earnings gaps are compressed at younger ages compared to later ages. Yet the recent literature on the role of ability in earnings exclusively analyzes younger workers. This suggests that recent studies *understate* the role of ability in accounting for wage differentials compared to its effect over the entire life cycle, say as measured by discounted lifetime earnings. Focusing on the young, we will misstate the consequences of explaining ability on the earnings differentials of the old as investments pay off.

This argument is traditional and it ignores the dynamics of skill prices in a period of rapid technical change. Investment in any form of capital entails forward-looking behavior comparing current costs to future returns. Human capital investment is no exception to this rule. In a period of rising prices for skilled labor and declining prices for unskilled labor, agents forecast the future returns and compare them with current costs (primarily forgone earnings) in deciding whether or not to invest. Ability-wage differentials estimated in different skill-price environments will depend on those environments. This makes problematic comparisons of estimates of these differentials based on different samples collected at different times.

Consider, for example, workers surprised by an increase in the demand for skilled labor that they think will not last. Unskilled workers are surprised by a decline in their market. The more skilled will invest *less* in the short run because their costs (forgone earnings) have gone up while the expected future rewards to skill have not changed. Reducing investment *raises* their earnings compared to those in a stationary economy. Conversely, if the less skilled experience what they perceive to be a temporary decline in their skill price, they invest more. Costs are down and long-term returns are unchanged. These investment effects widen skill differentials in the short run. Given the correlation between ability and skill, this effect leads to a widening of ability-wage differentials compared to those in a stationary economy, especially at younger ages. Conversely, if the increase in the price of skilled labor is perceived to be a permanent trend, and if the decrease in price of skilled labor is also perceived to be a permanent trend, then wage differentials by ability narrow at younger ages compared to what would occur in a stationary environment.

We argue in this chapter that the evidence on wage differentials is consistent with an analysis in which workers were surprised by the run-up of high skill prices and decline in low skill prices in the 1980s, and initially thought that the shock was temporary. High-skill workers invested less than they usually do, so their forgone earnings were lower than usual. Hence their earnings are higher than usual. Low-skill workers invested more than the norm and their forgone earnings were higher. Hence their earnings are lower than usual. Ability-wage differentials widened compared to what was observed in the 1960s and 1970s. There is no necessary conflict between an older generation of studies showing weak effects of controlling for ability in estimating the returns to education for samples of young people from the more placid 1960s and 1970s (see the survey in Griliches 1979) and later estimates based on samples of young people in the 1980s where much stronger effects of ability on earnings and effects for ability in diminishing the return to education are found.

In the course of investigating these issues, we encounter an important and hitherto neglected empirical problem associated with missing data. People with certain ability-education combinations are rarely observed, which makes it difficult or impossible to separate the effects of ability and education without imposing a lot of structure onto the data. For example, table 9.1 reveals that there are very few white males in the NLSY who are both in the lowest ability quartile and are college graduates. Given such a small sample size, the effect of college graduation on the wages of men of such ability cannot be reliably estimated. Furthermore, there are no white men in the lowest ability quartile with postgraduate education. For that ability quartile, not even a rough estimate of the wage gain of such education is possible.

Missing data also complicate attempts to identify a rise in the return to

TABLE 9.1

Percent of Highest Grade Completed by Ability Quartile, Age 30, White Males (1621 observations)

Highest Grade Completed	Quartile 1	Quartile 2	Quartile 3	Quartile 4
7	2.0	0.0	0.0	0.0
8	6.7	0.5	0.0	0.0
9	10.4	1.7	0.2	0.0
10	7.9	3.2	0.0	0.0
11	9.6	2.7	1.0	0.0
12	54.0	63.2	46.9	22.5
13	3.9	7.2	11.1	4.4
14	3.0	7.9	10.1	10.6
15	0.5	1.7	3.9	4.9
16	2.2	9.6	19.7	33.6
17	0.0	1.0	1.7	5.2
18	0.0	0.5	3.0	8.4
19	0.0	0.5	1.2	5.4
20	0.0	0.2	1.0	4.9

Note: Here ability is defined as general intelligence or g. We compute g as the ASVAB test score vector times the eigenvector associated with the largest eigenvalue in the test score covariance matrix. Sample includes all respondents who were employed, out of school, and had valid observations each year from age twenty-four to age thirty. Anyone receiving more schooling after age thirty was excluded.

ability over time. These estimates are usually derived from panel surveys. To follow the same people over time is also to follow them as they age. If the panel is not renewed with fresh cohorts, then it is very difficult to determine whether a trend (such as the recent rise in the return to education or ability) should be attributed to economywide change or simply to the fact that the survey respondents are aging. For example, it is difficult to tell whether the recent rise in the return to education or ability is due to economywide changes in the value of cognitive skills (a "time effect") or to the fact that as people age their ability becomes more valuable to employers (an "age effect"). There is an enormous difference between these two interpretations. One suggests that dramatic and important changes are occurring in the economy that may justify policy responses whereas the second suggests that nothing is changing in the economy as a whole. This problem is distinct from the standard problem of distinguishing age, period, and cohort effects that arises even in repeated cross sections or renewed panels.

The current literature copes with the problem of missing data in two distinct ways. Some authors impose linearity of time and/or age effects and arbitrarily suppress certain interactions. In Cawley, Heckman, and Vytlacil 1998 we demonstrate that the data are at odds with the widely used assumptions that time and age effects are linear, and we summarize that evidence here. Different ad hoc empirical specifications used in the literature explain part of the variation in reported estimates of the effects of ability on education across studies.

This chapter is organized into four sections. Section 1 summarizes our recent work on the role of ability in the recent rise in the return to education. The empirical estimates reported in this literature are sensitive to ad hoc solutions to the problem of missing data cells. The second section draws on Cawley, Heckman, and Vytlacil 1998 and discusses the identification problem that arises from using panel data to separate time and age effects and to identify a rising return to ability from panel data. Many researchers have coped with this problem by assuming that age and time effects are linear. We summarize a series of tests that reject this widely used assumption. When it is relaxed, the evidence indicates that the gap in wages between college- and high-school-educated men has widened over time for older workers of the highest ability groups. However, this pattern is not found for other ability groups and other schooling comparisons.

In the third section of this chapter, we use a model formulated by Heckman and Lochner (1996) and extended in Heckman, Lochner, and Taber (1998) to interpret this evidence and to examine the role of ability in explaining the increasing economic return to education. Simulations of these models demonstrate the importance of accounting for investment and recognizing whether or not workers know if demand shifts in favor of the skilled are permanent or transitory in using samples of young workers to infer the role of ability in accounting for the rise in the return to education. A model in which workers were surprised by the new labor market for skills that emerged in the early 1980s is consistent with the evidence.

Section 4 summarizes the chapter.

1. The Received Literature

Virtually all of the research that seeks to determine the role of ability in the rise in the economic return to education appeals to Mincer's (1974) model of earnings.[1] The goal of most papers we survey is to determine if "controlling for" ability reduces the rise in the return to schooling. The most influential of

---

[1] In the Mincer model, $\ell n\ w = \alpha_0 + \alpha_1 ed + \alpha_2 x$ where ed is schooling and x is experience. "α_1" is a rate of return under special conditions; see Heckman and Klenow (1997), Heckman, Taber and Lochner (1999), or Willis (1986) for a statement of these conditions. A hedonic model interprets the right-hand side variables as characteristics, or proxies for characteristics, valued in the labor market. Thus the coefficient on ability is sometimes interpreted as the "price" of ability, despite the fact that this model is inconsistent with a pure characteristics model. For more discussion, see Heckman and Scheinkman (1987).

these papers are by Blackburn and Neumark (1993) and Murnane, Willett, and Levy (1995), which we refer to as BN and MWL, respectively.

1.1 A Review of the Literature

Table 9.2 summarizes recent studies of the role of ability in explaining the rising return to schooling.[2] There are several features common to these studies. For example, most use the NLSY (National Longitudinal Survey of Youth), and all of the estimates are for the wages of young men (the oldest in any sample is thirty-one).[3]

There are, however, important differences in the literature, especially in the specification of age and time variables. MWL estimate their model for a single age group at two different times. Since correlations of ability and wages vary with age, the results of MWL do not apply to workers of all ages. BN estimate their model for a single experience group, using only entry wages, but samples across years are pooled. Other studies include many age or experience groups in their samples and assume that ability interacts with time and age measured in years (i.e., linear time multiplied by linear age or experience).

Some studies use age rather than work experience as a "control variable," ignoring Mincer's crucial distinction between the two. For example, MWL compare the college–high school wage differential over time at a given age, which implies that high school graduates have six years of work experience and college graduates have two years of work experience.

All studies show an increase in the return to schooling over time but they differ in how much it is moderated when cognitive ability is entered into the empirical analysis. MWL eliminate 38 percent of the increase for males and 100 percent for females between 1978 and 1986. BN report that the rise in the economic return to schooling is concentrated among the most able, but that controlling for ability alone does *not* reduce the rise in the return to schooling.[4] Grogger and Eide (1995) report that controlling for ability reduces, but does not eliminate, the rising return to schooling. They also find that the rise in the economic return to education is concentrated among the most able.

The literature reports mixed results on the economic return to ability over time. MWL find dramatic growth between 1978 to 1986. Grogger and Eide

---

[2] Because white males have received the most attention, we only survey empirical results for that group, noting that many authors fit models for women and obtain results that are *not* consistent with the results they obtain for males. (See, e.g., MWL and our discussion below.)

[3] MWL and Grogger and Eide (1995) also report evidence for young women.

[4] Herrnstein and Murray (1994) use this evidence to argue that the price of ability is rising and that society is becoming more meritocratic.

TABLE 9.2
Comparison of the Literature on Trends in Returns to Education and Cognitive Ability

	Bishop (1991) *Table 5-8*	*Blackburn/Neumark (1993)* *Table 4*
Sample	NLSY 1981–1986; includes those in school	NLSY white males, 1979–1987
Age Restriction	17 to 29	14 to 30
Dependent Variable	Log of hourly wage reported for each year	Log of first available hourly wage after completion of schooling
Regressors	Academic, computational, and technical ability (all drawn from ASVAB); years of schooling, years of college; actual experience; actual experience squared; potential experience; potential experience squared; interactions of date (year–1983) with the three ability measures, the two schooling measures, and actual experience; interactions of (age minus 22) with the three ability measures; interactions of actual experience with years of college and academic ability; interaction of academic ability and years of college; interactions of student status dummy with years of schooling and academic ability. Indicator variables for: school attendance, minority status, military, marital status, local unemployment rate, region, urban residence, children.	Years of education; interactions of time with education, experience, age, and union status dummy; dummy variables for urban residence, married with spouse present, and year. Academic ability and interactions of ability with education, education trend, age trend, and experience. Non-academic ability and its interacitons (with the same variables interacted with academic ability).
Parameterization of Time, Age, and Work Experience	Linear age, linear time, linear years of actual work experience	Linear time in interactions. Dummy variables for each year are also included as regressors. Linear age, linear years of actual experience.
Academic Ability Measure(s)	Average of 5 normalized ASVAB tests: AR, MK, PC, WK, GS. Renormalized to have a standard deviation of 1.	Average of 5 ASVAB tests demeaned by year of birth: AR, MK, PC, WK, GS. Standard deviation of .857.
Time Trend of Education Not Controlling for Ability	N.A.	Years of schooling trend coefficient is .0034.

(*table continues*)

TABLE 9.2 (*continued*)

	Bishop (1991) Table 5-8	Blackburn/Neumark (1992) Table 4
Time Trend of Education Controlling for Ability	Rising payoff to years of college (.0184) and falling payoff to years of education ($-.0055$) for men. For women, trend on years of schooling is not statistically significant and return to years of college (.0101) rises.	Controlling for ability, there is no statistically significant change over time in payoff to years of education.
Experience Trend of Education Controlling for Ability	$-.0139$ for men and $-.0072$ for women.	N.A.
Time Trend of Ability	Not statistically significant for either men or women.	Not statistically significant.
Age Trend of Ability	Not significant, but return to computational ability (Numerical Operations score) rises (.0097) for men.	Not significant if nonacademic ability (average of AS, EI, MC, NO demeaned by year of birth) included; .02 otherwise.
Experience Trend of Ability	Not significant for men or women.	$-.012$; however, when nonacademic ability and its interactions are included, it is not statistically significant.
Education-Ability Interaction	Years of college-ability interaction coefficient is .0124 for men and .0148 for women	Years of education-ability interaction coefficient is .015.
Time Trend of Education-Ability Interaction	N.A.	Coefficient is .0029.
	Grogger/Eide (1995) Tables 4 and 5	Murnane/Willett/Levy (1995) Tables 3, 4, and 5
Sample	NLS 1972 and HS&B 1980 (pooled) full-time workers who were not full-time students with hourly wages between $1 and $100	NLS 1972 HS&B 1980 persons out of school. Unweighted sample that overrepresents blacks and hispanics.
Age Restriction	23 to 25, 31	Six years after high school graduation: roughly age 24
Dependent Variable	Log of hourly wage for NLS 1977, 1978, 1979, and 1986 and HS&B 1986	Log of hourly wage in sixth year after HS graduation (1978 and 1986)

(*table continues*)

TABLE 9.2 (*continued*)

	Grogger/Eide (1995) Tables 4 and 5	Murnane/Willett/Levy (1995) Tables 3, 4, and 5
Regressors	Ability, work experience, and dummy variables for educational attainment (post-graduate degree, college degree, some college), race, cohort, part-time school enrollment, year, and for missing data. Education dummies are interacted with time trend and linear experience, separately.	Dummy variables for black, hispanic, attended high school in South, wages for part-time work, and single-parent household. Years of education; mother's highest grade completed; father's highest grade completed; number of siblings; years of full-time work experience; years of part-time work experience; ability; interaction of ability and schooling.
Parameterization of Time, Age, and Work Experience	Linear time, no age variables, linear years of actual work experience	Nonparametric time (regressions estimated separately for 1978 and 1986), age (all respondents are roughly 24 years of age), and work experience (all observations are six years after high school, which implies roughly six years of work experience for high school graduates and roughly two years of work expeience for college graduates). Linear years of full-time and part-time potential work experience are entered separately as regressors.
Academic Ability Measure(s)	Scores on ETS tests of math (standard deviations = 7.3 in NLS and 6.8 in HS&B), vocabulary, and mosaic, and dummy variables for high school grades	Scaled ETS math test score. Standard deviation of 7.12 in 1972 and 7.21 and 1980
Time Trend of Education Not Controlling for Ability	For men, .0135 for those with post-graduate degrees, .0169 for college graduates, and .0087 for those with some college. For women, the trend is not statistically significant for those with post-graduate degrees, and is .0096 for college graduates and .0075 for those with some college.	For men, years of schooling coefficient is .022 in 1978 and .044 in 1986 for men. For women, the schooling coefficient is .054 in 1978 and .065 in 1986 (all results conditional on age 24).

(*table continues*)

TABLE 9.2 (*continued*)

	Grogger/Eide (1995) Tables 4 and 5	Murnane/Willett/Levy (1995) Tables 3, 4, and 5
Time Trend of Education Controlling for Ability	Statistically insignificant for men and women with post-graduate degrees, .0131 for male college graduates, .0043 for female college graduates, .0066 for men with some college, and .004 for women with some college.	Inclusion of ability eliminates the rise in the college premium for women and reduces it from 100% to 62% for men. Specifically, including ability reduces the total education trend over eight years from .011 to zero for women, and from .022 to .008 for men (conditional on roughly 24 years of age).
Experience Trend of Education Controlling for Ability	Not statistically significant for women. For men: with post-graduate degrees: .0262; with college degrees: .0192; with some college: .0068.	N.A.
Time Trend of Ability	Trend on math test score is .0006 for males and .0008 for females.	For men, the ability coefficient almost triples from .004 in 1978 to .011 in 1986. For women, the ability coefficient almost doubles, from .009 in 1978, to .017 in 1986 (conditional on roughly 24 years of age).
Age Trend of Ability	N.A.	N.A.
Experience Trend of Ability	−.0002 for both men and women	N.A.
Education-Ability Interaction	N.A.	For men, .0034 in 1986 but statistically insignificant (with a coefficient of .0016) in 1978. The opposite pattern holds for women: .0016 in 1978 and statistically insignificant (with a coefficient of −.001) in 1986 (conditional on roughly 24 years of age)
Time Trend of Education-Ability Interaction	N.A.	The coefficients on education ability in two separate years imply a trend coefficient of .0002 for men and −.003 for women (conditional on roughly 24 years of age).

Note: N.A. stands for not applicable; that particular interaction was not tested. All reported coefficients are statistically significant unless explicitly reported otherwise.

(1995) also find statistically significant, albeit smaller, growth in this return over the same period. In a model with many interactions, BN estimate that there is no trend in the return to ability. Studies that include an age-ability interaction typically find no evidence of a rise in the economic return to ability over time.

1.2 Checking for Robustness

In Cawley, Heckman, and Vytlacil (1998), we examine two potential problems with this body of empirical research: the measures of cognitive ability used and the ranges of the ages of persons in the samples used to secure estimates. In an effort to examine the robustness of the BN finding, we determine if we can obtain comparable results using a measure of cognitive ability that is widely used in the psychology literature rather than the ad hoc measure used by BN. (See Carroll 1993, Herrnstein and Murray 1994, and Jensen 1987.) Instead of their average of five Armed Services Vocational Aptitude Battery (ASVAB) subtests, we use g.[5] Intuitively, g represents the combination of test scores that best explains the majority of variance in performance on all ten tests of cognitive ability in the NLSY. As demonstrated in Heckman (1995) and Cawley, Conneely, Heckman, and Vytlacil (1997), g explains much more of the variance of the test scores than any other principal component or *combinations* of test scores. In constructing g, tests that measure basic verbal and math skills receive a greater weight than tests of knowledge of electronics or auto shop or mechanical ability.

Our estimates, reported in table 9.3, indicate that a main result reported by BN does not apply when a more conventional measure of ability is used in place of theirs. The interaction between ability, education, and time is not statistically significant when g is used as a measure of ability.[6] (This is the $g \cdot$ education $\cdot$ time interaction). At a minimum this suggests that their result

---

[5] General intelligence is estimated by principal components analysis. Because age at the time of test influences performance on tests of cognitive ability, we residualized each subtest of the ASVAB tests on age at the time of test. The residuals were standardized to mean zero and variance one. Principal components were estimated from the standardized residuals. We calculated g by multiplying the test score vector by the eigenvector associated with the largest eigenvalue of the matrix of correlations among the standardized ASVAB scores. For a more complete description of g and its characteristics, see Cawley, Conneely, Heckman, and Vytlacil (1997). In our earlier work, we test and reject the hypothesis that unweighted averages of ASVAB scores, as used by BN or Hernstein and Murray, are better predictors of wages; g predicts better.

[6] The results in table 9.3 were produced using the first available wage after the last disenrollment from school, which is used by BN. We also reestimated their model using the wage after first disenrollment from school; these results are consistent with those for the first wage measure and so are not presented in this chapter but are available upon request.

TABLE 9.3

Blackburn and Neumark Specification, 1979–1987 (NLSY White Males, OLS Regression, Dependent Variable: Ln Wage, Number of Observations: 2,124, R^2: .188)

Variable	Coeff	Std Error	T-stat	P-val
Intercept	1.1939	.1597	7.4754	0
Years of completed schooling	.0644	.0136	4.7165	0
Education*Time	−.0079	.0035	−2.2456	.0247
General intelligence (G)	−.4492	.2428	−1.8502	.0643
G*Education	.0131	.0103	1.2742	.2026
G*Education*Time	.0001	.0029	.0391	.9688
G*Time	.0095	.0365	.2607	.7943
G*Work experience	−.0232	.0143	−1.6151	.1063
G*Age	.0166	.0121	1.368	.1713
Work experience*Time	.0068	.0031	2.2036	.0276
Age*Time	.0026	.0023	1.1039	.2696
Urban resident	.1511	.0277	5.4486	0
Married, spouse present	.138	.0363	3.8011	.0001
year = = 80	−.1508	.0664	−2.2702	.0232
year = = 81	−.1514	.1085	−1.3961	.1627
year = = 82	−.2499	−.1605	−1.5573	.1194
year = = 83	−.2796	.2122	−1.3176	.1876
year = = 84	−.1511	.2711	−.5576	.5771
year = = 85	−.0933	.3374	−.2766	.7821
year = = 86	−.1234	.3958	−.3119	.7552
year = = 87	.0862	.4589	.1878	.851

Note: The reported standard errors are Eicker-White robust standard errors. Regression uses first wage after the completion of schooling.

is fragile with respect to the choice of the ability measure used, although we argue that other factors also contribute to the fragility of their estimate.

Virtually all of the samples used to estimate the impact of ability on earnings are for young people. In the literature surveyed in table 9.2, the oldest person in any sample is thirty-one. Evidence for persons of this age group does not generalize to other age groups because the correlation of ability with earnings varies over the life cycle. See Griliches and Mason (1972) and Jencks (1972). Workers of greater ability invest more to acquire skills. Estimated relationships between earnings and cognitive ability are weak or even perverse at the very ages at which the empirical work in table 9.2 has been conducted. We develop this point further in section 4, where we consider somewhat more formally the implications of a dynamic model of human capital investment with ability.

Using our measure of ability, we examine whether the MWL findings hold for ages other than twenty-four. Our estimates are presented in tables 9.4a

TABLE 9.4A

Murnane-Willett-Levy Specification for Different Ages and Years
(NLSY Males, OLS Regression, Dependent Variable: Ln Wage)

Change in Education Coefficients	Change	Std Error	T-stat	P-val
Age 22: 1979–1986	.032	.025	1.28	.201
Age 22: 1979–1986 controlling for G	.017	.031	.548	.583
Age 23: 1980–1987	.054	.027	2	.046
Age 23: 1980–1987 controlling for G	.023	.028	.821	.411
Age 24: 1981–1988	−.002	.023	−.087	.931
Age 24: 1981–1988 controlling for G	−.025	.027	−.926	.354
Age 25: 1982–1989	.048	.023	2.087	.037
Age 25: 1982–1989 controlling for G	.024	.028	.857	.391
Age 26: 1983–1990	.024	.026	.923	.356
Age 26: 1983–1990 controlling for G	.024	.028	.857	.391
Age 27: 1984–1991	−.002	.021	−.095	.924
Age 27: 1984–1991 controlling for G	0	.025	0	1
Age 28: 1985–1992	.025	.022	1.136	.256
Age 28: 1985–1992 controlling for G	.017	.025	.68	.497
Age 29: 1986–1993	.012	.02	.6	.549
Age 29: 1986–1993 controlling for G	−.005	.023	−.217	.828
Age 30: 1987–1994	−.007	.022	−.318	.75
Age 30: 1987–1994 controlling for G	−.021	.026	−.808	.419

Notes: Change represents the difference between the later and earlier coefficient on education in a regression of ln wage on education, g, a dummy for residing in a single-parent household at age 14, number of siblings, mother and father's highest grade completed, dummy variables for residing in the South at age 14, black, and hispanic, and years (units of 50 weeks) of work experience. This regression was estimated for persons of different ages, and for persons of ($n −$ 1 to n) years of experience. This regression was estimated separately in each year. Standard errors, T-statistics, and P values apply to the change in coefficients between those two years.

Eicker-White robust standard errors are reported.

The dependent variable is log hourly wage in 1990 dollars.

Sample includes all valid employed out-of-school person-year observations.

NLSY sample weights are used.

and 9.4b. MWL use two data sources: the High School and Beyond, and the NLS-72. We use the NLSY and estimate a model similar to theirs.[7] Table 9.4a shows the change in the education coefficient over seven years in a

---

[7] We do not include as a regressor an indicator variable for a part-time wage, and we do not differentiate between part-time and full-time work experience. Also, our cognitive ability measure is g, whereas MWL use a math score.

TABLE 9.4B

Murnane-Willett-Levy Specification for Different Work Experience and Years
(NLSY Males, OLS Regression, Dependent Variable: Ln Wage)

Change in Education Coefficients	Change	Std Error	T-stat	P-val
2 Yrs Work Experience 1979–1986	.013	.038	.342	.732
2 Yrs Work Experience 1979–1986 controlling for G	−.021	.037	−.568	.57
3 Yrs Work Experience 1980–1987	.095	.029	3.276	.001
3 Yrs Work Experience 1980–1987 controlling for G	.058	.034	1.706	.088
4 Yrs Work Experience 1981–1988	.028	.024	1.167	.243
4 Yrs Work Experience 1981–1988 controlling for G	−.003	.03	−.1	.92
5 Yrs Work Experience 1982–1989	.055	.024	2.292	.022
5 Yrs Work Experience 1982–1989 controlling for G	.049	.029	1.69	.091
6 Yrs Work Experience 1983–1990	.075	.025	3	.003
6 Yrs Work Experience 1983–1990 controlling for G	.066	.031	2.129	.033
7 Yrs Work Experience 1984–1991	.046	.024	1.917	.055
7 Yrs Work Experience 1984–1991 controlling for G	.05	.03	1.667	.096
8 Yrs Work Experience 1985–1992	.078	.028	2.786	.005
8 Yrs Work Experience 1985–1992 controlling for G	.075	.033	2.273	.023
9 Yrs Work Experience 1986–1993	.067	.03	2.233	.026
9 Yrs Work Experience 1986–1993 controlling for G	.069	.038	1.816	.069
10 Yrs Work Experience 1987–1994	.046	.026	1.769	.077
10 Yrs Work Experience 1987–1994 controlling for G	.013	.032	.406	.685

Notes: Change represents the difference between the later and earlier coefficient on education
in a regression of ln wage on education, g, a dummy for residing in a single-parent household at
age 14, number of siblings, mother and father's highest grade completed, dummy variables for
residing in the South at age 14, black, and hispanic, and years (units of 50 weeks) of work
experience. This regression was estimated for persons of different ages, and for persons of (n −
1 to n) years of experience. This regression was estimated separately in each year. Standard
errors, T-statistics, and P values apply to the change in coefficients between those two years.

Eicker-White robust standard errors are reported.

The dependent variable is log hourly wage in 1990 dollars.

Sample includes all valid employed out-of-school person-year observations.

NLSY sample weights are used.

sample of males ages twenty-two through twenty-nine, before and after controlling for cognitive ability. We find that the change in the education coefficient that arises from introducing a measure of ability into the earnings function is statistically significant only at ages twenty-three and twenty-five.

By estimating their model for people age twenty-four, MWL compare college graduates with roughly two years of work experience to high school graduates with roughly six years of work experience. To compare these two groups at a uniform level of experience, we re-estimate the MWL model conditioning on years of work experience (calculated from reported weeks of work experience) instead of age. Results of this analysis are presented in table 9.4b. The increase in the return to education is generally statistically significant, and falls when we control for cognitive ability. This generally supports their analysis. However, the decline produced by controlling for ability varies by the age and experience of the worker. For example, among workers with three years of experience, the increase in the education coefficient is reduced by 40 percent when we control for cognitive ability. However, for those with seven, eight, or nine years of work experience, our estimate of the rise in the education premium is the same whether or not we control for cognitive ability.

Estimated interactions are not robust across specifications. No consensus view emerges from these tables. What is the source of this empirical discord? Part of the explanation is that the literature copes in different, ad hoc ways with fundamental identification problems, which we discuss in Cawley, Heckman, and Vytlacil (1998). We now summarize that analysis.

2. Estimating Interactions From Incomplete Data

One basic problem with the data used in all of these studies is that it is not possible to separate the effects of time and age without imposing a lot of structure on the data.[8] A Lexis diagram, a tool used by demographers that graphs age and time, is helpful in illustrating the problem of identifying age and time effects in a panel data set. Figure 9.1 is a Lexis diagram of a single age cohort followed over time. Darkened cells indicate the data that exist for the indicated age and time cells. If panel data consist of only a single age cohort, age and time are confounded; it is impossible to identify age and time effects. Even with multiple age cohorts (see, e.g., fig. 9.2 for the NLSY panel) there are many empty cells. "Main effects" for time or age are defined as averages over entire rows and columns. For example, the main time effect is the average year-specific change for workers of all ages. The main time

---

[8] For formal treatment of the issues discussed in this section, including definitions of unconditional and conditional time effects and a description of the identified linear combinations of interactions in the presence of incomplete data, see Cawley, Heckman, and Vytlacil (1998).

Age (a)

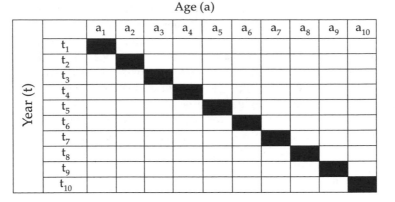

Figure 9.1. Lexis Diagram with a Single Age Cohort

effect cannot be identified in the NLSY because only workers of eight birth years are observed in any calendar year. Moreover, as the sample ages, the year effect is defined for older workers in later samples. No fixed age-weight year effect can be defined. Thus main effects for fixed sets of ages— or times—cannot be computed; as figure 9.2 shows, some of the required components are missing.

The empty data cells also represent an obstacle to identifying interactions between time and age. For example, because we cannot identify the main time effect, we also cannot identify all of the age-specific time effects. A pragmatic solution adopts a rule for "filling in" the empty data cells. The rule adopted reflects one's assumptions about the parametric structure of the

Age (a)

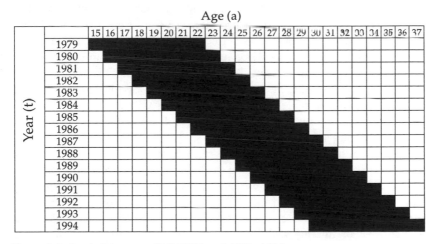

Figure 9.2. Lexis Diagram of NLSY Panel 1979–1994

data. For example, one could assume that the effects of time and age are linear, that is, that trends observed in nonempty data cells can safely be extended into the empty ones. Many interpretations are possible, however.

In the NLSY, only the blackened cells in figure 9.2 are available. The problem of empty off-diagonal cells substantially restricts what can be learned in two major ways. First, we cannot estimate the unconditional time and age effects. The unconditional time effect is the average time-specific effect of ability and schooling for a fixed set of ages, not just the ages observed in the data. Since we do not observe the same ages in every year (i.e., since we have empty off-diagonal cells), it is impossible to estimate these unconditional effects. Instead, we can estimate conditional main effects: age effects in the times observed, and the time effects for the ages observed.

The second major effect of empty data cells is to limit the number of identifiable interactions. Specifically, only interactions associated with nonempty data cells can be identified. If only one age cohort is observed (as in figure 9.1), no main effects or interactions are identified; they are hopelessly confounded as the single age cohort simultaneously ages and enters a new economic environment (see, e.g., Searle 1987). Given two age cohorts, all main effects are identified if interactions are assumed to be zero. (See Cawley, Heckman, and Vytlacil 1998 for details.) For three or more age cohorts, certain linear combinations of interactions are identified. Individual interactions cannot be identified. The problem is more severe at the boundary ages (for the youngest and oldest workers), where certain ages are observed for the first or last time. This feature of the identification problem is unfortunate because, as noted in section 1, considerable attention has been devoted to interactions at the youngest age groups in the NLSY.

The literature copes with this identification problem in various ways. It is not surprising that different strategies lead to very different results. Bishop (1991) assumes linear time and age effects. BN assume linear time effects in the interactions they estimate. Grogger and Eide (1995) assume linear experience effects and no age effects. BN analyze a particular experience group; MWL analyze two different experience groups for two different education groups. No author in table 9.2 fits a model with time and age effects estimated for each education-ability cell. Studies differ in the interactions that are estimated and suppressed.

We have outlined the limitations that stem from empty data cells. There is, however, an additional identification problem: data cells that are nonempty but contain little data. So far we have considered the problem of missing data with respect to age and time. In practice, this problem is compounded because estimates are often conditional on ability and education, making the problem one of missing and sparse data in a four-dimensional grid: age, time, ability, and education. It turns out that virtually all of the very able go to college; none of the low-ability people do (see table 9.1). The literature parses out ability and education effects through arbitrary linearity specifications and through arbitrary specifications of interactions, including setting many of them to zero. Different interactions are suppressed in different studies.

In Cawley, Heckman, and Vytlacil (1998), we present our own estimates of the wage returns to ability and education. We estimate conditional main time and age effects and the identified linear combinations of interactions nonparametrically. That is, we make no assumptions about how the effects of ability and education vary over time and age. In order to avoid making arbitrary functional form assumptions, we must look within groups of workers of identical age, education, and ability. We now briefly summarize our research.

2.1 New Evidence on the Effects of Ability on Earnings

Figure 9.3 shows the rising wage return to education over time for white males in the NLSY. Some researchers conclude that this trend is largely attributable to an increasing premium for ability. As figure 9.4 shows, this interpretation is consistent with the data. In fact, many hypotheses are consistent with the data: a rising return to education over age, a rising return to ability over age, a rising return to education over work experience, and a rising return to ability over work experience.

In Cawley, Heckman, and Vytlacil (1998) we use samples of white male workers to consider two questions. (1) Is the rising return to education attributable to a rising return to cognitive ability? To answer this question, we use a nonparametric approach. We estimate time effects within education-ability-age cells. That is, we estimate changes over time among workers of a given age with the same education and ability.

The second question we consider is: (2) Do we need to be so agnostic about the parameterization of time and age? By estimating time effects within education-ability-age cells, we obtain estimates for many small groups of workers and obtain estimates with higher standard errors than what we would get when we pool the data. If there are consistent patterns in the effects of age, for example, we could pool workers of all ages together and control for age with the regressor "years of age." This would produce estimates with lower standard errors. In order to test whether such an assumption is justified, we test the assumption of linear trends in time and age.

In a fully nonparametric analysis, we conclude that the wage premium for college graduation (over high school graduation) has risen since the mid 1980s for white males of the highest g quartile in their late twenties and early thirties. A parallel analysis controlling for experience, instead of age,

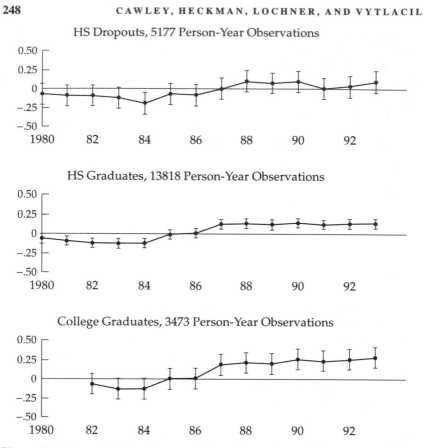

Figure 9.3. Return to Education over Time. Reported standard errors are Eicher-White robust standard errors. First-year coefficients are standardized to zero, not plotted. Standard errors shown as brackets. First-year coefficients normalized to zero.

finds a similar increase for most experience groups. This result is consistent with a central conclusion of BN. However, the high dependence between education and ability causes us to have insufficient data to examine the wage premium for college graduation for any other g quartile while being fully nonparametric, so we cannot tell whether the increasing college premium is occurring only for individuals of the highest g quartile. Even if we suppress interactions of age and time, we can only examine changes in the college premium for the highest two g quartiles, and in that case we do not find robust results for the third (the next to highest) quartile.[9] Likewise, empty

[9] In particular, we regressed log wages on age and year indicator variables within education-ability cells, thus suppressing interactions of age and time. In our main specification, we find a rising return to college graduation only in the highest g quartile. However, this result is highly sensitive to model specification—if we regress on experience instead of age, or use "Numerical

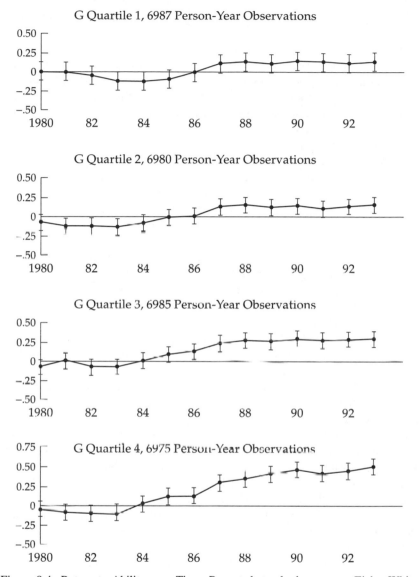

Figure 9.4. Return to Ability over Time. Reported standard errors are Eicher-White robust standard errors. Standard errors shown as brackets. 1979 coefficient standardized to zero, not plotted.

age-time cells limit our ability to make statements for other age groups. The literature makes comparisons across missing education-ability cells and

Operations" test scores instead of g, then we find the same increase in the college–high school wage differential in both the third and fourth g quartiles.

missing age-time cells by invoking a linearity assumption to fill in the missing cells.

A second question considered in Cawley, Heckman, and Vytlacil (1998) is whether we need to be fully nonparametric in age and time. Even though we cannot estimate all possible interactions because of the missing cell problem, we can estimate and test certain models. To answer the second question we first test whether age and time effects are equal across ability and education cells. We reject that hypothesis. Such effects should be estimated within education-ability cells.

Within each education-ability cell, we test whether all age-time interactions are zero. We also reject this hypothesis, which implies that in order to test for the linearity of time effects we must condition on age and vice versa. We follow this strategy[10] and reject the hypothesis that time effects are linear across education-ability-age cells and that age effects are linear across education-ability-time cells. From this series of tests, we conclude that there is no empirical justification for the widespread practice of assuming that the effects of time and age are linear.[11]

At the beginning of this section we asked two questions. The first was: How should attribution for the wage gain be divided between education and ability? In our research, we show that education and cognitive ability are so highly correlated that the wage effects of the two cannot be separated for most ability groups (see table 9.1). Thus a central policy question cannot be answered from these data.

We find that the college graduate–high school graduate wage differential has risen for those in the highest quartile of ability when we control for age or experience (for most experience groups). However, we cannot say whether this increasing wage differential is only for the most able without imposing incorrect structure on the data. Even when we do (incorrectly) impose the assumption that there are no age-time interactions, we find that the result (that the wage differential exists only for the most able) is highly sensitive to model specification—the result disappears when we regress on experience instead of age, and it disappears if we use an alternative measure of ability. Thus, the BN finding that the returns to education are greatest among the most able has to be qualified.

The second question we address is: Do we need to be nonparametric when estimating the effects of age and time? The answer is yes. We find no support for the widely accepted practice in the empirical literature of imposing linear effects of time and age. Imposing that assumption affects the estimates

---

[10] Specifically, for each age we consider whether the age-specific time trend is linear for that ability-education-age cell. The same approach is used for testing whether the time-specific age trend is linear.

[11] In results reported in Cawley, Heckman, and Vytlacil (1998), we also test and reject separable quadratic age and time specifications.

reported in the literature. Variations in identifying assumptions among different studies explain variations in the evidence reported in those studies.

A main lesson of this section can be summarized as follows. Suppose we observe that the interaction of education (or ability) and time is positive for the sample in 1979. This interaction would characterize young workers around age twenty. Now suppose that the interaction is zero in 1990. That would characterize workers around age thirty. There is no way to tell whether the rising return to ability or schooling has stopped or whether there is less of a rise in returns for older workers than younger workers. Thus, from the NLSY (and any data like it) we will never know whether the return to ability has continued to rise over time, because time effects may depend on age. Moreover, given the high correlation between ability and education, it is difficult—if not impossible—to separate out the effects of ability and education. We now demonstrate how a human capital model with post-school investment rationalizes the time-dependent age effects of the sort reported in the literature that survive our nonparametric analysis.

3. The Role of Ability and the Importance of Expectations about Demand Shocks in Earnings Equations

Thus far we have adhered to the economic model based on equation (1) that is implicit in recent studies of ability and earnings. Ability is a characteristic valued in the market in its own right or a proxy for such a characteristic. Ability has the same reward in all sectors of the economy.

Human capital theory suggests a more dynamic role for ability as it affects both endowments and investment over the life cycle. In this section we consider a dynamic relationship between ability and earnings over the life cycle, recognizing that ability not only affects current wage levels but it also affects how individuals choose to invest in their skills, thereby determining future wage levels as well. We also consider models of heterogeneous human capital in which human capital of different types commands different prices and ability is allowed to affect different schooling levels differently.

Ability can directly affect wages through three distinct mechanisms: (1) through its effect on the stock of human capital or current skill level, (2) through its effect on the proportion of time spent investing in new skills (or, alternatively, the amount of earnings forgone to acquire skill), and (3) through its effect on the wage return to each unit of human capital (or the price of one's skill). The coefficient on ability in a wage regression combines all three effects. Specifically, let R be the rental rate or price of human capital, let H be the personal stock of human capital, and I be the fraction of potential income forgone to invest in skills. The conventional human capital approach (e.g., Ben-Porath 1967 or Mincer 1974) models the wage at time t of a person age a as

$$W(a,t) = R(t)H(a,t) (1 - I(a,t)). \tag{2}$$

In logs,

$$\ell n \, W(a,t) = \ell n \, R(t) + \ell n \, H(a,t) + \ell n \, (1 - I(a,t)). \tag{3}$$

For each hour worked, individuals earn $R(t)$ for each unit of skill, $H(a,t)$, they possess. Thus, an individual's potential wage rate—the wage rate if all time is devoted to maximal output—is $R(t)H(a,t)$; however, if that individual chooses to spend some fraction of his or her time on the job investing in new skills, $I(a,t)$, that individual's observed wage will be less than his or her potential wage. (For example, in the early years of the life cycle when people forgo earnings to acquire skills, on-the-job investment can lower the measured earnings of college graduates to only 60 percent of potential earnings.) Post-school investment may include formal training, informal training on the job, or any activity that results in the worker producing less current output than he or she otherwise could.

A simple example of this phenomenon is a worker who spends some of her time learning a new computer program in order to perform her job faster or better in the future and as a result gets less work done in the short term. This model assumes that learning produces skills that are applicable generally in the market, so new skills can be used at any job. In this case, workers must pay for their training through forgone earnings. In general, the firm would not be willing to pay for the training, since the worker could always leave the firm, taking her skills elsewhere, once the training period has ended. Taking low-paying jobs with high learning content in order to eventually move to higher-paying occupations is one way such investment occurs (Rosen 1972).

In principle, ability can enter each component of equation (3). A higher-ability person is likely to have a higher level of skill at any age, and he may also receive a higher return on that skill. Thus, we might expect the potential wages (the wages that a person would earn if he spent no time investing in on-the-job training and used all of his time productively) of higher-ability individuals to be higher. However, high-ability individuals may also earn a higher return on their skill investments. Thus, they may spend more time investing in human capital, so the gap between their potential and observed wages will be larger.

Post-school investment activity is the greatest at the youngest ages. At young ages or low experience levels, investment differences among workers of different skill may be larger than differences in skill levels, so that the observed wage rates of young high-ability workers may be *lower* than the wage rates of young low-ability workers who invest less and have a higher

$1 - I$. These differences in investment productivity explain why wage differences among young workers are much smaller across different ability groups than are wage differences among older workers of heterogeneous abilities. Studies such as BN or MWL that estimate the impact of ability on the earnings of workers with low levels of work experience produce a distorted estimate of the effect of ability on life cycle earnings. Furthermore, differences in investment productivity among ability groups will lead to differential responses to changes in skill prices among ability groups in the economy (Heckman, Lochner, and Taber 1998).

Heckman and Lochner (1996) and Heckman, Lochner, and Taber (1998) investigate the role of ability and investment on earnings. They develop an empirically concordant model in which ability affects both initial human capital levels and the productivity of human capital investments made on the job, a model that explains rising wage inequality in the U.S. economy. They estimate human capital models with heterogeneous skills that allow different types of human capital to have different prices. In their models, ability is a determinant of initial endowments of skill and is a factor that influences the efficiency of human capital production on the job. The price of human capital R differs among schooling groups.

Using these models, we explore two different scenarios concerning shifts in demand toward more skilled labor and their effects on wage differentials by ability. The manner in which schooling-specific prices respond to shifts in demand is an important determinant of how investment and wages respond in the short run. Our simulations demonstrate the following points: (1) Post-school human capital investment is greatest at young ages for the most educated. As a result, college–high school wage differentials are smaller at the youngest ages compared to what they become at older ages. So are ability-wage differentials, because the more able are more likely to go to college and invest more on the job after they leave college. Since most of the empirical research on the effect of ability on earnings has been conducted on samples of young people, the evidence reported in the recent literature understates the role of ability in explaining wage differentials over most of the lifetime.

(2) A continuously operating anticipated shift in demand toward skilled labor *reduces* the college–high school wage differential at younger ages for the most able compared to what it would be in a stationary economy. As individuals age, the differential widens as the early post-school investments made by the more able pay off.

(3) A temporary shift in demand toward skilled labor leads to reduced post-school investment in on-the-job training in the short run by the most skilled and a temporary rise in the college–high school wage differential compared to what would occur in a stationary environment. This widens the college–high school wage differential, especially among workers of the

highest ability. This scenario seems most consistent with the evidence reported by BN that survives our nonparametric testing procedures. The college wage premium rises more for the most able due to a larger decline in post-school investment by high-ability workers during the period when skill prices are thought to be temporarily high.

3.1 Description of the Simulations

Heckman and Lochner (1996) estimate models for on-the-job training among workers of different ability and schooling levels using NLSY data. The more able have higher endowments of skill upon completing schooling and have greater efficiency in learning new skills on the job than do the less able. Their estimates are presented in figure 9.5, which plots actual versus fitted earnings for different ability quartiles for college and high school graduates. (The NLSY data stop after age thirty-one.) Not all ability quartiles are represented; this is a manifestation of the empty-cell problem discussed in section 2. In addition, as shown in section 2, all of the action in age-ability/age-experience interactions is for the top two quartiles of the ability distribution, so we confine our analysis to that group. We use Heckman and Lochner's model to simulate three hypothetical economies: (1) a base-case economy in which the rental rate for all types of human capital is constant and fixed at one for all years (there is no skill bias operating in this economy); (2) an economy with continuously rising skill prices for high-skill workers and declining prices for low-skill workers in which the rental rate (or price of skill) on human capital declines annually by 1 percent for high school graduates while the price for individuals with four or more years of college grows at 1 percent per year (agents are assumed to be aware of these trends and to act on them); and (3) an economy with a temporary rise in the price of skill. In this third simulated economy, the human capital rental rate for high school graduates falls by 3 percent for three years and then returns to its previous level, while the human capital rental rate for college graduates rises by 3 percent for the same three years and then returns to its previous level.

3.2 Simulation Results

We study the effects of ability, experience, and schooling on earnings in each of these simulated economies. Furthermore, we consider the effects of moving from the base-case economy to the two economies that differ in the permanence of the shift of demand in favor of skilled labor. We interpret these effects as "time" effects since many recent papers have argued that the time effects on wages seen in the data are the result of a shift to an economy

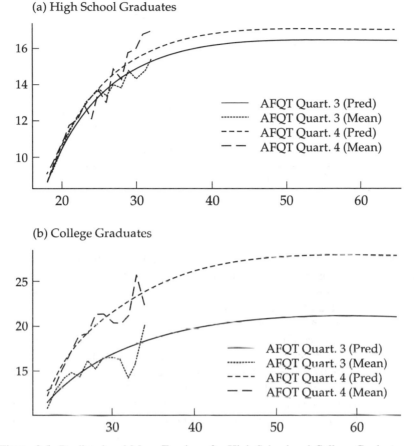

Figure 9.5. Predicted and Mean Earnings for High School and College Graduates

with rising returns to ability/skill. Whether that shift has been characterized by permanently rising prices for skill (simulated by economy 2) or a more temporary rise in high-skill rental rates followed by a subsequent decline (simulated by economy 3) has not been addressed in the literature. The time effects produced from these different economies are quite different, as we describe below. The evidence from the 1980s seems more consistent with a story that the change in the market for skills was perceived to be temporary.

Figure 9.6 addresses the first main point of this section. It plots the share of potential income forgone by workers of different education and ability classes. Human capital investment is an important component of wage growth, especially for high-ability and highly educated individuals. Failure to account for investment yields substantially lowers estimates of potential income for young/low-experience workers, especially for the more able and

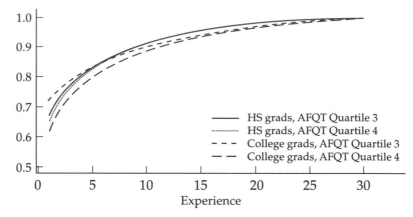

Figure 9.6. Observed Share of Total Income: 1 − I(t)

those with college degrees. For the college graduate, on-the-job investment can account for as much as 40 percent of total wages in early work years.

Among the most able, human capital investment is much higher for college graduates than for high school graduates. As a result, the college–high school wage differential based on observed earnings tends to substantially understate skill price differences for individuals of the highest ability. The consequences of investment are seen in figure 9.7, which shows the college–high school wage differential for quartiles 3 and 4 of the AFQT distribution. For the highest-ability group (quartile 4), the college–high school gap rises steadily in early years of employment. However, for workers in the third AFQT quartile, the initial wage gap declines, then rises after about ten years of experience.

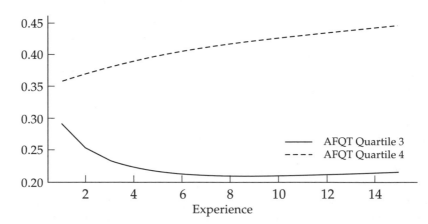

Figure 9.7. College–High School Log Wage Gap

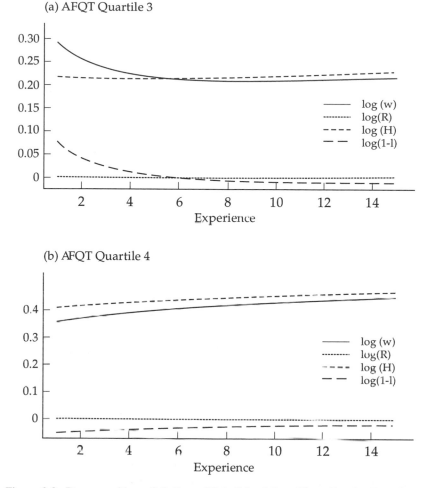

Figure 9.8. Decomposition of College–High School Log Wage Gap by Experience and AFQT

   These differentials are decomposed into the three components of equation (3) in figure 9.8a and b. These graphs show that the higher investment for college-educated young workers lowers the college–high school earnings differential for young workers in the highest ability quartile and raises the gap early on for those in the third ability quartile. For individuals with little work experience, there is a negative effect of ability on the college wage premium due to the higher investment by more able college graduates.
   Figure 9.9(1) shows the effect of moving to an economy with an anticipated permanently rising skill differential. The college–high school wage

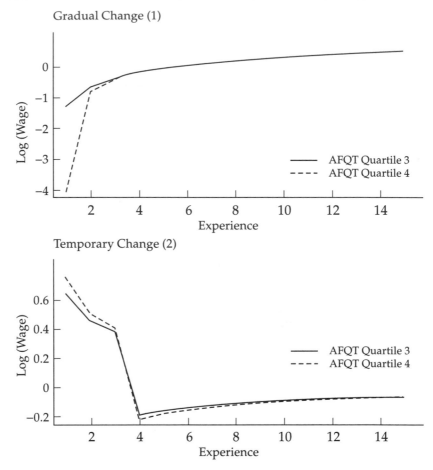

Figure 9.9. Effects of Increased Demand for Skill on the College–High School Log Wage Gap. (1) Change in log wages by ability quartile for an economy with gradually rising price of college labor and declining price of high school labor. (2) Change in log wages by ability quartile for an economy with a temporary rise in the price of college labor and temporary decline in the price of high school labor.

differential is *larger* for the second-highest ability group (quartile 3) than for the highest ability group (quartile 4) at younger ages. The disparity between the two ability groups disappears quickly, as both ability quartiles experience rising income as their post-school human capital stocks increase. A shift in demand toward high-skilled workers that produces continuously rising prices for high-skilled workers may reduce the estimated "return" to college at young ages for those who are most able. This arises because higher-ability college graduates respond to the increasing returns to human capital by raising their investment more than less able graduates in the first few years of

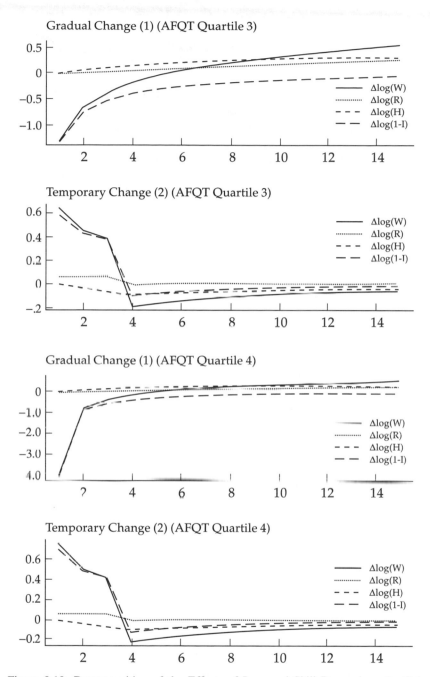

Figure 9.10. Decomposition of the Effects of Increased Skill Demand on the College–High School Log Wage Gap. (1) Change in log wages by ability quartile for an economy with gradually rising price of college labor and declining price of high school labor. (2) Change in log wages by ability quartile for an economy with a temporary rise in the price of college labor and temporary decline in the price of high school labor.

employment. (See figure 9.10 for a decomposition of the change in the wage gap into the three components of equation (3).) Although the value of a college education (in lifetime present value) is raised more for the most able, the wage levels of young workers do not reflect this. These findings caution against using samples of young workers to draw conclusions about the effects of both education on earnings and the interaction effect of ability and education on lifetime earnings.

We also examine the effects of a secular trend toward more-skilled labor on the mean log wages across both schooling classes within ability quartiles 3 and 4. Figure 9.11 shows how log wages within ability classifications fan

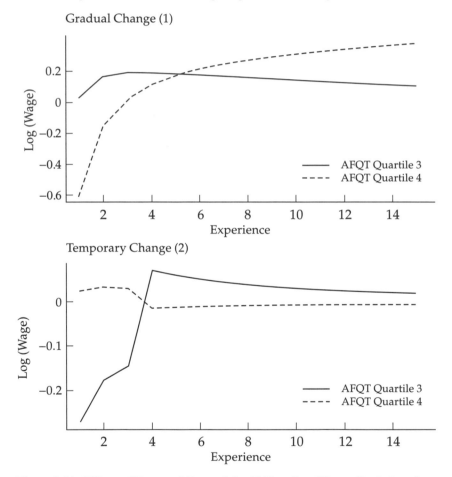

Figure 9.11. Effects of Increased Demand for Skill on Log Wages: Deviations from Initial Stationary Profile. (1) Change in log wages by ability quartile for an economy with gradually rising price of college labor and declining price of high school labor. (2) Change in log wages by ability quartile for an economy with a temporary rise in the price of college labor and temporary decline in the price of high school labor.

out in an economy with a rising price for skilled labor and a decline in the price of unskilled labor. While the highest ability workers (mostly college graduates) show a large drop in wages in the early years of their life cycles (again, due to increased investment), they quickly recover and receive the largest wage gains as a consequence of this shift in the economic regime. Workers in the third ability quartile see wage declines in nearly every period, since most of them are high school graduates experiencing a decline in their skill price. These effects arise primarily from the high correlation between ability and education. High-ability individuals typically graduate from college and thus experience positive growth in their rental rate on human capital. Lower-ability individuals are less likely to attend college. They experience declining rental rates. Thus our model of heterogeneous human capital with investment predicts a large ability effect on earnings, but a slightly negative ability-time interaction at young ages if the time effects are assumed to be generated by a permanently rising skill differential that is anticipated by the agents.[12] This scenario does not appear to be consistent with the evidence discussed in sections 1 and 2.

A temporary demand shift that results in a temporary rise in price of college human capital compared to high school human capital has exactly the opposite effect on investment and observed returns to schooling by ability to those just described (see figures 9.9 and 9.10). When current skill prices rise temporarily for the high-skill college graduates, they invest less and spend more time working. This is because the opportunity costs of investment rise more than the future returns from investment. For them, the motto "make hay before it rains" applies. The low-skill high school graduates invest more in the short run in response to the temporary decline in rental rates they experience. Work pays less now but their market will rebound. Thus it is profitable for them to invest in skills while the opportunity costs are low.

College graduates experience larger short-term wage increases than would be expected if investment levels were held constant, while high school graduates see larger declines in their earnings than would be predicted if investment responses were held constant. While the change in relative skill prices between college and high school graduates is 6 percent, the observed wage differences are much larger in the short run (see figure 9.10). Following the temporary change in skill prices, the ability-wage gap declines as the low-ability workers reap the benefits of their increased investment.

Furthermore, because the most able show larger investment responses, the college–high school wage gap increases the most for the most able. This accords well with the findings of Blackburn and Neumark (1993) that survive our tests. Once the rental rates return to their initial levels, the college–high school wage premium actually falls below its initial level for both the

---

[12] Selection effects on measured wage differentials caused by changes in college enrollment rates are modest. For that reason, we do not dwell on them in this chapter.

third and fourth ability quartiles. This is caused by the increased investment by high school graduates and the reduced investment by college graduates during the period of temporarily high relative skill prices.

These simulations highlight the role that post-school investment plays in determining wages. Changing skill prices may lead to different wage responses depending on how investment is affected. Economic changes that lead to permanently rising returns to skill that are understood to be permanent by agents can produce investment responses that lower the college–high school wage gap compared to what happens in a steady state environment, with the largest reductions occurring among the youngest and most able. On the other hand, changes in the economy that lead to sharp unexpected rises in returns to skill that are not expected to last indefinitely result in large increases in the college–high school wage differential, especially for the most able.

The increased college–high school wage premium observed in the samples from the 1980s suggests that the latter story may be closer to the truth. The increase in skill prices for high-skill workers and the decline in skill prices for low-skill workers was initially perceived to be a temporary phenomenon, and workers appear to have invested accordingly. This suggests that the ability differentials estimated in samples of young workers from the periods of the 1980s overstate long-run ability differentials that will be observed for other groups of young workers if the trend continues and is anticipated by later cohorts of labor market entrants. At older ages, ability differentials will narrow for the 1980s cohort of workers because the more able have invested less human capital in their youth and the less able have invested more. In the steady state, when agents learn about the new market for skills, ability-wage differentials will widen at the older ages as the more able invest more and these investments pay off. Our simulations suggest that as workers learn about the new labor market for skills and come to expect secular increases in skill differentials, ability-wage differentials at young ages will narrow as will education differentials within ability classes for younger workers.[13]

4. Conclusion

This chapter examines the role of ability in accounting for the rise in the economic return to education. We demonstrate that many empirical results

---

[13] The story from our model of "surprised workers" is also consistent with a model of perfect foresight with price cycles of the sort developed by Heckman, Lochner, and Taber (1998). The crucial feature of both models is that in the 1980s the price of high-skill labor was perceived to be high relative to what it would be in the future while the price of low-skill workers was perceived to be lower in the 1980s compared to what it would become.

reported in the literature are fragile to small variations in empirical specifications. We attribute this in part to an identification problem. The panel structure of the data and the stratification of persons by ability into schooling strata create many empty cells that compound the usual problems of identifying interactions. Different strategies for coping with this problem have led to different estimates of the role of ability in the rising return to schooling.

We summarize the nonparametric estimates of the identified parameters reported in Cawley, Heckman, and Vytlacil (1998). We find evidence that, within age groups, the college–high school premium has increased most for persons of high ability. A similar effect is found when we control for experience for persons with most levels of work experience. When we control for experience, the college–high school wage differential rises for both the third and fourth g quartile workers. The rise in the return to ability of college education compared to high school education is not confined to workers of the highest ability alone. When we use age instead of experience, the college–high school wage differential rises only in the fourth quartile of ability. Apart from these empirical regularities, few sturdy conclusions emerge about ability and its effect on the trend rise in the return to education. We show that a commonly used method of coping with the identification problem, assuming linear effects of age and time, is not supported by the data.

Simulations of a model of heterogeneous human capital and ability developed by Heckman and Lochner (1996) indicate that ability plays an important role in the correlation between education and wages because it influences the degree to which earnings are forgone to invest in human capital. The simulations also show dramatically different wage patterns for young workers who have a larger investment response than older workers. This suggests that the ability-wage differentials found in samples of young workers do not generalize to all workers and that the evidence from one economic environment does not generalize to another.

Our simulation of an economy with a temporary increase in the return to skill produces results that are similar to what is reported in the empirical literature. Specifically we obtain a rising college–high school wage gap, especially among the most able. Eventually, however, the wage gap falls below its initial level as the less skilled invest more than they would in a stationary environment and the more skilled invest less, and these investments pay off. This will lead to lower wage differentials by ability and schooling at later ages for these cohorts of workers. The lessons on the role of ability drawn from samples of young workers who were surprised by the new labor market for skills in the 1980s likely do not generalize to later periods, when the shift in the demand for skills came to be thought of as a permanent feature of the economic environment.

Appendix: Data

This chapter uses the data from the National Longitudinal Survey of Youth (NLSY). The NLSY, designed to represent the entire population of American youth, consists of a randomly chosen sample of 6,111 U.S. civilian youths, a supplemental sample of 5,295 randomly chosen minority and economically disadvantaged civilian youths, and a sample of 1,280 youths on active duty in the military. All youths were between fourteen and twenty-two years of age when the first of the annual interviews was conducted in 1979. The data set includes equal numbers of males and females. Sixteen percent of respondents are Hispanic and 25 percent are black. For our analysis, we restricted the sample to those not currently enrolled in school and receiving an hourly wage between $0.50 and $1,000 in 1990 dollars (all results in this chapter are reported in 1990 dollars). This chapter uses the NLSY weights for each year to produce a nationally representative sample. However, our sample is not nationally representative in age; we only observe a nine-year range of ages in any given year, and the oldest person in our 1994 sample is only thirty-seven.

References

Ben-Porath, Yoram. 1967. "The Production of Human Capital and the Life Cycle of Earnings." *Journal of Political Economy* 75, no. 4 (August): 352–365.

Bishop, John. 1991. "Achievement, Test Scores, and Relative Wages." In *Workers and Their Wages: Changing Patterns in the United States*, ed. M. H. Kosters, pp. 146–186. Washington, DC: American Enterprise Institute Press.

Blackburn, McKinley L., and David Neumark. 1993. "Omitted-Ability Bias and the Increase in the Return to Schooling." *Journal of Labor Economics* 11, no. 3: 521–544.

Carroll, John B. 1993. *Human Cognitive Ability: A Survey of Factor-Analytic Studies*, Cambridge: Cambridge University Press.

Cawley, John, Karen Conneely, James Heckman, and Edward Vytlacil. 1997. "Cognitive Ability, Wages, and Meritocracy." In *Intelligence, Genes, and Success: Scientists Respond to "The Bell Curve,"* ed. Bernie Devlin, Stephen Fienberg, Daniel Resnick, and Kathryn Roeder, pp. 179–192. New York: Springer Verlag.

Cawley, John, James Heckman, and Edward Vytlacil. 1998. "Cognitive Ability and the Rising Return to Education." National Bureau of Economic Research Working Paper no. 6388.

Griliches, Zvi. 1979. "Sibling Models and Data in Economics: Beginnings of a Survey." *Journal of Political Economy* 87, no. 5, part 2 (October): S37–S64.

Griliches, Zvi, and W. M. Mason. 1972. "Education, Income and Ability." *Journal of Political Economy* 80, part 2 (May/June): S74–S103.

Grogger, Jeff, and Eric Eide. 1995."Changes in College Skills and the Rise in the College Wage Premium." *Journal of Human Resources* (spring): 280–310.

Heckman, James J. 1995. "Lessons from *The Bell Curve.*" *Journal of Political Economy* 105, no. 5 (October): 1091–1120.

Heckman, James, and Peter Klenow. 1997. "Human Capital Policy." In *Capital Formation*, ed. M. Boskin. Hoover Economic Growth Conference. Stanford, CA: Hoover Institution.

Heckman, James, and Lance Lochner. 1996. "Dynamic Models of Human Capital Accumulation: Theory and Evidence and Application to the Evaluation of Tax and Training Policies." Keynote address to the Society of Economic Dynamics and Control, Mexico City, June 1996; also presented as an invited lecture at Latin American Econometric Society meetings, Rio de Janeiro, August 1996.

Heckman, James, Lance Lochner, and Christopher Taber. 1998. "Explaining Rising Wage Inequality: Explorations with a Dynamic General Equilibrium Model of Labor Earnings with Heterogeneous Agents." *Review of Economic Dynamics* 1: 1–58.

Heckman, James, Christopher Taber, and Lance Lochner. 1999. "General Equilibrium Cost-Benefit Analysis of Education and Tax Policies." In *Trade, Growth, and Development: Essays in Honor of Professor T. N. Srinivasan*, ed. G. Ranis and L. K. Raut, pp. 291–393. New York: Elsevier Science.

Heckman, James, and Jose Scheinkman. 1987. "The Importance of Bundling in a Gorman-Lancaster Model of Earnings." *Review of Economic Studies* 54, no. 2 (April): 243–255.

Herrnstein, Richard J., and Charles Murray. 1994. *The Bell Curve*. New York: Free Press.

Jencks, Christopher. 1972. *Inequality*. New York: Basic Books.

Jensen, Arthur. 1987. "The g Beyond Factor Analysis." In *The Influence of Cognitive Psychology on Testing and Measurement*, ed. R. R. Ronning, J. A. Glover, J. C. Conoley, and J. C. DeWitt, pp. 87–142. Hillsdale, NJ: Lawrence Erlbaum.

Mincer, Jacob. 1974. *Schooling, Experience, and Earnings*. New York: Columbia University Press.

Murnane, R. J., J. B. Willett, and F. Levy. 1995. "The Growing Importance of Cognitive Skills in Wage Determination." *Review of Economics and Statistics* 77, no. 2: 251–266.

Rosen, Sherwin. 1972. "Learning and Experience in the Labor Market." *Journal of Human Resources* 7, no. 3: 326–342.

Searle, Shayle. 1987. *Linear Models for Unbalanced Data*. New York: John Wiley and Sons.

Willis, Robert. 1986. "Wage Determinants: A Survey and Reinterpretation of Human Capital Earnings Functions." In *Handbook of Labor Economics*, ed. O. Ashenfelter and R. Layards, 1: 525–602. Amsterdam: North-Holland.

Part Four _____

POLICY OPTIONS

Ten

Inequality and Race: Models and Policy*

SHELLY J. LUNDBERG AND RICHARD STARTZ

RACE AND ETHNICITY play a central role in understanding the structure of inequality in the United States. In this chapter, we focus on the economic chasm between black and white America and on what economic theory can contribute to our understanding of both the sources of inequality and the design of effective policy. Our main conclusions are: (1) Modern theories of labor-market discrimination and of human capital investment in a social context provide support for activist government policies to combat racial inequality, and (2) not all policies that appear to be equity-enhancing will in fact have positive effects. It is good if equal opportunity policies are well-intentioned; it is better if they are well-informed.

In the original economic models of discrimination, the racial prejudice of firms, workers, and customers produced racial wage differentials; these differentials were difficult to sustain under market pressure. Though intuitively plausible, these models were thus limited as theoretical foundations for persistent income differentials between two groups with equal average productive capacity. In *The Bell Curve*, Herrnstein and Murray (1994) suggest that racial income differentials can be explained as the outcome of market forces determining the compensation of two groups not equal in innate productive capacity. The new economics of race, however, does not require differences in innate abilities to produce economic inequality, nor does it rely on noncompetitive labor markets. Models of statistical discrimination provide a plausible explanation for wage differentials due to information problems that are not eroded by competition, and recent theories of the intergenerational transmission of inequality trace persistent differences in the compensable skills of black and white workers to racially segregated communities.

Three themes run through this chapter.

The first theme is that the racial identification of workers can interact with the *social* processes of human capital accumulation in communities and human capital valuation by employers in ways that generate externalities. In the presence of such externalities, laissez-faire may not lead to efficient out-

* Department of Economics, University of Washington, Seattle, WA 98195-3330. The authors can be reached at lundberg@u.washington.edu. Financial support from the John D. and Catherine T. MacArthur Foundation is gratefully acknowledged.

comes. Well-focused policies can therefore improve *both* efficiency and equity.

Our second theme is that we need to understand both labor-market equilibrium and pre-labor-market behavior to explain the economic gulf between the races. Much of the economic literature has dealt with these two topics separately, but in the new economics of race there is an emphasis on the links between premarket investment in human capital and labor-market outcomes. New models of labor-market discrimination explain wage differentials in competitive labor markets that are maintained through informational externalities. The resulting wage structure reduces the incentives of black workers to invest in difficult-to-observe skills, and generates a racial gap in labor-market productivity. The new models of the intergenerational transmission of inequality center on group effects in the accumulation of human capital. These models show how past discrimination affects family and community resources and therefore contemporary economic equilibrium.

The third theme is that the microincentives of black and white agents matter for the design of effective policies. Well-intentioned but improperly focused policies may interact with the incentives and reactions of agents in such a way as to be ineffective or even reinforce negative externalities. We try in this chapter to outline some of the policy lessons learned and to point to questions that remain unresolved.

The new economics of race has focused on the causes of racial inequality, on the implications of anti-discrimination and other egalitarian policies for economic efficiency, and on the limits of government intervention in promoting both equitable and efficient outcomes. Some of the principal policy-relevant results are:

In the presence of labor-market discrimination, equal opportunity policies can improve labor-market efficiency as well as reduce inequality by increasing the incentives of minority workers to invest in human capital.

With imperfectly informed regulators, employers will attempt to evade equal opportunity restrictions. Affirmative action policies that regulate outcomes provide an enforcement mechanism that can be lower-cost than the regulation of process, but their long-run efficacy is uncertain. In some situations, affirmative action policies can eliminate negative group stereotypes and can therefore be self-enforcing; in others, affirmative action policies can reinforce negative stereotypes by reducing incentives for individual minority workers to excel.

When there are community effects on human capital accumulation and communities are economically or racially stratified, income inequality can persist over time in the absence of policy intervention, and small initial differences in income may be magnified by human capital spillovers. Community integration can improve the welfare of both high-income and low-income groups in the long run.

If both jobs and communities are racially segregated, labor-force integration is not an adequate substitute for community integration, and may not lead to long-run convergence of black and white income.

Financial transfers per se are unlikely to be effective responses to racial inequality, because they do not change incentives to acquire human capital.

With positive human capital spillovers, large temporary interventions may be effective while small permanent ones have no long-run effect.

This chapter has two parts. In the first we discuss appropriate policy toward ongoing de facto discrimination.[1] In the second we examine the legacy of past discrimination and the role of the social separation of black and white Americans as a transmission mechanism from the past to the present. In each case we try to link positive models with normative policy.

Labor-Market Discrimination and Anti-Discrimination Policy

Policies designed in the 1960s to combat racial discrimination in labor markets and educational opportunities have been scaled back in the 1990s, charged with being both unnecessary and unfair. The eradication of de jure discrimination eventually achieved wide public support, but policies to combat less transparent racial barriers in jobs and education have been more difficult to sell. Affirmative action, which denotes efforts to enforce some kind of proportional participation of blacks and whites in job categories, government contracts, and higher education, has been the principal target of criticism. Charges of "reverse discrimination" have mobilized long-standing public dissatisfaction with affirmative action initiatives, and in many arenas they have been, or are about to be, eliminated.

The attacks on and the defense of policies such as affirmative action involve arguments about the responses of both firms and workers to government intervention in hiring and compensation. Critics argue that employers will respond to the enforcement of affirmative action goals by hiring unqualified minority workers and that this leads to unfair reverse discrimination, to inefficient production, and to reduced incentives for minority workers to become qualified. Supporters of affirmative action respond that the hiring of

---

[1] There is ample evidence of ongoing racial discrimination in economic transactions, including evidence from controlled experiments. See, for example, Ayres and Siegelman (1995). Neal and Johnson (1996), who find that most of the wage gap between young black and white men can be attributed to "premarket factors," as manifested in a standardized test score, still find that one-third of the wage gap remains unexplained.

minority workers can improve information and thus efficiency in the labor market, breaking down unfavorable stereotypes and improving the incentives of formerly excluded workers to invest in job skills. Inherent in the discussion is a comparison of labor-market equilibria with and without anti-discrimination policy, with both firms and workers permitted to react to the (possibly imperfect) enforcement of such policies. Economic theory has much to contribute in sorting out the effects of regulation on market equilibria and, as we shall see, the results are sometimes surprising.

On what dimension can anti-discrimination policies be expected to "improve" labor-market equilibria? The obvious answer is that policies that reduce racial inequality lead to allocations that are preferred on equity grounds to those that would result in the absence of intervention. Competitive markets, under certain well-defined conditions, can be shown to produce goods and services efficiently in response to the signals of prices, so that no individual can be made better off without someone else being made worse off. However, if the distribution of incomes that results from the free play of markets is too unequal, then redistribution can improve social welfare. Such redistributions, if made through any mechanism other than lump-sum taxes and transfers, will tend to distort prices and incentives, and thus will be inefficient.

Much of the discussion of anti-discrimination policies, by economists and others, assumes that such intervention must involve an equity-efficiency trade-off: that improvements in the distribution of income through affirmative action come at the expense of reduced efficiency. Administrative costs must accompany any regulatory effort, but most concern over the costs of anti-discrimination policy centers on the distortion of private hiring and promotion decisions. Government pressure to employ and promote minority workers may force firms to misallocate labor and sacrifice production, though improved equity provides a countervailing benefit. However, the existence of the equity-efficiency trade-off is itself suspect, according to most economic models of racial inequality. There are two strands to this literature—one focusing on current labor-market discrimination and the other on the persistent effects of past discrimination on the human capital of minority workers. Both provide frameworks in which policies to reduce racial discrepancies in income may be both equity- and efficiency-enhancing.

Simple models of current labor-market discrimination provide a straightforward illustration of this point. If two groups of workers with equal productive capacity are treated differently by employers, then we say that there is discrimination in the labor market. This implies that discrimination is a market failure—a departure from the economists' paradigm of a perfect market. In a perfectly competitive labor market, workers of equal ability should receive equal compensation. If discrimination is due to market failure, then, by the theory of the second best, it may be possible to devise an intervention that both promotes equality and improves efficiency. Not all equity-enhancing policies will be efficient, of course, and much of the recent theoretical literature has concentrated on defining the conditions under which policies such as affirmative action lead to "good" or "bad" outcomes.

The general implications of economic models of labor-market discrimination for the sources of racial inequality can be summarized as follows:

"Taste" models of discrimination, or models based on racial prejudice, generally predict segregation of black and white workers by occupation or firm, rather than wage differentials.

"Statistical" models of discrimination, in which employers have imperfect information about the productivity of individual workers, result in labor-market equilibria in which employers use the perceived productivity of a group (for example, black or white workers) as a signal of the productivity of individual workers. Statistical discrimination can lead to racial wage and productivity differentials through the operation of a "self-fulfilling prophecy"—faced with a negative stereotype in the labor market about the productivity of black workers, black workers have less incentive to invest in human capital.

Models of Labor-Market Discrimination

Economists have experienced some difficulty in constructing models in which persistent racial wage differentials can coexist with reasonably well functioning labor markets. The search for a theoretical framework has led economists away from early models in which the source of income differentials is racial prejudice to more subtle arguments based on imperfections in information or intergenerational externalities. In the so-called taste models of Becker (1957) and Arrow (1973), discrimination is based on the personal prejudice of employers, who are willing to sacrifice profits to avoid hiring minority workers. Minority workers will be employed only at a lower wage that compensates employers for the disutility of their employment. With all workers identical, and with labor supplied inelastically, there is no efficiency loss associated with this discrimination, but there is redistribution to the disadvantage of minority workers. The wage differential itself, however, is vulnerable to competitive pressure. Low wages provide an opportunity for unprejudiced employers to earn higher profits by hiring the underpaid but equally productive minority workers. In the absence of complete unanimity in racial prejudice among entrepreneurs and potential entrepreneurs, discriminators will be penalized by the marketplace for their failure to maximize profits, and the wage differential will disappear as discriminating firms are driven out of business.

Variants of the taste model that attribute racial prejudice to workers or to customers lead to equilibria in which segregation provides an alternative to wage differentials. Prejudice by coworkers can lead to wage differentials if skill mismatches require integrated production, but there will be a tendency toward segregated firms and wage equality. The case of customer prejudice, in which the services of minority workers are undervalued relative to the services of majority workers, is somewhat distinct since it generates what is in effect a productivity difference between the two types of workers. Nevertheless, if the production of some goods involves no customer contact, we would expect minority workers to concentrate in this sector, where they experience no disadvantage. If customer demand for goods produced in this sector is large relative to the size of the minority workforce, customer prejudice will not result in discriminatory wage differentials in equilibrium.[2]

Wage differentials due to prejudice do require government action if prejudiced employers are able to collude to maintain racial barriers to employment. Monopoly profits accrue to the members of this coalition of employers, but an individual nonprejudiced employer will always have an incentive to depart from the agreement and hire minority workers cheaply. If supported by legal or institutional barriers and discriminatory social norms, however, such a coalition can persist for some time. Donohue and Heckman (1991) argue that this was the case in the American South until federal government actions in the 1960s helped break down the coalition by enforcing the desegregation of jobs and schools.[3]

Racial prejudice in the form of disutility associated with employing, working with, or being served by black workers is thus not completely convincing as the sole source of persistent wage differentials, and most economic models do not suggest a role for government action, rather than market forces, in eroding such differentials. An alternative source of labor-market discrimination can be found in imperfect information about worker productivity. Employers are uncertain about the productivity of individual workers and can observe only signals that predict productivity with some error. Under some circumstances, racial stereotypes in an employer's estimates of the productivity of individual workers can arise and persist. "Statistical discrimination" models are based on the notion that black workers are paid less because employers believe that they are less productive or have

[2] Kahn (1991) describes two cases in which wage differentials do result from customer discrimination and shows that a government policy requiring equal pay for equal work and proportional representation of minority workers in both sectors will eliminate the pay differential, reduce the real wages of white workers, and may increase or decrease the real wages of black workers.

[3] Race discrimination does not generally lead to efficiency losses in these models because their simplicity rules out many of the decisions that discrimination could distort, such as labor supply and human capital investment. The need to discuss a possible role for policy in removing such distortions is eliminated by the conclusion that market forces alone are expected to prevent them from persisting.

less accurate information about their productivity. If, in addition, individual investments in human capital respond to expected labor-market returns, these negative stereotypes can constitute a self-fulfilling prophecy, as workers who are expected to be less productive turn out to be, as a result of those expectations, less productive in fact.

Racial wage differentials can arise in models of statistical discrimination in two ways. In the signaling model of Arrow (1973) and Spence (1973), and the more recent work of Coate and Loury (1993b), the employment relation is characterized by multiple equilibria, in which the expectations of employers about worker productivity are confirmed by the actual productivity of workers, after human capital investments have been made and workers have been sorted into job categories. For historical reasons, black workers may be trapped in a low-wage, low-productivity equilibrium while white workers are in a high-wage, high-productivity equilibrium. In essence, race matters because employers think it does. Alternatively, statistical discrimination can be based on differences in the quality of information that employers receive about black and white workers. In Phelps (1972) and Aigner and Cain (1977), for example, personnel managers are predominately white and are more effective at assessing the skills of workers in their own group, so the "signal" they receive from white applicants has less noise. The offered wage will be a weighted average of the individual's own signal and the known average productivity of the group, but the weight placed on the individual signal will be higher for white workers than it is for black workers. Lundberg and Startz (1983) point out that a noisier signal results in a lower return to human capital investments that are not directly observable, so black workers are in equilibrium less productive and less well-paid. Race matters because black workers are "foreign" to employers.

Models of statistical discrimination have a couple of important characteristics in common. First, they generate racial wage differentials even though black and white workers have identical productive capacity and employers are profit-maximizing. It is not in the interests of any individual employer to deviate from the equilibrium wage pattern, and discrimination is not vulnerable to market forces as it is in the "taste" models.[4] Second, discrimination is inefficient, so there is a possible role for government anti-discrimination policy that is both equity- and efficiency-enhancing.[5] It is also possible, however, for government intervention to make things worse, and Coate and Loury concentrate on this case. The inefficiencies in statistical

---

[4] Although if the employer eventually becomes informed about the worker's productivity, wage contracts in which the newly hired worker posts a bond may be an alternative to wage differentials.

[5] Milgrom and Oster (1987) present an alternative information-based model of discrimination in which affirmative action is efficiency-enhancing.

discrimination models arise from underinvestments in human capital by black workers, whose decisions are distorted by labor-market discrimination.

How can anti-discrimination policy affect labor-market equilibrium in a model of statistical discrimination? Lundberg and Startz (1983) consider a policy that they label "equal opportunity," which consists of a prohibition of separate wage schedules for black and white workers. If firms are unable to perfectly observe individual productivity, but only a "test score," which is an unbiased but noisy predictor of productivity, a profit-maximizing wage schedule will rely both on average group productivity and the individual test score. The discriminatory equilibrium consists of two such wage schedules:

$$w_i^W = (1 - \beta^W)\overline{MP}^W + \beta^W T_i$$
$$w_i^B = (1 - \beta^B)\overline{MP}^B + \beta^B T_i$$

where $\overline{MP}^i$ is the average marginal product of workers in group j, T_i is the "test score" of worker i, and the coefficient β^j increases as the variance of the test score falls relative to the variance of marginal productivity. Since the signal-to-noise ratio of the test is assumed to be higher for white workers than for black workers, they face a higher return to increasing their test score ($\beta^W > \beta^B$), and therefore a higher expected return to investments in skills. These investments are not directly observable, consisting of acquired abilities in a general sense, rather than years of education or experience. This model generates underinvestment in such skills for both black and white workers, but the underinvestment is more severe for the group about whom the employers' information is of poorer quality.

Figure 10.1 provides a graphic illustration of the model, with the test score shown on the horizontal axis and the wage rate on the vertical. The solid lines marked "whites" and "blacks" show the wage schedules absent any investment in acquiring skills. Black workers are paid less on the margin than white workers (the slope of the black wage line is less than the slope of the white wage line), but average wages and average productivity are equal, as at point A. This is essentially the model of Aigner and Cain. When, however, workers can invest in productive skills that are not perfectly observable, black workers will have less incentive to invest than white workers. The resulting wage schedule for black workers is shown as the dashed lower line. Point B shows the equilibrium average wage and productivity for black workers. The privately rational lower marginal compensation for acquired skills leads to a social equilibrium in which, though black workers have native abilities equal to those of white workers, they nonetheless have lower productivity and lower wages.

"Equal opportunity" is a government policy requiring that employers offer the same wage schedule to both black and white workers. Profit-maximizing employers will then offer a schedule in which the test score coefficient is a weighted average of the two discriminatory coefficients, thus increasing the

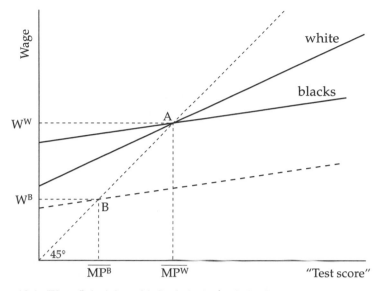

Figure 10.1. Wage Schedules with Statistical Discrimination

investments of black workers and decreasing those of whites. With the marginal cost of skills increasing, however, an equal opportunity policy will increase net social product. The practicalities of enforcing such a policy are not considered by Lundberg and Startz, but Lundberg (1991) examines the opportunities for evasion by employers. Restricting the employer's use of individual test scores in allocating workers may cause production losses by increasing inappropriate assignments of workers to jobs. The equal opportunity policy will therefore not be self-enforcing, and employers will try to evade it.[6] Suppose that another piece of information about individual workers, say height, is available to employers. Let height bear no relationship to the productive abilities of workers, but let it be correlated with group membership. If the anti-discrimination law requires that black and white workers be paid according to the same wage schedule, but does not specify what characteristics are allowable as determinants of wages, profit-maximizing employers will have an incentive to use apparently neutral characteristics, such as height, as a proxy for race in wage determination. It does not seem reasonable that the regulator will possess sufficient information about the true relationship between productivity and worker characteristics, or about the actual personnel policies of firms, to effectively prohibit such evasion.

[6] Not incorporated into the model is the possibility that personnel officers, with more experience in hiring minority workers under equal opportunity, will improve their ability to assess the productivity of these workers. If the abilities eventually equalize, policy intervention will become unnecessary.

An alternative to equal opportunity policies that attempt to regulate the process by which firms hire and compensate workers is an affirmative action policy, which monitors and regulates only the outcomes of the firm's personnel decisions. An affirmative action policy can be represented as a requirement that black workers be represented in each job category proportionate to their representation in the pool of qualified workers, or by the requirement that the compensation of black workers, conditional on the test score easily observed by both firm and regulators, be identical to that of white workers. The rationale for such a policy is that if the firm is not discriminating, we might expect to observe black workers represented proportionately in each job category. Affirmative action can thus be considered a policy that enables imperfectly informed regulators to enforce equal opportunity. Lundberg shows that affirmative action, by allowing employers to use all information about workers in a restricted manner, can result in lower costs of misallocating workers than an alternative "disparate impact" policy.

Coate and Loury (1993b) also consider an affirmative action–type policy, defining it in a similar way as a "results-oriented" rather than "process-oriented" anti-discrimination policy, and ruling out equal opportunity policies that require the regulator to observe all the information used by employers in making hiring and assignment decisions. In their model, however, the enforcement of affirmative action constraints on worker assignment can either improve or exacerbate the information problems that led to a discriminatory equilibrium. The key to this result is a statistical discrimination model in which, unlike in Lundberg and Startz's model, the actions of employers are discrete. Rather than establishing a wage schedule, employers assign workers to one of two jobs. Job one is more rewarding, but satisfactory performance requires that the worker be "qualified." Workers must undertake a costly investment to become qualified, and must do so before they know their job assignment. Employers observe only group identity and a noisy signal of the worker's qualifications. Employers choose a threshold standard for each group, assigning to job one all workers whose signal exceeds their group standard. A discriminatory equilibrium is one in which black workers are believed by employers to be less likely to be qualified, are subjected to a higher standard, and, in response to the reduced probability of being assigned to job one, are less likely to become qualified. Since there may be multiple equilibria, a negative stereotype held by the employer about black workers can be self-confirming, and black and white workers with identical productive capacity will experience different probabilities of being assigned to good jobs.

An affirmative action policy in this model consists of a requirement that equal proportions of black and white workers be assigned to the high-paid job, and it can have two very different effects, depending on the parameters of the model. Affirmative action may, by increasing the probability that a black worker will be assigned to job one, increase incentives to invest in becoming qualified, and thus eliminate the negative stereotype held by employers. A subsequent removal of the affirmative action constraint will yield a stable nondiscriminatory equilibrium. Alternatively, affirmative action can result in a "patronizing equilibrium" in which employers lower standards for assignment to job one and, by making this assignment easier to achieve, reduce investment incentives for black workers and exacerbate the employer's negative stereotype. In the latter case, affirmative action must be permanent to maintain equal job assignments for black and white workers.

Coate and Loury consider two policies other than affirmative action: a subsidy to employers for assigning black workers to job one and a subsidy to black workers for being assigned to job one. These policies have information requirements no more stringent than those required to enforce affirmative action. They show that a marginal subsidy cannot completely eliminate a negative stereotype about black workers, but that a large subsidy to employers can backfire, causing employers to lower their hiring standards so much that beliefs are revised so as to be even more negative than in the initial equilibrium. Subsidies to workers, however, present no such problem. A subsidy to workers always increases their performance, whereas a subsidy to employers that lowers their standards may lower workers' performance.

In an entirely different model in which taste discrimination makes employers less likely to hire black workers and reduces their human capital investment, Coate and Loury (1993a) show that affirmative action may result in a patronizing equilibrium similar to that in their informational model. Once again, forcing employers to change their hiring standards may either increase or decrease the marginal returns to human capital investment by black workers. In this model, a gradual policy of affirmative action in which the hiring target is increased slowly is more likely to be successful, since it enables the qualifications of black workers to increase with the target and prevents the reduction of hiring standards that will cause an abrupt affirmative action policy to fail.

The common thread through all the statistical discrimination models is that labor-market discrimination can affect workers' incentives to invest in human capital, and can therefore generate productivity differences. An effective anti-discrimination policy is one that, directly or indirectly, succeeds in equalizing the incentives, and therefore the productivity, of black and white workers.

The Intergenerational Transmission of Inequality

The study of intergenerational income mobility has a long history in both economics and sociology, but until recently it focused on the family as the mechanism by which economic status is transmitted to the next generation. Parents bequeath earnings ability as well as wealth to their offspring in the form of skills, attitudes toward education and work, and labor-market connections. If we think of an individual's stock of characteristics that are valued and remunerated by the labor market as being that worker's stock of human capital, then the human capital of children will be positively related to the human capital of their parents. Loury (1977) expanded this view to include the community environment as well as the home environment among the determinants of a child's opportunity to acquire human capital, and showed that if communities are organized along racial lines, equal opportunity in the labor market need not eradicate racial income differentials, even in the long run. The average stock of human capital in the community is termed "social capital" and is assumed to enter the production function for human capital of the next generation.[7] Social capital provides a mechanism whereby the human capital of one generation exerts a positive externality on the human capital of the next. Other writers have described this externality as operating through the provision of role models (Wilson 1987), employee referrals (Montgomery 1991), investments in community organizations and public educational facilities (Glomm and Ravikumar 1992), or "the maintenance of a rich and orderly environment in which learning can take place" (Lundberg and Startz 1998).

The new theory of the intergenerational transmission of inequality has contributed to our understanding of both the causes of inequality and the potential for remedial policy. Although the various models differ in important detail, they are alike in having a basic framework of competitive, individually rational behavior combined with a positive feedback operating through community effects or social capital. In broad sweep, the contributions to understanding the causes of inequality are:

Inequality today can be the historical legacy of past discrimination. Segregation perpetuates past discrimination even if there is no contemporary discrimination.

Residential stratification by income or skills can be the laissez-faire equilibrium of the economy.

Small differences in the initial conditions of the races may be magnified by the paths through which social capital is transmitted. Indeed, systems involving the formation of social capital can have highly nonlinear response mechanisms. Some models generate endogenous "poverty traps" in which a group may be perpetually caught through accidents of history.

---

[7] Related concepts are the "social capital" of Coleman (1988) and the "ethnic capital" of Borjas (1992, 1995).

Models of the Intergenerational Transmission of Inequality

The new models of the intergenerational transmission of inequality emphasize the effects of both segregation and positive feedback through social
capital on persistent group inequalities. Positive feedback arises because individual acquisition of human capital depends positively on social capital,
and social capital formation, in turn, depends positively on average individual human capital, resulting in a familiar multiplier effect. Segregation allows social capital, and therefore the human capital acquisition process, to
differ between two communities. Recent models vary in the microeconomic
source of the externality involved in social capital formation and in the
mechanism by which separation of the groups is maintained in equilibrium.
Temporarily setting aside the details, we begin with a generic illustrative
model.

The Simple Analytics of Social Capital and Segregation

The role of positive feedback loops in the formation of human and social
capital and the way this positive feedback interacts with segregation can be
illustrated in a simple analytical model. An individual's human capital, and
therefore her economic status, depends in part on her own ability and in part
on the social capital of her community. Social capital depends in part on the
average human capital of individuals in the community and in part on the
average human capital in the society at large. The relative importance of
these two components determines the role of segregation in the transmission
of historical differences. The model shows, in a generic way, that both social
capital and segregation matter for explaining the gap between the races.
Omitted, for the purpose of illustration, are the specific microchannels that
determine the importance of social capital and segregation.

We proceed in three steps. First, we characterize the process determining
individual human capital as a function of individual ability, of possible discrimination, and of the social capital available in a community. Second, we
define social capital as a function of the average level of human capital in
the black and white communities. Third, we solve for the equilibrium in
which levels of individual human capital and of social capital are mutually
consistent.

Suppose there are two groups, denoted W and B. Let A represent natural
ability, S social capital, and H human capital, so that A_i^B is the native ability
of ith person from group B, H_i^W is the human capital of the ith person from
group W, and so on. (Implicitly, we assume that economic status is proportional to human capital.) As a simplification, suppose that the human capital

development of the white majority can be taken to be unaffected by the black community. Let black human capital depend on individual ability and the social capital of the current and previous generation

$$H_{i,t}^B = A_{i,t}^B + \alpha[(1 - \gamma)S_t^B + \gamma S_{t-1}^B] \tag{1}$$

The social capital of the black community depends on the average (denoted by overbars) levels of human capital in the black and white communities.

$$S_t^B = \beta\overline{H}_t^B + (1 - \beta)\overline{H}_t^W \tag{2}$$

We can solve equations (1) and (2) for the average level of human capital.

$$H_t^B = \frac{1}{1 - \alpha\beta(1 - \gamma)}$$

$$\{A_t^B + \alpha(1 - \beta)[(1 - \gamma)H_t^w + \gamma h_{t-1}^w]\} + \frac{\alpha\beta\gamma}{1 - \alpha\beta(1 - \gamma)}H_{t-1}^B \tag{3}$$

Equation (3) is a distributed lag model. The parameter α, $0 \leq \alpha < 1$, controls the relative importance of individual ability versus social capital with the importance of social capital growing as α increases. The parameter β reflects the degree of segregation; in this simplified model we assume that the black community is a very small minority of the population, so that $\beta = 1$ is complete segregation and $\beta = 0$ is complete integration. Finally, the intergenerational transmission of social capital is very important as γ approaches 1 and is unimportant as γ approaches 0.

The purpose of this model is to show how the effects of past discrimination can persist into the present—indeed can be magnified—even though the inherent abilities of blacks and whites are equal and there is no contemporaneous discrimination. Persistent inequality requires both segregation and a social capital externality: neither is sufficient alone. This is seen formally here and in greater detail in Lundberg and Startz (1998). One can think of contemporaneous discrimination being modeled as a reduction in A: effectively society prevents blacks from utilizing their abilities fully in market activities. If social capital does not affect individual human capital acquisition, then $\alpha = 0$ in equation (3), and the reduction in A reduces human capital one-for-one. If $\alpha > 0$ the feedback through decreased social capital formation increases the damage done by discrimination. From equation (3), the short-run multiplier on discrimination is $\frac{1}{1 - \alpha\beta(1 - \gamma)}$. Solving for steady-state equilibrium, we can see that the multiplier increases to $\frac{1}{1 - \alpha\beta}$ in the long run.

What are the long-term effects of past discrimination? If social capital does not matter or society is completely integrated or there is no intergenerational transmission of social capital (α, β, $\gamma = 0$), then past discrimination has no legacy, as the lagged term at the right of equation (3) drops from the model. In general, however, all three elements contribute to the maintenance of racial human capital gaps long after the cessation of active discrimination. To focus on the role of segregation, suppose that the intergenerational transmission of social capital is very important. With $\alpha = \gamma = 1$ equation (3) simplifies to

$$H_t^B = \overline{A}_t^B + (1 - \beta)\overline{H}_{t-1}^W + \beta\overline{H}_{t-1}^B \qquad (4)$$

With complete integration, $\beta = 0$, earlier low levels of black human capital are irrelevant and discrimination has no lasting effect. In contrast, with complete segregation, $\beta = 1$, the effects of past discrimination on black human capital persist forever.

A principal aim of policy research is to identify the exact channels through which social capital formation and segregation operate. This simple model illustrates why social capital formation and segregation both matter. In a sense, a large part of the literature on intergenerational transmission can be viewed as explaining why α, β, $\gamma > 0$. Neither phenomenon is as simple as it appears in our model, and it is easy to identify some important questions. We take social capital formation in equation (2) to depend on a straightforward average of human capital. The real process might well depend on the tenth percentile or the ninetieth percentile rather than the mean. Perhaps this would help explain what appear to be threshold effects in phenomena such as racial "tipping" of neighborhoods. We treated the effect of segregation on black and white communities symmetrically in equation (2). It may be more realistic to set $\beta = 1$ to show the white community as more isolated from the black community than vice versa. We set human capital acquisition in equation (1) to depend on lagged social capital, but specific questions such as school integration rest precisely on the relative important of adult influence versus age-peers.

If social capital is transmitted through communities, then we need to understand how communities are formed. For our purposes, the literature on the intergenerational transmission of inequality can be classified according to whether separation of agents into groups is explained by income or by race. (The separation of classes is generally called "stratification" when groups are defined by income, and "segregation" when the separation is by race.) We begin with income stratification, which is of considerable interest for understanding inequality in general.

Stratification by Income

An exciting strand of the new literature examines the causes and effects of endogenous income stratification. Two questions arise. Why is it in the interest of an individual to stratify and, more specifically, why do high-income agents wish to isolate themselves? If there is an advantage to being among high-income agents, what mechanisms prevent low-income agents from mingling? The primary references are Bénabou (1993, 1994, 1996a) and Durlauf (1994, 1996).

The driving force in these models is the effect of spillovers between agents with different skill levels. In other words, agents gain from mingling with other agents, in either human capital accumulation or in production, and gain more from mingling with high-level (in skill or ability) agents than with low-level agents. It is frequently assumed that high-level agents gain more from being with other high-level agents than do low-level agents—at least in human capital acquisition. Thus, high-level agents are willing to spend more than low-level agents in order to stratify.

Nonetheless, an individual low-level agent would, ceteris paribus, also prefer to be with high-level agents. Two mechanisms that enforce the geographic separation of agents into two communities have been identified. The first is a market mechanism. Because the high-income community has desirable externalities, land rent in that community is bid up. This land rent rises to the point where agents are indifferent between earning a high income at the cost of expensive investment in human capital and high land rents and earning a low income with lower human capital investment and low rent. The second mechanism revolves around public choice. The high-income community may use the political mechanism to create artificially high zoning barriers or raise other expenses of living in the high-income community. These two mechanisms differ in their implications for both distributional and social efficiency issues.

Consider the market mechanism. That the poor and rich are both indifferent between living in either community is an equilibrium condition of the model. So, although these models have strong apparent results about income distribution, they do not speak to the distribution of economic welfare in the ways one might expect. This illustrates an important "bottleneck" in theories of purely endogenous stratification. If, as economists prefer, agents act only in isolation, without barriers modeled ex cathedra, then it is very difficult to derive an equilibrium in which living in a low-income community hurts the poor, despite the commonplace observation that stratification is worse for the poor than for the rich.

These stratified equilibria are generally socially inefficient. Bénabou (1993) emphasizes that education is geographically restricted but that production cuts across geographic areas. Externalities in education can lead to the wrong skill mix, considering the patterns of complementarity in production. In Bénabou's model, individual agents choose different investments in human capital to become "high-skill," "low-skill," or "unemployable." One possible equilibrium is for there to be a high-skill "suburb" and a "ghetto" of unemployed rather than low-skill workers. Although this pattern is privately optimal, the absence of low-skill workers is so damaging to production that even the high-skill workers are hurt.

What does this say about policy? Mandated integration would be Pareto-improving. This point is worth reiterating. This is a carefully specified model in which all agents could be made better off if integration could be costlessly imposed. Note, however, that stratification arises out of individual, not collective, action, so one cannot simply eliminate de jure rules. It is also noteworthy that Bénabou distinguishes between segregation in the workplace and in human capital accumulation. The inefficient equilibrium arises even though the workplace is fully integrated. (This is also an important element in Lundberg and Startz 1998.)

Public choice mechanisms for maintaining separation are developed in Fernandez and Rogerson (1996). In these models, the high-skill agents "capture" part of the externality generated by their skills by raising barriers to prevent the low-skilled from sharing them. These barriers can include exclusive zoning or high property tax rates. Since these choices are made in voting models, not in markets, it is unsurprising that the result is not socially efficient. These models also correspond to some traditional ideas about integrationist public policy: reducing zoning barriers, imposing scatter-site housing, and the like. Because the high-skilled workers in these models are capturing rents they are likely to resist such measures.

Models of purely endogenous stratification show how small, nonzero differences in initial conditions can be greatly magnified. The endogenous stratification models of Bénabou (1996a) and Durlauf (1994) show how small initial differences in human capital can lead to complete stratification. In Bénabou this separation occurs because of the positive feedback in which it is in the private interest of the agents with slightly better than average endowments to live only with agents with high human capital, which raises the private return to human capital acquisition, further increasing the incentive of those who are better off to live among themselves. Over time, the separation becomes complete. Durlauf presents a stochastic model with similar economics. Here the "small" differences can arise out of shocks rather than initial conditions. Depending on the parameters and shocks, a community can develop where there is so little incentive to acquire human capital that a "poverty trap" ensues from which families never escape.

In addition to the positive prediction, these models have a strong policy implication. Bénabou (1994) shows that stratification "is *independent of financial resources* . . . [and] *redistributive policies have no effect* on either the distribution of educational attainment or the efficiency of equilibrium" (italics in the original). Durlauf (1996) shows a similar result. In this context, policies that attempt to treat inequality without understanding the incentive mechanisms that cause inequality are likely to be unsuccessful.

Finally, Bénabou (1996b) presents a model in which stratification is given *exogenously* by skill level (and concomitantly by income) and which considers short-run versus long-run efficiency issues. The productive relationships in his model are such that homogeneity of skills is efficient for society. This presents an interesting intertemporal policy trade-off. In static equilibrium, segregation by skill is more efficient than integration. So in the short run integration policy is costly. However, integration leads to more homogenous skills in the future, whereas segregation does the opposite. Thus, in the long run integration is more efficient. Depending on parameter values, the net present value of this dynamic effect can outweigh the static inefficiency. In this way there is a trade-off between equity and efficiency in the short run, but integration is more equitable and more efficient in the long run.

Segregation by Race

It is a fact of American life that society is stratified by race as well as income, and that race has a strong effect on measures of attainment even after socioeconomic background and other measurable aspects of family resources have been controlled for. We would like to treat the racial segregation of neighborhoods and social networks as the endogenous outcomes of individual choices of community and friends. Yet economic models have almost nothing to say about racial segregation, other than to appeal to "tastes."[8] The endogenous stratification models do not address this issue directly but they do suggest that, given stratification of communities by race as well as income, it may not be surprising that initial differences in human capital arising out of America's racial history have persisted and that these persistent differences may be large. In addition, it seems reasonable to speculate that whatever forces generate racial segregation, they are probably reinforced by the kind of income stratification described above.

Lundberg and Startz (1998) take racial segregation to be exogenous, although mobility is allowed between white and black communities at some cost. The model applies the techniques of "new growth theory" to persistent racial inequality in the United States using the analogy of the "two nations" of black and white America. In this model agents live two periods, investing in costly human capital in the first and producing and receiving income in the second. In the first period, the cost of acquiring human capital depends

---

[8] Economists also explain preferences for steak over meatloaf as a matter of taste, but taking tastes about race as a biological imperative is neither very helpful nor, given the difference between American and other cultures on this question, probably very accurate. The social formation of preferences is obviously a relevant issue here, but we know very little about how externalities in social formation of preferences compare to externalities in the social formation of productive capacity.

on the social capital in the community of parents' residence. In the second period, workers contribute to the social capital of their residence community and engage in work whose productivity depends on both their own human capital and the social capital of the community in which they work. In addition, there may be spillovers in human capital acquisition in which the social capital of the better-off group provides some benefit to the worse-off group. Without such spillovers, a human capital gap generated by past discrimination will be permanent—income of the two groups will never converge, even if there is no contemporary discrimination.

One policy conclusion is fairly immediate. Simple financial transfers to the black community will have little effect on inequality except for the dollar value of the transfer itself. Unlike subsidies for human capital acquisition, financial transfers do not affect incentives to acquire human capital and therefore have no effect on the dynamics of social capital formation and inequality. (The same conclusion is reached in Bénabou 1994 and Durlauf 1996.) Once the question of subsidies is raised one should consider whether a given dollar devoted to subsidizing human capital acquisition is more efficiently spent as a direct subsidy to an individual or directly on community infrastructure. This last question has received little attention to date.

Since the 1960s there has been a great deal of workplace integration but relatively little residential integration. In Lundberg and Startz, workplace mobility is permitted, but there is a transition cost paid by a black worker who acquires a "white" job. Those with the most to gain move first, and as black workers "migrate" to an originally white work world, the dynamics of human capital accumulation depend on whether their human capital continues to contribute to the social capital of those "left behind." Suppose, first, that when black workers move to a majority job, they take their human capital out of the origin community. The future social capital of the minority community is reduced as its most able workers leave. As a result, opportunities in the minority community deteriorate. Each successive period, the next most able group of minority workers leaves, and conditions spiral downward, as in Wilson's description of the creation of an underclass.[9]

In contrast, suppose the most able black workers obtain "majority" jobs

[9] There is an important policy point here that probably should not need to be said, but which probably does. Following an analysis that shows that movement of the most able hurts those left behind, someone will surely leap to the conclusion that an appropriate policy goal would be to discourage the movement of the most able. Typically, economists qua economists have not much to say about ethical values, although implicitly most economists consider social welfare to depend on individual well-being as opposed to group well-being. Many of the policies discussed here focus on a racially identified group, and it is easy to focus on group welfare while ignoring redistribution within the group. To be blunt, it would require an unusual set of ethics to argue that the cost of remedying past oppression should be borne by those moderately hurt for the benefit of those severely hurt, while both the inheritors of the oppressors and neutral parties are excluded from any costs.

but remain living in segregated communities. These job migrants have both positive and negative effects on the social capital of the black community. The workers taking majority jobs acquire more human capital than they otherwise would, and so their direct effect on the black community's social capital is positive. However the workers taking majority jobs are the most able and their exit reduces the average human capital in minority jobs and the investment incentives of those who remain. The net effect on the minority community and on racial inequality depends on the parameters of the model. One possible outcome is a stable equilibrium with a permanent income disparity between the two communities. In equilibrium, the black community contains a mix of majority and minority job-holders, and the negative effect of the marginal migrant on minority jobs is just equal to the positive direct contribution to social capital.

One of the most important policy lessons of models with positive feedbacks is that the effects of both the size and timing of policies can be highly nonlinear. Consider a subsidy to human capital acquisition in the minority community in a model with "migration." Such a subsidy has two positive effects on the minority. First, it raises the level of minority human capital. Second, it reduces the incentives to "migrate" so that the minority community retains more of its more able workers. Figure 10.2 shows an example pattern taken from Lundberg and Startz (1998).

Figure 10.2 shows human capital on the vertical axis and time on the horizontal. During the period of complete segregation, conditions in the minority community decline relative to the majority community. During the period we label "reparation," human capital acquisition is subsidized. The effect of a small subsidy is a small improvement over what conditions would have otherwise been. A moderate subsidy improves conditions more and slows "migration" substantially. However, migration is slowed, not halted. Contrast this with a subsidy large enough to reverse the incentives to migrate. As time passes, more and more able workers find it unnecessary to move. Eventually the minority community reaches parity with the majority community and the subsidy can be eliminated. If discount rates are low, the net present value of the cost of the subsidy is smaller for a large, short subsidy than for a small, long subsidy.

In a model with complete segregation, the effect of past discrimination is permanent. However, apart from this extreme case, there are forces that may eventually erode the gap. If the barriers between communities are permeable, then the social capital of the white community will spill over to the black community (and vice versa). If education, both formal and informal, is highly integrated, then the relative economic status of African Americans will rise relatively quickly. Unfortunately, the degree of segregation between the races at the stage of human capital accumulation is high in the United States—in contrast, for example, to separation by religious affiliation. In

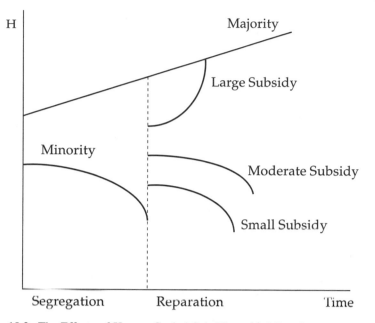

Figure 10.2. The Effects of Human Capital Subsidies with Migration

other countries religion or language may play a role similar to that of race in the United States, and a cross-national correlation of cultural separation and income inequality would be of considerable interest.

What Have We Learned about Policy?

The policies that are the heritage of the civil rights movement have failed to close the economic gap between blacks and whites, and have fallen into disfavor with much of the public. The new economics of race provides a fresh look at the sources of racial inequality that may change our views regarding the proper role of government intervention and the appropriate policy levers to promote racial equality. We begin this section with a review of policy implications of these models. Finally, we bring together some general threads running through this literature and then raise some more speculative issues—questions opened, but not settled, by the new models of racial inequality.

Specific policy results include:

When labor-market discrimination is the result of imperfect information, equal opportunity policies can improve efficiency. Imperfect information generates suboptimal incentives to acquire human capital, and this departure from optimality is greater for the discriminated-against group—equalizing the marginal returns to investment raises net efficiency (Lundberg and Startz 1983).

Outcomes-oriented affirmative action policies may be more efficient than process-oriented equal opportunity policies because they allow employers more flexibility in allocating labor while meeting a target (Lundberg 1991).

In statistical discrimination models with discrete job assignment, affirmative action policies can either increase or decrease the human capital of minority workers, and thus can either eliminate or reinforce a negative stereotype. It may be more effective to attack negative stereotypes through subsidies for human capital accumulation by black workers than through restrictions on employment decisions (Coate and Loury 1993b).

In the presence of community effects in the accumulation of social capital and economic stratification, integration can be Pareto-improving (Bénabou 1993). Even when integration has short-run costs, they may be outweighed by long-run benefits (Bénabou 1996b).

Labor-force integration does not eliminate the need for community integration in combatting the effects of historical discrimination because social capital at the community level is an important determinant of human capital accumulation (Bénabou 1993, Lundberg and Startz 1998).

Financial remediation in the form of transfers is ineffective in reducing inequality, as opposed to subsidies for human capital acquisition (Bénabou 1994, Durlauf 1996, Lundberg and Startz 1998).

In models with multiple equilibria, strong short-run measures are more cost-effective than weak permanent measures (Coate and Loury 1993b, Lundberg and Startz 1998).

General Lessons and Unanswered Questions

Pervasive and persistent discrepancies between the outcomes experienced by two groups, defined according to an economically irrelevant criterion (race), require a positive explanation. Absent such explanation, there is a natural tendency to attribute differences in outcome to inherent differences between the races. The new economic models of race explain such discrepancies in a manner consistent with the operation of market forces, as the results of group-specific externalities (i.e., imperfect information and use of race as a signal, community effects plus racial segregation). Therefore, policy need not involve an equity-efficiency trade-off—we are already in a second-best world.

Discussions of remedial policies on racial inequality, and income distribution generally, are often phrased in terms of an equity/efficiency trade-off. In a world of competitive markets where incentives and exchange between individuals are mediated only through prices and wages, government intervention can only help one individual at the expense of another. However, the new economic models of race and income distribution are characterized by social externalities that make it possible to design policies that increase equity while increasing the size of the social pie. Markets are competitive, but incentives are also transmitted through a variety of community effects. In modern treatments of both contemporary discrimination and of the contemporary legacy of historical discrimination incentives are mediated through a variety of community effects such as "social capital" and "group reputation." The repeated theme is that there are positive feedback loops in which the behavior of individuals affects the attributes of communities and in which the attributes of communities affect the opportunities and incentives of individuals. Intervention at the right point in a system with positive feedback creates productive, effective policies. But the wrong sort of intervention, however well-intentioned, can reinforce the mechanisms in the economy that push the races apart.

Crucial to the design of effective policy interventions is a deeper understanding of how the positive feedbacks through social capital and group reputation operate. The new economic models of race demonstrate that microincentives matter—that the effectiveness of affirmative action may rest upon the relative importance of discrete labor-market hurdles rather than continuous reward structures, or upon how rapidly employer stereotypes adjust relative to the speed of worker qualification adjustments—yet we have little solid evidence concerning the relevant magnitudes. A central issue concerns the definition and measurement of social capital. Does an aggregate measure of income or education capture this idea adequately, or do we need a multidimensional concept that incorporates community infrastructure, family interactions, or "culture"? Is social capital to be defined geographically, or by social networks?[10] Do averages serve as sufficient statistics for social capital, or do the extremes exert some independent influence on behavior? A tendency to target averages, or the worst off, may be misguided if the activities of the most fortunate in the community have a disproportionate impact on social capital as, for example, role models. If, as Wilson suggests, the exit of the middle class from urban ghettos has been the cause of rapid deterioration in the social capital of these communities, then this may alter trade-offs between services to the very poor and services such as public education and police protection that are of value to the middle class as well. Policies are

---

[10] Borjas (1995) presents some evidence that both geographic proximity and social ties defined by ethnic affiliation play some role in the intergenerational transmission of status.

most effective when they change the incentives of those agents whose decisions are close to the margin, so identifying these agents is an important element of policy design. This kind of fine-tuning is difficult and requires much more empirical knowledge than we currently possess, but it is essential with limited policy resources.

The possible interactions of policies that attempt to influence social capital is another important, but relatively untouched, issue in the design of effective policy to reduce racial inequality. Some social scientists have argued that successful policy needs to deal with urban poverty on several fronts.[11] Should finite resources be used on a broad front or in a focused attack? Should all efforts be directed toward improving public schools—or is such an effort doomed without adequate transportation to take urban workers to suburban jobs? Can improved public safety return businesses to the urban core—or is increased small business capital required first? The apparent ineffectiveness of interventions such as Head Start to improve educational prospects for African-American children suggests that narrowly focused policies in the face of multidimensional racial barriers may be doomed to failure.[12]

Given that conservation of public resources frequently requires that policies be targeted, what are the merits of using race rather than income as a screen? The case for race-based policy is that effective policies are likely to be ones that operate on the externalities that generate or perpetuate inequality. For example, in models of statistical discrimination, a policy that succeeds in changing the equilibrium informational content of racial identification enough to outweigh the cost of restricting privately efficient employer decisions is an effective policy, and is of necessity race-based whether accomplished via affirmative action or training subsidies. An analogous income-based rule, say one that subsidized or targeted a particular income-decile, would be less cost-effective. Policies designed to repair a community's "social capital" need not be overtly race-based, but since American society is racially segregated both residentially and through the social networks of friendship and kinship, community-targeted policies will be racially unbalanced.

Whatever the theoretical merits of race-tested policies, their use is clearly limited by current public distaste. Regulations that forbid overt, identifiable, discriminatory acts remain popular, but policies that are believed to simply favor particular groups have come under increasing fire. Policies that are geographically based, such as one that targets schools in low-income areas, are less automatically objectionable even though their impact is not racially

[11] William Julius Wilson, Stice Memorial Lectures, University of Washington, 1995.

[12] Currie and Thomas (1995) note that the failure of Head Start to improve outcomes for African-American children may be due either to "inadequacies in these programs" or to "the limited opportunities available to African-American children afer they leave the program."

neutral. The efficacy of such targeting depends in part on the extent to which racially segregated social capital is based on geography rather than social networks. In other words, "neighborhood" and "community" are not necessarily synonymous, and the latter is likely to be more racially segregated than the former.

Do we need to regard social networks, and therefore social capital externalities, as themselves endogenous? Economists have had relatively little to say about these questions, but they are important for interpreting the policy implications of the theoretical models. For example, "integration" is used to describe the removal of barriers between groups over which social capital is defined, that is, increasing cross-group spillovers. Yet it is not at all clear what integration implies in terms of more concrete policies. As an example of the kinds of question that arise: Is it sufficient that black and white students attend the same college courses and eat in the same student cafeteria, if they still eat at self-segregated tables? Externalities that operate through physical proximity are easily manipulated in an algebraic model, but are perhaps less amenable to politically acceptable changes. While the new economics of race has contributed a great deal about the broad brush of policy, we need to know much more about which specific policies and which policy combinations have the best chance of success.

References

Aigner, Dennis J., and Glen G. Cain. 1977. "Statistical Theories of Discrimination in Labor Markets." *Industrial and Labor Relations Review* 30 (January): 175–187.

Arrow, Kenneth J. 1973. "The Theory of Discrimination." In *Discrimination in Labor Markets*, ed. Orley Ashenfelter and Albert Rees, pp. 3–33. Princeton, NJ: Princeton University Press.

Ayres, Ian, and Peter Siegelman. 1995. "Race and Gender Discrimination in Bargaining for a New Car." *American Economic Review* 85 (June): 304–321.

Becker, Gary. 1957. *The Economics of Discrimination.* Chicago: University of Chicago Press.

Bénabou, Roland. 1993. "Workings of a City: Location, Education, and Production." *Quarterly Journal of Economics* 108 (August): 619–652.

———. 1994. "Human Capital, Inequality, and Growth: A Local Perspective." *European Economic Review* 38 (April): 817–826.

———. 1996a. "Equity and Efficiency in Human Capital Investment: The Local Connection." *Review of Economic Studies* 63 (April): 237–264.

———. 1996b. "Heterogeneity, Stratification, and Growth: Macroeconomic Implications of Community Structure and School Finance." *American Economic Review* 86 (June): 584–609.

Borjas, George J. 1992. "Ethnic Capital and Intergenerational Mobility." *Quarterly Journal of Economics* 107 (February): 123–150.

Borjas, George J. 1995. "Ethnicity, Neighborhoods, and Human-Capital Externalities." *American Economic Review* 85 (June): 365–390.

Coate, Stephen, and Glenn C. Loury. 1993a. "Antidiscrimination Enforcement and the Problem of Patronization." *American Economic Review Papers and Proceedings* 83 (May): 92–98.

————. 1993b. "Will Affirmative-Action Policies Eliminate Negative Stereotypes?" *American Economic Review* 83 (December): 1220–1240.

Coleman, James S. 1988. "Social Capital in the Creation of Human Capital." *American Journal of Sociology* 94: S95–S120.

Currie, Janet, and Duncan Thomas. 1995. "Does Head Start Make a Difference?" *American Economic Review* 85 (June): 341–364.

Donohue, John H., and James Heckman. 1991. "Continuous Versus Episodic Change: The Impact of Civil Rights Policy on the Economic Status of Blacks." *Journal of Economic Literature* 29 (December): 1603–1643.

Durlauf, Steven N. 1994. "Spillovers, Stratification, and Inequality," *European Economic Review* 38 (April): 836–845.

————. 1996. "A Theory of Persistent Income Inequality." *Journal of Economic Growth* 1 (March): 75–94.

Fernandez, Raquel, and Richard Rogerson. 1996. "Income Distribution, Communities and the Quality of Public Education: A Policy Analysis." *Quarterly Journal of Economics* 111 (February): 135–164.

Glomm, Gerhard, and B. Ravikumar. 1992. "Public versus Private Investment in Human Capital: Endogenous Growth and Income Inequality." *Journal of Political Economy* 100 (August): 818–834.

Herrnstein, Richard J., and Charles Murray. 1994. *The Bell Curve: Intelligence and Class Structure in American Life*. New York: Free Press.

Kahn, Lawrence M. 1991. "Customer Discrimination and Affirmative Action." *Economic Inquiry* 29 (July): 555–571.

Loury, Glenn C. 1977. "A Dynamic Theory of Racial Income Differences." In *Women, Minorities, and Employment Discrimination*, ed. Phyllis A. Wallace and Annette M. LaMond, pp. 153–186. Lexington, MA: D. C. Heath and Co.

Lundberg, Shelly J. 1991. "The Enforcement of Equal Opportunity Laws under Imperfect Information: Affirmative Action and Alternatives." *Quarterly Journal of Economics* 106 (February): 309–326.

Lundberg, Shelly J., and Richard Startz. 1983. "Private Discrimination and Social Intervention in Competitive Labor Markets." *American Economic Review* 73 (June): 340–347.

————. 1998. "On the Persistence of Racial Inequality." *Journal of Labor Economics* 16 (April): 292–323.

Milgrom, Paul, and Sharon Oster. 1987. "Job Discrimination, Market Forces, and the Invisibility Hypothesis." *Quarterly Journal of Economics* 102 (August): 453–476.

Montgomery, James D. 1991. "Social Networks and Persistent Inequality in the Labor Market: Toward an Economic Analysis." *American Economic Review* 81 (December): 1408–1418.

Neal, Derek, and William Johnson. 1996. "The Role of Premarket Factors in Black-White Wage Differences." *Journal of Political Economy* 104 (October): 1603–1643.

Phelps, Edmund S. 1972. "The Statistical Theory of Racism and Sexism." *American Economic Review* 62 (September): 659–661.

Spence, Michael. 1973. "Job Market Signalling." *Quarterly Journal of Economics* 87: 355–374.

Wilson, William Julius. 1987. *The Truly Disadvantaged: The Inner City, the Underclass, and Public Policy*. Chicago: University of Chicago Press.

———. Stice Memorial Lectures, University of Washington, 1995.

Eleven

Conceptual Problems in the Enforcement
of Anti-Discrimination Laws

GLENN LOURY

THIS CHAPTER considers some problems that arise for anti-discrimination enforcement due to the limited availability of information to an enforcement agent. I intend to stress that under these circumstances enforcement efforts, if not carried out properly, can be counterproductive. Specifically, employment quotas for a group of persons thought to be victims of discrimination can alter employers' and workers' incentives so as to produce undesirable results. Because employers' hiring decisions and workers' investment decisions each depend on perceptions of how the other behaves, one needs an equilibrium model of labor-market interactions to study the issues with which I am concerned. Two such models are provided in what follows.

These models correspond to the two theories of employment discrimination that are most prominent in the literature. The first theory, proposed by Gary Becker (1957), posits that some employers, harboring a "taste" for discrimination against some groups of workers, experience disutility from hiring them. The result can be reduced labor-market opportunities for these workers. The second theory, introduced by Kenneth Arrow (1973), postulates that employers treat some workers differently than others because of disparate statistical generalizations about worker productivity in the various groups. When an individual worker's productivity is not observable, employers may use the information contained in group averages to make their decisions. Arrow showed that this reliance on group averages can lead to discrimination against one group in favor of another, even when the objective capacities of the groups are the same and when the employers hold no invidious motives.

These two theories do not, of course, exhaust the possible explanations of dicrimination that one might offer. But they are a useful context within which to examine the issues that most concern me. These issues have to do with how laws against employment discrimination can be enforced, and what some unintended consequences of enforcement efforts might be. In practice a government determined to prohibit race or sex discrimination in employment faces a difficult problem. If the regulator had unlimited information he might, by observing the outcome of every employment decision made by a firm, be able to determine if that firm is using exactly the same criteria to select among applicants from different groups. Absent such information, however, enforcement must rest upon means other than exhaustive observation. One response is to compare the numbers of various groups in a particular firm with their population proportions. If there is a significant divergence, the firm might be asked to account for it. Absent a compelling justification, the difference would be presumed to be evidence of bias.

This technique is implicit in one of the key provisions of the U.S. Civil Rights Act of 1991, which holds any employment practice having a "disparate impact" on women or minorities to be unlawful unless the firm can demonstrate that the practice constitutes a "business necessity" (Epstein 1992). (This method is also commonly used in the private sector, by universities in their admissions decisions, and by government agencies in their procurement decisions.) Goals for the employment of minority and women personnel are set for particular enterprises by reference to population percentages of the various groups, sometimes with the comparison population defined so as to approximate the pool of potential employees with skills relevant to the task in question. Enforcement methods such as this have a quota-like quality, in that they specify target numerical outcomes rather than focusing on the particular selection procedures being used.

Objections can be raised against this type of numerical enforcement policy. If the distribution of skills across groups differs in ways not taken into account when the numerical target is set, the representation of women and minorities in the population may overstate their actual employment rates under nondiscriminatory hiring rules. Firms then bear the burden of proving that any difference in group hiring rates is due to a disparity in group skills, which can be quite difficult to do to the satisfaction of a court. Anticipating this difficulty, firms may instead respond to the enforcement regime by adopting hiring rules in favor of women and minorities, so as to avoid costly litigation.

This concern about quotas motivated much of the conservative criticism of the Civil Rights Act of 1991. Yet this criticism misses a basic point: If discrimination is in fact taking place, then it reduces the incentives for the workers being discriminated against to acquire skills. When minority workers expect to face biased hiring rules, their returns from acquiring job-relevant skills are lowered. Thus group disparities in skills may simply reflect the presence of employment discrimination. Hence, a regulator may be justified in placing a "burden of proof" on firms whose workforce exhibits substantial underrepresentation of minorities in certain jobs. The ultimate effects of this burden may be to induce firms that would otherwise discriminate to offer equal opportunities to all workers, which might lead to the elimination of any existing skill disparities across groups.

This is the view taken by many liberal advocates of stronger civil rights laws. Yet this view also overlooks an important point, illustrated by the models to follow. Quota-like enforcement policies do not necessarily move workers' incentives in the right direction. If the policy forces firms (even those who would discriminate in the absence of the quota) to set lower standards for minorities, then minority workers may be persuaded that they can get desired jobs without making costly investment in skills. But if fewer members of some group acquire skills, firms will be forced to continue patronizing them in order to achieve parity. Thus skill disparities might persist, or even worsen, under such policies.

Model 1: Taste Discrimination

What follows is a simple taste discrimination model that illustrates these problems. In the model, discrimination reduces the incentives to invest and hence creates skill disparities between groups. These disparities are not necessarily eliminated by statistical enforcement policies because of the adverse incentives such policies can create. *The model suggests that a* gradual *policy, in which representation targets are ratcheted up through time, will be more likely to eliminate both discrimination and skill disparities than a radical policy which, starting from a situation in which skill disparities are significant, demands immediate proportional representation* (see proposition 3).

Consider a labor market consisting of a large number of firms, each of which hires its workforce from a common population. A large number of prospective employees, drawn randomly from this population, approaches each firm seeking employment. These workers belong to one of two identifiable groups, denoted W or B; λ *is the fraction of* Ws in the population, and hence is also the probability that a given applicant for employment is a W. When a firm encounters a worker it must decide whether to "accept" or "reject" the applicant. A firm engages in discrimination if it uses a different rule when deciding whether to accept Bs than it does when deciding about Ws.

Workers are either "qualified" or "unqualified." Firms observe a worker's qualifications before deciding to accept or reject. An accepted worker gains the gross benefit ω, irrespective of her qualifications; a rejected worker's gross payoff is zero. The monetary return to a firm from accepting a worker is $x_q > 0$ if she is qualified, and $-x_u < 0$ if she is unqualified. The return to any firm from rejecting any worker is zero. Thus, absent nonmonetary motives, firms would accept all qualified workers and reject all unqualified ones.

Following Becker, I assume firms have a taste for discrimination in that they experience some psychic cost from accepting a B. This cost is greater the larger the ratio of Bs to Ws among the pool of acceptees. Specifically, let r be the ratio of accepted Bs to Bs for a firm. For some $\gamma > 0$, if a worker is a B then accepting him has the psychic cost to that firm of γr. This means that the net return of accepting a B worker is $x_q - \gamma r$ if he is qualified, and $-x_u - \gamma r$ if he in unqualified. The payoff parameters x_q, x_u, ω, and γ are exogenous. In particular, firms are not allowed to offer lower wages to Bs as compensation for their psychic costs. The focus here is on the implications of enforcement against discriminatory hiring by firms in a world where equal-pay laws are perfectly enforced.

To complete the description of the model I must consider how workers decide whether or not to become qualified. I assume that prior to encountering a firm, a worker can make some costly investment. Once the investment is made, a worker is qualified; otherwise, she is unqualified. The cost to a worker of this investment varies in the population, but is distributed in the same way among Bs and Ws. Let c denote an individual's investment cost, and $G(c)$ the fraction of workers in either groups with cost no greater than c. A worker makes this investment if the expected return from doing so is no less than her cost. I assume that $G(0) = 0$, $G'(c) > 0$, and $G(\omega) < 1$.

The timing of events in this model is as follows: First, each worker decides whether to invest. Then all workers are randomly matched with firms. Finally, each firm observes the group identities and qualifications of its applicants and makes its acceptance decisions. A worker's decision about investment depends on his cost, c, and the group to which he belongs. A firm's decision about whether to accept a given worker depends on that worker's qualifications and the group to which he belongs. An *equilibrium* is a set of decision rules for all workers and firms such that each is a rational (i.e., return-maximizing) response to the others. I shall assume that firms' taste for discrimination is sufficiently great, in the following sense:

$$\text{Assumption 1: } \gamma > Max\{\frac{x_q^2}{4x_u} ; \frac{\lambda x_q}{2(1 - \lambda)}\}. \tag{2.1}$$

The purpose of this assumption will become apparent momentarily.

Let us find the equilibrium of this model in the absence of anti-discrimination enforcement. Consider first the behavior of firms. No firm accepts an unqualified B or rejects a qualified W. Doing so would both lower a firm's monetary returns and increase its psychic costs. I claim that under assumption 1 firms reject unqualified Ws and accept qualified Bs as long as the B/W ratio is not too great. To see this, suppose a firm follows some decision rule that results in the acceptance of n_b Bs and n_w Ws. That firm then has a ratio of Bs to Ws among its accepted workers of $r \equiv \frac{n_b}{n_w}$, and so it incurs the psychic cost $\gamma r n_b = \frac{\gamma n_b^2}{n_w}$ due to its discriminatory taste. Hence its marginal psychic cost of accepting another B is $\frac{2\gamma n_b}{n_w} = 2\gamma r$, while its marginal psychic benefit of accepting another W (thereby reducing the B/W ratio) is γr^2. Since the direct monetary benefit of accepting a qualified B is x_q, the rational firm accepts an additional qualified B if and only if $x_q \geq 2\gamma r$. That is, a qualified B is accepted as long as the B/W ratio among accepted workers, r, satisfies the inequality: $r \leq r^* \equiv \frac{x_q}{2\gamma}$. Furthermore, since the monetary cost of accepting an unqualified W is x_u, it pays for a firm to do so only if $x_u \leq \gamma r^2$. But we know that firms do not permit r to exceed r^*. So accepting an unqualified W does not pay if $x_u > \gamma r^{*2} = \frac{x_q^2}{4\gamma}$, which is assured by assumption 1. We conclude that a rational firm rejects unqualified Bs and Ws, accepts qualified Ws, and accepts a qualified B only if $r \leq r^*$.

Let $\pi_b(\pi_w)$ be the fraction of group B (group W) who invest. Since workers are randomly matched with firms and there are many workers per firm, the Law of Large Numbers implies that the shares of qualified Ws and Bs in a firm's applicant pool are approximately $\lambda\pi_w$ and $(1 - \lambda)\pi_b$, respectively. Let $\bar{r} = \frac{1-\lambda}{\lambda}$ be the ratio of Bs to Ws in the population. By the foregoing reasoning if $\bar{r}\left(\frac{\pi_b}{\pi_w}\right) \leq r$ then a firm can expect to accept all of its qualified B applicants, while if $\bar{r}\left(\frac{\pi_b}{\pi_w}\right) > r^*$ a firm will accept some, but not all, qualified Bs. In fact, one sees readily that if firms behave rationally and assumption 1 holds, then a qualified B is accepted with probability $\delta(\pi_b, \pi_w)$, where:

$$\delta(\pi_b, \pi_w) \equiv Min\{\frac{\pi_w r^*}{\pi_b \bar{r}}; 1\} \tag{2.2}$$

So Bs are discriminated against in equilibrium if workers qualify at rates such that $\left(\frac{\pi_b}{\pi_w}\right) > \left(\frac{r^*}{\bar{r}}\right)$. That is, even though firms dislike accepting Bs, since it is economically advantageous to do so they act on this preference only when Bs are sufficiently numerous among their qualified applicants.

Now we can see that, under assumption 1, discrimination must occur in the equilibrium of this model. Suppose no discrimination was practiced. Then B and W workers with costs $c \leq \omega$ will invest, the fraction of each group becoming qualified will be $\pi_b = \pi_w = G(\omega)$, and thus $\frac{\pi_b}{\pi_w}$ will equal 1. But assumption 1 implies $\frac{r^*}{\bar{r}} \frac{\lambda x_q}{2\gamma(1-\lambda)} < 1$ which, by the foregoing argument, means that rational firms will desire to discriminate against Bs. This contradicts the initial presumption that they do not.

On the other hand, if qualified Bs face some probability $\delta < 1$ of being accepted, then each B worker expects the average return $\omega\delta$ from investing. So only those Bs with $c \leq \omega\delta$ invest, implying $\pi_b = G(\omega\delta)$. Since Ws are accepted if and only if they invest we have $\pi_w = G(\omega)$. Therefore, in equilibrium each firm will accept all qualified Ws and some but not all qualified Bs, maintaining a B/W ratio just equal to r^*, and implying a probability of acceptance for qualified Bs equal to δ^*, where δ^* solves the equation:

$$\delta \cdot G(\delta\omega) = \left[\frac{r^*}{\bar{r}}\right] \cdot G(\omega) \tag{2.3}$$

It is easily seen that (2.3) has a unique solution δ, with $0 < \delta^* < 1$. Moreover, δ^* is a decreasing function of λ, and it is an increasing function of x_q and of λ. That is, discrimination against Bs is greater in equilibrium the greater the psychic cost to firms of accepting them, the greater their percentage of the workforce, and the smaller the economic benefit to firms of employing qualified workers.

Let us now consider the effect of anti-discrimination enforcement efforts in this context. I will assume, for the reasons mentioned above, that the government uses a quota-like enforcement strategy, comparing the aggregate number of workers in each group accepted by each firm with some standard, and finding the firm in violation if its employment ratio of Bs to Ws is not sufficiently high. Specifically, suppose that the regulator selects some target ratio $\hat{r} > r^*$ *and* announces that any firm found with a B/W ratio less than $\hat{r}$ will face costly legal proceedings. Let the anticipated costs of these proceedings be so great that no firm wants to risk being found in violation. Then firms will adapt to this regulatory regime by altering their acceptance rules to ensure that $r \geq \hat{r}$. I will assess the effects of this kind of regulation by analyzing how the equilibrium outcome of our simple model changes under this constraint.

The objective of population proportional representation corresponds to a target $\hat{r} = \bar{r}$. However, a regulator might also want to consider more modest objectives. I conduct the analysis under the assumption that the target is set to increase the representation of Bs, but not beyond their relative number in the population, so $\hat{r}$ lies somewhere between r^* and $\bar{r}$: $r^* < \hat{r} \leq \bar{r}$.

To analyze the impact of this constraint, notice first that if the taste for discrimination γ is too large, and the representation target $\hat{r}$ too severe, then the enforcement policy may cause the market to collapse, with no workers being accepted and none investing. To see this, observe that the constraint $r \geq \bar{r}$ will bind for all firms, since a firm in strict compliance (with $r > \hat{r}$) can reject an additional B while remaining in compliance. With $r > \hat{r} > r^*$ *we* know that $2\gamma r$, the marginal benefit of rejecting another B, exceeds x_q, the loss to the firm of rejecting a qualified B. Now, because the constraint is binding, firms will never accept unqualified Ws. So the firm's problem under the regulatory constraint reduces to choosing how many qualified Ws to accept, with Bs then accepted at a rate sufficient to ensure compliance with the anti-discrimination mandate.

Compliance requires there be $\hat{r}$ Bs for each W among the accepted. Therefore, the net benefit from accepting a qualified W, taking account of monetary and psychic returns and of the regulatory constraint, is $x_q + \hat{r}x_q - \gamma\hat{r}^2$ if the marginal B accepted is qualified, and is $x_q - \hat{r}x_u - \gamma\hat{r}^2$ if the marginal B is unqualified. Thus, if $x_q + \hat{r}x_q - \gamma\hat{r}^2 < 0$ firms will reject all their applicants, and the collapse of the market is assured. To avoid this outcome for all $\hat{r} \in (r^*, \bar{r}]$ requires that $x_q + \hat{r}x_q - \gamma\hat{r}^2 > 0$, which amounts to the following:

$$\text{Assumption 2: } \gamma < \left(\frac{\varkappa_q}{1 - \lambda}\right) \cdot \left(\frac{\lambda}{1 - \lambda}\right) \tag{2.4}$$

Assumptions 1 and 2 together simply state that firms dislike Bs enough to discriminate against them in the absence of regulation, but not so much as to forgo all operations if required to employ qualified Bs at a rate equal to their presence in the population.

Under assumption 2 firms gain by accepting qualified Ws so long as compliance with the regulation can be maintained by accepting qualified Bs. If the ratio of Bs to Ws among a firm's qualified applicants is less than $\hat{r}$, the firm will need to consider whether it pays to accept any unqualified Bs. From the above discussion, this will be worthwhile if:

$$\varkappa_q > \varkappa_u \hat{r} + \gamma \hat{r}^2 \tag{2.5}$$

Hence, there are two cases of interest, depending on whether $\varkappa_q < \varkappa_u \hat{r} + \gamma \hat{r}^2$ [case 1], or $\varkappa_q > \varkappa_u \hat{r} + \gamma \hat{r}^2$ [case 2]. Under case 1, firms accept the maximal number of qualified Ws consistent with being able to remain in compliance by accepting only qualified Bs. Under case 2, firms accept all qualified Ws and as many Bs as necessary to remain in compliance, even if some unqualified Bs must be accepted. For $\hat{r}$ near $\bar{r}$, equation (2.5) is more demanding than assumption 2. Still, it can be shown that values for the parameters $\varkappa_q$, $\varkappa_u$, and γ exist satisfying equation (2.5) for all $\hat{r} \in (r^*, \bar{r}]$, and satisfying assumption 1, if $\lambda > \frac{1}{2}$.

It is now possible to describe how the government's quota-like enforcement policy alters the equilibrium of the model.

Proposition 1: In case 1 there is a unique equilibrium for each statistical enforcement policy $\hat{r} \in (r^*, \bar{r}]$. In this equilibrium all unqualified workers are rejected, all qualified Ws are accepted, and qualified Bs are accepted with probability $\delta(\hat{r})$, $0 < \delta(\hat{r}) \le 1$. This probability $\delta(\hat{r})$ exceeds the *laissez faire* acceptance rate δ^*, is strictly increasing in $\hat{r}$, and satisfies $\delta(\bar{r}) = 1$. Indeed, $\delta(r)$ solves the equation: $\delta G(\delta \omega) = \left(\frac{r}{\bar{r}}\right) \cdot G(\omega)$.

Proof: If Bs and Ws invest at rates π_b and π_w then the fractions of a firm's applicants who are qualified Bs and Ws are $(1 - \lambda)\pi_b$ and $\lambda \pi_w$, respectively. In case 1 firms accept none of the unqualified, and among the qualified all Ws and some Bs if $\frac{\hat{r}}{\bar{r}} < \frac{\pi_b}{\pi_w}$ and all Bs and some Ws if $\frac{\hat{r}}{\bar{r}} > \frac{\pi_b}{\pi_w}$. But when $\hat{r} \in (r^*, \bar{r}]$ an equilibrium with $\frac{\hat{r}}{\bar{r}} > \frac{\pi_b}{\pi_w}$ is impossible, since accepting all Bs and not all Ws from among the qualified means that $\pi_b > \pi_w$, and so $\frac{\hat{r}}{\bar{r}} > 1$, a contradiction. Thus, equilibrium necessarily entails acceptance from among the qualified of all Ws, and some fraction $\delta = \left(\frac{\hat{r}}{\bar{r}}\right) \cdot \left(\frac{\pi_b}{\pi_w}\right)$ of Bs, where $\pi_w = G(\omega)$ and $\pi_b = G(\delta \omega)$. So, the equilibrium acceptance rate for qualified Bs, $\delta(\hat{r})$, solves: $\delta G(\delta \omega) = \left(\frac{\hat{r}}{\bar{r}}\right) \cdot G(\omega)$. This solution is unique, exceeds δ^* for all $\hat{r} \in (r^*, \bar{r}]$, is increasing in $\hat{r}$, and equals 1 when $\hat{r} = \bar{r}$. ∎

So in case 1 the use of a quota-like enforcement strategy is sure to produce desirable results. Setting the target $\hat{r}$ equal to the population ratio $\bar{r}$

implies an outcome with no discrimination and no skill disparity between groups. More generally, a stricter target leads to less discrimination by firms and less of a skill disparity between the groups. Matters are not so comforting in case 2.

Proposition 2: In case 2 the equilibrium described in proposition 1 continues to exist. In addition, however, other equilibria may also exist. In these other equilibria all qualified workers are accepted, all unqualified Ws are rejected, but unqualified Bs are accepted with positive probability. A necessary and sufficient condition for the existence of these additional equilibria is that, for some $\delta \in (0,1), \delta \cdot [1 - G(\omega\delta)] > [1 - \left(\frac{\hat{r}}{\bar{r}}\right) \cdot G(\omega)]$.

Proof: In case 2 firms accept unqualified Bs if and only if this is necessary to remain in compliance when accepting all the qualified Ws. In the equilibrium of proposition 1 compliance can be achieved by accepting all qualified Ws and no unqualified Bs, since $\frac{\pi_b}{\pi_w} \geq \frac{\hat{r}}{\bar{r}}$. So this remains an equilibrium in case 2. We seek to identify other (patronizing) equilibria, where $\frac{\pi_b}{\pi_w} < \frac{\hat{r}}{\bar{r}}$, in case 2. In such an equilibrium, to comply while accepting all qualified Ws, firms must accept all qualified Bs and the fraction $\sigma = [\left(\frac{\hat{r}}{\bar{r}}\right)\pi_w - \pi_b]/(1 - \pi_b)$ of unqualified Bs. But then, a B's return from investing is $\delta = 1 - \sigma = [1 - \left(\frac{\hat{r}}{\bar{r}}\right)\pi_w]/(1 - \pi_b)$. Hence the fractions $\pi_b = G(\omega\delta)$ and $\pi_\omega = G(\omega)$ of Bs and Ws would invest. So a patronizing equilibrium exists if $\delta = [1 - \left(\frac{\hat{r}}{\bar{r}}\right)G(\omega)]/[1 - G(\omega\delta)]$ has a solution for some $\delta \in (0,1)$. A necessary and sufficient condition for this to occur is that $\delta \geq [1 - \left(\frac{\hat{r}}{\bar{r}}\right) G(\omega)]/[1 - G(\omega\delta)]$ for some $\delta \subset$ in $(0,1)$. Indeed, if this inequality holds strictly then at least two patronizing equilibria exist. ∎

In case 2 and under the above-stated condition the use of a quota-like enforcement policy can lead firms to patronize Bs in equilibrium by accepting some even when unqualified, despite the presence of a distaste for accepting Bs. Firms accept unqualified Bs because it is necessary to do so in order to meet the hiring target. But by doing so, firms act to lower the incentive for Bs to invest, thereby inducing a skill disparity disfavoring Bs. Indeed, the skill disparity may actually widen as a result of the regulator's intervention, as compared to the discriminatory equilibrium without intervention. Note that the condition in proposition 2 will be more easily satisfied when $\hat{r}$ is larger. *Equilibria in which Bs are patronized are more likely to exist when the target is more ambitious.*

Intuitively, what happens in a patronizing equilibrium may be seen by considering how firms react to the initial imposition of some hiring target $\hat{r} > r^*$. Prior to the regulation a "surplus" of qualified Bs exists—that is, more Bs invest than find employment ($\delta^* < 1$). So if the target is modest ($\hat{r} \approx r^*$) firms anticipate meeting it by accepting only qualified Bs. But this raises δ, increasing Bs' incentives to invest. So the new equilibrium is as described in proposition 1, with more Bs accepted and the skill gap narrowed.

However, if case 2 applies and if the target is sufficiently ambitious ($\hat{r} \approx \bar{r}$), then firms perceive a "shortage" of qualified Bs relative to the numbers needed to be in compliance while accepting all qualified Ws. They therefore switch from discriminating against qualified Bs to favoring unqualified Bs. This response can actually lower Bs' incentives to invest, leading to a patronizing equilibrium such as that described in proposition 2.

How likely is it that such an equilibrium would arise? This question can be addressed by imagining successive cohorts of workers interacting with firms over time. A dynamic adjustment process is defined for a given hiring target $\hat{r}$ by assuming that firms hire optimally from the workers in each cohort, while investment decisions in cohort $t + 1$ are based on the acceptance rules applied by firms to cohort t. By iterating this process I trace out a long-run response to the enforcement policy. The fraction of Bs investing initially is denoted by π_b^0. Since, in case 2, firms always accept all of the qualified and none of the unqualified Ws, we know that the constant fraction $\pi_\omega = G(\omega)$ of Ws invest in each cohort.

Let π_b^t be Bs' investment rate on cohort t. If $\frac{\pi_b^t}{\pi_w} \geq \frac{\hat{r}}{\bar{r}}$, firms accept a qualified B with probability $\delta^t \equiv \left(\frac{\hat{r}}{\bar{r}}\right) \cdot \frac{\pi_w}{\pi_b^t}$) to comply, so Bs in cohort $t + 1$ invest at rate $\pi_b^{t+1} = G(\omega\delta^t)$. If $\frac{\pi_b^t}{\pi_w} < \frac{\hat{r}}{\bar{r}}$, all qualified Bs and the fraction $\sigma^t = [(\frac{\hat{r}}{\bar{r}}) \pi_\omega - \pi_b^t]/(1 - \pi_b^t)$ of unqualified Bs are accepted, so Bs' in cohort $t + 1$ invest at rate $\pi_b^{t+1} = G(\omega(1 - \sigma^t))$. Thus $\{\pi_b^t\}$, $t \geq 0$, solves:

$$\pi_b^{t+1} = G(\omega \cdot \left[\frac{\hat{r}}{\bar{r}}\right] \cdot \left[\frac{\pi_\omega}{\pi_b^t}\right]), \qquad\qquad for \ \frac{\pi_b^t}{\pi_\omega} \geq \frac{\hat{r}}{\bar{r}} \qquad (2.6)$$

$$\pi_b^{t+1} = G(\omega \cdot \left[1 - \left(\frac{\hat{r}}{\bar{r}}\right)\pi_\omega\right]/[1 - \pi_b^t]), \quad for \ \frac{\pi_b^t}{\pi_\omega} < \frac{\hat{r}}{\bar{r}} \qquad (2.7)$$

The stationary points of this difference equation correspond exactly to the fraction of Bs who invest in the equilibria of our model. Hence, if a patronizing equilibrium exists then equation (2.6) has a stationary point π_b^* at which $\frac{\pi_b^*}{\pi_w} < \frac{\hat{r}}{\bar{r}}$. Detailed study of equation (2.6) leads to the following result:

Proposition 3: If a patronizing equilibrium exists from enforcement policy $\hat{r} \in (r \cdot, \bar{r}]$ then one also exists from any $r' \in (r \cdot, \bar{r}]$. Let $\underline{r} \equiv \inf\{r \in (r \cdot, \bar{r}] |$ a pat. equil. exists from r\}. If $\frac{\omega G'(\omega)}{1 - G(\omega)} > 1$ then $\underline{r} < \bar{r}$, and $\exists$ a continuous, increasing function $\tilde{\pi}_b : (\underline{r}, \bar{r}] \rightarrow (0, \pi_\omega]$ with $\tilde{\pi}_p(\bar{r}) = \pi_\omega$ such that $\forall \hat{r} \in (\underline{r}, \bar{r}]$, equation (2.6) converges to a patronizing equilibrium whenever $\pi_b^0 < \tilde{\pi}_b(\hat{r})$.

Sketch of Proof: Figure 11.1 graphs the difference equation, equation (2.6). Notice that if a patronizing equilibrium exists at all, then this equation has at least two stationary points that are less than $\frac{\hat{r}}{\bar{r}} \cdot \pi_\omega$. Denote by $\tilde{\pi}(\hat{r})$ the largest of these stationary points. With this definition it is a straightforward exercise to verify the claims in the proposition. ■

To see the implications of this result, note that $\pi b^0 < \pi_\omega$ *necessarily*, or else there is no need for regulation. Now, suppose that $\varkappa_q > \varkappa_u\bar{r} + \gamma\bar{r}^2$ and

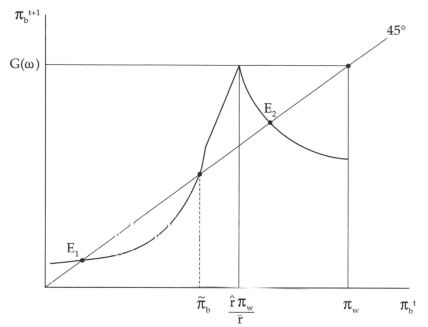

Figure 11.1. E_1 is a (locally stable) patronizing equilibrium.

that $\frac{\omega G'(\omega)}{1-G(\omega)} > 1$. Then proposition 3 states that *a patronizing outcome is the inevitable result of the regulator seeking fully proportional representation* $[\hat{r} = \bar{r}]$. But since the threshold investment rate $\tilde{\pi}_b(\hat{r})$ is increasing in $\hat{r}$, the regulator could avoid an equilibrium in which Bs are patronized by setting a more modest target. For example, it is easy to see that a target equal to the *laissez-faire* ratio of qualified Bs to Ws $[\hat{r} = \bar{r} \cdot \frac{G(\delta^*\omega)}{G(\omega)}]$ never leads to patronization.

These results show that anti-discrimination enforcement may embody an awkward trade-off: A policy of proportional representation of Bs risks inducing a patronizing outcome, whereas a more modest target, though less prone to that problem, will not fully eliminate discrimination. Yet the model also suggests a way around this trade-off. Rather than settling immediately upon the proportional target $\hat{r} = \bar{r}$, the regulator could instead operate a gradual policy, with the target being ratcheted up in a series of steps.

Suppose, for example, that the adjustment process described in equation (2.6) operates quickly relative to the rate at which the policy target is changed. Then, if the regulator always sets the new target r' so that the currently prevailing investment rate among Bs, π_b, satisfies $\pi b > \tilde{\pi}_b(r')$, a patronizing outcome can be avoided. But, by proposition 1, each time the target is raised the rate of investment among Bs improves, which permits the target to be raised further without risk of patronization. By proceeding in this way, this process can eventually reduce both discrimination and also skill disparities between the groups to an arbitrarily small level (though it can never completely eliminate them).

Model 2: Statistical Discrimination

I now consider a model based on Arrow's theory of statistical discrimination. In this model firms have no desire to avoid hiring Bs per se. However, because firms cannot observe a worker's qualifications directly, they use group-based stereotypes about workers when making hiring decisions. These stereotypes can become a self-fulfilling prophecy, as explained more fully below. A regulator may then want to intervene so as to break the firms of the habit of relying on stereotypes. *But the model to follow shows that such intervention, when it takes a quota-like form, can be self-defeating* (see proposition 5).

My concern is with the standards employees use to assign workers to desirable positions, the effort workers invest to acquire skills useful in those positions, and the ways in which assignment and investment decisions are affected by group hiring standards. Consider the interaction between an employer and a large number of workers divided into two racial groups, Bs and Ws; again λ denotes the fraction of Ws in this population. The employer observes a worker's color, and so can treat B and W workers differently. The sole action of the employer is to assign each worker to one of two positions, called task "zero" and task "one." Assignment to task one may be thought of as giving the worker a promotion; it is the more desirable, but also more demanding, of the two positions.

I assume that all workers perform satisfactorily at task zero. Workers decide, before the employer assigns them to a task and without the employer's knowledge, whether to invest in the acquisition of a skill essential for effective performance at task one. The investment is costly for a worker to make. The size of this cost varies from worker to worker, though in a manner that is statistically the same for each racial group. Imagine, for example, that more able workers find it easier to acquire the skill needed for task one, and that the distribution of ability is the same within each group. Let c denote a worker's cost. I assume that each worker's cost is a random draw from a uniform distribution on the interval $[0,1]$, regardless of her group.

The employer cannot observe a particular worker's cost (ability). What he can observe is the group identity of each worker and the outcome of a skills test, to be described momentarily. Although the two groups have the same distribution of ability, they need not exhibit the same pattern of investment. Workers with the same investment cost but belonging to different groups might make different investment decisions, if they anticipate they will receive different treatment by the employer.

I assume that a worker obtains a premium whenever she gains assignment to task one, whether she has acquired the needed skill or not. However, since an unskilled worker performs inadequately, the employer wants a worker in task one if and only if she has the acquired requisite skill. Otherwise he wants that worker to go to task zero. The employer's profits are greatest when all skilled workers are assigned to task one and all unskilled workers to task zero. Specifically, let ω be the premium a worker puts on assignment to task one. Let $x_1 > 0$ be the employer's net gain from assigning an investing worker to task one instead of task zero; and let $x_0 > 0$ be his net gain from assigning a noninvesting worker to task zero rather than task one. Define $r \equiv \frac{x_1}{x_0}$.

The employer wants to match workers to their most productive tasks. Lacking any prior information, the employer "tests" a worker's qualification for doing task one. That is, he gathers what information he can (from an interview, analysis of previous work history, written exam, etc.) in order to assess the worker's capabilities. Let θ denote the test outcome. I assume that three test outcomes are possible: (1) it is clear that the worker can do task one ($\theta = $ "pass"); (2) it is clear that she cannot ($\theta = $ "fail"); and (3) it is uncertain whether the worker can do task one ($\theta = $ "unclear"). I assume that if a worker invests she cannot fail the test, and if a worker does not invest she cannot pass the test. Let $p_1(p_0)$ be the probability that an investing (noninvesting) worker gets an unclear test result. So $1 - p_1$ is the probability that an investing worker passes the test, and $1 - p_0$ is the probability that a noninvesting worker fails it. I require the following assumption:

$$Assumption\ 3:\ p_1 > p_0 > 1 - \frac{1}{\omega} \qquad (3.1)$$

Assumption 3 implies that the test is better at revealing noninvestors than investors, but not so good as to induce all workers to invest.

I now consider the behavior of the workers and employer in this model. Let $A(i, \theta)$ denote the probability that the employer assigns to task one a worker from group i with test outcome θ, for $i \in \{B, W\}$ and $\theta \in T = \{pass, fail, unclear\}$. A strategy for the employer is any function $A : \{B, W\} \times T \rightarrow [0, 1]$. Let $I(i, c)$ denote the probability that a group i worker with cost c invest in the skill needed to do task one, for $i \in \{B, W\}$ and $c \in [0, 1]$. A strategy for workers is any function $I : \{B, W\} \times [0, 1] \rightarrow [0, 1]$. The sequence of events is that each worker, knowing his color and his investment cost, decides whether to acquire the skill needed for task one. The employer then encounters the workers, gives them the test, and, on the basis of the test outcome and (possibly) the worker's color, assigns the workers to a task.

An equilibrium, then, is a pair of functions $< A^*, I^* >$ such that each strategy maximizes that decision maker's anticipated net reward, given the available information and the strategies employed by the other agents. I show that despite the absence of any racially invidious motive on the part of the employer, discrimination against Bs can arise in an equilibrium of this model.

To find the equilibria I begin by considering the employer's decision in each contingency. Clearly she assigns anyone passing the test to task one, and anyone failing it to task zero, regardless of color: $A^* (i, pass) = 1$ and $A^* (i, fail) = 0$ in any equilibrium. Let $\alpha_i \equiv A^* (i, unclear)$ denote the equilibrium probability a worker in group i who gets an unclear test outcome is assigned to task one. When $\theta = unclear$ the employer must assess the conditional probability that the worker has invested, $\xi_i \equiv \Pr[I^* (i, c) = 1 | \theta = unclear]$, in order to decide which assignment is best. Her net expected return from putting the worker in task one rather than task zero is $\xi_i x_1 - (1 - \xi_i) x_0$. Thus, if $\xi_i > (\frac{x_0}{x_0 + x_1})$, then we must have $\alpha_i = 1$, while if $\xi_i < (\frac{x_0}{x_0 + x_1})$ then we must have $\alpha_i = 0$. Note that $\frac{x_0}{x_0 + x_1} = \frac{1}{1+r}$.

Given an unclear test result, the odds that the worker producing it has invested depend on the mean rate of investing in that worker's group and the likelihood that investors and noninvestors get unclear results. Let $\pi_i \equiv \int_0^1 I^* (i, c)dc$, the mean equilibrium investment rate in group i, $i \in \{B, W\}$. Bayes's Rule then implies that $\xi_i = \frac{\pi_i p_1}{\pi_i p_1 + (1 - \pi_i)p_0}$. We conclude that there exists a threshold investment rate π^* such that, in equilibrium, $\pi_i > \pi^*$ implies $\alpha_i = 1$, and $\pi_i < \pi^*$ implies $\alpha_i = 0$, where $\pi^* \equiv \frac{p_0}{p_0 + p_1 r}$. We may interpret this result as follows: For a given group of workers, only if the employer believes the fraction of investors is sufficiently large will he give any one of them the "benefit of the doubt" in the face of an unclear test outcome. Define the employer's best response correspondence, $\phi_e (\pi)$, as follows:

$$\alpha_i \in \phi_e(\pi_i) \equiv \begin{cases} \{1\} & \text{if } \pi_i > \pi^*, \\ [0, 1] & \text{if } \pi_i = \pi^*, \\ \{0\} & \text{if } \pi_i < \pi^* \end{cases} \tag{3.2}$$

I call the employer "optimistic" about group i when $\pi_i \geq \pi^*$, and "pessimistic" when $\pi_i < \pi^*$. I call the employer "liberal" toward group i if $\alpha_i = 1$, and "conservative" if $\alpha_i = 0$. I say the employer "discriminates" against Bs in a given equilibrium if he is conservative toward Bs while being liberal toward Ws.

To see how equilibria with discrimination can occur in this model, we must consider the workers' behavior. A worker invests only if she expects the gain to exceed the cost. Since in any equilibrium passing workers always gain assignment to task one and failing workers never do, the key issue for workers contemplating whether or not to invest is what happens if the test outcome is unclear. It is easy to see that $I^* (i, c) = 1$ in equilibrium if $c < c_i^*$, and I^* $(i, c) = 0$ if $c > c_i^*$ for $c_i^* \equiv \omega \cdot [\alpha_i(1 - p_0) + (1 - \alpha_i)(1 - p_1)]$. So $\pi_i = \int_0^1 I^* (i, c)dc = c_i^*$ in any equilibrium. Define the workers' best response function, $\phi_\varphi (\alpha)$, as follows:

$$\pi_i = \phi_\omega(\alpha_i) \equiv \omega \cdot [\alpha_i(1 - p_0) + (1 - \alpha_i)(1 - p_1)] \qquad (3.3)$$

If a group of workers expect liberal treatment from the employer then $\alpha_i = 1$, and the fraction $\pi_l \equiv \omega(1 - p_0)$ invest. If a group of workers anticipates conservative treatment then $\alpha_i = 0$, and the fraction $\pi_c \equiv \omega(1 - p_1)$ invest. Assumption 3 implies that $0 < \pi_c < \pi_l < 1$. Our earlier analysis shows that in any equilibrium the following relationship obtains:

$$\alpha_i \in \phi_e(\phi_\omega(\alpha_i)), \ i \in \{B,W\} \qquad (3.4)$$

This equation states that the employer's behavior is optimal toward each group of workers, given their respective mean investment rates, and at the same time workers' investment decisions are optimal, given the employer's behavior toward their group when the test outcome is unclear. We adopt the following assumption:

$$\textit{Assumption 4:} \quad \frac{1}{\omega(1 - p_0)} < 1 + \frac{rp_1}{p_0} < \frac{1}{\omega(1 - p_1)}$$

Proposition 4: Given assumption 3, a discriminatory equilibrium exists in which the employer is optimistic about and liberal toward Ws, who invest at rate π_l, while being pessimistic about and conservative toward Bs, who invest at rate π_c, if (and, with weak inequalities, only if) assumption 4 holds.

Sketch of Proof: Figure 11.2 graphs the best response relations $\phi_e (\pi)$ and $\phi_\omega (\alpha)$ in the (α, π) unit square. Then, in view of equation (3.4), the result should be obvious. ∎

Assumption 4 is simply the requirement that $\pi_c < \pi^* < \pi_l$. This condition requires that r, the relative employer benefit of correctly assigning an investing worker as compared to correctly assigning a noninvesting worker, is neither too large nor too small. In a discriminatory equilibrium the employer, by treating the groups differently in the event of an unclear test outcome, creates unequal incentives for workers in the two groups to become skilled. Although the employer's differential treatment is justified by his (correct in equilibrium) belief that workers in the two groups have unequal mean investment rates, this investment disparity is itself due to his differential treatment. That is, in a discriminatory equilibrium the belief that Bs are on average less skillful that Ws is a self-fulfilling prophecy.

In a discriminatory equilibrium, when the employer is not acting in a "color-blind" fashion, it is natural for an anti-discrimination enforcement agent to try to correct this discrimination by forcing the employer to assign workers from each group to each task at the same rate. This enforcement official might proceed in one of two ways. Ideally, she would insist on color-

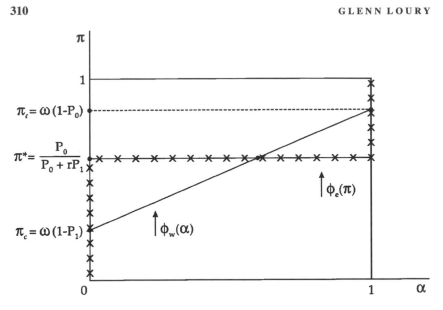

Figure 11.2. Proof that a discriminatory equilibrium exists under A4

blind behavior by forbidding the employer to treat Ws and Bs with unclear tests any differently. That is, the official would require $A(B, \theta) = A(W, \theta)$, $\forall \theta \in T$. This would be difficult to implement, however. Consider the informational demands of such a policy. The enforcement agent would have to observe all information upon which an employer might base his assignment (interviews, work history, etc.) to determine if Bs and Ws are really being treated the same. In most situations this is not possible.

As a second way of proceeding, the enforcement agent might take a more "results-oriented" rather than "process-oriented" approach. Here, the government monitors the rate at which workers in the respective groups are assigned to various positions, insisting on proportional representation. This quota-like policy, which I will refer to as "affirmative action," leads both the employer and the government to depart from purely color-blind practice. The government must monitor the racial composition of the employer's workforce in each task, while the employer, if she is to comply with the policy, must calibrate her hiring policy, given the workers' investment strategies, so as to anticipate achieving equal proportionate representation. I will now examine in the context of the model set out above whether this intervention eliminates the B/W difference in investment incentives that prevailed in the discriminatory equilibrium.

Suppose that we start in a discriminatory equilibrium in which $\pi_\omega = \pi_l$ and $\pi_b = \pi_c$. Let the anti-discrimination enforcement authorities enact a policy requiring that each group be assigned to each task at the same overall rate. Initially the employer is violating this policy. Indeed, if ρ_i is the rate group i workers are assigned to task one, then

$$\rho_i = \int_0^1 \{\Sigma_\theta \Pr[\theta]I^*(i,c)\} \cdot A^*(i,\theta)\}dc, \qquad (3.5)$$

so $\rho_\omega = \pi_1 + (1 - \pi_1)p_0 > \pi_l > \pi_c > \rho_b = \pi_c(1 - p_1)$ in the initial situation.

Therefore, in order to comply with the affirmative action mandate the employer must either assign more Bs or fewer Ws to task one. Since he is maximizing his profits in the initial equilibrium, both alternatives lower his net payoff. Which course is least undesirable to him, however, depends on the relative numbers of B and B workers in the population. In general the employer will try to minimize the number of instances where, in order to comply with the enforcement policy, he has to assign a worker of either group to a task that he believes will not be most profitable for him. If Bs are comparatively few, then by reassigning some Bs to task one instead of task zero he could meet the enforcement mandate with a relatively small number of unprofitable assignments. On the other hand, if Bs are numerous in comparison to Ws, then by reassigning some Ws to task zero instead of task one, he could meet the government's hiring requirement at least cost to himself.

Specifically, there exists a number $\lambda^* \in (0,1)$ such that when $\lambda > \lambda^*$ the employer always responds to anti-discrimination enforcement efforts by reassigning Bs from task zero to task one, and never by reassigning Ws from task one to task zero. To see this, consider reassigning either ΔB more blacks in task one, or alternatively ΔW more whites to task zero, where the object in each case is to reduce the difference in the proportions of black and white workers going into task one by the same amount. So $\frac{\Delta B}{1-\lambda} = \frac{\Delta W}{\lambda}$, or equivalently, $\Delta W - (\frac{\lambda}{1-\lambda}) \Delta B$. In the initial equilibrium the mean investment rate among Ws is $\pi_\omega = \pi_l$, so the employer expects to lose $\xi_1 x_1 - (1 - \xi_1)x_0$ on each W unclear test outcome who is reassigned, where $\xi_1 = \pi_l p_1/[\pi_l p_1 + (1 - \pi_l)p_0]$. On the other hand, if a B who *fails* the test is reassigned to task one from task zero the employer is sure to lose x_0. Hence it is less costly to the employer to accomplish a given increase in the relative representation of Bs in task one by reassigning B and not W workers if $\frac{\lambda}{1-\lambda} \cdot [\xi_1 x_1 - (1 - \xi_1)x_0]$, which obtains for λ sufficiently large, as long as $\pi_l > \pi^*$. This is formalized below:

Assumption 5: $\lambda > \lambda^* \equiv \left[1 + \left(\frac{p_0}{p_1}\right) \cdot \left(\frac{1 - \pi_l}{\pi_l}\right) \right] / [1 + r] \quad (3.6)$

An equilibrium under affirmative action is a pair of strategies $\langle I'(i, c), A'(i, \theta)\rangle$ such that workers are responding optimally to A', while the employer is responding optimally to I' subject to the constraint $\rho_\omega = \rho_b$. This constraint may be stated formally as:

$$\int_0^1 \{\Sigma_\theta \ \Pr[\theta|I'(B,c)] \cdot A'(B,\theta)\}dc =$$

$$\int_0^1 \{\Sigma_\theta \ \Pr[\theta|I'(W,c)] \cdot A'(W,\theta)\}dc \qquad (3.7)$$

Starting from the initial discriminatory equilibrium $\langle I^*, A^* \rangle$, the employer would not expect to meet the enforcement agent's equal representation mandate by simply following a color-blind policy, since the initial mean investment rate is smaller among Bs than Ws. Moreover, under assumption 5, since the employer does not reassign any W workers, her best response, consistent with the anti-discrimination requirements, to the workers' strategy I^* must involve putting B workers who fail the test, and who the employer therefore knows are unqualified, into task one. When she does this I say that she "patronizes" B workers. Let β denote the probability that a B worker who fails the test is nevertheless assigned to task one. I call β the employer's "degree of patronization."

The degree of patronization necessary for the employer to assure equal group representation in task one depends on the mean rates of investment in the two groups. The investment rate among Ws is fixed at π_l, since no Ws are going to be reassigned. Let $\pi_b \leq \pi_l$ be given. Equal task one representation requires $\pi_b + (1 - \pi_b)[p_0 + \beta(1 - p_0)] = \pi_l + (1 - \pi_l)p_0$, or:

$$\beta = \frac{\pi_l - \pi_b}{1 - \pi_b} \qquad (3.8)$$

On the other hand, if the employer is liberal toward Bs with an unclear test outcome, and uses degree of patronization $\beta > 0$ with Bs failing the test, then the resulting incentive for Bs to invest will be less than the incentive for Ws to invest. Any positive degree of patronization lowers a B worker's expected gain from investing, compared to merely being treated liberally but not patronized, because a positive degree of patronization raises the chance for a noninvestor to get into task one without affecting the fact that an investor is certain to gain that assignment. Specifically, an investing B worker gains ω with probability one; a non-investing B gains ω with probability $p_0 + \beta(1 - p_0)$. So investment for a B worker is optimal only if $c \leq \omega(1 - p_0)(1 - \beta) = \pi_l(1 - \beta)$. We conclude that when B workers are making a best response to the employer's enforcement-influenced assignment strategy, they are investing at a mean rate π_b given below:

$$\pi_b = \pi_l(1 - \beta) \qquad (3.9)$$

Combining equations (3.8) and (3.9), we see that Bs' mean investment rate in any equilibrium under affirmative action satisfies:

$$\pi_b' = \frac{\pi_l(1 - \pi_l)}{1 - \pi_b'}, \quad and \quad \pi_b' \le \pi_l$$

$$(3.10)$$

Thus two equilibrium situations are possible under affirmative action: $\pi_b' = \pi_l$, and $\pi_b' = 1 - \pi_l$. The second situation occurs if and only if $\pi_l > \frac{1}{2}$. The first situation has an obvious interpretation. Should the employer come to believe that Bs are investing at rate π_l, the same as Ws, he would want to be liberal but not patronizing toward them, and would comply with the government's mandate by doing so. If Bs expect the degree of patronization to be zero, they, like Ws, would invest at rate π_l. When this equilibrium arises the employer's initial discriminatory beliefs have been eliminated by the use of the affirmative action enforcement tool. The government's insistence on equal representation for each group creates a situation in which the opportunities, and so the distributions of skills, for each group of workers are equalized. Having achieved this result, affirmative action policy can "wither away" because the employer's discriminatory beliefs, which justified (for him) the initial unequal treatment of Bs, have been dispelled.

A second situation has a rather less obvious, but no less important, interpretation: the employer continues to think Bs invest at a lower mean rate than Ws. She therefore persists in patronizing them to some degree. But because Bs when patronized have a lower incentive to invest than Ws, the employer's belief that patronization is needed becomes a self-fulfilling prophecy. In this instance, rather than creating equality of opportunity, the enforcement policy leads to a situation in which, in order to meet the equal representation requirement, the employer discriminates in favor of unskilled Bs. Because noninvesting Bs have superior opportunities, the return to acquiring a skill is lower for Bs than Ws, and relatively fewer Bs invest. So the employer has to continually favor B workers in order to comply with the government's mandate. In this equilibrium affirmative action, far from "withering away," sets in motion a sequence of events that guarantee that it may have to maintain indefinitely.[1] The incentives for the employer, and hence for B and W workers, are altered by the government's use of a color-conscious enforcement strategy in such a way that a group difference in workers' acquisition of skills is sustained.[2] This is precisely the unintended negative consequence of racial preferences to which I alluded in the introduction.

[1] This conclusion is true only if the mean investment rate among Bs in this second equilibrium is low enough that the employer would want to be conservative toward them were he not constrained to meet the government's mandate, that is, if $1 - \pi_l < \pi^*$.

[2] The Bs' skill acquisition rate in this equilibrium ($\pi_b' = 1 - \pi_l$) could even turn out to be smaller than in the initial discriminatory equilibrium (π_c). Thus $1 - \pi_l < \pi_c$ if $\pi_l + \pi_c > 1$, or equivalently, if $\omega (2 - p_0 - p_1) > 1$. Hence if the worker's value of getting task one is big enough, and/or the test is sufficiently accurate, then this extreme illustration of the "law of unintended consequences" will, in fact, obtain in this model.

It is therefore of some interest to determine which of these two equilibria under affirmative action will actually obtain. At the initial discriminatory equilibrium the employer thinks she needs some patronization, but her use of it alters Bs' investment incentives. As B workers change their behavior, the degree of patronization the employer believes to be necessary also changes. Imagine an adjustment process, similar to that employed in the study of the previous model in this chapter, in which the employer and B workers alter their behavior over a sequence of stages, each party reacting to the behavior observed from the other at the previous stage of adjustment. It is plausible to postulate that the equilibrium reached under affirmative action is the one that eventually emerges from this iterative process of adjustment.

Proposition 5: If $\pi_l > \frac{1}{2}$, and if assumptions 3–5 hold, then the adjustment process described above converges monotonically to an equilibrium under affirmative action in which the degree of patronization is positive.

Proof: Let π_b^t be the mean investment rate among Bs at stage t of this adjustment process, $t = 1, 2, \ldots$ At stage one $\pi_b^1 = \pi_c < \pi_l$. To comply with the affirmative action mandate the employer adopts that degree of patronization β^t which, given π_b^t, satisfies equation (3.8): $\beta^t = \frac{\pi_l - \pi_b^t}{1 - \pi_b^t}$. Given degree of patronization β^t, the mean investment rate of Bs at stage $t + 1$, using equation (3.9), is $\pi_b^{t+1} = \pi_l(1 - \beta^t)$. Combining these results leads to the difference equation:

$$\beta^{t+1} = \frac{\beta^t}{\left(\frac{1 - \pi_l}{\pi_l}\right) + \beta^t}, \quad \beta^1 = \frac{\pi_l - \pi_c}{1 - \pi_c} \tag{3.11}$$

It is straightforward to verify the following: If $\pi_l \leq \frac{1}{2}$, then $\{\beta^t\} \to 0$ and $\{\pi_b^t\} \to \pi_l$ as $t \to \infty$. If $\pi_l > \frac{1}{2}$, then $\{\beta^t\} \to 1 - \left(\frac{1 - \pi_l}{\pi_l}\right) > 0$, and $\{\pi_b^t\} \to 1 - \pi_l$ as $t \to \infty$. ∎

Another way of saying this is that *the undesirable outcome obtains under affirmative action if, when facing a liberal employer, the average worker would strictly prefer to invest in the skill needed for task one.* The average worker will want to invest when facing a liberal employer only if the expected return from doing so exceeds his investment cost. This expected return is greater the greater the gain to a worker from being assigned to task one, and the lower the probability that a noninvestor goes undetected by the test. Thus, the higher the value of assignment to task one, relative to the average worker's investment cost, and the more powerful the test for identifying noninvestors, the more likely that a patronizing equilibrium will arise under affirmative action. The patronizing outcome is also more likely when the disadvantaged group is a relatively small fraction of the total population.[3]

---

[3] Coate and Loury (1993) develop a more general model along these lines. They provide sufficient conditions for a patronizing equilibrium to exist.

Conclusions

The point of this exercise has been to illustrate, with the aid of formal economic reasoning, that the concerns expressed by some critics of quota-like anti-discrimination enforcement policies should be taken seriously. *My main result in these two simple models of worker-employer interaction is that, even when minority and majority groups have equal abilities on average, requiring equal representation of their members in high-level positions may distort incentives so as to produce an unintended consequence. Specifically, minorities may underinvest in the skills needed to perform adequately in such positions, relative to the investment rate of majority workers. That is, policies intended to assure equality of achievement may end up producing inequality of skills.*

The analysis suggests two general conclusions. First, the asymmetry of information between employers and government concerning the qualifications of workers who may or may not be subject to discrimination constitutes a serious obstacle to effective anti-discrimination policies. In both the taste discrimination and the statistical discrimination models, it is the inability of the enforcement agent to prescribe detailed procedural employment methodologies that forces reliance upon quota-like techniques. As is clear from the results of this chapter, these techniques can backfire.

A second implication is that gradualism is preferable to radical intervention when attempting to correct for group disparities thought to be the result of discrimination. When discrimination does occur, it discourages skill acquisition. A radical effort to enforce equality of representation can thus create bottlenecks, since there may actually be a shortage of qualified minority workers. Intervention that aims for increased, though less than fully proportional, minority representation allows time for the pool of qualified minority workers to expand in response to the improved opportunities, after which the enforcement goal can be made more ambitious. In this way, the chance of producing unintended negative consequences can be minimized.

This chapter is not meant to be an attack on the practice of preferential treatment for minority workers. Whatever the political and legal merits of such policies, I have shown that there are circumstances, involving either invidious discrimination or rational but self-fulfilling employer stereotypes, when the use of quota-like policies can have desirable results. However, this is not necessarily the case. It is important therefore that we try to understand, in the many concrete circumstances in which preferences are now employed, just when the risks of generating negative unintended consequences of the sort I identify here are worth taking. Too often both advocates and critics are content to base their arguments entirely on first principles, without reference to the direct or indirect consequences of this contentious policy. Further study will be required to identify practically significant cases that exemplify the effects uncovered here.

References

Arrow, Kenneth. 1973. "The Theory of Discrimination." In *Discrimination in Labor Markets*, ed. Orley Ashenfelter and Albert Rees, pp. 3–33. Princeton, NJ: Princeton University Press.

Becker, Gary. 1957. *The Economics of Discrimination*. Chicago: University of Chicago Press.

Coate, Stephen, and Glenn Loury. 1993. "Will Affirmative Action Policies Eliminate Negative Stereotypes?" *American Economic Review* 83, no. 5 (December): 1220–1240.

Epstein, Richard. 1992. *Forbidden Grounds: The Case against Employment Discrimination Laws*. Cambridge, MA: Harvard University Press.

Twelve

Meritocracy, Redistribution, and the Size of the Pie*

ROLAND BÉNABOU

THIS CHAPTER examines how ambiguous notions such as "meritocracy," "equality of opportunity," and "equality of outcomes" can be given a formal content and related to more standard economic concepts such as social mobility, income inequality, and efficiency. It then proceeds to examine how redistributive policies affect each of these criteria of social justice and economic performance. This is done using a dynamic, optimizing model of earnings determination that incorporates ability, effort, family background, educational bequests, and redistributive policies. Because of endogenous labor supply and missing credit markets, redistribution has both adverse and beneficial effects on investment and output.

Writers on distributive justice have put forward very different views of what an individual "deserves" or is "entitled to." At one end is Rawls (1971), who sees no moral justification for differences in welfare among individuals. Innate talent and socioeconomic background are equally arbitrary forms of luck, which in themselves merit no reward. Some inequality is necessary to provide incentives for people to produce, but it should be kept to the minimum level consistent with maximizing the welfare of the most disadvantaged individual. At the other end are libertarians such as Nozick (1974), who view individuals as entitled to the entire endowment with which they came into the world, comprising both their own qualities and whatever was inherited from parents or other altruistic donors.[1] Common perceptions of fairness fall between these two extremes, with the line often drawn between innate qualities of the individual, which are mostly seen as true merits, and inherited economic and social advantages, which are not. For instance, Loury (1981) states that "it is widely held that differences in ability provide

* Prepared for the conference on "Meritocracy and Inequality" organized by the MacArthur Foundation at the University of Wisconsin–Madison. I am grateful to J. P. Benoit, Jason Cummins, Jordi Gali, and especially Efe Ok for useful suggestions and references. Financial support from the National Science Foundation (SBR-9601319) and the C. V. Starr Center is gratefully acknowledged.

[1] With the proviso that the capital thus transmitted should not have been acquired unjustly in the past, through expropriation, exploitation, or the like. But while Nozick briefly concedes that a principle of "just redress" is necessary, he remains remarkably silent on what it should be.

ethical grounds for differences in rewards," and then proceeds to define measures of meritocracy based on the correlation between talent and income. Roemer (1995) goes further and proposes that resources be redistributed so as to equalize utility among people whose performance deviates to a similar extent from the predicted median for individuals with whom they share a set of basic characteristics, observed early in life.

Although surely arbitrary, this distinction between background and ability or talent seems to underlie two recurrent themes in discussions of social justice: *equality of opportunity* which is seen as desirable, and *equality of outcomes,* which is not. I begin this chapter by discussing potential measures of each, based on the extent to which individual ability is rewarded both relative to background and in absolute terms. Even in the context of a simple abstract model, it is clear that redistributive policies (or exogenous technological change) will generally affect these two notions in opposite ways, so they cannot be examined separately. I therefore discuss possible indexes of meritocracy that take the form of "meritocratic utility functions" defined over these two "goods."

To see whether these concepts are useful, I then examine whether they are good indicators of the effects of *redistribution* on social mobility, income inequality, and growth. These effects, which constitute the chapter's second main focus, are studied in the context of a dynamic optimizing model where heterogeneous families accumulate human capital. Because the idea of meritocracy is often associated with that of maximizing the size of the economic "pie"—albeit at some cost in terms of insurance or social preference for equality—I focus on the path of total output as the main indicator (or component) of efficiency. The exposition is centered on the case of progressive income taxation, but I also discuss the similar effects of progressive education finance (equalization of school inputs). Equality of opportunity is shown to be closely related to social mobility. Perhaps more surprisingly, meritocratic utility functions, introduced to represent competing notions of distributive justice, turn out to reflect fairly accurately the main channels through which redistribution affects growth. Equality of outcomes dulls individuals' incentives to provide the effort required to translate ability into earnings, and this contributes to lower output. Enforcing greater equality of opportunities, on the other hand, yields efficiency gains when there are imperfections in the markets for loans and insurance. For instance, reallocating educational funds toward poorer, liquidity-constrained families who have a higher return on human capital investment tends to raise the economy's growth rate (e.g., Loury 1981, Galor and Zeira 1993, Bénabou 1996b). It also provides valuable insurance against idiosyncratic shocks (e.g., Varian 1980, Persson 1983). Most of these benefits are shown to occur in future periods, through a gradual reduction in inequality and the inefficiency of human capital investment that it implies. In contrast, the costs are all contemporaneous. Thus society may be faced with an intertemporal trade-off: maximizing long-run growth in every period does not result in maximizing long-run output.

As explained above, the analysis generally validates the common intuition that meritocracy, appropriately defined, is desirable not only on grounds of fairness but also on grounds of efficiency. Indeed, long-run output takes a form very similar to the meritocratic utility function posited in the first part of the chapter. There are differences, however, arising in particular from the complementarity between the inputs into human capital accumulation that are being redistributed (money and the school resources it buys) and those that are not (neighborhood effects, social capital) or even cannot be redistributed (parental characteristics). Meritocracy calls for greater redistribution in the presence of these complementarities, whereas efficiency pushes the other way, unless some of these nonpurchased inputs can be simultaneously redistributed. I extend the model to show how residential stratification and human capital heritability affect the desirability of redistribution (through tax or education policy) from either point of view.

1. Measures of Meritocracy

1.1 Equality of Opportunity versus Equality of Outcomes

A recurrent theme in discussions of meritocracy is *equality of opportunity*, which means that family origins should not constitute a significant advantage or handicap in pursuing economic success. One intuitive measure of this is the fraction of variance in income that is attributable to an individual's own qualities, or lack thereof, rather than to his or her background. Starting with the simplest case, suppose that a person's (lifetime) income can be written as

$$y = \bar{y} + \lambda a + \mu b, \tag{1}$$

where b represents social background (e.g., family resources) and a some intrinsic quality of the individual (e.g., cognitive ability), which for now is taken to be independent of b. Both are normalized to have mean zero, so $\bar{y} = E[y]$. One can then define meritocracy in opportunities as:

$$M^{opp} \equiv \frac{Var[\lambda a]}{Var[y]} = \frac{\lambda^2 \sigma_a}{\lambda^2 \sigma_a + \mu^2 \sigma_d^2} \tag{2}$$

This is also the squared correlation between income and ability, which Loury (1981) proposed as a definition of "weak meritocracy." It is also the main definition of equality of opportunity discussed in Atkinson (1980). It increases as $\mu \sigma_b$ is reduced, say by equalizing school expenditures or neighborhood compositions, or as $\lambda \sigma_a$ rises, say because technological progress increases the return to ability. In the more realistic case where a and b are correlated one must decide what part of their covariance represents qualities it is "meritocratic" to reward, as opposed to inequitable disparities in opportunity. For instance, it is generally viewed as unmeritocratic that children's educational opportunities should be constrained by parental wealth; inherited talent or beauty, on the other hand, seem somehow less objectionable. But this is a thin line to draw, and one that can shift rapidly with technology. Family resources already determine, through the quality of pre- and postnatal care, some permanent characteristics of children's health and physical appearance that directly affect their productive abilities. With the continued progress of genetic engineering, disparities in wealth will increasingly translate into different abilities to ensure that children are born with desirable traits (or at least free of undesirable ones), whether physical, cognitive, or behavioral.

It seems hard to avoid carrying this logic to its natural conclusion, namely, that inherited advantages or disadvantages of any kind make opportunities unequal. In that case one simply replaces a by $a' = a - E[a|b]$ in the computation of M^{opp}.[2] Thus if intelligence, initiative, or beauty is partly inherited and contributes to earnings, its predicted component is counted as part of b. Only innovations, including market luck, are part of the individual's intrinsic "merit." This information-based definition may seem unusual, but I do not see that ethical considerations provide a convincing rationale for drawing the line elsewhere. The distinction commonly made between traits whose transmission is mediated by socioeconomic resources and those inherited through other channels seems to reflect instead a practical concern about what can or cannot be redistributed across families. Fortunately, the issues, results, and policy trade-offs to be discussed in the remainder of this chapter are not critically predicated on a specific definition.

For instance, although a general distinction between background and intrinsic qualities captures an important component of what most people mean by "meritocracy," the picture is incomplete. What is missing is the converse notion that imposing *equality of outcomes* is unmeritocratic, as the following example will make clear. Let income still be determined by equation (1), but suppose now that the government taxes it at the rate τ and redistributes it in an egalitarian manner. Posttax income is therefore:

$$\hat{y} \equiv (1 - \tau)y + \tau\bar{y} = \bar{y} + \lambda(1 - \tau)a + \mu(1 - \tau)b. \qquad (3)$$

This equalization could also take the form of pay scales or wage norms within the firm, as in Scandinavian countries, or arise through technological

---

[2] More generally, if ability and background are multidimensional vectors A and B, one simply replaces λa by $y - E[y|B]$ in equation (2). Thus income is decomposed into the part that is predictable on the basis of family and social characteristics and that which is not.

complementarity between the labor inputs of workers with different levels of human capital (defined as y). What do such redistributions imply for meritocracy? According to any informational criterion such as equation (2), *nothing!* Yet one would usually think that such a society is less meritocratic the higher its τ. This is most clearly the case when $\mu = 0$, so that income (or marginal product) reflects only a person's own ability or talent; nonetheless rewards are equalized among individuals, perhaps even to the point where $\tau = 1$. Similarly, while the most salient feature of Roemer-type (1995) redistributive schemes is that people are rewarded only for the "distance traveled" from the median of their peer group, equal attention needs to be paid to the steepness or flatness of this reward schedule for "personal responsibility."

These considerations argue for a two-dimensional measure of meritocracy, capturing both:

1. *Equality of opportunities:* the extent to which talent, rather than background, is a determinant of income or rewards. This is measured by M^{opp} defined in equation (2).

2. *Inequality of outcomes,* with respect to ability: the extent to which talent (or market luck) is rewarded in absolute terms.[3] This is measured by $M^{out} \equiv \lambda(1 - \tau)$.

This makes clear that there can be no single, value-free definition of meritocracy, but only preference orderings over values of (M^{opp}, M^{out}). The relative importance placed on each of these desirable attributes can then be summarized through a *meritocracy utility function:*

$$M = W(M^{opp}, M^{out}) \qquad (4)$$

with the standard properties: W is increasing in both arguments, quasiconcave, and $W_{12} > 0$, as illustrated in figure 12.1. I shall also impose the normalization that $W = 0$ when either M^{opp} or M^{out} is zero. These conditions correspond to the following limiting cases:

a. *"Aristocracy":* when $M^{opp} \to 0$, all income-generating characteristics are passed down from parents to children. Whether they consist of education expenditures, social connections, family human capital or even inherited intelligence, as some have recently argued, is irrelevant. An individual has no opportunity to advance on his own "merits."

b. *"Mediocracy":* when $M^{out} \to 0$, talent is not rewarded, that is, irrelevant to the determination of income. Note from the above tax example that when $M^{out} \to 0$ the same need not be true of M^{opp} because μ may be changing together with λ.

---

[3] Rewards to effort (which is endogenously chosen, given ability and background) are discussed in section 1.2.

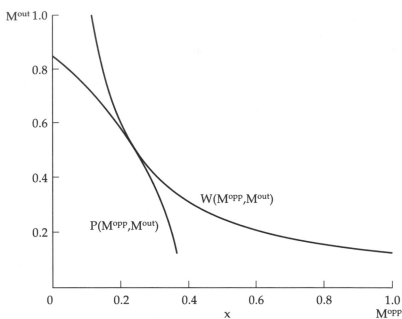

Figure 12.1. Meritocratic Utility Function and Meritocracy Possibility Frontier

This elementary model is static. Once *intergenerational dynamics* are brought into the picture, however, it becomes apparent that most policies will cause M^{opp} and M^{out} to move in opposite directions. Summarily put, parents' outcomes determine children's opportunities, and vice versa. For instance, redistributing each generation's income at the rate τ clearly reduces M^{out}, but if parental resources affect educational opportunities ($b = \theta\hat{y} + (1 - \theta)c$, where c captures nonpecuniary background variables) it reduces σ_b^2 and therefore raises M^{opp}. Similarly, redistributing educational funds or subsidizing schooling for the poor increases M^{opp} but it also lowers the utility or real income of parents, that is, reduces M^{out} once outcomes are appropriately measured.[4] Indeed, the quality of the schools and neighborhoods where their child is educated is an integral part of parents' reward, and in particular of their reward for ability. These observations suggest that policy outcomes are constrained to lie on a *meritocracy possibility frontier* $P(M^{opp}, M^{out})$, subject to which one would like to maximize the meritocratic welfare function $W(M^{opp}, M^{out})$, as illustrated in figure 12.1.

To assess whether these notions are really meaningful, one needs a more proper economic model of intergenerational dynamics and redistribution. I

---

[4] These arguments will be made more formal in section 3 using the dynamic model developed in section 2.

develop such a model in section 2 and show in section 3 that notions like $W(M^{opp}, M^{out})$ and $P(M^{opp}, M^{out})$ indeed provide useful (albeit imperfect) intuitions both on *social mobility* and on the *efficiency costs and benefits* of redistribution. But first I turn to the issue of effort decisions.

1.2 Rewards to Effort

Is a society that rewards effort necessarily more meritocratic? A common view of distributive justice indeed holds that individuals should be held responsible for the actions that are under their control but not for their innate attributes, which are not (e.g., Roemer 1995). However, different propensities to work must ultimately reflect different (perceived) returns to effort, hence differences in either background or ability. Formally, let income net of effort costs be determined by:

$$\max_e\{\bar{y} + \lambda a + \mu b + ve - e^2/2(\gamma a + \delta b)\}. \tag{1'}$$

Then:

$$M^{out} = \lambda + \gamma v^2,$$

$$M^{opp} = \frac{(\lambda + \gamma v^2)^2 \sigma_a^2}{(\lambda + \gamma v^2)^2 \sigma_a^2 + (\mu + \delta v^2)^2 \sigma_b^2}.$$

While a higher return to effort v always improves M^{out}, its effect on M^{opp} depends on the behavior of $(\lambda + \gamma v^2)/(\mu + \delta v^2)$. Equality of opportunity increases or decreases depending on $\gamma/\delta \gtrless \mu/\lambda$, that is, on the relative *ability-intensity* of effort, compared to that of other determinants of income. To make things concrete, suppose that the cost or perceived cost of graduating from high school is much higher in a community with poor role models and peers. To the extent that the sorting of families into towns and neighborhoods reflects differences in parents' wealth, education, or even tastes, the differences in studying effort (attendance, homework, etc.) observed between the children of poor and better-off communities will not reflect differences in their individual merits.

2. Inequality, Redistribution, and Growth

I now turn to a truly dynamic, optimizing model of earnings determination, which embodies the effects of luck (genetic or other), effort, family background, educational bequests, and redistributive policies. It will allow me to relate the dual notions of meritocracy defined above to more standard economic variables such as social mobility, income inequality, or productive efficiency, and to clearly demonstrate the costs and benefits of redistribution. The model is more fully developed in Bénabou (1996c, 1997) and the reader is referred to these papers for proofs, which will be omitted here. The second paper also provides a quantitative analysis through numerical simulations.

2.1 The Model

A continuum $i \in [0,1]$ of infinite-lived agents or dynasties maximizes the intertemporal utility

$$U_0^i = E \left[\sum_{t=0}^{\infty} \rho^t (\ln c_t^i - \delta(l_t^i)^\eta) \right] \tag{5}$$

subject to:

$$c_t^i + e_t^i = \hat{y}_t^i \tag{6}$$

$$y_t^i = (h_t^i)^\lambda (l_t^i)^\mu \tag{7}$$

$$h_{t+1}^i = \kappa \xi_{t+1}^i (h_t^i)^\alpha (e_t^i)^\beta. \tag{8}$$

In period or generation t, agent i produces output y_t^i using his or her human capital h_t^i and labor input l_t^i. Taxes and transfers, specified below, then transform this gross income into *net* income, denoted $\hat{y}_t^i$. Both consumption c_t^i and education expenditures e_t^i are financed out of these current resources, reflecting agents' inability to borrow for human-capital investment. Insurance markets are also incomplete, so that the random shocks ξ_t^i cannot be diversified away. The simplest interpretation of ξ_t^i is as the child's innate ability, as in Loury (1981), but it can also stand for other forms of luck. This shock is assumed to be i.i.d., without much loss of generality since children already inherit some of their parents' productive potential through the term $(h_t^i)^\alpha$. This nonpecuniary effect of family background on the young's human capital can thus be viewed as a convenient stand-in for genetic inheritance.[5] More generally, if the home environment provides important inputs that affect children's ability to learn in school, α is large. Social-capital spillovers at the level of the school, the neighborhood, or the community have the same effect when these "clubs" are highly segregated by income and occu-

---

[5] Allowing for first-order serial correlation in ξ_t^i involves additional algebra but is not very difficult. The main features of this extended model are qualitatively similar to those of the original one with a higher α. For instance, there is greater intergenerational persistence of income, and the growth benefits of redistribution arising from capital market imperfections are attenuated due to the complementarity between education expenditures and the non-redistributed input (talent, parental human capital).

pation; see section 4.2. I shall assume $\xi_t^i \sim \mathcal{N}(-s^2/2, s^2)$, so that $E[\xi] = 1$, and $\ln h_0^i \sim \mathcal{N}(m_0, \Delta_0^2)$. I also restrict $\eta \geq 1 > \rho$ and $\alpha + \beta\lambda < 1$.

Let us now turn to public policy. Income redistribution is almost always modeled as a combination of linear taxes and lump-sum transfers, making posttax income an arithmetic average of an individual's own income and the aggregate level. In reality, most countries have *progressive* taxes and transfers; moreover, the fairness and efficiency implications of increasing marginal rates are important issues in discussions of meritocracy. I shall therefore use here the same progressive scheme as in Bénabou (1996c, 1997), which makes disposable income a geometric average of an individual's own resources and some economywide aggregate:

$$\hat{y}_t^i = (y_t^i)^{1-\tau t}\,(\tilde{y}_t)^{\tau t}, \tag{9}$$

where $\tilde{y}_t$ is defined by the balanced-budget constraint:

$$\int_0^1 (y_t^i)^{1-\tau t}\,(\tilde{y}_t)^{\tau t}\,di = \int_0^1 y_t^i\,di \equiv y_t. \tag{10}$$

Note that $\tilde{y}_t$ is the break-even point where pre- and posttax income coincide, and that $\tilde{y}_t > y_t$ when $\tau_t > 0$, in contrast to the usual linear case. Indeed, the elasticity τ_t measures the degree of *progressivity* of the fiscal scheme, or conversely its regressivity when it is negative.[6] As usual, tax rates $\tau_t > 1$ must be excluded because they are not incentive-compatible. Redistributive policies other than income taxation, such as education finance or residential integration, will be discussed in section 4.

2.2 Savings and Effort

Intuition suggests that the anticipation of future taxes $\{\tau_t\}_{t=1}^\infty$ will negatively affect parents' incentives to invest in their children's education. While this is correct, it can be shown that the policy described by equations (9)–(10) can be combined with an investment subsidy, financed by a proportional tax on consumption, to ensure that the savings rate never deviates from its optimal level, $\bar{s} \equiv \beta\lambda/(1 - \rho\alpha)$. Moreover, for any envisioned sequence $\{\tau_t\}_{t=0}^\infty$, this complementary scheme is Pareto-optimal: it will be unanimously supported by every family in every generation.[7] For brevity I shall directly assume here that agents save a constant fraction $\bar{s}$ of their post-tax income,

[6] Since writing Bénabou (1996c and 1998) and the first version of the present chapter, I have become aware of a couple of articles in the public finance literature that used a similar geometric scheme in a static context, most notably Persson (1983).

[7] The first-best savings rate $\bar{s}$ corresponds to agents' choice in the absence of all taxes or subsidies, as there are no externalities in this model. The political unanimity result is proved in

$$e_t^i = \mathcal{S}\, \hat{y}_t^i, \tag{11}$$

as in a Solow model. The only margin subject to distortion is therefore labor supply, and the dynamic optimization problem faced by an agent with human capital h is:

$$V_t(h) = \max_l \left\{ \ln[(1 - \mathcal{S})(h^\lambda l^\mu)^{1-\tau t}(\tilde{y}_t)^{\tau t}] - \delta l^\eta + \right.$$
$$\left. \rho E V_{t+1}[\kappa \xi h^\alpha(\mathcal{S}(h^\lambda l^\mu)^{(1-\tau_t)}(\tilde{y}_t)^{\tau t})^\beta] \right\}. \tag{12}$$

It can be solved under any tax profile $\{\tau_t\}_{t=0}^\infty$, but for simplicity I shall restrict attention from here on to time-invariant policies, $\tau_t \equiv \tau$. One can then show the following result.

Proposition 1: *Let the rate of fiscal progressivity be $\tau_t = \tau$ for all t. Agents then choose in every period a common, constant labor supply:*

$$l = \left(\frac{(\mu/\delta\eta)(1 - \tau)(1 - \rho\alpha)}{1 - \rho(\alpha + \beta\lambda(1 - \tau))} \right)^{1/\eta}. \tag{13}$$

A more progressive tax system reduces the return to effort because it impounds each generation's current consumption (numerator) as well as its ability to pass on human capital to its offspring (denominator). Because of the second effect, the distortion is greater the more forward-looking agents are, and the more lasting human capital is : $-l'(\tau)$ increases with ρ and α. Finally, note that it would be straightforward to allow an individual's effort to vary with his ability ξ_t^i or background h_t^i, as in section 1.2. Replacing in equation (5) the cost of effort δ by $\delta\, (\xi_t^i)^{-\nu}\, (h_t^i)^{-\nu'}$ leaves the model's structure unchanged, up to a renormalization of the parameters.

2.3 Individual and Aggregate Dynamics

Taking logs in equations (7)–(8), the accumulation of human capital becomes:

$$\ln h_{t+1}^i = \ln \xi_{t+1}^i + \ln \kappa + \beta\ln\mathcal{S} + \beta\mu(1 - \tau)$$
$$\ln l + (\alpha + \beta\lambda(1 - \tau))\ln h_t^i + \beta\tau \ln \tilde{y}_t. \tag{14}$$

It is easy to see that human wealth and income always remain *log-normally distributed* across families. Indeed, suppose that $\ln h_t^i \sim \mathcal{N}(m_t, \Delta_t^2)$; the production function (7) then implies

$$\ln y_t^i \sim \mathcal{N}(\lambda m_t + \mu\ln l, (\lambda\Delta_t)^2), \tag{15}$$

Bénabou (1996c), and under more general preferences in Bénabou (1998). The latter paper also derives the equilibrium path of savings rates when corrective consumption taxes and investment subsidies are not available.

and the budget constraint (10) allows us to compute the break-even point of the tax-and-transfer scheme:

$$\ln \bar{y}_t = \ln y_t + (1 - \tau)(\lambda\Delta_t)^2/2 =$$
$$\lambda m_t + \mu\ln l + (2 - \tau)(\lambda\Delta_t)^2/2. \tag{16}$$

Substituting into equation (14) yields next period's distribution, $\ln h^i_{t+1}$ $\sim \mathcal{N}(m_{t+1}, \Delta^2_{t+1})$, as a function of the current one.

Proposition 2: *The cross-sectional distribution of human capital evolves according to the linear difference equations:*

$$m_{t+1} = \ln \hat{\kappa} + \beta\mu\ln l + (\alpha + \beta\lambda)m_t + \beta\tau(2 - \tau)(\lambda\Delta_t)^2/2$$
$$\Delta^2_{t+1} = (\alpha + \beta\lambda(1 - \tau))^2 \Delta^2_t + s^2$$

where $\ln \hat{\kappa} \equiv \ln\kappa - s^2/2 + \beta\ln\hat{s}$ *is a constant. The distribution of income is then given by equation (15).*

Two important terms appear in these expressions. The first is $\alpha + \beta\lambda(1 - \tau)$, which measures the degree of persistence of inequalities in human capital and income, or conversely the lack of *social mobility*. I will show in section 3 that it is directly related to the index of "equality of opportunity," M^{opp}. The other critical term is $\beta\tau(2 - \tau)(\lambda\Delta_t)^2/2$ $= \beta(1 - (1 - \tau)^2)(\lambda\Delta_t)^2/2$, which captures the gains in *aggregate welfare* achieved by redistributing income at the rate τ in period t—keeping labor supply constant. These arise primarily from two sources:

(a) redistribution provides insurance against the idiosyncratic shock ξ^i_{t+1};
(b) it tends to raise total output $y_{t+1} \equiv E[y^i_{t+1}]$, through a reallocation of capital from low to high marginal product investments.

Because this chapter's main concern is with the links between meritocracy, redistribution, and the size of the economic "pie," I shall from here on focus only on the second of these effects.[8] Proposition 2 easily leads to the following result, where $\ln\tilde{\kappa} \equiv \lambda(\ln\kappa + \beta\ln\hat{s}) - \lambda(1 - \lambda)s^2/2$ is a constant.

Proposition 3: *Income inequality reduces the growth rate of per-capita income,*

$$\ln y_{t+1} - \ln y_t = \ln \tilde{\kappa} + \mu(1 - \alpha)\ln l(\tau) -$$
$$(1 - \alpha - \beta\lambda)\ln y_t - \mathfrak{L}(\tau)(\lambda\Delta_t)^2/2, \tag{17}$$

to an extent measured by

$$\mathfrak{L}(\tau) \equiv \alpha + \beta\lambda(1 - \tau)^2 - (\alpha + \beta\lambda(1 - \tau))^2. \tag{18}$$

---

[8] It is not difficult, however, to compute from equation (14) and proposition 2 a family's expected intertemporal welfare, which embodies the insurance effect. On the insurance value of redistributive taxation (in a static model) see also Varian (1980) and Persson (1983).

This loss factor is positive for all τ and minimized at $\bar{\tau} \equiv 1 - \alpha/(1 - \beta\lambda)$.

These results have simple interpretations. The first three terms in equation (17) give the growth rate of a *representative agent* economy, where everyone has the same level of human capital. Convergence to the steady-state $\ln y_\infty$ occurs at the rate $(1 - \alpha - \beta\lambda)$. As usual, continual growth could be sustained by incorporating spillovers to preserve constant returns. The last term shows that *inequality* constitutes a *drag on growth*, in line with the empirical findings of Alesina and Rodrik (1994), Persson and Tabellini (1994), and Perotti (1996), among others. The reason is that credit market imperfections result in a misallocation of education resources: given that $\alpha + \lambda\beta < 1$, families with low human capital have a higher return than wealthier ones, but are constrained to lower levels of investment by their inability to borrow. This differential marginal productivity of education expenditures reflects the presence of decreasing returns in educational investment ($\lambda\beta < 1$), which are only partially mitigated by the positive impact of family background ($(h_t^i)^\alpha$ in equation (8)).[9] The role of decreasing returns can be made more apparent by rewriting:

$$\mathfrak{L}(\tau) \equiv \alpha + \beta\lambda(1 - \tau) - (\alpha + \beta\lambda(1 - \tau))^2 - \beta\lambda(1 - \tau - (1 - \tau)^2).$$

Under a tax rate τ, y_{t+1}^i is proportional to $(y_t^i)^{\alpha + \beta\lambda(1 - \tau)} (\tilde{y}_t)^{\beta\lambda\tau}$, and the difference of the first two terms in $\mathfrak{L}(\tau)$ directly measures the *concavity* of this accumulation technology. The last term embodies the extent to which $\tilde{y}_t > y_t$, which in turn is due to the concavity (progressivity) of the fiscal scheme $\hat{y}_{t+1}^i = (y_t^i)^{1 - \tau} \tilde{y}_t$ with respect to y_t^i.

The role of credit market imperfections in generating a dependence of aggregate growth on the distribution of income and wealth has been explored in a number of papers such as Loury (1981), Galor and Zeira (1993), Banerjee and Newman (1993), Perotti (1993), Saint-Paul and Verdier (1993), Bénabou (1996b, 1996c), Aghion and Bolton (1997), or Piketty (1997). The potential for growth-increasing redistributions is a general feature of these models (most of which abstract from labor supply), although in some of them the presence of a fixed cost in the investment technology implies that regressive policies may be called for at the early stages of development. Calibrated simulations on U.S. data suggest that the long-run gains from

---

[9] This complementarity between background and purchased inputs explains why the tax rate $\bar{\tau}$ that minimizes the growth losses from inequality $\mathfrak{L}(\tau)$ decreases with α. In its absence ($\alpha = 0$), and with fixed labor supply ($l'(\tau) = 0$), the growth-maximizing tax rate would be $\tau = 1$; such is for instance the case in Loury (1981) or Piketty (1997). One could easily incorporate into the model additional features that make inequality either more costly or more desirable: complementarity or substitutability in the production of goods and human capital, costs of crime, and the like. These additional components of L are studied in Bénabou (1996b) and to some extent in section 4.2, but for now I intentionally focus on a "benchmark" case with no externalities of any kind.

redistributing resources (either directly or through income transfers) toward educational investment by poor families or communities could be quite large, amounting to several percentage points of GDP (Fernandez and Rogerson 1998, Bénabou 1998).

2.4 Short- and Long-Run Effects of Redistribution

Consider the economy at a given point in time. The degree of inequality Δ_t^2 is given, as the result of historical accidents and past policies. The degree of progressivity $\tau_{SR}^*(\Delta_t)$ that maximizes the current growth rate is determined as the solution to:[10]

$$\mu(1 - \alpha)l'(\tau)/l(\tau) = \mathcal{L}'(\tau)(\lambda\Delta_t)^2/2. \tag{19}$$

The marginal distortion to labor supply is optimally balanced with the marginal gain from relaxing the liquidity constraints on poor families' investment. As a result, τ_{SR}^* increases with Δ_t^2 but remains bounded above by $\bar{\tau} \equiv$ argmax2^c ($\sim$). This static trade-off, however, is only part of the story. Looking more than one period ahead reveals another, dynamic effect of redistribution: increasing τ_t at time t reduces Δ_{t+1}^2 and, more generally, all future variances. Similarly, if the tax rate is permanently set to τ, inequality converges to:

$$\Delta_\infty^2 (\tau) = \frac{s^2}{1 - (\alpha + \beta\lambda(1 - \tau))^2}. \tag{20}$$

By lessening future growth losses due to the combination of inequality of resources with imperfect markets, this *homogenizing effect* on the distribution of human capital and income generates an important intertemporal trade-off.[11]

Proposition 4: Much of the benefit from an increase in redistribution occurs in future periods, whereas all of the costs are contemporaneous. Therefore, maximizing short-run growth in every period will not result in maximizing long-run growth or output.

Formally, long-run output, which is obtained by taking limits in equation (17),

---

[10] Throughout this section I shall implicitly assume strict quasi-concavity of the relevant objective functions. This condition was always satisfied in numerical simulations.

[11] Writing $l'(\tau)$ in equation (19) implicitly assumes that agents always expect the current tax rate to remain constant in the future. But the result stated in proposition 4 applies in the general case: for any given expected sequence $\{\tau_{t+k}\}_{k=1}^\infty$, a change in τ_t can be shown to affect labor supply l_t and the loss factor $L(\tau_t)$ only in the current period, but inequality $\{\Delta_{t+k}^2\}_{k=1}^\infty$ in all future periods.

$$\ln y_\infty = \frac{\theta + (1 - \alpha)\mu\ln l(\tau) - \mathfrak{L}(\tau)\lambda^2\Delta_\infty^2(\tau)/2}{1 - \alpha - \beta\lambda}. \tag{21}$$

is maximized by the tax rate τ_{LR}^* defined as the solution to:

$$\mu(1 - \alpha)l'(\tau)/l(\tau) = \mathfrak{L}'(\tau)\lambda^2\Delta_\infty^2(\tau)/2 + \mathfrak{L}(\tau)\lambda^2(\Delta_\infty^2)'(\tau)/2. \tag{22}$$

Let $\Delta_{LR}^* \equiv \Delta_\infty(\tau_{LR}^*)$ denote the associated level of inequality; it is easy to see that $\tau_{LR}^* > \tau_{SR}^*(\Delta_{LR}^*)$. Thus, starting from the steady-state $(\tau_{LR}^*, \Delta_{LR}^*)$, a tax cut would boost growth *for a while* but eventually lower output *permanently* —as well as increase income disparities. Conversely, suppose that in every period τ is set so as to maximize current growth: $\tau_t = \tau_{SR}^*(\Delta_t^2)$. The economy will converge to the steady-state $(\tau_{SR}^*, \Delta_{SR}^*)$ located at the intersection of the upward-sloping locus defined by equation (19) and the downward-sloping locus given by equation (20); note that $\tau_{SR}^* < \tau_{LR}^*$. Starting from this steady state, higher long-run output can be achieved at the cost of an *initial phase* of slower growth, through a permanent increase in the rate of tax progressivity.

This intertemporal trade-off, which also occurs when evaluating individual or aggregate welfare rather than per capita income, makes clear the importance of the horizon over which policies are evaluated by governments and voters. It arises, fundamentally, from the fact that incomplete markets make the entire *distribution* of income a *state variable* relevant to the economy's aggregate behavior.[12] To obtain a similar reversal between the short- and long-run effects of tax policy in a standard growth model one would have to introduce a form of "time to build" delay between government spending (say, on infrastructure) and its productivity benefits.

Bénabou (1996b) shows that a similar trade-off is likely to apply to other forms of redistribution, which involve *social capital* rather than financial resources. That paper develops a general analysis of the costs and benefits of mixing together heterogeneous populations in the presence of human capital spillovers or production complementarities. It explains in particular how policies promoting the *residential integration* of neighborhoods, or *affirmative action* in education or at the workplace, may reduce growth in the short run yet still increase it in the long run.

3. Meritocracy, Social Mobility, and Growth

Do more meritocratic societies grow faster? To address this question, let us now relate the determinants of growth to the dual notions of meritocracy discussed in section 1. Recall that $\ln \hat{y}_{t_t + 1}^i = (1 - \tau)(\lambda\ln h_{t + 1}^i + \mu\ln l)$

---

[12] This is also the property that allows for multiple long-run equilibria in models such as those of Banerjee and Newman (1993), Piketty (1997), and Bénabou (1996c).

$+ \tau \ln \tilde{y}_t$, while $\ln h^i_{t+1}$ is explained in terms of ability $\ln \xi^i_t$ and background $\ln h^i_t$ by equation (14). The proportion of variance in $\ln \hat{y}^i_{t+1}$, $\ln y^i_{t+1}$ or $\ln h^i_{t+1}$ that is due to the individual's own ability is therefore

$$M^{opp}_t = \frac{s^2}{\Delta^2_{t+1}} = 1 - (\alpha + \beta\lambda(1 - \tau))^2 \frac{\Delta^2_t}{\Delta^2_{t+1}}. \tag{23}$$

Over time, this measure of *equality of opportunity* tends to:

$$M^{opp}_\infty = 1 - (\alpha + \beta\lambda(1 - \tau))^2, \tag{24}$$

which, in our economy, is an exact measure of *social mobility*.[13] As to *inequality of outcomes*, measured by the elasticity of posttax income to ability, it is simply:

$$M^{out} = \lambda(1 - \tau). \tag{25}$$

Let us now temporarily "forget" the dependence of $\mathfrak{L}(\tau)$ on τ, denoting it simply as $\mathfrak{L}$. The accumulation equation (17) can be rewritten as:

$$\ln y_{t+1} - \ln y_t = \theta - \mu \frac{(1 - \alpha)}{\eta}$$

$$\ln\left(\frac{\lambda}{M^{out}} - \frac{\rho\beta\lambda}{1 - \rho\alpha}\right) - (1 - \alpha - \beta\lambda)\ln y_t - \mathfrak{L}\frac{\lambda^2 s^2/2}{M^{opp}_{t-1}},$$

which makes apparent that *both dimensions of meritocracy contribute positively to growth:* inequality of outcomes sharpens individual incentives for effort, whereas equality of opportunities improves the allocation of investment. The trade-off between equality of opportunity and equality of outcomes therefore *differs from the standard one* between equity and efficiency. In particular, M^{opp} enhances both equality and aggregate growth. Naturally, the beneficial effects of meritocratic values on the economy's growth path are also reflected in the long-run level of per capita income y_∞, which by equation (21) is proportional to:

$$W(M^{out}, M^{opp}) \equiv$$

$$\left(\frac{\lambda}{M^{out}} - \frac{\rho\beta\lambda}{1 - \rho\alpha}\right)^{-\mu(1 - \alpha)/\eta} \times \exp\left(- \mathfrak{L}\frac{\lambda^2 s^2/2}{M^{opp}_\infty}\right). \tag{26}$$

It is rather striking that W has all the properties discussed in section 1 for indexes of meritocracy: $W_1 > 0$, $W_2 > 0$, and $W(M,M') = 0$ whenever $MM' = 0$; moreover, $W_{12} > 0$ and W is quasi-concave (even concave at high enough values) in (M,M'). Introduced to represent competing notions of distributive justice, *meritocratic utility functions* turn out to also capture the

---

[13] For a general survey of mobility measures, see Fields and Ok (1999).

two main forces that shape efficiency. Moreover, these two effects are indeed tied together by movements along a convex *meritocracy possibility frontier:*

$$M_\infty^{opp} + (\alpha + \beta M^{out})^2 = 1. \tag{27}$$

If $\mathfrak{L}$ was actually a constant we could interpret it as measuring the relative weight of M_∞^{opp} with respect to M^{out} in W (slope of the iso-meritocracy curves) and we would be exactly in the case of Figure 12.1.[14] The analogy is imperfect, however, because $\mathfrak{L}(\tau)$ is *not* a constant preference parameter, but an *endogenous* measure of the productivity gains obtained by reducing disparities in educational opportunity: it varies together with $(M_\infty^{opp}, M^{out})$ in response to the progressivity rate τ. This more subtle but important effect marks the limit of the general intuition that meritocracy and efficiency go together. I explore this issue further in section 4.2.

When computing equality of opportunity and equality of outcomes I focused for simplicity on current income as a measure of individual reward. In a dynamic model one should more properly use expected *intertemporal utilities*, which take into account the value to parents of their children's welfare. To see that this leads to very similar results, observe that consumption is proportional to posttax income $\hat{y}_t^i$, which has elasticity $\lambda(1 - \tau)$ with respect to human capital; h_t^i, in turn, follows an autoregressive process with innovations ξ_t^i and persistence coefficient $p(\tau) \equiv \alpha + \beta(1 - \tau)$. Therefore:

$$\hat{M}_t^{opp} \equiv \frac{Var[\ln \xi_t^i]}{Var[U_t^i]} = \frac{s^2}{s^2 + p(\tau)^2 \Delta_{t-1}^2}, \text{ so that } M_\infty^{opp} = 1 - p(\tau)^2; \tag{28}$$

$$\hat{M}^{out} \equiv \frac{\partial U_t^i}{\partial \ln \xi_t^i} = \frac{\lambda(1 - \tau)}{1 - \rho p(\tau)}. \tag{29}$$

It is clear that M^{out} and M_t^{opp} (which is unchanged) are constrained to lie on a possibility frontier very similar to equation (27), and that $\ln y_\infty$ can again be expressed as a function of M^{out}, M_t^{opp}, and $\mathfrak{L}$.[15]

4. Education Finance, Family Background, and Social Capital

4.1 Redistributing Education Funding versus Redistributing Income

A welfare-based measure of equality of outcomes becomes indispensable when redistribution occurs directly at the level of education funding rather

---

[14] Note from equation (26) that this slope also depends positively on λ and s^2, both of which tend (ceteris paribus) to increase long-run income dispersion. This accords well with intuition: inequality of opportunity (a strong dependence of children's education and income on parental background) should be more of a concern the more unequal families' resources are.

[15] Ex-ante or aggregate welfare in the steady state, $\lim_{k \to \infty} (E[U_{t+k}^i | h_t^i])$, also depends on M^{out}, M_t^{opp}, and $\mathfrak{L}$. But in addition it incorporates the insurance value of redistribution.

than through progressive income taxation. Such is the case when the state provides free universal public education or transfers that aim to equalize school budgets between rich and poor communities. The distributional and efficiency properties of alternative systems of education finance have been investigated in a number of papers (e.g., Loury 1981, Glomm and Ravikumar 1992, Bénabou 1996a and 1996b, Fernandez and Rogerson 1996 and 1998, and Gradstein and Justman 1998). Here I shall simply explain the close similarity—except for one important difference—with the income redistributions studied earlier.

Suppose that earnings are left untaxed but educational monies are redistributed according to a progressive scheme.[16] Thus e_t^i is replaced in equation (8) by $\hat{e}_t^i$, with:

$$\hat{e}_t^i = (e_t^i)^{1-\tau}(\hat{s}\bar{y}_t)^\tau, \tag{30}$$

where $\hat{s}$ and $\bar{y}_t$ are defined as before. The case $\tau = 0$ corresponds to laissez-faire, while at the other extreme $\tau = 1$ imposes egalitarian funding. This policy has implications very similar to those of income taxation, and in particular gives rise to the same trade-off between distortions to $l(\tau)$ and gains from relaxing both present and future wealth constraints. With respect to meritocracy, it is easy to see that equality of opportunity $\hat{M}_t^{opp}$ remains unchanged, while the utility-based $\hat{M}^{out}$ is now equal to the expression in (29) except that $1 - \tau$ does not appear in the numerator any more. This reduced impact on outcomes reflects the fact that parental consumption now escapes redistribution, and indicates that distortions to effort will be smaller than under progressive income taxation. It also implies that if human capital is the main transmission mechanism for intergenerational income differences, as in our model, progressive *education finance* is *more meritocratic* than progressive *income taxation*. If other channels such as financial bequests are important, on the other hand, the increase in M^{out} obtained by redistributing only e^i rather than all of y^i must, once again, be traded against a reduction in M^{opp}.

4.2 The Role of Family and Social Inputs to Education

In addition to teachers, classrooms, books, and other school resources, the accumulation of human capital involves important nonpurchased inputs, provided either by the family or by the local community. Examples of neighborhood influences include peer effects, role models, job contacts, local norms of behavior, and crime. Altering through law or financial incentives the so-

---

[16] In addition, there may be a flat consumption tax whose proceeds are used to finance educational subsidies, so that the savings rate remains equal to $\hat{s}$. See the discussion in section 2.2, and Bénabou (1998) for more details.

cioeconomic mix of schools, communities, or even firms amounts to a redistribution of these various forms of "social capital" (a term coined by Loury 1977), which can be studied in a way similar to redistributions of income. Conversely, the presence of socioeconomic background as a complement to expenditures in the education production function affects the effectiveness of income redistribution and school finance reform. This is one of the main sources of divergence between meritocracy and efficiency.

Let us start by recalling the claim in section 2 that the transmission of human capital within the family and the impact of social capital in segregated communities can both be captured by the term $(h_t^i)^\alpha$ in equation (8). In the latter case, this reflects a more general technology of the form

$$h_{t+1}^i = \kappa \xi_{t+1}^i \, (h_t^i)^\alpha (e_t^i)^\beta (L_t^i)^\gamma, \tag{31}$$

where the local spillover L_t^i is measured by a CES average of education levels in the community or "club" Ω_t^i where individual (i, t) is educated

$$L_t^i = \left(\int_{j \in \Omega_t^i} (h_t^j)^{\frac{\varepsilon-1}{\varepsilon}} \, dj \right)^{\frac{\varepsilon}{\varepsilon-1}}. \tag{32}$$

By allowing the *elasticity of complementarity* $1/\varepsilon$ to vary between $+\infty$ and $-\infty$, this specification captures all cases between the two extremes where local interactions are dominated by the lower or by the upper tail of the human capital distribution ($L_t^i = \min\{h_t^j, j \in \Omega_t^i\}$ and $L_t^i = \max\{h_t^j, j \in \Omega_t^i\}$, respectively). Perfectly segregated communities correspond to $L_t^i = h_t^i$, while perfectly integrated ones yield $L_t^i = L_t$ where this index is computed over a representative sample of the economy's population. A rise in the degree of socioeconomic *stratification* such as an exodus of better-off families to the suburbs, can therefore be represented in the transmission equation $h_{t+1}^i = \kappa \cdot \xi_{t+1}^i \cdot (h_t^i)^\alpha (e_t^i)^\beta (L_t)^\gamma$ by an increase in α and a corresponding decline in γ. This extension leaves the general structure of the model unchanged, and in particular, human capital remains distributed log-normally over time, $\ln h_t^i \sim \mathcal{N}(m_t, \Delta_t^2)$. Thus:

$$\ln L_t = m_t + \Delta_t^2 (\varepsilon - 1)/2\varepsilon = \ln y_t - \Delta_t^2/2\varepsilon, \tag{33}$$

and the economy's dynamics are obtained by simply replacing $\ln \kappa$ with $\ln \kappa + \gamma(m_t + \Delta_t^2(\varepsilon - 1)/2\varepsilon)$ in equation (14). The law of motion for cross-sectional inequality Δ_t^2 is then unchanged from proposition 2 and so is intergenerational mobility $p(\tau) = \alpha + \beta\lambda (1 - \tau)$. As to growth in per capita income, it becomes:

$$\ln y_{t+1} - \ln y_t = \theta - (1 - \alpha - \beta\lambda - \gamma)\ln y_t \\ + (1 - \alpha - \gamma)\mu \ln l(\tau) - \mathfrak{L}(\tau)(\lambda\Delta_t)^2/2 \tag{34}$$

where θ is still a constant but $\mathcal{L}(\tau)$ is now:

$$\mathcal{L}(\tau) \equiv \alpha + \beta\lambda (1 - \tau)^2 - (\alpha + \beta\lambda (1 - \tau))^2 \\ + \lambda\gamma (1/\varepsilon - (1 - \lambda)) \tag{35}$$

which, of course, reduces to equation (17) in the absence of local spillovers. Note that when $\alpha + \beta\lambda + \gamma = 1$ the economy experiences continual growth, and redistributive policies as well as the extent of socioeconomic stratification affect the asymptotic growth rate. Two related questions can be addressed with this model.

First, what are the effects of greater socioeconomic segregation on the macroeconomy? This problem is analyzed in detail in Bénabou (1996b), so here I will just sketch the answer.[17] In the short run, the impact on growth reflects the response of $\mathcal{L}$ to a simultaneous increase in α and decrease in γ, with $\alpha + \gamma$ constant. The last term in equation (35) shows that whether this is beneficial or detrimental depends in particular on the balance between the *costs of heterogeneity* at the *local* and *global* levels: the former reflect the degree of interdependence $1/\varepsilon$ between peers or neighbors, while the latter arise from decreasing returns to individual human capital in production (recall that aggregate output is $y = l^\mu \int_0^1 (h^i)^\lambda \, di$). In the long run, the homogenization effect also comes into play: steady-state disparities in education and income increase with segregation, and this rise in Δ_∞^2 is always detrimental. Therefore the potential trade-off between short-run and long run output growth discussed in section 2.4 for income redistributions also arises for redistributions of social capital.

The second question is how the presence of family or social inputs to education affects the desirability of redistributing financial resources, both from the point of view of meritocratic values and from that of long-run aggregate income (or efficiency more generally). Focusing for simplicity on income redistributions, note first that a rise in α lowers $\hat{M}_\infty^{opp} - M_\infty^{opp} = 1 - (\alpha + \beta\lambda (1 - \tau))^2$ and increases $\partial\hat{M}_\infty^{opp}/\partial\tau$. Therefore, in response to an increase in segregation, *equality of opportunity* unambiguously calls for an offsetting increase in redistribution. The picture is a little less clear-cut concerning *inequality in outcomes*. The income-based definition $M^{out} = \lambda (1 - \tau)$ remains unaffected but the utility-based measure $\hat{M}^{out} = \lambda (1 - \tau)/(1 - pp(\tau))$ rises, and so does $\partial M_\infty^{out}/\partial\tau$: high-ability parents now enjoy more effective channels through which to pass human capital on to their offspring, and this is more valuable the lower the future tax rates. Whether more or less redistribution is called for thus depends on the specific form of $W(M^{opp}, M^{out})$, that is, on the relative weights placed on the two meritocratic values. Nonetheless, in plausible situations where the discount factor ρ is not too high—or, equivalently, when equality of outcomes is

---

[17] That paper provides a general treatment of dynamic economies with both local and economywide spillovers of the form (32).

judged mostly in terms of lifetime income rather than intergenerational welfare—the concern for equality of opportunity will dominate, leading to an increase in τ.

Things are quite different from the point of view of *efficiency*. Focusing once more on long-run output, let us now examine how $\partial \ln y_\infty / \partial \tau$ or, equivalently, how

$$\frac{\partial}{\partial \tau} \left((1 - \alpha - \gamma)\mu \ln l(\tau) - \mathcal{L}(\tau)\frac{\lambda^2 \Delta_\infty^2(\tau)}{2} \right) \tag{36}$$

varies with α, keeping $\alpha + \gamma$ constant. There are three effects:

a. As explained following proposition 1, an increase in α magnifies the effort disincentive $-\partial \ln l(\tau)/\partial \tau$, because when human capital depreciates more slowly it becomes more sensitive to permanent changes in taxation.

b. For any given distribution of backgrounds, a greater α also magnifies the efficiency loss from a marginal increase in redistribution: $\mathcal{L}(\tau)$ is maximized at $\bar{\tau} = 1 - \alpha/(1 - \beta\lambda)$, which varies inversely with α.[18]

c. On the other hand, the efficiency value of reducing permanent inequality $\Delta_\infty^2 = s^2/\hat{M}_\infty^{opp}$ calls for responding to a rise in α with greater progressivity: one can show that $\partial^2(\Delta_\infty^2)/\partial \tau \partial \alpha < 0$.

The balance of these three effects is generally too complicated to determine analytically, but in simple cases where it can be done—and in all the simulations of the model—the first two dominate. For instance, proposition 1 and equation (20) imply that when $\alpha = 0$, $\mathcal{L}(\tau)\Delta_\infty^2(\tau)$ is minimized by $\tau = 1$. For $\alpha > 0$, however, the solution can be shown to be interior. This suggests that $\partial \tau_{LR}^*/\partial \alpha < 0$, even before distortions to labor supply are taken into account.

These results accord well with intuition: when families or communities provide complementary inputs to education expenditures, factors that magnify disparities in background make redistribution less efficient, even though more of it would be called for from the point of view of meritocracy (or at least from that of equal opportunity). Compounding this problem is the fact that disparities in nonpurchased or background inputs are likely to arise independent of capital market imperfections and therefore to persist in the face of extensive redistribution—which, in turn, they make less efficient. This is obvious when h^α just reflects family human capital, but it also applies to social capital. Indeed, significant socioeconomic stratification can arise even with perfect credit markets, whether due to some group's preference for racial separation or to differences in families' valuations of community quality.

---

[18] See Arrow (1971) for an early analysis of the impact of such complementarities between background and inputs on the optimal degree of redistribution, in a static model.

The distributional, growth, and policy implications of endogenous community composition in the presence of local human-capital spillovers are studied in Bénabou (1993, 1996a), Durlauf (1996, 1999), Cooper (1998), and Lundberg and Startz (1994), among others.

5. Conclusion

There is no value-free definition of meritocracy. Redistributive policies such as progressive income taxation or education finance typically involve a trade-off along a "meritocracy possibility frontier" linking equality of opportunity with equality of outcomes. This trade-off differs from the conventional one between equity and efficiency, because equalizing the young's opportunities for human-capital investment enhances not only social mobility but also the growth of aggregate output. The model presented in this chapter shows precisely how this positive contribution of educational or even fiscal redistributions to the size of the economic pie must be weighed against the concomitant disincentive effect of imposing a greater equality of outcomes among adults. The optimal degree of redistribution also reflects how family inputs and social capital affect the productivity of education expenditures, and incorporates the efficiency value of reducing inequality of resources in future generations.

References

Aghion, P., and B. Bolton. 1997. "A Trickle-Down Theory of Growth and Development with Debt Overhang." *Review of Economics Studies* 64, no. 2: 151–172.

Alesina, A., and D. Rodrik. 1994. "Distributive Politics and Economic Growth." *Quarterly Journal of Economics* 109: 465–490.

Arrow, K. 1971. "Equality in Public Expenditure." *Quarterly Journal of Economics* 85, no. 3: 409–415.

Atkinson, A. 1980. *Social Justice and Public Policy.* Cambridge, MA: MIT Press. Chapter 4, "Income Distribution and Inequality of Opportunity."

Banerjee, A., and A. Newman. 1993. "Occupational Choice and the Process of Development." *Journal of Political Economy* 101: 274–298.

Bénabou, R. 1993. "Workings of a City: Location, Education and Production." *Quarterly Journal of Economics* 108: 619–652.

———. 1996a. "Equity and Efficiency in Human Capital Investment: the Local Connection." *Review of Economic Studies* 63, no. 2: 237–264.

———. 1996b. "Heterogeneity, Stratification, and Growth: Macroeconomic Implications of Community Structure and Education Finance." *American Economic Review* 86, no. 3: 584–609.

———. 1996c. "Unequal Societies." NBER Working Paper no. 5583, May.

Bénabou, R. 1998. "Macroeconomics and Public Finance with Heterogeneous Agents: What Levels of Redistribution Maximize Output and Efficiency?" IDEI, mimeo, November.

Cooper, S. 1998. "A Positive Theory of Income Redistribution." *Journal of Economic Growth* 3, no. 2 (June): 171–195.

Durlauf, S. 1996. "A Theory of Persistent Income Inequality." *Journal of Economic Growth* 1, 1: 75–94.

———. 1999. "Neighborhood Feedbacks, Endogenous Stratification, and Income Inequality." In *Proceedings of the Sixth International Symposium on Economic Theory and Econometrics,* ed. W. Barnett, G. Gandolfo and C. Hillinger, pp. 505–534. Cambridge: Cambridge University Press.

Fernandez, R., and R. Rogerson. 1996. "Income Distribution, Communities and the Quality of Public Education." *Quarterly Journal of Economics* 111: 135–164.

———. 1998. "Public Education and the Dynamics of Income Distribution: A Quantitative Evaluation of Education Finance Reform." *American Economic Review* 88, no. 4 (September): 813–833.

Fields, G., and E. Ok. 1999. "The Measurement of Income Mobility: An Introduction to the Literature." Forthcoming in *Handbook of Inequality Measurement,* ed. Jacques Silber. Dordrecht, Germany: Kluwer Academic Press.

Galor, O., and J. Zeira. 1993. "Income Distribution and Macroeconomics." *Review of Economic Studies* 60: 35–52

Glomm, G., and B. Ravikumar. 1992. "Public vs. Private Investment in Human Capital: Endogenous Growth and Income Inequality." *Journal of Political Economy* 100: 818–834.

Gradstein, M., and M. Justman, 1997. "Democratic Choice of an Education System: Implications for Growth and Income Distribution." *Journal of Economic Growth* 2, no. 2: 169–184.

Loury, G. 1977. "A Dynamic Theory of Racial Income Differences." in *Women, Minorities and Employment Discrimination,* ed. A. Le Mond, pp. 153–186. Lexington, MA: D. C. Heath.

———. 1981. "Intergenerational Transfers and the Distribution of Earnings." *Econometrica* 49: 843–867.

Lundberg, S., and R. Startz. 1994. "On the Persistence of Racial Inequality." University of Washington, Institute for Economic Research Working Paper no. 94-07, September.

Nozick, R. 1974. *Anarchy, State and Utopia.* New York: Basic Books.

Perotti, R. 1993. "Political Equilibrium, Income Distribution, and Growth." *Review of Economic Studies* 60: 755–776.

Persson, M. 1983. "The Distribution of Abilities and the Progressive Income Tax." *Journal of Public Economics* 22: 73–88.

Persson, T., and G. Tabellini. 1991. "Is Inequality Harmful for Growth? Theory and Evidence." *American Economic Review* 48: 600–621.

Piketty, T. 1997. "The Dynamics of the Wealth Distribution and Interest Rate with Credit-Rationing." *Review of Economic Studies* 64, no. 2: 173–190.

Rawls, J. 1971. *A Theory of Justice.* Cambridge, MA: Harvard University Press.

Roemer, J. 1995. "Equality and Responsibility." *Boston Review* 20, no. 2: 3–7.

Saint-Paul, G., and T. Verdier. 1993. "Education, Democracy and Growth." *Journal of Development Economics* 42, no. 2: 399–407.

Varian, H. 1980. "Redistributive Taxation as Social Insurance." *Journal of Public Economics* 14: 49–62.

Index